Manners, Custom And Dress During The Middle Ages And During The Renaissance Period

Table of Contents

Fac–simile of a miniature from the *Breviary* of the Cardinal Grimani, attributed to Memling. Bibl. of S. Marc, Venice. (From a copy in the possession of M. Ambroise Firmin–Didot.)

The King inclines his sceptre towards the Queen indicating his appreciation of her person and her gifts; five ladies attend the Queen and five of the King's courtiers stand on his right hand.]

Manners, Customs, and Dress During the Middle Ages, and During the Renaissance Period.

By Paul Lacroix (Bibliophile Jacob), Curator of the Imperial Library of the Arsenal, Paris.

Illustrated with Nineteen Chromolithographic Prints by F. Kellerhoven and upwards of *Four Hundred Engravings on Wood*.

Preface.

The several successive editions of "The Arts of the Middle Ages and Period of the Renaissance" sufficiently testify to its appreciation by the public. The object of that work was to introduce the reader to a branch of learning to which access had hitherto appeared only permitted to the scientific. That attempt, which was a bold one, succeeded too well not to induce us to push our researches further. In fact, art alone cannot acquaint us entirely with an epoch. "The arts, considered in their generality, are the true expressions of society. They tell us its tastes, its ideas, and its character." We thus spoke in the preface to our first work, and we find nothing to modify in this opinion. Art must be the faithful expression of a society, since it represents it by its works as it has created them—undeniable witnesses of its spirit and manners for future generations. But it must be acknowledged that art is only the consequence of the ideas which it expresses; it is the fruit of civilisation, not its origin. To understand the Middle Ages and the Renaissance, it is necessary to go back to the source of its art, and to know the life of our fathers; these are two inseparable things, which entwine one another, and become complete one by the other.

The Manners and Customs of the Middle Ages:—this subject is of the greatest interest, not only to the man of science, but to the man of the world also. In it, too, "we retrace not only one single period, but two periods quite distinct one from the other." In the first, the public and private customs offer a curious mixture of barbarism and civilisation. We find barbarian, Roman, and Christian customs and character in presence of each other, mixed up in the same society, and very often in the same individuals. Everywhere the most adverse and opposite tendencies display themselves. What an ardent struggle during that long period! and how full, too, of emotion is its picture! Society tends to reconstitute itself in every aspect. She wants to create, so to say, from every side, property, authority, justice, &c., &c., in a word, everything which can establish the basis of public life; and this new order of things must be established by means of the elements supplied at once by the barbarian, Roman, and Christian world—a prodigious creation, the working of which occupied the whole of the Middle Ages. Hardly does modern society, civilised by Christianity, reach the fullness of its power, than it divides itself to follow different paths. Ancient art and literature resuscitates because custom *insensibly* takes that direction. Under that influence, everything is modified both in private and public life. The history of the human race does not present a subject more vast or more interesting. It is a subject we have chosen to succeed our first book, and which will be followed by a similar study on the various aspects of Religious and Military Life.

This work, devoted to the vivid and faithful description of the Manners and Customs of the Middle Ages and Renaissance, answers fully to the requirements of contemporary times. We are, in fact, no longer content with the chronological narration and simple nomenclatures which formerly were considered sufficient for education. We no longer imagine that the history of our institutions has less interest than that of our wars, nor that the annals of the humbler classes are irrelevant to those of the privileged orders. We go further still. What is above all sought for in historical works nowadays is the physiognomy, the inmost character of past generations. "How did our fathers live?" is a daily question. "What institutions had they? What were their political rights? Can you not place before us their pastimes, their hunting parties, their meals, and all sorts of scenes, sad or gay, which composed their home life? We should like to follow them in public and private occupations, and to know their manner of living hourly, as we know our own."

In a high order of ideas, what great facts serve as a foundation to our history and that of the modern world! We have first royalty, which, weak and debased under the Merovingians, rises and establishes itself energetically under Pepin and Charlemagne, to degenerate under Louis le Debonnaire and Charles le Chauve. After having dared a second time to found the Empire of the Caesars, it quickly sees its sovereignty replaced by feudal rights, and all its rights usurped by the nobles, and has to struggle for many centuries to recover its rights one by one.

Feudalism, evidently of Germanic origin, will also attract our attention, and we shall draw a rapid outline of this legislation, which, barbarian at the onset, becomes by degrees subject to the rules of moral progress. We shall ascertain that military service is the essence itself of the "fief," and that thence springs feudal right. On our way we shall protest against civil wars, and shall welcome emancipation and the formation of the communes. Following the thousand details of the life of the people, we shall see the slave become serf, and the serf become peasant. We shall assist at the dispensation of justice by royalty and nobility, at the solemn sittings of parliaments, and we shall see the complicated details of a strict ceremonial, which formed an integral part of the law, develop themselves before us. The counters of dealers, fairs and markets, manufactures, commerce, and industry, also merit our attention; we must search deeply into corporations of workmen and tradesmen, examining their statutes, and initiating ourselves into their business. Fashion and dress are also a manifestation of public and private customs; for that reason we must give them particular attention.

And to accomplish the work we have undertaken, we are lucky to have the conscientious studies of our old associates in the great work of the Middle Ages and the Renaissance to assist us: such as those of Emile Begin, Elzear Blaze, Depping, Benjamin Guerard, Le Roux de Lincy, H. Martin, Mary–Lafon, Francisque Michel, A. Monteil, Rabutau, Ferdinand Sere, Horace de Viel–Castel, A. de la Villegille, Vallet de Viriville.

As in the volume of the Arts of the Middle Ages, engraving and chromo–lithography will come to our assistance by reproducing, by means of strict fac–similes, the rarest engravings of the fifteenth and sixteenth centuries, and the most precious miniatures of the manuscripts preserved in the principal libraries of France and Europe. Here again we have the aid of the eminent artist, M. Kellerhoven, who quite recently found means of reproducing with so much fidelity the gems of Italian painting.

Paul Lacroix (Bibliophile Jacob).

Manners, Customs, and Dress During the Middle Ages, and During the Renaissance Period.

Condition of Persons and Lands.

Disorganization of the West at the Beginning of the Middle Ages.—Mixture of Roman, Germanic, and Gallic Institutions.—Fusion organized under Charlemagne.—Royal Authority.—Position of the Great Feudalists.—Division of the Territory and Prerogatives attached to Landed Possessions.—Freemen and Tenants.—The Laeti, the Colon, the Serf, and the Labourer, who may be called the Origin of the Modern Lower Classes.—Formation of Communities.—Right of Mortmain.

The period known as the Middle Ages, says the learned Benjamin Guerard, is the produce of Pagan civilisation, of Germanic barbarism, and of Christianity. It began in 476, on the fall of Agustulus, and ended in 1453, at the taking of Constantinople by Mahomet II., and consequently the fall of two empires, that of the West and that of the East, marks its duration. Its first act, which was due to the Germans, was the destruction of political unity, and this was destined to be afterwards replaced by religions unity. Then we find a multitude of scattered and disorderly influences growing on the ruins of central power. The yoke of imperial dominion was broken by the barbarians; but the populace, far from acquiring liberty, fell to the lowest degrees of servitude. Instead of one despot, it found thousands of tyrants, and it was but slowly and with much trouble that it succeeded in freeing itself from feudalism. Nothing could be more strangely troubled than the West at the time of the dissolution of the Empire of the Caesars; nothing more diverse or more discordant than the interests, the institutions, and the state of society, which were delivered to the Germans (Figs. 1 and 2). In fact, it would be impossible in the whole pages of history to find a society formed of more heterogeneous or incompatible elements. On the one side might be placed the Goths, Burgundians, Vandals, Germans, Franks, Saxons, and Lombards, nations, or more strictly hordes, accustomed to rough and successful warfare, and, on the other, the Romans, including those people who by long servitude to Roman dominion had become closely allied with their conquerors (Fig. 3). There were, on both sides, freemen, freedmen, colons, and slaves; different ranks and degrees being, however, observable both in freedom and servitude. This hierarchical principle applied itself even to the land, which was divided into freeholds, tributary lands,

lands of the nobility, and servile lands, thus constituting the freeholds, the benefices, the fiefs, and the tenures. It may be added that the customs, and to a certain degree the laws, varied according to the masters of the country, so that it can hardly be wondered at that everywhere diversity and inequality were to be found, and, as a consequence, that anarchy and confusion ruled supreme.

[Illustration: Figs. 1 and 2.—Costumes of the Franks from the Fourth to the Eighth Centuries, collected by H. de Vielcastel, from original Documents in the great Libraries of Europe.]

[Illustration: Fig. 3.—Costumes of Roman Soldiers. Fig. 4.—Costume of German Soldiers. From Miniatures on different Manuscripts, from the Sixth to the Twelfth Centuries.]

The Germans (Fig. 4) had brought with them over the Rhine none of the heroic virtues attributed to them by Tacitus when he wrote their history, with the evident intention of making a satire on his countrymen. Amongst the degenerate Romans whom those ferocious Germans had subjugated, civilisation was reconstituted on the ruins of vices common in the early history of a new society by the adoption of a series of loose and dissolute habits, both by the conquerors and the conquered.

[Illustration: Fig. 5.—Costumes of Slaves or Serfs, from the Sixth to the Twelfth Centuries, collected by H. de Vielcastel, from original Documents in the great Libraries of Europe.]

In fact, the conquerors contributed the worse share (Fig. 5); for, whilst exercising the low and debasing instincts of their former barbarism, they undertook the work of social reconstruction with a sort of natural and innate servitude. To them, liberty, the desire for which caused them to brave the greatest dangers, was simply the right of doing evil—of obeying their ardent thirst for plunder. Long ago, in the depths of their forests, they had adopted the curious institution of vassalage. When they came to the West to create States, instead of reducing personal power, every step in their social edifice, from the top to the bottom, was made to depend on individual superiority. To bow to a superior was their first political principle; and on that principle feudalism was one day to find its base.

Servitude was in fact to be found in all conditions and ranks, equally in the palace of the sovereign as in the dwellings of his subjects. The vassal who was waited on at his own table by a varlet, himself served at the table of his lord; the nobles treated each other likewise, according to their rank; and all the exactions which each submitted to from his superiors, and required to be paid to him by those below him, were looked upon not as onerous duties, but as rights and honours. The sentiment of dignity and of personal independence, which has become, so to say, the soul of modern society, did not exist at all, or at least but very slightly, amongst the Germans. If we could doubt the fact, we have but to remember that these men, so proud, so indifferent to suffering or death, would often think little of staking their liberty in gambling, in the hope that if successful their gain might afford them the means of gratifying some brutal passion.

[Illustration: Fig. 6.—King or Chief of Franks armed with the Seramasax, from a Miniature of the Ninth Century, drawn by H. de Vielcastel.]

When the Franks took root in Gaul, their dress and institutions were adopted by the Roman society (Fig. 6). This had the most disastrous influence in every point of view, and it is easy to prove that civilisation did not emerge from this chaos until by degrees the Teutonic spirit disappeared from the world. As long as this spirit reigned, neither private nor public liberty existed. Individual patriotism only extended as far as the border of a man's family, and the nation became broken up into clans. Gaul soon found itself parcelled off into domains which were almost independent of one another. It was thus that Germanic genius became developed.

[Illustration: Fig. 7.—The King of the Franks, in the midst of the Military Chiefs who formed his *Treuste*, or armed Court, dictates the Salic Law (Code of the Barbaric Laws).—Fac-simile of a Miniature in the "Chronicles of St. Denis," a Manuscript of the Fourteenth Century (Library of the Arsenal).]

The advantages of acting together for mutual protection first established itself in families. If any one suffered from an act of violence, he laid the matter before his relatives for them jointly to seek reparation. The question was then settled between the families of the offended person and the offender, all of whom were equally associated in the object of vindicating a cause which interested them alone, without recognising any established authority, and without appealing to the law. If the parties had sought the protection or advice of men of power, the quarrel might at once take a wider scope, and tend to kindle a feud between two nobles. In any case the King only interfered when the safety of his person or the interests of his dominions were threatened.

Penalties and punishments were almost always to be averted by a money payment. A son, for instance, instead of avenging the death of his father, received from the murderer a certain indemnity in specie, according to legal tariff; and the law was thus satisfied.

The tariff of indemnities or compensations to be paid for each crime formed the basis of the code of laws amongst the principal tribes of Franks, a code essentially barbarian, and called the Salic law, or law of the Salians (Fig. 7). Such, however, was the spirit of inequality among the German races, that it became an established principle for justice to be subservient to the rank of individuals. The more powerful a man was, the more he was protected by the law; the lower his rank, the less the law protected him.

The life of a Frank, by right, was worth twice that of a Roman; the life of a servant of the King was worth three times that of an ordinary individual who did not possess that protecting tie. On the other hand, punishment was the more prompt and rigorous according to the inferiority of position of the culprit. In case of theft, for instance, a person of importance was brought before the King's tribunal, and as it respected the rank held by the accused in the social hierarchy, little or no punishment was awarded. In the case of the same crime by a poor man, on the contrary, the ordinary judge gave immediate sentence, and he was seized and hung on the spot.

Inasmuch as no political institutions amongst the Germans were nobler or more just than those of the Franks and the other barbaric races, we cannot accept the creed of certain historians who have represented the Germans as the true regenerators of society in Europe. The two sources of modern civilisation are indisputably Pagan antiquity and Christianity.

After the fall of the Merovingian kings great progress was made in the political and social state of nations. These kings, who were but chiefs of undisciplined bands, were unable to assume a regal character, properly so called. Their authority was more personal than territorial, for incessant changes were made in the boundaries of their conquered dominions. It was therefore with good reason that they styled themselves kings of the Franks, and not kings of France.

Charlemagne was the first who recognised that social union, so admirable an example of which was furnished by Roman organization, and who was able, with the very elements of confusion and disorder to which he succeeded, to unite, direct, and consolidate diverging and opposite forces, to establish and regulate public administrations, to found and build towns, and to form and reconstruct almost a new world (Fig. 8). We hear of him assigning to each his place, creating for all a common interest, making of a crowd of small and scattered peoples a great and powerful nation; in a word, rekindling the beacon of ancient civilisation. When he died, after a most active and glorious reign of forty–five years, he left an immense empire in the most perfect state of peace (Fig. 9). But this magnificent inheritance was unfortunately destined to pass into unworthy or impotent hands, so that society soon fell back into anarchy and confusion. The nobles, in their turn invested with power, were continually at war, and gradually weakened the royal authority—the power of the kingdom—by their endless disputes with the Crown and with one another.

[Illustration: Fig. 8.—Charles, eldest Son of King Pepin, receives the News of the Death of his Father and the Great Feudalists offer him the Crown.—Costumes of the Court of Burgundy in the Fifteenth Century.—Fac–simile of a Miniature of the "History of the Emperors" (Library of the Arsenal).]

[Illustration: Fig. 9. Portrait of Charlemagne, whom the Song of Roland names the King with the Grizzly Beard.—Fac–simile of an Engraving of the End of the Sixteenth Century.]

The revolution in society which took place under the Carlovingian dynasty had for its especial object that of rendering territorial what was formerly personal, and, as it were, of destroying personality in matters of government.

The usurpation of lands by the great having been thus limited by the influence of the lesser holders, everybody tried to become the holder of land. Its possession then formed the basis of social position, and, as a consequence, individual servitude became lessened, and society assumed a more stable condition. The ancient laws of wandering tribes fell into disuse; and at the same time many distinctions of caste and race disappeared, as they were incompatible with the new order of things. As there were no more Salians, Ripuarians, nor Visigoths among the free men, so there were no more colons, laeti, nor slaves amongst those deprived of liberty.

[Illustrations: Figs. 10 and 11.—Present State of the Feudal Castle of Chateau–Gaillard aux Andelys, which was considered one of the strongest Castles of France in the Middle Ages, and was rebuilt in the Twelfth Century by Richard Coeur de Lion.]

Heads of families, on becoming attached to the soil, naturally had other wants and other customs than those which they had delighted in when they were only the chiefs of wandering adventurers. The strength of their followers was not now so important to them as the security of their castles. Fortresses took the place of armed bodies; and at this time, every one who wished to keep what he had, entrenched himself to the best of his ability at his own residence. The banks of rivers, elevated positions, and all inaccessible heights, were occupied by towers and castles, surrounded by ditches, which served as strongholds to the lords of the soil. (Figs. 10 and 11). These places of defence soon became points for attack. Out of danger at home, many of the nobles kept watch like birds of prey on the surrounding country, and were always ready to fall, not only upon their enemies, but also on their neighbours, in the hope either of robbing them when off their guard, or of obtaining a ransom for any unwary traveller who might fall into their hands. Everywhere society was in ambuscade, and waged civil war—individual against individual—without peace or mercy. Such was the reign of feudalism. It is unnecessary to point out how this system of perpetual petty warfare tended to reduce the power of centralisation, and how royalty itself was weakened towards the end of the second dynasty. When the descendants of Hugh Capet wished to restore their power by giving it a larger basis, they were obliged to attack, one after the other, all these strongholds, and practically to re–annex each fief, city, and province held by these petty monarchs, in order to force their owners to recognise the sovereignty of the King. Centuries of war and negotiations became necessary before the kingdom of France could be, as it were, reformed.

[Illustration: Fig. 12.—Knights and Men–at–arms, cased in Mail, in the Reign of Louis le Gros, from a Miniature in a Psalter written towards the End of the Twelfth Century.]

The corporations and the citizens had great weight in restoring the monarchical power, as well as in forming French nationality; but by far the best influence brought to bear in the Middle Ages was that of Christianity. The doctrine of one origin and of one final destiny being common to all men of all classes constantly acted as a strong inducement for thinking that all should be equally free. Religious equality paved the way for political equality, and as all Christians were brothers before God, the tendency was for them to become, as citizens, equal also in law.

This transformation, however, was but slow, and followed concurrently the progress made in the security of property. At the onset, the slave only possessed his life, and this was but imperfectly guaranteed to him by the laws of charity; laws which, however, year by year became of greater power. He afterwards became *colon*, or labourer (Figs. 13 and 14), working for himself under certain conditions and tenures, paying fines, or services, which, it is true, were often very extortionate. At this time he was considered to belong to the domain on which he was born, and he was at least sure that that soil would not be taken from him, and that in giving part of his time to his master, he was at liberty to enjoy the rest according to his fancy. The farmer afterwards became proprietor of the soil he cultivated, and master, not only of himself, but of his lands; certain trivial obligations or fines being all that was required of him, and these daily grew less, and at last disappeared altogether. Having thus obtained a footing in society, he soon began to take a place in provincial assemblies; and he made the last bound on the road of social progress, when the vote of his fellow–electors sent him to represent them in the parliament of the kingdom. Thus the people who had begun by excessive servitude, gradually climbed to power.

[Illustration: Fig. 13.—Labouring Colons (Twelfth Century), after a Miniature in a Manuscript of the Ste. Chapelle, of the National Library of Paris.]

We will now describe more in detail the various conditions of persons of the Middle Ages.

The King, who held his rights by birth, and not by election, enjoyed relatively an absolute authority, proportioned according to the power of his abilities, to the extent of his dominions, and to the devotion of his vassals. Invested with a power which for a long time resembled the command of a general of an army, he had at first no other ministers than the officers to whom he gave full power to act in the provinces, and who decided arbitrarily in the name of, and representing, the King, on all questions of administration. One minister alone approached the King, and that was the chancellor, who verified, sealed, and dispatched all royal decrees and orders.

As early, however, as the seventh century, a few officers of state appeared, who were specially attached to the King's person or household; a count of the palace, who examined and directed the suits brought before the throne; a mayor of the palace, who at one time raised himself from the administration of the royal property to the supreme power; an arch–chaplain, who presided over ecclesiastical affairs; a lord of the bedchamber, charged with the treasure of the chamber; and a count of the stables, charged with the superintendence of the stables.

[Illustration: Fig. 14.—Labouring Colons (Twelfth Century), after a Miniature in a Manuscript of the Ste. Chapelle, of the National Library of Paris.]

For all important affairs, the King generally consulted the grandees of his court; but as in the five or six first centuries of monarchy in France the royal residence was not permanent, it is probable the Council of State was composed in part of the officers who followed the King, and in part of the noblemen who came to visit him, or resided near the place he happened to be inhabiting. It was only under the Capetians that the Royal Council took a permanent footing, or even assembled at stated periods.

In ordinary times, that is to say, when he was not engaged in war, the King had few around him besides his family, his personal attendants, and the ministers charged with the dispatch of affairs. As he changed from one of his abodes to another he only held his court on the great festivals of the year.

[Illustration: Fig. 15.—The Lords and Barons prove their Nobility by hanging their Banners and exposing their Coats–of–arms at the Windows of the Lodge of the Heralds.—After a Miniature of the "Tournaments of King Rene" (Fifteenth Century), MSS. of the National Library of Paris.]

Up to the thirteenth century, there was, strictly speaking, no taxation and no public treasury. The King received, through special officers appointed for the purpose, tributes either in money or in kind, which were most variable, but often very heavy, and drawn almost exclusively from his personal and private properties. In cases of emergency only, he appealed to his vassals for pecuniary aid. A great number of the grandees, who lived far from the court, either in state offices or on their own fiefs, had establishments similar to that of the King. Numerous and considerable privileges elevated them above other free men. The offices and fiefs having become hereditary, the order of nobility followed as a consequence; and it then became highly necessary for families to keep their genealogical histories, not only to gratify their pride, but also to give them the necessary titles for the feudal advantages they derived by birth. (Fig. 15). Without this right of inheritance, society, which was still unsettled in the Middle Ages, would soon have been dissolved.

This great principle, sacred in the eyes both of great and small, maintained feudalism, and in so doing it maintained itself amidst all the chaos and confusion of repeated revolutions and social disturbances.

We have already stated, and we cannot sufficiently insist upon this important point, that from the day on which the adventurous habits of the chiefs of Germanic origin gave place to the desire for territorial possessions, the part played by the land increased insensibly towards defining the position of the persons holding it. Domains became small kingdoms, over which the lord assumed the most absolute and arbitrary rights. A rule was soon established, that the nobility was inherent to the soil, and consequently that the land ought to transmit to its possessors the rights of nobility.

This privilege was so much accepted, that the long tenure of a fief ended by ennobling the commoner. Subsequently, by a sort of compensation which naturally followed, lands on which rent had hitherto been paid became free and noble on passing to the possession of a noble. At last, however, the contrary rule prevailed, which caused the lands not to change quality in changing owners: the noble could still possess the labourers's lands without losing his nobility, but the labourer could be proprietor of a fief without thereby becoming a noble.

To the *comites*, who, according to Tacitus, attached themselves to the fortunes of the Germanic chiefs, succeeded the Merovingian *leudes*, whose assembly formed the King's Council. These *leudes* were persons of great importance owing to the number of their vassals, and although they composed his ordinary Council, they did not hesitate at times to declare themselves openly opposed to his will.

[Illustration: Fig. 16.—Knight in War–harness, after a Miniature in a Psalter written and illuminated under Louis le Gros.]

The name of *leudes* was abandoned under the second of the then French dynasties, and replaced by that of *fideles*, which, in truth soon became a common designation of both the vassals of the Crown and those of the nobility.

Under the kings of the third dynasty, the kingdom was divided into about one hundred and fifty domains, which were called great fiefs of the crown, and which were possessed in hereditary right by the members of the highest nobility, placed immediately under the royal sovereignty and dependence.

[Illustration: Fig. 17.—King Charlemagne receiving the Oath of Fidelity and Homage from one of his great Feudatories or High Barons.—Fac-simile of a Miniature in Cameo, of the "Chronicles of St. Denis." Manuscript of the Fourteenth Century (Library of the Arsenal).]

Vassals emanating directly from the King, were then generally designated by the title of *barons*, and mostly possessed strongholds. The other nobles indiscriminately ranked as *chevaliers* or *cnights*, a generic title, to which was added that of *banneret*, The fiefs of *hauberk* were bound to supply the sovereign with a certain number of knights covered with coats of mail, and completely armed. All knights were mounted in war (Fig. 16); but knights who were made so in consequence of their high birth must not be confounded with those who became knights by some great feat in arms in the house of a prince or high noble, nor with the members of the different orders of chivalry which were successively instituted, such as the Knights of the Star, the Genet, the Golden Fleece, Saint-Esprit, St. John of Jerusalem, &c. Originally, the possession of a benefice or fief meant no more than the privilege of enjoying the profits derived from the land, a concession which made the holder dependent upon the proprietor. He was in fact his "man," to whom he owed homage (Fig. 17), service in case of war, and assistance in any suit the proprietor might have before the King's tribunal. The chiefs of German bands at first recompensed their companions in arms by giving them fiefs of parts of the territory which they had conquered; but later on, everything was equally given to be held in fief, namely, dignities, offices, rights, and incomes or titles.

It is important to remark (and it is in this alone that feudalism shows its social bearing), that if the vassal owed obedience and devotion to his lord, the lord in exchange owed protection to the vassal. The rank of "free man" did not necessarily require the possession of land; but the position of free men who did not hold fiefs was extremely delicate and often painful, for they were by natural right dependent upon those on whose domain they resided. In fact, the greater part of these nobles without lands became by choice the King's men, and remained attached to his service. If this failed them, they took lands on lease, so as to support themselves and their families, and to avoid falling into absolute servitude. In the event of a change of proprietor, they changed with the land into new hands. Nevertheless, it was not uncommon for them to be so reduced as to sell their freedom; but in such cases, they reserved the right, should better times come, of re—purchasing their liberty by paying one—fifth more than the sum for which they had sold it.

We thus see that in olden times, as also later, freedom was more or less the natural consequence of the possession of wealth or power on the part of individuals or families who considered themselves free in the midst of general dependence. During the tenth century, indeed, if not impossible, it was at least difficult to find a single inhabitant of the kingdom of France who was not "the man" of some one, and who was either tied by rules of a liberal order, or else was under the most servile obligations.

The property of the free men was originally the "*aleu*," which was under the jurisdiction of the royal magistrates. The *aleu* gradually lost the greater part of its franchise, and became liable to the common charges due on lands which were not freehold.

In ancient times, all landed property of a certain extent was composed of two distinct parts: one occupied by the owner, constituted the domain or manor; the other, divided between persons who were more or less dependent, formed what were called *tenures*. These *tenures* were again divided according to the position of those who occupied them: if they were possessed by free men, who took the name of vassals, they were called benefices or fiefs; if they were let to laeti, colons, or serfs, they were then called colonies or demesnes.

[Illustration: Fig. 18.—Ploughmen.—Fac—simile of a Miniature in a very ancient Anglo—Saxon Manuscript published by Shaw, with legend "God Spede ye Plough, and send us Korne enow."]

The *laeti* occupied a rank between the colon and the serf. They had less liberty than the colon, over whom the proprietor only had an indirect and very limited power. The colon only served the land, whilst the laeti, whether agriculturists or servants, served both the land and the owner (Fig. 18). They nevertheless enjoyed the right of possession, and of defending themselves, or prosecuting by law. The serf, on the contrary, had neither city, tribunal, nor family. The laeti had, besides, the power of purchasing their liberty when they had amassed sufficient for the purpose.

Serfs occupied the lowest position in the social ladder (Fig. 19). They succeeded to slaves, thus making, thanks to Christianity, a step towards liberty. Although the civil laws barely protected them, those of the Church continually stepped in and defended them from arbitrary despotism. The time came when they had no direct masters, and when the almost absolute dependence of serfs was changed by the nobles requiring them to farm the land and pay tithes and fees. And lastly, they became farmers, and regular taxes took the place of tithes and fees.

The colons, laeti, and serfs, all of whom were more or less tillers of the soil, were, so to speak, the ancestors of "the people" of modern times; those who remained devoted to agriculture were the ancestors of our peasants; and those who gave themselves up to trades and commerce in the towns, were the originators of the middle classes.

[Illustration: Fig. 19.—Serf or Vassal of Tenth Century, from Miniatures in the "Dialogues of St. Gregory," Manuscript No. 9917 (Royal Library of Brussels).]

As early as the commencement of the third royal dynasty we find in the rural districts, as well as in the towns, a great number of free men: and as the charters concerning the condition of lands and persons became more and more extended, the tyranny of the great was reduced, and servitude decreased. During the following centuries, the establishment of civic bodies and the springing up of the middle classes (Fig. 20) made the acquisition of liberty more easy and more general. Nevertheless, this liberty was rather theoretical than practical; for if the nobles granted it nominally, they gave it at the cost of excessive fines, and the community, which purchased at a high price the right of self–administration, did not get rid of any of the feudal charges imposed upon it.

[Illustration: Fig. 20.—Bourgeois at the End of Thirteenth Century.—Fac–simile of Miniature in Manuscript No. 6820, in the National Library of Paris.]

Fortunately for the progress of liberty, the civic bodies, as if they had been providentially warned of the future in store for them, never hesitated to accept from their lords, civil or ecclesiastical, conditions, onerous though they were, which enabled them to exist in the interior of the cities to which they belonged. They formed a sort of small state, almost independent for private affairs, subject to the absolute power of the King, and more or less tied by their customs or agreements with the local nobles. They held public assemblies and elected magistrates, whose powers embraced both the administration of civil and criminal justice, police, finance, and the militia. They generally had fixed and written laws. Protected by ramparts, each possessed a town–hall (*hotel de ville*), a seal, a treasury, and a watch—tower, and it could arm a certain number of men, either for its own defence or for the service of the noble or sovereign under whom it held its rights.

In no case could a community such as this exist without the sanction of the King, who placed it under the safeguard of the Crown. At first the kings, blinded by a covetous policy, only seemed to see in the issue of these charters an excellent pretext for extorting money. If they consented to recognise them, and even to help them against their lords, it was on account of the enormous sacrifices made by the towns. Later on, however, they affected, on the contrary, the greatest generosity towards the vassals who wished to incorporate themselves, when they had understood that these institutions might become powerful auxiliaries against the great titulary feudalists; but from the reign of Louis XI., when the power of the nobles was much diminished, and no longer inspired any terror to royalty, the kings turned against their former allies, the middle classes, and deprived them successively of all the prerogatives which could prejudice the rights of the Crown.

The middle classes, it is true, acquired considerable influence afterwards by participation in the general and provincial councils. After having victoriously struggled against the clergy and nobility, in the assemblies of the three states or orders, they ended by defeating royalty itself.

Louis le Gros, in whose orders the style or title of *bourgeois* first appears (1134), is generally looked upon as the founder of the franchise of communities in France; but it is proved that a certain number of communities or corporations were already formally constituted, before his accession to the throne.

The title of bourgeois was not, however, given exclusively to inhabitants of cities. It often happened that the nobles, with the intention of improving and enriching their domains, opened a kind of asylum, under the attractive title of *Free Towns*, or *New Towns*, where they offered, to all wishing to establish themselves, lands, houses, and a more or less extended share of privileges, rights, and liberties. These congregations, or families, soon became boroughs, and the inhabitants, though agriculturists, took the name of bourgeois.

[Illustration: Fig. 21.—Costume of a Vilain or Peasant, Fifteenth Century, from a Miniature of "La Danse Macabre," Manuscript 7310 of the National Library of Paris.]

17

There was also a third kind of bourgeois, whose influence on the extension of royal power was not less than that of the others. There were free men who, under the title of bourgeois of the King (bourgeois du Roy), kept their liberty by virtue of letters of protection given them by the King, although they were established on lands of nobles whose inhabitants were deprived of liberty. Further, when a *vilain* —that is to say, the serf, of a noble—bought a lease of land in a royal borough, it was an established custom that after having lived there a year and a day without being reclaimed by his lord and master, he became a bourgeois of the King and a free man. In consequence of this the serfs and vilains (Fig. 21) emigrated from all parts, in order to profit by these advantages, to such a degree, that the lands of the nobles became deserted by all the serfs of different degrees, and were in danger of remaining uncultivated. The nobility, in the interests of their properties, and to arrest this increasing emigration, devoted themselves to improving the condition of persons placed under their dependence, and attempted to create on their domains *boroughs* analogous to those of royalty. But however liberal these ameliorations might appear to be, it was difficult for the nobles not only to concede privileges equal to those emanating from the throne, but also to ensure equal protection to those they thus enfranchised. In spite of this, however, the result was that a double current of enfranchisement was established, which resulted in the daily diminution of the miserable order of serfs, and which, whilst it emancipated the lower orders, had the immediate result of giving increased weight and power to royalty, both in its own domains and in those of the nobility and their vassals.

These social revolutions did not, of course, operate suddenly, nor did they at once abolish former institutions, for we still find, that after the establishment of communities and corporations, several orders of servitude remained.

At the close of the thirteenth century, on the authority of Philippe de Beaumanoir, the celebrated editor of "Coutumes de Beauvoisis," there were three states or orders amongst the laity, namely, the nobleman (Fig. 22), the free man, and the serf. All noblemen were free, but all free men were not necessarily noblemen. Generally, nobility descended from the father and franchise from the mother. But according to many other customs of France, the child, as a general rule, succeeded to the lower rank of his parents. There were two orders of serfs: one rigorously held in the absolute dependence of his lord, to such a degree that the latter could appropriate during his life, or after death if he chose, all he possessed; he could imprison him, ill–treat him as he thought proper, without having to answer to any one but God; the other, though held equally in bondage, was more liberally

18

treated, for "unless he was guilty of some evil–doing, the lord could ask of him nothing during his life but the fees, rents, or fines which he owed on account of his servitude." If one of the latter class of serfs married a free woman, everything which he possessed became the property of his lord. The same was the case when he died, for he could not transmit any of his goods to his children, and was only allowed to dispose by will of a sum of about five sous, or about twenty–five francs of modern money.

As early as the fourteenth century, serfdom or servitude no longer existed except in "mortmain," of which we still have to speak.

[Illustration: The Court of Mary of Anjou, Wife of Charles VII.

Her chaplain the learned Robert Blondel presents her with the allegorical Treatise of the *"Twelve Perils of Hell."* Which he composed for her (1455). Fac–simile of a miniature from this work. Bibl. de l'Arsenal, Paris.]

Mortmain consisted of the privation of the right of freely disposing of one's person or goods. He who had not the power of going where he would, of giving or selling, of leaving by will or transferring his property, fixed or movable, as he thought best, was called a man of mortmain.

[Illustration: Fig. 22.—Italian Nobleman of the Fifteenth Century. From a Playing–card engraved on Copper about 1460 (Cabinet des Estampes, National Library of Paris).]

This name was apparently chosen because the hand, "considered the symbol of power and the instrument of donation," was deprived of movement, paralysed, in fact struck as by death. It was also nearly in this sense, that men of the Church were also called men of mortmain, because they were equally forbidden to dispose, either in life, or by will after death, of anything belonging to them.

There were two kinds of mortmain: real and personal; one concerning land, and the other concerning the person; that is to say, land held in mortmain did not change quality, whatever might be the position of the person who occupied it, and a "man of mortmain" did not cease to suffer the inconveniences of his position on whatever land he went to establish himself.

The mortmains were generally subject to the greater share of feudal obligations formerly imposed on serfs; these were particularly to work for a certain time for their lord without receiving any wages, or else to pay him the *tax* when it was due, on certain definite occasions, as for example, when he married, when he gave a dower to his daughter, when he was taken prisoner of war, when he went to the Holy Land, &c., &c. What particularly characterized the condition of mortmains was, that the lords had the right to take all their goods when they died without issue, or when the children held a separate household; and that they could not dispose of anything they possessed, either by will or gift, beyond a certain sum.

The noble who franchised mortmains, imposed on them in almost all cases very heavy conditions, consisting of fees, labours, and fines of all sorts. In fact, a mortmain person, to be free, not only required to be franchised by his own lord, but also by all the nobles on whom he was dependent, as well as by the sovereign. If a noble franchised without the consent of his superiors, he incurred a fine, as it was considered a dismemberment or depreciation of the fief.

As early as the end of the fourteenth century, the rigorous laws of mortmain began to fall into disuse in the provinces; though if the name began to disappear, the condition itself continued to exist. The free men, whether they belonged to the middle class or to the peasantry, were nevertheless still subject to pay fines or obligations to their lords of such a nature that they must be considered to have been practically in the same position as mortmains. In fact, this custom had been so deeply rooted into social habits by feudalism, that to make it disappear totally at the end of the eighteenth century, it required three decrees of the National Convention (July 17 and October 2, 1793; and 8 Ventose, year II.—that is, March 2, 1794).

It is only just to state, that twelve or fourteen years earlier, Louis XVI. had done all in his power towards the same purpose, by suppressing mortmain, both real or personal, on the lands of the Crown, and personal mortmain (i.e. the right of following mortmains out of their original districts) all over the kingdom.

[Illustration: Fig. 23.—Alms Bag taken from some Tapestry in Orleans, Fifteenth Century.]

Privileges and Rights. Feudal and Municipal.

Elements of Feudalism.—Rights of Treasure–trove, Sporting, Safe
Conducts, Ransom, Disinheritance, &c.—Immunity of the Feudalists.—Dues
from the Nobles to their Sovereign.—Law and University Dues.—Curious
Exactions resulting from the Universal System of Dues.—Struggles to
Enfranchise the Classes subjected to Dues.—Feudal Spirit and Citizen
Spirit.—Resuscitation of the System of Ancient Municipalities in Italy,
Germany, and France.—Municipal Institutions and Associations.—The
Community.—The Middle–Class Cities (*Cites Bourgeoises*).—Origin of
National Unity.

So as to understand the numerous charges, dues, and servitudes, often as quaint as
iniquitous and vexations, which weighed on the lower orders during the Middle Ages, we
must remember how the upper class, who assumed to itself the privilege of oppression on
lands and persons under the feudal System, was constituted.

The Roman nobles, heirs to their fathers' agricultural dominions, succeeded for the most
part in preserving through the successive invasions of the barbarians, the influence
attached to the prestige of birth and wealth; they still possessed the greater part of the
land and owned as vassals the rural populations. The Grerman nobles, on the contrary,
had not such extended landed properties, but they appropriated all the strongest positions.
The dukes, counts, and marquises were generally of German origin. The Roman race,
mixed with the blood of the various nations it had subdued, was the first to infuse itself
into ancient Society, and only furnished barons of a secondary order.

These heterogeneous elements, brought together, with the object of common dominion,
constituted a body who found life and motion only in the traditions of Rome and ancient
Germany. From these two historical sources, as is very judiciously pointed out by M.
Mary–Lafon, issued all the habits of the new society, and particularly the rights and
privileges assumed by the nobility.

These rights and privileges, which we are about to pass summarily in review, were
numerous, and often curious: amongst them may be mentioned the rights of
treasure–trove, the rights of wreck, the rights of establishing fairs or markets, rights of

marque, of sporting, &c.

The rights of treasure–trove were those which gave full power to dukes and counts over all minerals found on their properties. It was in asserting this right that the famous Richard Coeur de Lion, King of England, met his death. Adhemar, Viscount of Limoges, had discovered in a field a treasure, of which, no doubt, public report exaggerated the value, for it was said to be large enough to model in pure gold, and life–size, a Roman emperor and the members of his family, at table. Adhemar was a vassal of the Duke of Guienne, and, as a matter of course, set aside what was considered the sovereign's share in his discovery; but Richard, refusing to concede any part of his privilege, claimed the whole treasure. On the refusal of the viscount to give it up he appeared under arms before the gates of the Castle of Chalus, where he supposed that the treasure was hidden. On seeing the royal standard, the garrison offered to open the gates. "No," answered Richard, "since you have forced me to unfurl my banner, I shall only enter by the breach, and you shall all be hung on the battlements." The siege commenced, and did not at first seem to favour the English, for the besieged made a noble stand. One evening, as his troops were assaulting the place, in order to witness the scene, Richard was sitting at a short distance on a piece of rock, protected with a target—that is, a large shield covered with leather and blades of iron—which two archers held over him. Impatient to see the result of the assault, Richard pushed down the shield, and that moment decided his fate (1199). An archer of Chalus, who had recognised him and was watching from the top of the rampart, sent a bolt from a crossbow, which hit him full in the chest. The wound, however, would perhaps not have been mortal, but, shortly after, having carried the place by storm, and in his delight at finding the treasure almost intact, he gave himself up madly to degrading orgies, during which he had already dissipated the greater part of his treasure, and died of his wound twelve days later; first having, however, graciously pardoned the bowman who caused his death.

The right of shipwrecks, which the nobles of seaboard countries rarely renounced, and of which they were the more jealous from the fact that they had continually to dispute them with their vassals and neighbours, was the pitiless and barbaric right of appropriating the contents of ships happening to be wrecked on their shores.

[Illustration: Figs. 24 and 25.—Varlet or Squire carrying a Halberd with a thick Blade; and Archer, in Fighting Dress, drawing the String of his Crossbow with a double–handled Winch.—From the Miniatures of the "Jouvencel," and the "Chroniques" of Froissart, Manuscripts of the Fifteenth Century (Imperial Library of Paris).]

When the feudal nobles granted to their vassals the right of assembling on certain days, in order to hold fairs and markets, they never neglected to reserve to themselves some tax on each head of cattle, as well as on the various articles brought in and put up for sale. As these fairs and markets never failed to attract a great number of buyers and sellers, this formed a very lucrative tax for the noble (Fig. 26).

[Illustration: Fig. 26.—Flemish Peasants at the Cattle Market.—Miniature of the "Chroniques de Hainaut." Manuscripts of the Fifteenth Century, vol. ii. fol. 204 (Library of the Dukes of Burgundy, Brussels).]

The right of *marque*, or reprisal, was a most barbarous custom. A famous example is given of it. In 1022, William the Pious, Count of Angouleme, before starting for a pilgrimage to Rome, made his three brothers, who were his vassals, swear to live in honourable peace and good friendship. But, notwithstanding their oath, two of the brothers, having invited the third to the Easter festivities, seized him at night in his bed, put out his eyes so that he might not find the way to his castle, and cut out his tongue so that he might not name the authors of this horrible treatment. The voice of God, however, denounced them, and the Count of Angouleme, shuddering with horror, referred the case to his sovereign, the Duke of Aquitaine, William IV., who immediately came, and by fire and sword exercised his right of *marque* on the lands of the two brothers, leaving them nothing but their lives and limbs, after having first put out their eyes and cut out their tongues, so as to inflict on them the penalty of retaliation.

The right of sporting or hunting was of all prerogatives that dearest to, and most valued by the nobles. Not only were the severest and even cruellest penalties imposed on "vilains" who dared to kill the smallest head of game, but quarrels frequently arose between nobles of different degrees on the subject, some pretending to have a feudal privilege of hunting on the lands of others (Fig. 27). From this tyrannical exercise of the right of hunting, which the least powerful of the nobles only submitted to with the most violent and bitter feelings, sprung those old and familiar ballads, which indicate the popular sentiment on the subject. In some of these songs the inveterate hunters are condemned, by the order of Fairies or of the Fates, either to follow a phantom stag for everlasting, or to hunt, like King Artus, in the clouds and to catch a fly every hundred years.

The right of jurisdiction, which gave judicial power to the dukes and counts in cases arising in their domains, had no appeal save to the King himself, and this was even often contested by the nobles, as for instance, in the unhappy case of Enguerrand de Coucy. Enguerrand had ordered three young Flemish noblemen, who were scholars at the Abbey of "St. Nicholas des Bois," to be seized and hung, because, not knowing that they were on the domain of the Lord of Coucy, they had killed a few rabbits with arrows. St. Louis called the case before him. Enguerrand answered to the call, but only to dispute the King's right, and to claim the judgment of his peers. The King, without taking any notice of the remonstrance, ordered Enguerrand to be locked up in the big tower of the Louvre, and was nearly applying the law of *retaliation* to his case. Eventually he granted him letters of pardon, after condemning him to build three chapels, where masses were continually to be said for the three victims; to give the forest where the young scholars had been found hunting, to the Abbey of "St. Nicholas des Bois;" to lose on all his estates the rights of jurisdiction and sporting; to serve three years in the Holy Land; and to pay to the King a fine of 12,500 pounds tournois. It must be remembered that Louis IX., although most generous in cases relating simply to private interests, was one of the most stubborn defenders of royal prerogatives.

A right which feudalists had the greatest interest in observing, and causing to be respected, because they themselves might with their wandering habits require it at any moment, was that of *safe convoy*, or *guidance*. This right was so powerful, that it even applied itself to the lower orders, and its violation was considered the most odious crime; thus, in the thirteenth century, the King of Aragon was severely abused by all persons and all classes, because in spite of this right he caused a Jew to be burned so as not to have to pay a debt which the man claimed of him.

[Illustration: Fig. 27.—Nobleman in Hunting Costume, preceded by his Servant, trying to find the Scent of a Stag.—From a Miniature in the Book of Gaston Phoebus ("Des Deduitz de la Chasse des Bestes Sauvaiges").—Manuscript of the Fourteenth Century (National Library of Paris).]

The right of "the Crown" should also be mentioned, which consisted of a circle of gold ornamented in various fashions, according to the different degrees of feudal monarchy, which vassals had to present to their lord on the day of his investiture. The right of seal was a fee or fine they had to pay for the charters which their lord caused to be delivered to them.

The duty of *aubaine* was the fine or due paid by merchants, either in kind or money, to the feudal chief, when they passed near his castle, landed in his ports, or exposed goods for sale in his markets.

The nobles of second order possessed among their privileges that of wearing spurs of silver or gold according to their rank of knighthood; the right of receiving double rations when prisoners of war; the right of claiming a year's delay when a creditor wished to seize their land; and the right of never having to submit to torture after trial, unless they were condemned to death for the crime they had committed. If a great baron for serious offences confiscated the goods of a noble who was his vassal, the latter had a right to keep his palfrey, the horse of his squire, various pieces of his harness and armour, his bed, his silk robe, his wife's bed, one of her dresses, her ring, her cloth stomacher, &c.

The nobles alone possessed the right of having seats of honour in churches and in chapels (Fig. 28), and to erect therein funereal monuments, and we know that they maintained this right so rigorously and with so much effrontery, that fatal quarrels at times arose on questions of precedence. The epitaphs, the placing of tombs, the position of a monument, were all subjects for conflicts or lawsuits. The nobles enjoyed also the right of *disinheritance*, that is to say, of claiming the goods of a person dying on their lands who had no direct heir; the right of claiming a tax when a fief or domain changed hands; the right of *common oven*, or requiring vassals to make use of the mill, the oven, or the press of the lord. At the time of the vintage, no peasant might sell his wine until the nobles had sold theirs. Everything was a source of privilege for the nobles. Kings and councils waived the necessity of their studying, in order to be received as bachelors of universities. If a noble was made a prisoner of war, his life was saved by his nobility, and his ransom had practically to be raised by the "vilains" of his domains. The nobles were also exempted from serving in the militia, nor were they obliged to lodge soldiers, &c. They had a thousand pretexts for establishing taxes on their vassals, who were generally considered "taxable and to be worked at will." Thus in the domain of Montignac, the Count of Perigord claimed among other things as follows: "for every case of censure or complaint brought before him, 10 deniers; for a quarrel in which blood was shed, 60 sols; if blood was not shed, 7 sols; for use of ovens, the sixteenth loaf of each baking; for the sale of corn in the domain, 43 setiers: besides these, 6 setiers of rye, 161 setiers of oats, 3 setiers of beans, 1 pound of wax, 8 capons, 17 hens, and 37 loads of wine." There were a multitude of other rights due to him, including the provostship fees, the fees on deeds, the tolls and furnaces of towns, the taxes on salt, on leather, corn, nuts; fees for the right of fishing; for the right of sporting, which last gave the lord a certain part or quarter of the game killed, and, in addition, the *dime* or tenth part of all the corn, wine, &c., &c.

[Illustration: Fig. 28.—Jean Jouvenel des Ursins, Provost of the Merchants of Paris, and Michelle de Vitry, his Wife, in the Reign of Charles VI.—Fragment of a Picture of the Period, which was in the Chapel of the Ursinus, and is now in the Versailles Museum.]

This worthy noble gathered in besides all this, during the religious festivals of the year, certain tributes in money on the estate of Montignac alone, amounting to as much as 20,000 pounds tournois. One can judge by this rough sketch, of the income he must have had, both in good and bad years, from his other domains in the rich county of Perigord.

It must not be imagined that this was an exceptional case; all over the feudal territory the same state of things existed, and each lord farmed both his lands and the persons whom feudal right had placed under his dependence.

[Illustration: Fig. 29.—Dues on Wines, granted to the Chapter of Tournai by King Chilperic.—From the Windows of the Cathedral of Tournai, Fifteenth Century.]

To add to these already excessive rates and taxes, there were endless dues, under all shapes and names, claimed by the ecclesiastical lords (Figs. 29 and 30). And not only did the nobility make without scruple these enormous exactions, but the Crown supported them in avenging any act, however opposed to all sense of justice; so that the nobles were really placed above the great law of equality, without which the continuance of social order seemed normally impossible.

The history of the city of Toulouse gives us a significant example on this subject.

[Illustration: Fig. 30.—The Bishop of Tournai receiving the Tithe of Beer granted by King Chilperic.—From the Windows of the Cathedral of Tournai, Fifteenth Century.]

On Easter Day, 1335, some students of the university, who had passed the night of the anniversary of the resurrection of our Saviour in drinking, left the table half intoxicated, and ran about the town during the hours of service, beating pans and cauldrons, and making such a noise and disturbance, that the indignant preachers were obliged to stop in the middle of their discourses, and claimed the intervention of the municipal authorities of Toulouse. One of these, the lord of Gaure, went out of church with five sergeants, and tried himself to arrest the most turbulent of the band. But as he was seizing him by the body, one of his comrades gave the lord a blow with a dagger, which cut off his nose, lips, and part of his chin. This occurrence aroused the whole town. Toulouse had been insulted in the person of its first magistrate, and claimed vengeance. The author of the deed, named Aimeri de Berenger, was seized, judged, condemned, and beheaded, and his body was suspended on the *spikes* of the Chateau Narbonnais.

[Illustration: Fig. 31.—Fellows of the University of Paris haranguing the Emperor Charles IV. in 1377.—From a Miniature of the Manuscript of the "Chroniques de St. Denis," No. 8395 (National Library of Paris).]

Toulouse had to pay dearly for the respect shown to its municipal dignity. The parents of the student presented a petition to the King against the city, for having dared to execute a noble and to hang his body on a gibbet, in opposition to the sacred right which this noble had of appealing to the judgment of his peers. The Parliament of Paris finally decided the matter with the inflexible partiality to the rights of rank, and confiscated all the goods of the inhabitants, forced the principal magistrates to go on their knees before the house of Aimeri de Berenger, and ask pardon; themselves to take down the body of the victim, and to have it publicly and honourably buried in the burial–ground of the Daurade. Such was the sentence and humiliation to which one of the first towns of the south was subjected, for having practised immediate justice on a noble, whilst it would certainly have suffered no vindication, if the culprit condemned to death had belonged to the middle or lower orders.

We must nevertheless remember that heavy dues fell upon the privileged class themselves to a certain degree, and that if they taxed their poor vassals without mercy, they had in their turn often to reckon with their superiors in the feudal hierarchy.

Albere, or right of shelter, was the principal charge imposed upon the noble. When a great baron visited his lands, his tenants were not only obliged to give him and his followers shelter, but also provisions and food, the nature and quality of which were all arranged beforehand with the most extraordinary minuteness. The lesser nobles took advantage sometimes of the power they possessed to repurchase this obligation; but the rich, on the contrary, were most anxious to seize the occasion of proudly displaying before their sovereign all the pomp in their power, at the risk even of mortgaging their

27

revenues for several years, and of ruining their vassals. History is full of stories bearing witness to the extravagant prodigalities of certain nobles on such occasions.

Payments in kind fell generally on the abbeys, up to 1158. That of St. Denis, which was very rich in lands, was charged with supplying the house and table of the King. This tax, which became heavier and heavier, eventually fell on the Parisians, who only succeeded in ridding themselves of it in 1374, when Charles V. made all the bourgeois of Paris noble. In the twelfth century, all furniture made of wood or iron which was found in the house of the Bishop at his death, became the property of the King. But in the fourteenth century, the abbots of St. Denis, St. Germain des Pres, St. Genevieve (Fig. 32), and a few priories in the neighbourhood of Paris, were only required to present the sovereign with two horse–loads of produce annually, so as to keep up the old system of fines.

This system of rents and dues of all kinds was so much the basis of social organization in the Middle Ages, that it sometimes happened that the lower orders benefited by it.

Thus the bed of the Bishop of Paris belonged, after his death, to the poor invalids of the Hotel Dieu. The canons were also bound to leave theirs to that hospital, as an atonement for the sins which they had committed. The Bishops of Paris were required to give two very sumptuous repasts to their chapters at the feasts of St. Eloi and St. Paul. The holy men of St. Martin were obliged, annually, on the 10th of November, to offer to the first President of the Court of Parliament, two square caps, and to the first usher, a writing–desk and a pair of gloves. The executioner too received, from various monastic communities of the capital, bread, bottles of wine, and pigs' heads; and even criminals who were taken to Montfaucon to be hung had the right to claim bread and wine from the nuns of St. Catherine and the Filles Dieux, as they passed those establishments on their way to the gibbet.

[Illustration: Fig. 32.—Front of the Ancient Church of the Abbey of Sainte–Genevieve, in Paris, founded by Clovis, and rebuilt from the Eleventh to Thirteenth Centuries.—State of the Building before its Destruction at the End of the Last Century.]

Fines were levied everywhere, at all times, and for all sorts of reasons. Under the name of *epices*, the magistrates, judges, reporters, and counsel, who had at first only received sweetmeats and preserves as voluntary offerings, eventually exacted substantial tribute in current coin. Scholars who wished to take rank in the University sent some small pies, costing ten sols, to each examiner. Students in philosophy or theology gave two suppers to the president, eight to the other masters, besides presenting them with sweetmeats, &c. It would be an endless task to relate all the fines due by apprentices and companions before they could reach mastership in their various crafts, nor have we yet mentioned certain fines, which, from their strange or ridiculous nature, prove to what a pitch of folly men may be led under the influence of tyranny, vanity, or caprice.

Thus, we read of vassals descending to the humiliating occupation of beating the water of the moat of the castle, in order to stop the noise of the frogs, during the illness of the mistress; we elsewhere find that at times the lord required of them to hop on one leg, to kiss the latch of the castle–gate, or to go through some drunken play in his presence, or sing a somewhat broad song before the lady.

At Tulle, all the rustics who had married during the year were bound to appear on the Puy or Mont St. Clair. At twelve o'clock precisely, three children came out of the hospital, one beating a drum violently, the other two carrying a pot full of dirt; a herald called the names of the bride–grooms, and those who were absent or were unable to assist in breaking the pot by throwing stones at it, paid a fine.

At Perigueux, the young couples had to give the consuls a pincushion of embossed leather or cloth of different colours; a woman marrying a second time was required to present them with an earthen pot containing twelve sticks of different woods; a woman marrying for the third time, a barrel of cinders passed thirteen times through the sieve, and thirteen spoons made of wood of fruit–trees; and, lastly, one coming to the altar for the fifth time was obliged to bring with her a small tub containing the excrement of a white hen!

"The people of the Middle Ages and the Renaissance period were literally tied down with taxes and dues of all sorts," says M. Mary–Lafon. "If a few gleams of liberty reached them, it was only from a distance, and more in the hope of the future than as regarded the present. As an example of the way people were treated, a certain Lord of Laguene, spoken of in the old chronicles of the south, may be mentioned. Every year, this cunning baron assembled his tenants in the village square. A large maypole was planted, and on the top was attached a wren. The lord, pointing to the little bird, declared solemnly, that if any 'vilain' succeeded in piercing him with an arrow he should be exempt from that year's dues. The vilains shot away, but, to the great merriment of their lord, never hit, and so had to continue paying the dues."

[Illustration: Fig. 33.—Ramparts of the Town of Aigues–Mortes, one of the Municipalities of Languedoc.]

One can easily understand how such a system, legalised by law, hampered the efforts for freedom, which a sense of human dignity was constantly raising in the bosoms of the oppressed. The struggle was long, often bloody, and at times it seemed almost hopeless, for on both sides it was felt that the contest was between two principles which were incompatible, and one of which must necessarily end by annihilating the other. Any compromise between the complete slavery and the personal freedom of the lower orders, could only be a respite to enable these implacable adversaries to reinforce themselves, so as to resume with more vigour than ever this desperate combat, the issue of which was so long to remain doubtful.

[Illustration: Louis IV Leaving Alexandria on the 24th of April 1507 To chastise the city of Genoa.

From a miniature by Jean Marot. No 5091, Bibl. nat'le de Paris.]

These efforts to obtain individual liberty displayed themselves more particularly in towns; but although they became almost universal in the west, they had not the same importance or character everywhere. The feudal system had not everywhere produced the same consequences. Thus, whilst in ancient Gaul it had absorbed all social vitality, we find that in Germany, the place of its origin, the Teutonic institutions of older date gave a comparative freedom to the labourers. In southern countries again we find the same beneficial effect from the Roman rule.

On that long area of land reaching from the southern slope of the Cevennes to the Apennines, the hand of the barbarian had weighed much less heavily than on the rest of Europe. In those favoured provinces where Roman organization had outlived Roman patronage, it seems as if ancient splendour had never ceased to exist, and the elegance of customs re–flourished amidst the ruins. There, a sort of urban aristocracy always continued, as a balance against the nobles, and the counsel of elected *prud'hommes*, the syndics, jurors or *capitouls*, who in the towns replaced the Roman *honorati* and *curiales*, still were considered by kings and princes as holding some position in the state. The municipal body, larger, more open than the old "ward," no longer formed a corporation of unwilling aristocrats enchained to privileges which ruined them. The principal cities on the Italian coast had already amassed enormous wealth by commerce, and displayed the most remarkable ardour, activity, and power. The Eternal City, which was disputed by emperors, popes, and barons of the Roman States, bestirred itself at times to snatch at the ancient phantom of republicanism; and this phantom was destined soon to change into reality, and another Rome, or rather a new Carthage, the lovely Venice, arose free and independent from the waves of the Adriatic (Fig. 34).

In Lombardy, so thickly colonised by the German conquerors, feudalism, on the contrary, weighed heavily; but there, too, the cities were populous and energetic, and the struggle for supremacy continued for centuries in an uncompromising manner between the people and the nobles, between the Guelphs and the Ghibellines.

In the north and east of the Gallic territory, the instinct of resistance did not exist any the less, though perhaps it was more intermittent. In fact, in these regions we find ambitious nobles forestalling the action of the King, and in order to attach towns to themselves and their houses, suppressing the most obnoxious of the taxes, and at the same time granting legal guarantees. For this the Counts of Flanders became celebrated, and the famous Heribert de Vermandois was noted for being so exacting in his demands with the great, and yet so popular with the small.

[Illustration: Fig. 34.—View of St. Mark's Place, Venice, Sixteenth Century, after Cesare Vecellio.]

The eleventh century, during which feudal power rose to its height, was also the period when a reaction set in of the townspeople against the nobility. The spirit of the city revived with that of the bourgeois (a name derived from the Teutonic word *burg*, habitation) and infused a feeling of opposition to the system which followed the conquest of the Teutons. "But," says M. Henri Martin, "what reappeared was not the Roman municipality of the Empire, stained by servitude, although surrounded with glittering pomp and gorgeous arts, but it was something coarse and almost semi−barbarous in form, though strong and generous at core, and which, as far as the difference of the times would allow, rather reminds us of the small republics which existed previous to the Roman Empire."

Two strong impulses, originating from two totally dissimilar centres of action, irresistibly propelled this great social revolution, with its various and endless aspects, affecting all central Europe, and being more or less felt in the west, the north, and the south. On one side, the Greek and Latin partiality for ancient corporations, modified by a democratic element, and an innate feeling of opposition characteristic of barbaric tribes; and on the other, the free spirit and equality of the old Celtic tribes rising suddenly against the military hierarchy, which was the offspring of conquest. Europe was roused by the double current of ideas which simultaneously urged her on to a new state of civilisation, and more particularly to a new organization of city life.

Italy was naturally destined to be the country where the new trials of social regeneration were to be made; but she presented the greatest possible variety of customs, laws, and governments, including Emperor, Pope, bishops, and feudal princes. In Tuscany and Liguria, the march towards liberty was continued almost without effort; whilst in Lombardy, on the contrary, the feudal resistance was very powerful. Everywhere, however, cities became more or less completely enfranchised, though some more rapidly than others. In Sicily, feudalism swayed over the countries; but in the greater part of the peninsula, the democratic spirit of the cities influenced the enfranchisement of the rural population. The feudal caste was in fact dissolved; the barons were transformed into patricians of the noble towns which gave their republican magistrates the old title of consuls. The Teutonic Emperor in vain sought to seize and turn to his own interest the sovereignty of the people, who had shaken off the yokes of his vassals: the signal of war was immediately given by the newly enfranchised masses; and the imperial eagle was obliged to fly before the banners of the besieged cities. Happy indeed might the cities of Italy have been had they not forgotten, in their prosperity, that union alone could give them the possibility of maintaining that liberty which they so freely risked in continual quarrels amongst one another!

[Illustration: Fig. 35.—William, Duke of Normandy, accompanied by Eustatius, Count of Boulogne, and followed by his Knights in arms.—Military Dress of the Eleventh Century, from Bayeux Tapestry said to have been worked by Queen Matilda.]

The Italian movement was immediately felt on the other side of the Alps. In Provence, Septimanie, and Aquitaine, we find, in the eleventh century, cities which enjoyed considerable freedom. Under the name of communities and universities, which meant that all citizens were part of the one body, they jointly interfered in the general affairs of the kingdom to which they belonged. Their magistrates were treated on a footing of equality with the feudal nobility, and although the latter at first would only recognise them as "good men" or notables, the consuls knew how to make a position for themselves in the hierarchy. If the consulate, which was a powerful expression of the most prominent system of independence, did no succeed in suppressing feudalism in Provence as in Italy, it at least so transformed it, that it deprived it of its most unjust and insupportable elements. At Toulouse, for instance (where the consuls were by exception called *capitouls*, that is to say, heads of the chapters or councils of the city), the lord of the country seemed less a feudal prince in his capital, than an honorary magistrate of the bourgeoisie. Avignon added to her consuls two *podestats* (from the Latin *potestas*, power). At Marseilles, the University of the high city was ruled by a republic under the presidency of the Count of Provence, although the lower city was still under the sovereignty of a viscount. Perigueux, which was divided into two communities, "the great and the small fraternity," took up arms to resist the authority of the Counts of Perigord; and Arles under its *podestats* was governed for some time as a free and imperial town. Amongst the constitutions which were established by the cities, from the eleventh to the sixteenth centuries, we find admirable examples of administration and government, so that one is struck with admiration at the efforts of intelligence and patriotism, often uselessly lavished on such small political arenas. The consulate, which nominally at least found its origin in the ancient grandeur of southern regions, did not spread itself beyond Lyons. In the centre of France, at Poictiers, Tours, Moulin, &c., the urban progress only manifested itself in efforts which were feeble and easily suppressed; but in the north, on the contrary, in the provinces between the Seine and the Rhine, and even between the Seine and the Loire, the system of franchise took footing and became recognised. In some places, the revolution was effected without difficulty, but in others it gave rise to the most determined struggles. In Normandy, for instance, under the active and intelligent government of the dukes of the race of Roll or Rollon, the middle class was rich and even warlike. It had access to the councils of the duchy; and when it was contemplated to invade England, the Duke William (Fig. 35) found support from the middle class, both in money and men. The case was the same in Flanders, where the towns of Ghent (Fig. 36), of Bruges, of Ypres, after being enfranchised but a short time developed with great rapidity. But in the other counties of western France, the greater part of the towns were still much oppressed by the counts and bishops. If some obtained certain franchises, these privileges were their ultimate ruin, owing to the ill faith of their nobles. A town between the Loire and the Seine gave the signal which caused the regeneration of the North. The inhabitants of Mans formed a community or association, and took an oath that they would obtain and maintain certain rights. They rebelled about 1070, and forced the count and his noble vassals to grant them the freedom which they had sworn to obtain, though William of Normandy very soon restored the rebel city to order, and dissolved the presumptuous community. However, the example soon bore fruit. Cambrai rose in its turn and proclaimed the "Commune," and although its bishop, aided by treason and by the Count of Hainault, reduced it to obedience, it only seemed to succumb for a time, to renew the struggle with greater success at a subsequent period.

[Illustration: Fig. 36.—Civic Guard of Ghent (Brotherhood of St. Sebastian), from a painting on the Wall of the Chapel of St. John and St. Paul, Ghent, near the Gate of Bruges.]

We have just mentioned the Commune; but we must not mistake the true meaning of this word, which, under a Latin form (*communitas*), expresses originally a Germanic idea, and in its new form a Christian mode of living. Societies of mutual defence, guilds, &c., had never disappeared from Germanic and Celtic countries; and, indeed, knighthood itself was but a brotherhood of Christian warriors. The societies of the *Paix de Dieu*, and of the *Treve de Dieu*, were encouraged by the clergy in order to stop the bloody quarrels of the nobility, and formed in reality great religious guilds. This idea of a body of persons taking some common oath to one another, of which feudalism gave so striking an example, could not fail to influence the minds of the rustics and the lower classes, and they only wanted the opportunity which the idea of the Commune at once gave them of imitating their superiors.

They too took oaths, and possessed their bodies and souls in "common;" they seized, by force of strategy, the ramparts of their towns; they elected mayors, aldermen, and jurors, who were charged to watch over the interests of their association. They swore to spare neither their goods, their labour, nor their blood, in order to free themselves; and not content with defending themselves behind barricades or chains which closed the streets, they boldly took the offensive against the proud feudal chiefs before whom their fathers had trembled, and they forced the nobles, who now saw themselves threatened by this armed multitude, to acknowledge their franchise by a solemn covenant.

It does not follow that everywhere the Commune was established by means of insurrection, for it was obtained after all sorts of struggles; and franchises were sold in some places for gold, and in others granted by a more or less voluntary liberality.

Everywhere the object was the same; everywhere they struggled or negotiated to upset, by a written constitution or charter, the violence and arbitrary rule under which they had so long suffered, and to replace by an annual and fixed rent, under the protection of an independent and impartial law, the unlimited exactions and disguised plundering so long made by the nobility and royalty. Circumstanced as they were, what other means had they to attain this end but ramparts and gates, a common treasury, a permanent military force, and magistrates who were both administrators, judges, and captains? The hotel de ville, or mansion–house, immediately became a sort of civic temple, where the banner of the Commune, the emblems of unity, and the seal which sanctioned the municipal acts were preserved. Then arose the watch–towers, where the watchmen were unceasingly posted night and day, and whence the alarm signal was ever ready to issue its powerful sounds when danger threatened the city. These watch–towers, the monuments of liberty, became as necessary for the burghers as the clock–towers of their cathedrals, whose brilliant peals and joyous chimes gave zest to the popular feasts (Fig. 37). The mansion–houses built in Flanders from the fourteenth to the sixteenth centuries, under municipal influence, are marvels of architecture.

[Illustration: Fig. 37.—Chimes of the Clock of St. Lambert of Liege.]

Who is there who could thoroughly describe or even appreciate all the happy or unhappy vicissitudes relating to the establishment of the Communes? We read of the Commune of Cambrai, four times created, four times destroyed, and which was continually at war with the Bishops; the Commune of Beauvais, sustained on the contrary by the diocesan prelate against two nobles who possessed feudal rights over it; Laon, a commune bought for money from the bishop, afterwards confirmed by the King, and then violated by fraud and treachery, and eventually buried in the blood of its defenders. We read also of St. Quentin, where the Count of Vermandois and his vassals voluntarily swore to maintain the right of the bourgeois, and scrupulously respected their oath. In many other localities the feudal dignitaries took alarm simply at the name of Commune, and whereas they would not agree to the very best arrangements under this terrible designation, they did not hesitate to adopt them when called either the "laws of friendship," the "peace of God," or the "institutions of peace." At Lisle, for instance, the bourgeois magistrates took the name of *appeasers*, or watchers over friendship. At Aire, in Artois, the members of friendship mutually, not only helped one another against the enemy, but also assisted one another in distress.

[Illustration: Fig. 38.—The Deputies of the burghers of Ghent, in revolt against their Sovereign Louis II., Count of Flanders, come to beg him to pardon them, and to return to their Town. 1397—Miniature from Froissart, No. 2644 (National Library of Paris)]

Amiens deserves the first place amongst the cities which dearly purchased their privileges. The most terrible and sanguinary war was sustained by the bourgeois against their count and lord of the manor, assisted by King Louis le Gros, who had under similar circumstances just taken the part of the nobles of Laon.

From Amiens, which, having been triumphant, became a perfect municipal republic, the example propagated itself throughout the rest of Picardy, the Isle of France, Normandy, Brittany, and Burgundy, and by degrees, without any revolutionary shocks, reached the region of Lyons, where the consulate, a characteristic institution of southern Communes, ended.

From Flanders, also, the movement spread in the direction of the German Empire; and there, too, the struggle was animated, and victorious against the aristocracy, until at last the great system of enfranchisement prevailed; and the cities of the west and south formed a confederation against the nobles, whilst those in the north formed the famous Teutonic Hanse, so celebrated for its maritime commerce.

The centre of France slowly followed the movement; but its progress was considerably delayed by the close influence of royalty, which sometimes conceded large franchises, and sometimes suppressed the least claims to independence. The kings, who willingly favoured Communes on the properties of their neighbours, did not so much care to see them forming on their own estates; unless the exceptional position and importance of any town required a wise exercise of tolerance. Thus Orleans, situated in the heart of the royal domains, was roughly repulsed in its first movement; whilst Mantes, which was on the frontier of the Duchy of Normandy, and still under the King of England, had but to ask in order to receive its franchise from the King of France.

It was particularly in the royal domains that cities were to be found, which, although they did not possess the complete independence of communes, had a certain amount of liberty and civil guarantees. They had neither the right of war, the watch-tower, nor the exclusive jurisdiction over their elected magistrates, for the bailiffs and the royal provosts represented the sovereign amongst them (Fig. 39).

[Illustration: Fig. 39.—Bailliage, or Tribunal of the King's Bailiff.—Fac−simile of an Engraving on Wood in the Work of Josse Damhoudere, "Praxis Rerum Civilium." (Antwerp, 1557, in 4to.).]

In Paris, less than anywhere, could the kings consent to the organization of an independent political System, although that city succeeded in creating for itself a municipal existence. The middle−class influence originated in a Gallo−Roman corporation. The Company of *Nautes* or "the Corporation of the Water Trade," formed a centre round which were successively attached various bodies of different trades. Gradually a strong concourse of civic powers was established, which succeeded in electing a municipal council, composed of a provost of merchants, four aldermen, and twenty−six councillors of the town. This council afterwards succeeded in overstepping the royal influence at difficult times, and was destined to play a prominent part in history.

There also sprang up a lower order of towns or boroughs than these bourgeois cities, which were especially under the Crown. Not having sufficient strength to claim a great amount of liberty, they were obliged to be satisfied with a few privileges, conceded to them by the nobles, for the most part with a political end. These were the Free Towns or New Towns which we have already named.

However it came about, it is certain that although during the tenth century feudal power was almost supreme in Europe, as early as the twelfth century the municipal system had gained great weight, and was constantly progressing until the policy of the kingdom became developed on a more and more extended basis, so that it was then necessary for it to give up its primitive nature, and to participate in the great movement of consolidisation and national unity. In this way the position of the large towns in the state relatively lost their individual position, and became somewhat analogous, as compared with the kingdom at large, to that formerly held by bourgeois in the cities. Friendly ties arose between provinces; and distinct and rival interests were effaced by the general aspiration towards common objects. The towns were admitted to the states general, and the citizens of various regions mixed as representatives of the *Tiers Etat*. Three orders thus met, who were destined to struggle for predominance in the future.

We must call attention to the fact that, as M. Henri Martin says, by an apparent contradiction, the fall of the Communes declared itself in inverse ratio to the progress of the *Tiers Etat*. By degrees, as the government became more settled from the great fiefs being absorbed by the Crown, and as parliament and other courts of appeal which emanated from the middle class extended their high judiciary and military authority, so the central power, organized under monarchical form, must necessarily have been less disposed to tolerate the local independence of the Communes. The State replaced the Commune for everything concerning justice, war, and administration. No doubt some valuable privileges were lost; but that was only an accidental circumstance, for a great social revolution was produced, which cleared off at once all the relics of the old age; and when the work of reconstruction terminated, homage was rendered to the venerable name of "Commune," which became uniformly applied to all towns, boroughs, or villages into which the new spirit of the same municipal system was infused.

[Illustration: Fig. 40.—Various Arms of the Fifteenth Century.]

Private Life in the Castles, the Towns, and the Rural Districts.

The Merovingian Castles.—Pastimes of the Nobles; Hunting, War.—Domestic Arrangements.—Private Life of Charlemagne.—Domestic Habits under the Carlovingians.—Influence of Chivalry.—Simplicity of the Court of Philip Angustus not imitated by his Successors.—Princely Life of the Fifteenth Century.—The bringing up of Latour Landry, a Noble of Anjou.—Varlets, Pages, Esquires, Maids of Honour.—Opulence of the Bourgeoisie.—"Le Menagier de Paris."—Ancient Dwellings.—State of Rustics at various Periods.—"Rustic Sayings," by Noel du Fail.

Augustin Thierry, taking Gregory of Tours, the Merovingian Herodotus, as an authority, thus describes a royal domain under the first royal dynasty of France:—

"This dwelling in no way possessed the military aspect of the chateau of the Middle Ages; it was a large building surrounded with porticos of Roman architecture, sometimes built of carefully polished and sculptured wood, which in no way was wanting in elegance. Around the main body of the building were arranged the dwellings of the officers of the palace, either foreigners or Romans, and those of the chiefs of companies, who, according to Germanic custom, had placed themselves and their warriors under the King, that is to say, under a special engagement of vassalage and fidelity. Other houses, of less imposing appearance, were occupied by a great number of families, who worked at all sorts of trades, such as jewellery, the making of arms, weaving, currying, the embroidering of silk and gold, cotton, &c.

"Farm–buildings, paddocks, cow–houses, sheepfolds, barns, the houses of agriculturists, and the cabins of the serfs, completed the royal village, which perfectly resembled, although on a larger scale, the villages of ancient Germany. There was something too in the position of these dwellings which resembled the scenery beyond the Rhine; the greater number of them were on the borders, and some few in the centre of great forests, which have since been partly destroyed, and the remains of which we so much admire."

[Illustration: Fig. 41.—St. Remy, Bishop of Rheims, begging of Clovis the restitution of the Sacred Vase taken by the Franks in the Pillage of Soissons.—Costumes of the Court of Burgundy in the Fifteenth Century.—Fac–simile of a Miniature on a Manuscript of the "History of the Emperors" (Library of the Arsenal).]

Although historical documents are not very explicit respecting those remote times, it is only sufficient to study carefully a very small portion of the territory in order to form some idea of the manners and customs of the Franks; for in the royal domain we find the existence of all classes, from the sovereign himself down to the humblest slave. As regards the private life, however, of the different classes in this elementary form of society, we have but approximate and very imperfect notions.

It is clear, however, that as early as the beginning of the Merovingian race, there was much more luxury and comfort among the upper classes than is generally supposed. All the gold and silver furniture, all the jewels, and all the rich stuffs which the Gallo–Romans had amassed in their sumptuous dwellings, had not been destroyed by the barbarians. The Frank Kings had appropriated the greater part; and the rest had fallen into the hands of the chiefs of companies in the division of spoil. A well–known anecdote, namely, that concerning the Vase of Soissons (Fig. 41), which King Clovis wished to preserve, and which a soldier broke with an axe, proves that many gems of ancient art must have disappeared, owing to the ignorance and brutality of the conquerors; although it is equally certain that the latter soon adopted the tastes and customs of the native population. At first, they appropriated everything that flattered their pride and sensuality. This is how the material remains of the civilisation of the Gauls were preserved in the royal and noble residences, the churches, and the monasteries. Gregory of Tours informs us, that when Fredegonde, wife of Chilperic, gave the hand of her daughter Rigouthe to the son of the Gothic king, fifty chariots were required to carry away all the valuable objects which composed the princess's dower. A strange family scene, related by the same historian, gives us an idea of the private habits of the court of that terrible queen of the Franks. "The mother and daughter had frequent quarrels, which sometimes ended in the most violent encounters. Fredegonde said one day to Rigouthe, 'Why do you continually trouble me? Here are the goods of your father, take them and do as you like with them.' And conducting her to a room where she locked up her treasures, she opened a large box filled with valuables. After having pulled out a great number of jewels which she gave to her daughter, she said, 'I am tired; put your own hands in the box, and take what you find.' Rigouthe bent down to reach the objects placed at the bottom of the box; upon which Fredegonde immediately lowered the lid on her daughter, and pressed upon it with so much force that the eyes began to start out of the princess's head. A maid began screaming, 'Help! my mistress is being murdered by her mother!' and Rigouthe was saved from an untimely end." It is further related that this was only one of the minor crimes attributed by history to Fredegonde *the Terrible*, who always carried a dagger or poison about with her.

Amongst the Franks, as amongst all barbaric populations, hunting was the pastime preferred when war was not being waged. The Merovingian nobles were therefore determined hunters, and it frequently happened that hunting occupied whole weeks, and took them far from their homes and families. But when the season or other circumstances prevented them from waging war against men or beasts, they only cared for feasting and gambling. To these occupations they gave themselves up, with a determination and wildness well worthy of those semi–civilised times. It was the custom for invited guests to appear armed at the feasts, which were the more frequent, inasmuch as they were necessarily accompanied with religious ceremonies. It often happened that these long repasts, followed by games of chance, were stained with blood, either in private quarrels or in a general *melee*. One can easily imagine the tumult which must have arisen in a numerous assembly when the hot wine and other fermented drinks, such as beer, &c., had excited every one to the highest pitch of unchecked merriment.

[Illustration: Fig. 42.—Costumes of the Women of the Court from the Sixth to the Tenth Centuries, from Documents collected by H. de Vielcastel, in the great Libraries of Europe.]

Some of the Merovingian kings listened to the advice of the ministers of the Catholic religion, and tried to reform these noisy excesses, and themselves abandoned the evil custom. For this purpose they received at their tables bishops, who blessed the assembly at the commencement of the meal, and were charged besides to recite chapters of holy writ, or to sing hymns out of the divine service, so as to edify and occupy the minds of the guests.

Gregory of Tours bears witness to the happy influence of the presence of bishops at the tables of the Frank kings and nobles; he relates, too, that Chilperic, who was very proud of his theological and secular knowledge, liked, when dining, to discuss, or rather to pronounce authoritatively his opinion on questions of grammar, before his companions in arms, who, for the most part, neither knew how to read nor write; he even went as far as to order three ancient Greek letters to be added to the Latin alphabet.

[Illustration: Fig. 43.—Queen Fredegonde, seated on her Throne, gives orders to two young Men of Terouanne to assassinate Sigebert, King of Austrasia.—Window in the Cathedral of Tournai, Fifteenth Century.]

The private properties of the Frank kings were immense, and produced enormous revenues. These monarchs had palaces in almost all the large towns; at Bourges, Chalons–sur–Saone, Chalons–sur–Marne, Dijon, Etampes, Metz, Langres, Mayence, Rheims, Soissons, Tours, Toulouse, Treves, Valenciennes, Worms, &c. In Paris, they occupied the vast residence now known as the *Thermes de Julien* (Hotel de Cluny), which then extended from the hill of St. Genevieve as far as the Seine; but they frequently left it for their numerous villas in the neighbourhood, on which occasions they were always accompanied by their treasury.

All these residences were built on the same plan. High walls surrounded the palace. The Roman *atrium*, preserved under the name of *proaulium* (*preau*, ante–court), was placed in front of the *salutorium* (hall of reception), where visitors were received. The *consistorium*, or great circular hall surrounded with seats, served for legislation, councils, public assemblies, and other solemnities, at which the kings displayed their royal pomp.

The *trichorium*, or dining–room, was generally the largest hall in the palace; two rows of columns divided it into three parts; one for the royal family, one for the officers of the household, and the third for the guests, who were always very numerous. No person of

41

rank visiting the King could leave without sitting at his table, or at least draining a cup to his health. The King's hospitality was magnificent, especially on great religious festivals such as Christmas and Easter.

The royal apartments were divided into winter and summer rooms. In order to regulate the temperature hot or cold water was used, according to the season; this circulated in the pipes of the *hypocauste*, or the subterranean furnace which warmed the baths. The rooms with chimneys were called *epicaustoria* (stoves), and it was the custom hermetically to close these when any one wished to be anointed with ointments and aromatic essences. In the same manner as the Gallo–Roman houses, the palaces of the Frank kings and principal nobles of ecclesiastical or military order had *thermes*, or bath–rooms: to the *thermes* were attached a *colymbum*, or washhouse, a gymnasium for bodily exercise, and a *hypodrome*, or covered gallery for exercise, which must not be confounded with the *hippodrome*, a circus where horse–races took place.

Sometimes after the repast, in the interval between two games of dice, the nobles listened to a bard, who sang the brilliant deeds of their ancestors in their native tongue.

Under the government of Charlemagne, the private life of his subjects seems to have been less rough and coarse, although they did not entirely give up their turbulent pleasures. Science and letters, for a long time buried in monasteries, reappeared like beautiful exiles at the imperial court, and social life thereby gained a little charm and softness. Charlemagne had created in his palace, under the direction of Alcuin, a sort of academy called the "School of the Palace," which followed him everywhere. The intellectual exercises of this school generally brought together all the members of the imperial family, as well as all the persons of the household. Charlemagne, in fact, was himself one of the most attentive followers of the lessons given by Alcuin. He was indeed the principal interlocutor and discourser at the discussions, which were on all subjects, religions, literary, and philosophical.

[Illustration: Fig. 44.—Costumes of the Nobility from the Seventh to the Ninth Centuries, from Documents gathered by H. de Vielcastel from the great Libraries of Europe.]

Charlemagne took as much pains with the administration of his palace as he did with that of his States. In his "Capitulaires," a work he wrote on legislature, we find him descending to the minutest details in that respect. For instance, he not only interested himself in his warlike and hunting equipages, but also in his kitchen and pleasure gardens. He insisted upon knowing every year the number of his oxen, horses, and goats; he calculated the produce of the sale of fruits gathered in his orchards, which were not required for the use of his house; he had a return of the number of fish caught in his ponds; he pointed out the shrubs best calculated for ornamenting his garden, and the vegetables which were required for his table, &c.

The Emperor generally assumed the greatest simplicity in his dress. His daily attire consisted of a linen shirt and drawers, and a woollen tunic fastened with a silk belt. Over this tunic he threw a cloak of blue stuff, very long behind and before, but very short on each side, thus giving freedom to his arms to use his sword, which he always wore. On his feet he wore bands of stuffs of various colours, crossed over one another, and covering his legs also. In winter, when he travelled or hunted on horseback, he threw over his shoulders a covering of otter or sheepskin. The changes in fashion which the custom of the times necessitated, but to which he would never submit personally, induced him to issue several strenuous orders, which, however, in reality had hardly any effect.

He was most simple as regards his food and drink, and made a habit of having pious or historical works read to him during his repasts. He devoted the morning, which with him began in summer at sunrise, and in winter earlier, to the political administration of his empire. He dined at twelve with his family; the dukes and chiefs of various nations first waited on him, and then took their places at the table, and were waited on in their turn by the counts, prefects, and superior officers of the court, who dined after them. When these had finished the different chiefs of the household sat down, and they were succeeded lastly by servants of the lower order, who often did not dine till midnight, and had to content themselves with what was left. When occasion required, however, this powerful Emperor knew how to maintain the pomp and dignity of his station; but as soon as he had done what was necessary, either for some great religious festival or otherwise, he returned, as if by instinct, to his dear and native simplicity.

It must be understood that the simple tastes of Charlemagne were not always shared by the princes and princesses of his family, nor by the magnates of his court (Fig. 45). Poets and historians have handed down to us descriptions of hunts, feasts, and ceremonies, at which a truly Asiatic splendour was displayed. Eginhard, however, assures us that the sons and daughters of the King were brought up under their father's eye in liberal studios; that, to save them from the vice of idleness, Charlemagne required his sons to devote themselves to all bodily exercises, such as horsemanship, handling of arms, &c., and his daughters to do needlework and to spin. From what is recorded, however, of the frivolous habits and irregular morals of these princesses, it is evident that they but imperfectly realised the end of their education.

[Illustration: Fig. 45.—Costumes of the Ladies of the Nobility in the Ninth Century, from a Miniature in the Bible of Charles the Bold (National Library of Paris).]

Science and letters, which for a time were brought into prominence by Charlemagne and also by his son Louis, who was very learned and was considered skilful in translating and expounding Scripture, were, however, after the death of these two kings, for a long time banished to the seclusion of the cloisters, owing to the hostile rivalry of their successors, which favoured the attacks of the Norman pirates. All the monuments and relics of the Gallo-Roman civilisation, which the great Emperor had collected, disappeared in the civil wars, or were gradually destroyed by the devastations of the northerners.

The vast empire which Charlemagne had formed became gradually split up, so that from a dread of social destruction, in order to protect churches and monasteries, as well as castles and homesteads, from the attacks of internal as well as foreign enemies, towers and impregnable fortresses began to rise in all parts of Europe, and particularly in France.

[Illustration: Fig. 46.—Towers of the Castle of Semur, and of the Castle of Nogent-le-Rotrou (Present Condition).—Specimens of Towers of the Thirteenth Century.]

During the first period of feudalism, that is to say from the middle of the ninth to the middle of the twelfth centuries, the inhabitants of castles had little time to devote to the pleasures of private life. They had not only to be continually under arms for the endless quarrels of the King and the great chiefs; but they had also to oppose the Normans on one side, and the Saracens on the other, who, being masters of the Spanish peninsula, spread like the rising tide in the southern counties of Languedoc and Provence. It is true that the Carlovingian warriors obtained a handsome and rich reward for these long and sanguinary efforts, for at last they seized upon the provinces and districts which had been originally entrusted to their charge, and the origin of their feudal possession was soon so far forgotten, that their descendants pretended that they held the lands, which they had really usurped regardless of their oath, from heaven and their swords. It is needless to say, that at that time the domestic life in these castles must have been dull and monotonous; although, according to M. Guizot, the loneliness which was the resuit of this rough and laborious life, became by degrees the pioneer of civilisation.

"When the owner of the fief left his castle, his wife remained there, though in a totally different position from that which women generally held. She remained as mistress, representing her husband, and was charged with the defence and honour of the fief. This high and exalted position, in the centre of domestic life, often gave to women an opportunity of displaying dignity, courage, virtue, and intelligence, which would otherwise have remained hidden, and, no doubt, contributed greatly to their moral development, and to the general improvement of their condition.

[Illustration: Fig. 47.—Woman under the Safeguard of Knighthood, allegorical Scene.—Costume of the End of the Fifteenth Century, from a Miniature in a Latin Psalm Book (Manuscript No. 175, National Library of Paris).]

"The importance of children, and particularly of the eldest son, was greater in feudal houses than elsewhere.... The eldest son of the noble was, in the eyes of his father and of all his followers, a prince and heir–presumptive, and the hope and glory of the dynasty. These feelings, and the domestic pride and affection of the various members one to another, united to give families much energy and power..... Add to this the influence of Christian ideas, and it will be understood how this lonely, dull, and hard castle life was, nevertheless, favourable to the development of domestic society, and to that improvement in the condition of women which plays such a great part in the history of our civilisation."

[Illustration: Fig. 48.—Court of Love in Provence in the Fourteenth Century (Manuscript of the National Library of Paris).]

Whatever opinion may be formed of chivalry, it is impossible to deny the influence which this institution exercised on private life in the Middle Ages. It considerably modified custom, by bringing the stronger sex to respect and defend the weaker. These warriors, who were both simple and externally rough and coarse, required association and intercourse with women to soften them (Fig. 47). In taking women and helpless widows under their protection, they were necessarily more and more thrown in contact with them. A deep feeling of veneration for woman, inspired by Christianity, and, above all, by the worship of the Virgin Mary, ran throughout the songs of the troubadours, and produced a sort of sentimental reverence for the gentle sex, which culminated in the authority which women had in the courts of love (Fig. 48).

We have now reached the reign of Philip Augustus, that is to say, the end of the twelfth century. This epoch is remarkable, not only for its political history, but also for its effect on civilisation. Christianity had then considerably influenced the world; arts, sciences, and letters, animated by its influence, again began to appear, and to add charms to the leisure of private life. The castles were naturally the first to be affected by this poetical and intellectual regeneration, although it has been too much the custom to exaggerate the ignorance of those who inhabited them. We are too apt to consider the warriors of the Middle Ages as totally devoid of knowledge, and as hardly able to sign their names, as far as the kings and princes are concerned. This is quite an error; for many of the knights composed poems which exhibit evidence of their high literary culture.

It was, in fact, the epoch of troubadours, who might be called professional poets and actors, who went from country to country, and from castle to castle, relating stories of good King Artus of Brittany and of the Knights of the Round Table; repeating historical poems of the great Emperor Charlemagne and his followers. These minstrels were always accompanied by jugglers and instrumentalists, who formed a travelling troop (Fig. 49), having no other mission than to amuse and instruct their feudal hosts. After singing a few fragments of epics, or after the lively recital of some ancient fable, the jugglers would display their art or skill in gymnastic feats or conjuring, which were the more appreciated by the spectators, in that the latter were more or less able to compete with them. These wandering troops acted small comedies, taken from incidents of the times. Sometimes, too, the instrumentalists formed an orchestra, and dancing commenced. It may be here remarked that dancing at this epoch consisted of a number of persons forming large circles, and turning to the time of the music or the rhythm of the song. At least the dances of the nobles are thus represented in the MSS. of the Middle Ages. To these amusements were added games of calculation and chance, the fashion for which had much increased, and particularly such games as backgammon, draughts, and chess, to which certain knights devoted all their leisure.

From the reign of Philip Augustus, a remarkable change seems to have taken place in the private life of kings, princes, and nobles. Although his domains and revenues had always been on the increase, this monarch never displayed, in ordinary circumstances at least, much magnificence. The accounts of his private expenses for the years 1202 and 1203 have been preserved, which enable us to discover some curious details bearing witness to the extreme simplicity of the court at that period. The household of the King or royal family was still very small: one chancellor, one chaplain, a squire, a butler, a few Knights of the Temple, and some sergeants–at–arms were the only officers of the palace. The king and princes of his household only changed apparel three times during the year.

[Illustration: Fig. 49.—King David playing on the Lyre, surrounded by four Musicians.—Costumes of the Thirteenth Century (from a Miniature in a Manuscript Psalter in the Imperial Library, Paris).]

The children of the King slept in sheets of serge, and their nurses were dressed in gowns of dark–coloured woollen stuff, called *brunette*. The royal cloak, which was of scarlet, was jewelled, but the King only wore it on great ceremonies. At the same time enormous expenses were incurred for implements of war, arrows, helmets with visors, chariots, and for the men–at–arms whom the King kept in his pay.

Louis IX. personally kept up almost similar habits. The Sire de Joinville tells us in his "Chronicles," that the holy King on his return from his first crusade, in order to repair the damage done to his treasury by the failure of this expedition, would no longer wear costly furs nor robes of scarlet, and contented himself with common stuffs trimmed with hare–skin. He nevertheless did not diminish the officers of his household, which had already become numerous; and being no doubt convinced that royalty required magnificence, he surrounded himself with as much pomp as the times permitted.

Under the two Philips, his successors, this magnificence increased, and descended to the great vassals, who were soon imitated by the knights "bannerets." There seemed to be a danger of luxury becoming so great, and so general in all classes of feudal society, that in 1294 an order of the King was issued, regulating in the minutest details the expenses of each person according to his rank in the State, or the fortune which he could prove. But this law had the fate of all such enactments, and was either easily evaded, or was only partially enforced, and that with great difficulty. Another futile attempt to put it in practice was made in 1306, when the splendour of dress, of equipages, and of table had become still greater and more ruinous, and had descended progressively to the bourgeois and merchants.

It must be stated in praise of Philip le Bel (Fig. 50) that, notwithstanding the failure of his attempts to arrest the progress of luxury, he was not satisfied with making laws against the extravagances of his subjects, for we find that he studied a strict economy in his own household, which recalled the austere times of Philip Augustus. Thus, in the curious regulations relating to the domestic arrangements of the palace, the Queen, Jeanne de Navarre, was only allowed two ladies and three maids of honour in her suite, and she is said to have had only two four-horse carriages, one for herself and the other for these ladies. In another place these regulations require that a butler, specially appointed, "should buy all the cloth and furs for the king, take charge of the key of the cupboards where these are kept, know the quantity given to the tailors to make clothes, and check the accounts when the tailors send in their claims for the price of their work."

[Illustration: Fig. 50.—King Philip le Bel in War-dress, on the Occasion of his entering Paris in 1304, after having conquered the Communes of Flanders.—Equestrian Statue placed in Notre Dame, Paris, and destroyed in 1772.—Fac-simile of a Woodcut from Thevet's "Cosmographie Universelle," 1575.]

After the death of the pious Jeanne de Navarre, to whom perhaps we must attribute the wise measures of her husband, Philip le Bel, the expenses of the royal household materially increased, especially on the occasions of the marriages of the three young sons of the King, from 1305 to 1307. Gold, diamonds, pearls, and precious stones were employed profusely, both for the King's garments and for those of the members of the royal family. The accounts of 1307 mention considerable sums paid for carpets, counterpanes, robes, worked linen, &c. A chariot of state, ornamented and covered with paintings, and gilded like the back of an altar, is also mentioned, and must have been a great change to the heavy vehicles used for travelling in those days.

Down to the reign of St. Louis the furniture of castles had preserved a character of primitive simplicity which did not, however, lack grandeur. The stone remained uncovered in most of the halls, or else it was whitened with mortar and ornamented with moulded roses and leaves, coloured in distemper. Against the wall, and also against the pillars supporting the arches, arms and armour of all sorts were hung, arranged in suits, and interspersed with banners and pennants or emblazoned standards. In the great middle hall, or dining-room, there was a long massive oak table, with benches and stools of the same wood. At the end of this table, there was a large arm-chair, overhung with a canopy of golden or silken stuff, which was occupied by the owner of the castle, and only relinquished by him in favour of his superior or sovereign. Often the walls of the hall of state were hung with tapestry, representing groves with cattle, heroes of ancient history, or events in the romance of chivalry. The floor was generally paved with hard stone, or covered with enamelled tiles. It was carefully strewn with scented herbs in summer, and straw in winter. Philip Augustus ordered that the Hotel Dieu of Paris should receive the herbs and straw which was daily removed from the floors of his palace. It was only very much later that this troublesome system was replaced by mats and carpets.

The bedrooms were generally at the top of the towers, and had little else by way of furniture, besides a very large bed, with or without curtains, a box in which clothes were kept, and which also served as a seat, and a *priedieu* chair, which sometimes contained prayer and other books of devotion. These lofty rooms, whose thick walls kept out the heat in summer, and the cold in winter, were only lighted by a small window or loophole, closed with a square of oiled paper or of thin horn.

A great change took place in the abodes of the nobility in the fourteenth and fifteenth centuries (Fig. 51). We find, for instance, in Sauval's "History and Researches of the Antiquities of the City of Paris," that the abodes of the kings of the first dynasty had been transformed into Palaces of Justice by Philip le Bel; the same author also gives us a vivid description of the Chateau du Louvre, and the Hotel St. Paul, which the kings inhabited when their court was in the capital. But even without examining into all the royal abodes, it will suffice to give an account of the Hotel de Boheme, which, after having been the home of the Sires de Nesles, of Queen Blanche of Castille, and other great persons, was given by Charles VI., in 1388, to his brother, the famous Duke Louis of Orleans.

[Illustration: Fig. 51.—The Knight and his Lady.—Costumes of the Court of Burgundy in the Fourteenth Century; Furnished Chamber.—Miniature in "Othea," Poem by Christine de Pisan (Brussels Library).]

"I shall not attempt," says Sauval, "to speak of the cellars and wine-cellars, the bakehouses, the fruiteries, the salt-stores, the fur-rooms, the porters' lodges, the stores, the guard-rooms, the wood-yard, or the glass-stores; nor of the servants; nor of the place where *hypocras* was made; neither shall I describe the tapestry-room, the linen-room, nor the laundry; nor, indeed, any of the various conveniences which were then to be found in the yards of that palace as well as in the other abodes of the princes and nobles.

"I shall simply remark, that amongst the many suites of rooms which composed it, two occupied the two first stories of the main building; the first was raised some few steps above the ground–floor of the court, and was occupied by Valentine de Milan; and her husband, Louis of Orleans, generally occupied the second. Each of these suites of rooms consisted of a great hall, a chamber of state, a large chamber, a wardrobe, some closets, and a chapel. The windows of the halls were thirteen and a half feet[A] high by four and a half wide. The state chambers were eight 'toises,' that is, about fifty feet and a half long. The duke and duchess's chambers were six 'toises' by three, that is, about thirty–six feet by eighteen; the others were seven toises and a half square, all lighted by long and narrow windows of wirework with trellis–work of iron; the wainscots and the ceilings were made of Irish wood, the same as at the Louvre."

[Footnote A: French feet.]

In this palace there was a room used by the duke, hung with cloth of gold, bordered with vermilion velvet embroidered with roses; the duchess had a room hung with vermilion satin embroidered with crossbows, which were on her coat of arms; that of the Duke of Burgundy was hung with cloth of gold embroidered with windmills. There were, besides, eight carpets of glossy texture, with gold flowers; one representing "The Seven Virtues and the Seven Vices;" another the history of Charlemagne; another that of St. Louis. There were also cushions of cloth of gold, twenty–four pieces of vermilion leather of Aragon, and four carpets of Aragon leather, "to be placed on the floor of rooms in summer." The favourite arm–chair of the princess is thus described in an inventory:—"A chamber chair with four supports, painted in fine vermilion, the seat and arms of which are covered with vermilion morocco, or cordovan, worked and stamped with designs representing the sun, birds, and other devices, bordered with fringes of silk and studded with nails."

Among the ornamental furniture were—"A large vase of massive silver, for holding sugar–plums or sweetmeats, shaped like a square table, supported by four satyrs, also of silver; a fine wooden casket, covered with vermilion cordovan, nailed, and bordered with a narrow gilt band, shutting with a key."

[Illustration: Fig. 52.—Bronze Chandeliers of the Fourteenth Century (Collection of M. Ach. Jubinal).]

In the daily life of Louis of Orleans and his wife, everything corresponded with the luxury of their house. Thus, for the amusement of their children, two little books of pictures were made, illuminated with gold, azure, and vermilion, and covered with vermilion leather of Cordova, which cost sixty *sols parisis, i.e. four hundred francs. But it was in the custom of New Year's gifts that the duke and duchess displayed truly royal magnificence, as we find described in the accounts of their expenses. For instance, in 1388 they paid four hundred francs of gold for sheets of silk to give to those who received the New Year's gifts from the King and Queen. In 1402, one hundred pounds (tournois) were given to Jehan Taienne, goldsmith, for six silver cups presented to Jacques de Poschin, the Duke's squire. To the Sire de la Tremouille Valentine gives "a cup and basin of gold;" to Queen Isabella, "a golden image of St. John, surrounded with nine rubies, one sapphire, and twenty–one pearls;" to Mademoiselle de Luxembourg, "another small golden sacred image, surrounded with pearls;" and lastly, in an account of 1394, headed, "Portion of gold and silver jewels bought by Madame la Duchesse d'Orleans as a New Year's gift," we find "a clasp of gold, studded with one large ruby and six large pearls, given to the King; three paternosters for the King's daughters, and two large diamonds for the Dukes of Burgundy and Berry."*

[Illustration: Fig. 53.—Styli used in writing in the Fourteenth Century.]

Such were the habits in private life of the royal princes under Charles VI.; and it can easily be shown that the example of royalty was followed not only by the court, but also in the remotest provinces. The great tenants or vassals of the crown each possessed several splendid mansions in their fiefs; the Dukes of Burgundy, at Souvigny, at Moulins, and at Bourbon l'Archambault; the Counts of Champagne, at Troyes; the Dukes of Burgundy, at Dijon; and all the smaller nobles made a point of imitating their superiors. From the fifteenth to the sixteenth centuries, the provinces which now compose France were studded with castles, which were as remarkable for their interior, architecture as for the richness of their furniture; and it may be asserted that the luxury which was displayed in the dwellings of the nobility was the evidence, if not the result, of a great social revolution in the manners and customs of private life.

At the end of the fourteenth century there lived a much–respected noble of Anjou, named Geoffroy de Latour–Landry, who had three daughters. In his old age, he resolved that, considering the dangers which might surround them in consequence of their inexperience and beauty, he would compose for their use a code of admonitions which might guide them in the various circumstances of life.

[Illustration: A Young Mother's Retinue

Representing the Parisian costumes at the end of the fourteenth century. Fac–simile of a miniature from the latin *Terence* of King Charles VI. From a manuscript in the Bibl. de l'Arsenal.]

This book of domestic maxims is most curious and instructive, from the details which it contains respecting the manners and customs, mode of conduct, and fashions of the nobility of the period (Fig. 54). The author mostly illustrates each of his precepts by examples from the life of contemporary personages.

[Illustration: Fig. 54.—Dress of Noble Ladies and Children in the Fourteenth Century.—Miniature in the "Merveilles du Monde" (Manuscript, National Library of Paris).]

The first advice the knight gives his daughters is, to begin the day with prayer; and, in order to give greater weight to his counsel, he relates the following anecdote: "A noble had two daughters; the one was pious, always saying her prayers with devotion, and regularly attending the services of the church; she married an honest man, and was most happy. The other, on the contrary, was satisfied with hearing low mass, and hurrying once or twice through the Lord's Prayer, after which she went off to indulge herself with sweetmeats. She complained of headaches, and required careful diet. She married a most excellent knight; but, one evening, taking advantage of her husband being asleep, she shut herself up in one of the rooms of the palace, and in company with the people of the household began eating and drinking in the most riotous and excessive manner. The knight awoke; and, surprised not to find his wife by his side, got up, and, armed with a stick, betook himself to the scene of festivity. He struck one of the domestics with such force that he broke his stick in pieces, and one of the fragments flew into the lady's eye and put it out. This caused her husband to take a dislike to her, and he soon placed his affections elsewhere."

"My pretty daughters," the moralising parent proceeds, "be courteous and meek, for nothing is more beautiful, nothing so secures the favour of God and the love of others. Be then courteous to great and small; speak gently with them.... I have seen a great lady take

52

off her cap and bow to a simple ironmonger. One of her followers seemed astonished. 'I prefer,' she said, 'to have been too courteous towards that man, than to have been guilty of the least incivility to a knight.'"

[Illustration: Fig. 55.—Noble Lady and Maid of Honour, and two Burgesses with Hoods (Fourteenth Century), from a Miniature in the "Merveilles du Monde" (Manuscript in the Imperial Library of Paris).]

Latour–Landry also advised his daughters to avoid outrageous fashions in dress. "Do not be hasty in copying the dress of foreign women. I will relate a story on this subject respecting a bourgeoise of Guyenne and the Sire de Beaumanoir. The lady said to him, 'Cousin, I come from Brittany, where I saw my fine cousin, your wife, who was not so well dressed as the ladies of Guyenne and many other places. The borders of her dress and of her bonnet are not in fashion.' The Sire answered, 'Since you find fault with the dress and cap of my wife, and as they do not suit you, I shall take care in future that they are changed; but I shall be careful not to choose them similar to yours.... Understand, madam, that I wish her to be dressed according to the fashion of the good ladies of France and this country, and not like those of England. It was these last who first introduced into Brittany the large borders, the bodices opened on the hips, and the hanging sleeves. I remember the time, and saw it myself, and I have little respect for women who adopt these fashions.'"

Respecting the high head–dresses "which cause women to resemble stags who are obliged to lower their heads to enter a wood," the knight relates what took place in 1392 at the fete of St. Marguerite. "There was a young and pretty woman there, quite differently dressed from the others; every one stared at her as if she had been a wild beast. One respectable lady approached her and said, 'My friend, what do you call that fashion?' She answered, 'It is called the "gibbet dress."' 'Indeed; but that is not a fine name!' answered the old lady. Very soon the name of 'gibbet dress' got known all round the room, and every one laughed at the foolish creature who was thus bedecked." This head–dress did in fact owe its name to its summit, which resembled a gibbet.

These extracts from the work of this honest knight, suffice to prove that the customs of French society had, as early as the end of the fourteenth century, taken a decided character which was to remain subject only to modifications introduced at various historical periods.

Amongst the customs which contributed most to the softening and elegance of the feudal class, we must cite that of sending into the service of the sovereign for some years all the youths of both sexes, under the names of varlets, pages, squires, and maids of honour. No noble, of whatever wealth or power, ever thought of depriving his family of this apprenticeship and its accompanying chivalric education.

Up to the end of the twelfth century, the number of domestic officers attached to a castle was very limited; we have seen, for instance, that Philip Augustus contented himself with a few servants, and his queen with two or three maids of honour. Under Louis IX. this household was much increased, and under Philippe le Bel and his sons the royal household had become so considerable as to constitute quite a large assemblage of young men and women. Under Charles VI., the household of Queen Isabella of Bavaria alone amounted to forty-five persons, without counting the almoner, the chaplains, and clerks of the chapel, who must have been very numerous, since the sums paid to them amounted to the large amount of four hundred and sixty francs of gold per annum.

[Illustration: Fig. 56.—Court of the Ladies of Queen Anne of Brittany, Miniature representing this lady weeping on account of the absence of her husband during the Italian war.—Manuscript of the "Epistres Envoyees au Roi" (Sixteenth Century), obtained by the Coislin Fund for the Library of St. Germain des Pres in Paris, now in the Library of St. Petersburg.]

Under Charles VIII., Louis XII., and Francis I., the service of the young nobility, which was called "apprenticeship of honour or virtue," had taken a much wider range; for the first families of the French nobility were most eager to get their children admitted into the royal household, either to attend on the King or Queen, or at any rate on one of the princes of the royal blood. Anne of Brittany particularly gave special attention to her female attendants (Fig. 56). "She was the first," says Brantome in his work on "Illustrious Women," "who began to form the great court of ladies which has descended to our days; for she had a considerable retinue both of adult ladies and young girls. She never refused to receive any one; on the contrary, she inquired of the gentlemen of the court if they had any daughters, ascertained who they were, and asked for them." It was thus that the Admiral de Graville (Fig. 57) confided to the good Queen the education of his daughter Anne, who at this school of the Court of Ladies became one of the most distinguished women of her day. The same Queen, as Duchess of Brittany, created a company of one hundred Breton gentlemen, who accompanied her everywhere. "They never failed," says the author of "Illustrious Women," "when she went to mass or took a walk, to await her return on the little terrace of Blois, which is still called the *Perche aux Bretons*. She gave it this name herself; for when she saw them she said, 'There are my Bretons on the perch waiting for me.'"

We must not forget that this queen, who became successively the wife of Charles VIII. and of Louis XII., had taken care to establish a strict discipline amongst the young men and women who composed her court. She rightly considered herself the guardian of the honour of the former, and of the virtue of the latter; therefore, as long as she lived, her court was renowned for purity and politeness, noble and refined gallantry, and was never allowed to degenerate into imprudent amusements or licentious and culpable intrigues.

Unfortunately, the moral influence of this worthy princess died with her. Although the court of France continued to gather around it almost every sort of elegance, and although it continued during the whole of the sixteenth century the most polished of European courts, notwithstanding the great external and civil wars, yet it afforded at the same time a sad example of laxity of morals, which had a most baneful influence on public habits; so much so that vice and corruption descended from class to class, and contaminated all orders of society. If we wished to make investigations into the private life of the lower orders in those times, we should not succeed as we have been able to do with that of the upper classes; for we have scarcely any data to throw light upon their sad and obscure history. Bourgeois and peasants were, as we have already shown, long included together with the miserable class of serfs, a herd of human beings without individuality, without significance, who from their birth to their death, whether isolated or collectively, were the "property" of their masters. What must have been the private life of this degraded multitude, bowed down under the most tyrannical and humiliating dependence, we can scarcely imagine; it was in fact but a purely material existence, which has left scarcely any trace in history.

[Illustration: Fig. 57.—Louis de Mallet, Lord of Graville, Admiral of France, 1487, in Costume of War and Tournament, from an Engraving of the Sixteenth Century (National Library of Paris, Cabinet des Estampes).]

Many centuries elapsed before the dawn of liberty could penetrate the social strata of this multitude, thus oppressed and denuded of all power of action. The development was slow, painful, and dearly bought, but at last it took place; first of all towns sprang up, and with them, or rather by their influence, the inhabitants became possessed of social life. The agricultural population took its social position many generations later.

As we have already seen, the great movement for the creation of communes and bourgeoisies only dates from the unsettled period ranging from the eleventh to the thirteenth centuries, and simultaneously we see the bourgeois appear, already rich and luxurious, parading on all occasions their personal opulence. Their private life could only be an imitation of that in the chateaux; by degrees as wealth strengthened and improved their condition, and rendered them independent, we find them trying to procure luxuries equal or analogous to those enjoyed by the upper classes, and which appeared to them the height of material happiness. In all times the small have imitated the great. It was in vain that the great obstinately threatened, by the exercise of their prerogatives, to try and crush this tendency to equality which alarmed them, by issuing pecuniary edicts, summary laws, coercive regulations, and penal ordinances; by the force of circumstances the arbitrary restrictions which the nobility laid upon the lower classes gradually disappeared, and the power of wealth displayed itself in spite of all their efforts to suppress it. In fact, occasions were not wanting in which the bourgeois class was able to refute the charge of unworthiness with which the nobles sought to stamp it. When taking a place in the council of the King, or employed in the administration of the provinces, many of its members distinguished themselves by firmness and wisdom; when called upon to assist in the national defence, they gave their blood and their gold with noble self–denial; and lastly, they did not fail to prove themselves possessed of those high and delicate sentiments of which the nobility alone claimed the hereditary possession.

[Illustration: Fig. 58.—Burgess of Ghent and his Wife, in ceremonial Attire, kneeling in Church, from a painted Window belonging to a Chapel in that Town (Fifteenth Century).]

"The bourgeois," says Arnaud de Marveil, one of the most famous troubadours of the thirteenth century, "have divers sorts of merits: some distinguish themselves by deeds of honour, others are by nature noble and behave accordingly. There are others thoroughly brave, courteous, frank, and jovial, who, although poor, find means to please by graceful speech, frequenting courts, and making themselves agreeable there; these, well versed in courtesy and politeness, appear in noble attire, and figure conspicuously at the tournaments and military games, proving themselves good judges and good company."

Down to the thirteenth century, however rich their fathers or husbands might be, the women of the bourgeoisie were not permitted, without incurring a fine, to use the ornaments and stuffs exclusively reserved for the nobility. During the reigns of Philip Augustus and Louis IX., although these arbitrary laws were not positively abolished, a heavy blow was inflicted on them by the marks of confidence, esteem, and honour which these monarchs found pleasure in bestowing on the bourgeoisie. We find the first of these kings, when on the point of starting for a crusade, choosing six from amongst the principal members of the *parloir aux bourgeois* (it was thus that the first Hotel de Ville, situated in the corner of the Place de la Greve, was named) to be attached to the Council of Regency, to whom he specially confided his will and the royal treasure. His grandson made a point of following his grandsire's example, and Louis IX. showed the same appreciation for the new element which the Parisian bourgeoisie was about to establish in political life by making the bourgeois Etienne Boileau one of his principal ministers of police, and the bourgeois Jean Sarrazin his chamberlain.

Under these circumstances, the whole bourgeoisie gloried in the marks of distinction conferred upon their representatives, and during the following reign, the ladies of this class, proud of their immense fortunes, but above all proud of the municipal powers held by their families, bedecked themselves, regardless of expense, with costly furs and rich stuffs, notwithstanding that they were forbidden by law to do so.

Then came an outcry on the part of the nobles; and we read as follows, in an edict of Philippe le Bel, who inclined less to the bourgeoisie than to the nobles, and who did not spare the former in matters of taxation:—"No bourgeois shall have a chariot nor wear gold, precious stones, or crowns of gold or silver. Bourgeois, not being either prelates nor dignitaries of state, shall not have tapers of wax. A bourgeois possessing two thousand pounds (tournois) or more, may order for himself a dress of twelve sous six deniers, and for his wife one worth sixteen sous at the most." The sou, which was but nominal money, may be reckoned as representing twenty francs, and the denier one franc, but allowance must be made for the enormous difference in the value of silver, which would make twenty francs in the thirteenth century represent upwards of two hundred francs of present currency.

[Illustration: Fig. 59.—The new–born Child, from a Miniature in the "Histoire de la Belle Helaine" (Manuscript of the Fifteenth Century, National Library of Paris).]

But these regulations as to the mode of living were so little or so carelessly observed, that all the successors of Philippe le Bel thought it necessary to re–enact them, and, indeed, Charles VII., one century later, was obliged to censure the excess of luxury in dress by an edict which was, however, no better enforced than the rest. "It has been shown to the said lord" (the King Charles VII.), "that of all nations of the habitable globe there are none so changeable, outrageous, and excessive in their manner of dress, as the French nation, and there is no possibility of discovering by their dress the state or calling of persons, be they princes, nobles, bourgeois, or working men, because all are allowed to dress as they think proper, whether in gold or silver, silk or wool, without any regard to their calling."

At the end of the thirteenth century, a rich merchant of Valenciennes went to the court of the King of France wearing a cloak of furs covered with gold and pearls; seeing that no one offered him a cushion, he proudly sat on his cloak. On leaving he did not attempt to take up the cloak; and on a servant calling his attention to the fact he remarked, "It is not the custom in my country for people to carry away their cushions with them."

Respecting a journey made by Philippe le Bel and his wife Jeanne de Navarre to the towns of Bruges and Ghent, the historian Jean Mayer relates that Jeanne, on seeing the costly array of the bourgeois of those two rich cities, exclaimed, "I thought I was the only queen here, but I see more than six hundred!"

In spite of the laws, the Parisian bourgeoisie soon rivalled the Flemish in the brilliancy of their dress. Thus, in the second half of the fourteenth century, the famous Christine de Pisan relates that, having gone to visit the wife of a merchant during her confinement, it was not without some amazement that she saw the sumptuous furniture of the apartment in which this woman lay in bed (Fig. 59). The walls were hung with precious tapestry of Cyprus, on which the initials and motto of the lady were embroidered; the sheets were of fine linen of Rheims, and had cost more than three hundred pounds; the quilt was a new invention of silk and silver tissue; the carpet was like gold. The lady wore an elegant dress of crimson silk, and rested her head and arms on pillows, ornamented with buttons of oriental pearls. It should be remarked that this lady was not the wife of a large merchant, such as those of Venice and Genoa, but of a simple retail dealer, who was not above selling articles for four sous; such being the case, we need not be surprised that Christine should have considered the anecdote "worthy of being immortalised in a book."

It must not, however, be assumed that the sole aim of the bourgeoisie was that of making a haughty and pompous display. This is refuted by the testimony of the "Menagier de Paris," a curious anonymous work, the author of which must have been an educated and enlightened bourgeois.

The "Menagier," which was first published by the Baron Jerome Pichon, is a collection of counsels addressed by a husband to his young wife, as to her conduct in society, in the world, and in the management of her household. The first part is devoted to developing the mind of the young housewife; and the second relates to the arrangements necessary for the welfare of her house. It must be remembered that the comparatively trifling duties relating to the comforts of private life, which devolved on the wife, were not so numerous in those days as they are now; but on the other hand they required an amount of practical knowledge on the part of the housewife which she can nowadays dispense with. Under this head the "Menagier" is full of information.

After having spoken of the prayers which a Christian woman should say morning and evening, the author discusses the great question of dress, which has ever been of supreme importance in the eyes of the female sex: "Know, dear sister," (the friendly name he gives his young wife), "that in the choice of your apparel you must always consider the rank of your parents and mine, as also the state of my fortune. Be respectably dressed, without devoting too much study to it, without too much plunging into new fashions. Before leaving your room, see that the collar of your gown be well adjusted and is not put on crooked."

[Illustration: Fig. 60.—Sculptured Comb, in Ivory, of the Sixteenth Century (Sauvageot Collection)]

Then he dilates on the characters of women, which are too often wilful and unmanageable; on this point, for he is not less profuse in examples than the Chevalier de Latour–Landry, he relates an amusing anecdote, worthy of being repeated and remembered.

"I have heard the bailiff of Tournay relate, that he had found himself several times at table with men long married, and that he had wagered with them the price of a dinner under the following conditions: the company was to visit the abode of each of the husbands successively, and any one who had a wife obedient enough immediately, without contradicting or making any remark, to consent to count up to four, would win the bet; but, on the other hand, those whose wives showed temper, laughed, or refused to obey, would lose. Under these conditions the company gaily adjourned to the abode of Robin, whose wife, called Marie, had a high opinion of herself. The husband said before all, 'Marie, repeat after me what I shall say.' 'Willingly, sire.' 'Marie, say, "One, two, three!"' But by this time Marie was out of patience, and said, 'And seven, and twelve, and fourteen! Why, you are making a fool of me!' So that husband lost his wager.

"The company next went to the house of Maitre Jean, whose wife, Agnescat well knew how to play the lady. Jean said, 'Repeat after me, one!' 'And two!' answered Agnescat disdainfully; so he lost his wager. Tassin then tried, and said to dame Tassin, 'Count one!' 'Go upstairs!' she answered, 'if you want to teach counting, I am not a child.' Another said, 'Go away with you; you must have lost your senses,' or similar words, which made the husbands lose their wagers. Those, on the contrary, who had well-behaved wives gained their wager and went away joyful."

This amusing quotation suffices to show that the author of the "Menagier de Paris" wished to adopt a jocose style, with a view to enliven the seriousness of the subject he was advocating.

The part of his work in which he discusses the administration of the house is not less worthy of attention. One of the most curious chapters of the work is that in which he points out the manner in which the young bourgeoise is to behave towards persons in her service. Rich people in those days, in whatever station of life, were obliged to keep a numerous retinue of servants. It is curious to find that so far back as the period to which we allude, there was in Paris a kind of servants' registry office, where situations were found for servant-maids from the country. The bourgeois gave up the entire management of the servants to his wife; but, on account of her extreme youth, the author of the work in question recommends his wife only to engage servants who shall have been chosen by Dame Agnes, the nun whom he had placed with her as a kind of governess or companion.

"Before engaging them," he says, "know whence they come; in what houses they have been; if they have acquaintances in town, and if they are steady. Discover what they are capable of doing; and ascertain that they are not greedy, or inclined to drink. If they come from another country, try to find out why they left it; for, generally, it is not without some serious reason that a woman decides upon a change of abode. When you have engaged a maid, do not permit her to take the slightest liberty with you, nor allow her to speak disrespectfully to you. If, on the contrary, she be quiet in her demeanour, honest, modest, and shows herself amenable to reproof, treat her as if she were your daughter.

"Superintend the work to be done; and choose among your servants those qualified for each special department. If you order a thing to be done immediately, do not be satisfied with the following answers: 'It shall be done presently, or to–morrow early;' otherwise, be sure that you will have to repeat your orders."

[Illustration: Fig. 61.—Dress of Maidservants in the Thirteenth Century.—Miniature in a Manuscript of the National Library of Paris.]

To these severe instructions upon the management of servants, the bourgeois adds a few words respecting their morality. He recommends that they be not permitted to use coarse or indecent language, or to insult one another (Fig. 61). Although he is of opinion that necessary time should be given to servants at their meals, he does not approve of their remaining drinking and talking too long at table: concerning which practice he quotes a proverb in use at that time: "Quand varlet presche a table et cheval paist en gue, il est temps qu'on l'en oste: assez y a este;" which means, that when a servant talks at table and a horse feeds near a watering–place it is time he should be removed; he has been there long enough.

[Illustration: Fig. 62.—Hotel des Ursins, Paris, built during the Fourteenth Century, restored in the Sixteenth, and now destroyed.—State of the North Front at the End of the last Century.]

The manner in which the author concludes his instruction proves his kindness of heart, as well as his benevolence: "If one of your servants fall sick, it is your duty, setting everything else aside, to see to his being cured."

It was thus that a bourgeois of the fifteenth century expressed himself; and as it is clear that he could only have been inspired to dictate his theoretical teachings by the practical experience which he must have gained for the most part among the middle class to which he belonged, we must conclude that in those days the bourgeoisie possessed considerable knowledge of moral dignity and social propriety.

It must be added that by the side of the merchant and working bourgeoisie—who, above all, owed their greatness to the high functions of the municipality—the parliamentary bourgeoisie had raised itself to power, and that from the fourteenth century it played a considerable part in the State, holding at several royal courts at different periods, and at last, almost hereditarily, the highest magisterial positions. The very character of these great offices of president, or of parliamentary counsel, barristers, &c., proves that the holders must have had no small amount of intellectual culture. In this way a refined taste was created among this class, which the protection of kings, princes, and lords had alone hitherto encouraged. We find, for example, the Grosliers at Lyons, the De Thous and Seguiers in Paris, regardless of their bourgeois origin, becoming judicious and zealous patrons of poets, scholars, and artists.

A description of Paris, published in the middle of the fifteenth century, describes amongst the most splendid residences of the capital the hotels of Juvenal des Ursins (Fig. 62), of Bureau de Dampmartin, of Guillaume Seguin, of Mille Baillet, of Martin Double, and particularly that of Jacques Duchie, situated in the Rue des Prouvaires, in which were collected at great cost collections of all kinds of arms, musical instruments, rare birds, tapestry, and works of art. In each church in Paris, and there were upwards of a hundred, the principal chapels were founded by celebrated families of the ancient bourgeoisie, who had left money for one or more masses to be said daily for the repose of the souls of their deceased members. In the burial–grounds, and principally in that of the Innocents, the monuments of these families of Parisian bourgeoisie were of the most expensive character, and were inscribed with epitaphs in which the living vainly tried to immortalise the deeds of the deceased. Every one has heard of the celebrated tomb of Nicholas Flamel and Pernelle his wife (Fig. 63), the cross of Bureau, the epitaph of Yolande Bailly, who died in 1514, at the age of eighty–eight, and who "saw, or might have seen, two hundred and ninety–five children descended from her."

In fact, the religious institutions of Paris afford much curious and interesting information relative to the history of the bourgeoisie. For instance, Jean Alais, who levied a tax of one denier on each basket of fish brought to market, and thereby amassed an enormous fortune, left the whole of it at his death for the purpose of erecting a chapel called St. Agnes, which soon after became the church of St. Eustace. He further directed that, by way of expiation, his body should be thrown into the sewer which drained the offal from the market, and covered with a large stone; this sewer up to the end of the last century was still called Pont Alais.

[Illustration: Fig. 63.—Nicholas Flamel and Pernelle, his Wife, from a Painting executed at the End of the Fifteenth Century, under the Vaults of the Cemetery of the Innocents, in Paris.]

Very often when citizens made gifts during their lifetime to churches or parishes, the donors reserved to themselves certain privileges which were calculated to cause the motives which had actuated them to be open to criticism. Thus, in 1304, the daughters of Nicholas Arrode, formerly provost of the merchants, presented to the church of St. Jacques–la–Boucherie the house and grounds which they inhabited, but one of them reserved the right of having a key of the church that she might go in whenever she pleased. Guillaume Haussecuel, in 1405, bought a similar right for the sum of eighteen *sols parisis* per annum (equal to twenty–five francs); and Alain and his wife, whose house was close to two chapels of the church, undertook not to build so as in any way to shut out the light from one of the chapels on condition that they might open a small window into the chapel, and so be enabled to hear the service without leaving their room.

[Illustration: Fig. 64.—Country Life—Fac–simile of a Woodcut in a folio Edition of Virgil, published at Lyons in 1517.]

We thus see that the bourgeoisie, especially of Paris, gradually took a more prominent position in history, and became so grasping after power that it ventured, at a period which does not concern us here, to aspire to every sort of distinction, and to secure an important social standing. What had been the exception during the sixteenth century became the rule two centuries later.

We will now take a glance at the agricultural population (Fig. 64), who, as we have already stated, were only emancipated from serfdom at the end of the eighteenth century.

But whatever might have been formerly the civil condition of the rural population, everything leads us to suppose that there were no special changes in their private and domestic means of existence from a comparatively remote period down to almost the present time.

A small poem of the thirteenth century, entitled, "De l'Oustillement au Vilain," gives a clear though rough sketch of the domestic state of the peasantry. Strange as it may seem, it must be acknowledged that, with a few exceptions resulting from the progress of time, it would not be difficult, even at the present day, to find the exact type maintained in the country districts farthest away from the capital and large towns; at all events, they were faithfully represented at the time of the revolution of 1789.

[Illustration: Fig. 65.—Sedentary Occupations of the Peasauts.—Fac–simile from an Engraving on Wood, attributed to Holbein, in the "Cosmographie" of Munster (Basle, 1552, folio).]

We gather from this poem, which must be considered an authentic and most interesting document, that the *manse* or dwelling of the villain comprised three distinct buildings; the first for the corn, the second for the hay and straw, the third for the man and his family. In this rustic abode a fire of vine branches and faggots sparkled in a large chimney furnished with an iron pot–hanger, a tripod, a shovel, large fire–irons, a cauldron and a meat–hook. Next to the fireplace was an oven, and in close proximity to this an enormous bedstead, on which the villain, his wife, his children, and even the stranger who asked for hospitality, could all be easily accommodated; a kneading trough, a table, a bench, a cheese cupboard, a jug, and a few baskets made up the rest of the furniture. The villain also possessed other utensils, such as a ladder, a mortar, a hand–mill—for every one then was obliged to grind his own corn; a mallet, some nails, some gimlets, fishing lines, hooks, and baskets, &c.

[Illustration: Fig. 66.—Villains before going to Work receiving their Lord's Orders.—Miniature in the "Proprietaire des Choses."—Manuscript of the Fifteenth Century (Library of the Arsenal, in Paris).]

His working implements were a plough, a scythe, a spade, a hoe, large shears, a knife and a sharpening stone; he had also a waggon, with harness for several horses, so as to be able to accomplish the different tasks required of him under feudal rights, either by his proper lord, or by the sovereign; for the villain was liable to be called upon to undertake every kind of work of this sort.

His dress consisted of a blouse of cloth or skin fastened by a leather belt round the waist, an overcoat or mantle of thick woollen stuff, which fell from his shoulders to half–way down his legs; shoes or large boots, short woollen trousers, and from his belt there hung his wallet and a sheath for his knife (Figs. 66 and 71). He generally went bareheaded, but in cold weather or in rain he wore a sort of hat of similar stuff to his coat, or one of felt with a broad brim. He seldom wore *mouffles*, or padded gloves, except when engaged in hedging.

A small kitchen–garden, which he cultivated himself, was usually attached to the cottage, which was guarded by a large watch–dog. There was also a shed for the cows, whose milk contributed to the sustenance of the establishment; and on the thatched roof of this and his cottage the wild cats hunted the rats and mice. The family were never idle, even in the bad season, and the children were taught from infancy to work by the side of their parents (Fig. 65).

If, then, we find so much resemblance between the abodes of the villains of the thirteenth century and those of the inhabitants of the poorest communes of France in the present day, we may fairly infer that there must be a great deal which is analogous between the inhabitants themselves of the two periods; for in the chateaux as well as in the towns we find the material condition of the dwellings modifying itself conjointly with that of the moral condition of the inhabitants.

[Illustration: Fig. 67.—The egotistical and envious Villain.—From a Miniature in "Proverbes et Adages, &c.," Manuscript of the La Valliere Fund, in the National Library of Paris, with this legend:

 "Attrapez y sont les plus fins:
 Qui trop embrasse mal estraint."

("The cleverest burn their fingers at it,
And those who grasp all may lose all.")]

Another little poem entitled, "On the Twenty–four Kinds of Villains," composed about the same period as the one above referred to, gives us a graphic description of the varieties of character among the feudal peasants. One example is given of a man who will not tell a traveller the way, but merely in a surly way answers, "You know it better than I" (Fig. 67). Another, sitting at his door on a Sunday, laughs at those passing by, and says to himself when he sees a gentleman going hawking with a bird on his wrist, "Ah! that bird will eat a hen to–day, and our children could all feast upon it!" Another is described as a sort of madman who equally despises God, the saints, the Church, and the nobility. His neighbour is an honest simpleton, who, stopping in admiration before the doorway of

Notre Dame in Paris in order to admire the statues of Pepin, Charlemagne, and their successors, has his pocket picked of his purse. Another villain is supposed to make trade of pleading the cause of others before "Messire le Bailli;" he is very eloquent in trying to show that in the time of their ancestors the cows had a free right of pasture in such and such a meadow, or the sheep on such and such a ridge; then there is the miser, and the speculator, who converts all his possessions into ready money, so as to purchase grain against a bad season; but of course the harvest turns out to be excellent, and he does not make a farthing, but runs away to conceal his ruin and rage. There is also the villain who leaves his plough to become a poacher. There are many other curious examples which altogether tend to prove that there has been but little change in the villager class since the first periods of History.

[Illustration: Fig. 68.—The covetous and avaricious Villain.—From a Miniature in "Proverbes et Adages, &c," Manuscript in the National Library of Paris, with this legend:

"Je suis icy levant les yeulx
Eu ce haut lieu des attendens,
En convoitant pour avoir mieulx
Prendre la lune avec les dens."

("Even on this lofty height
We yet look higher,
As nothing will satisfy us
But to clutch the moon.")]

Notwithstanding the miseries to which they were generally subject, the rural population had their days of rest and amusement, which were then much more numerous than at present. At that period the festivals of the Church were frequent and rigidly kept, and as each of them was the pretext for a forced holiday from manual labour, the peasants thought of nothing, after church, but of amusing themselves; they drank, talked, sang, danced, and, above all, laughed, for the laugh of our forefathers quite rivalled the Homeric laugh, and burst forth with a noisy joviality (Fig. 69).

The "wakes," or evening parties, which are still the custom in most of the French provinces, and which are of very ancient origin, formed important events in the private lives of the peasants. It was at these that the strange legends and vulgar superstitions, which so long fed the minds of the ignorant classes, were mostly created and propagated. It was there that those extraordinary and terrible fairy tales were related, as well as those of magicians, witches, spirits, &c. It was there that the matrons, whose great age justified their experience, insisted on proving, by absurd tales, that they knew all the marvellous secrets for causing happiness or for curing sickness. Consequently, in those days the most enlightened rustic never for a moment doubted the truth of witchcraft.

In fact, one of the first efforts at printing was applied to reproducing the most ridiculous stories under the title of the "Evangile des Conuilles ou Quenouilles," and which had been previously circulated in manuscript, and had obtained implicit belief. The author of this remarkable collection asserts that the matrons in his neighbourhood had deputed him to put together in writing the sayings suitable for all conditions of rural life which were believed in by them and were announced at the wakes. The absurdities and childish follies which he has dared to register under their dictation are almost incredible.

The "Evangile des Quenouilles," which was as much believed in as Holy Writ, tells us, amongst other secrets which it contains for the advantage of the reader, that a girl wishing to know the Christian name of her future husband, has but to stretch the first thread she spins in the morning across the doorway; and that the first man who passes and touches the thread will necessarily have the same name as the man she is destined to marry.

Another of the stories in this book was, that if a woman, on leaving off work on Saturday night, left her distaff loaded, she might be sure that the thread she would obtain from it during the following week would only produce linen of bad quality, which could not be bleached; this was considered to be proved by the fact that the Germans wore dark-brown coloured shirts, and it was known that the women never unloaded their distaffs from Saturday to Monday.

Should a woman enter a cow-house to milk her cows without saying "God and St. Bridget bless you!" she was thought to run the risk of the cows kicking and breaking the milk-pail and spilling the milk.

[Illustration: Fig. 69.—Village Feast.—Fac-simile of a Woodcut of the "Sandrin ou Verd Galant," facetious Work of the End of the Sixteenth Century (edition of 1609).]

This silly nonsense, compiled like oracles, was printed as late as 1493. Eighty years later a gentleman of Brittany, named Noel du Fail, Lord of Herissaye, councillor in the Parliament of Rennes, published, under the title of "Rustic and Amusing Discourses," a work intended to counteract the influence of the famous "Evangile des Quenouilles." This new work was a simple and true sketch of country habits, and proved the elegance and artless simplicity of the author, as well as his accuracy of observation. He begins thus: "Occasionally, having to retire into the country more conveniently and uninterruptedly to finish some business, on a particular holiday, as I was walking I came to a neighbouring village, where the greater part of the old and young men were assembled, in groups of separate ages, for, according to the proverb, 'Each seeks his like.' The young were practising the bow, jumping, wrestling, running races, and playing other games. The old were looking on, some sitting under an oak, with their legs crossed, and their hats lowered over their eyes, others leaning on their elbows criticizing every performance, and refreshing the memory of their own youth, and taking a lively interest in seeing the gambols of the young people."

The author states that on questioning one of the peasants to ascertain who was the cleverest person present, the following dialogue took place: "The one you see leaning on his elbow, hitting his boots, which have white strings, with a hazel stick, is called Anselme; he is one of the rich ones of the village, he is a good workman, and not a bad writer for the flat country; and the one you see by his side, with his thumb in his belt, hanging from which is a large game bag, containing spectacles and an old prayer book, is called Pasquier, one of the greatest wits within a day's journey—nay, were I to say two I should not be lying. Anyhow, he is certainly the readiest of the whole company to open his purse to give drink to his companions." "And that one," I asked, "with the large Milanese cap on his head, who holds an old book?" "That one," he answered, "who is scratching the end of his nose with one hand and his beard with the other?" "That one," I replied, "and who has turned towards us?" "Why," said he, "that is Roger Bontemps, a merry careless fellow, who up to the age of fifty kept the parish school; but changing his first trade he has become a wine–grower. However, he cannot resist the feast days, when he brings us his old books, and reads to us as long as we choose, such works as the 'Calondrier des Bergers,' 'Fables d'Esope,' 'Le Roman de la Rose,' 'Matheolus,' 'Alain Chartier,' 'Les Vigiles du feu Roy Charles,' 'Les deux Grebans,' and others. Neither, with his old habit of warbling, can he help singing on Sundays in the choir; and he is called Huguet. The other sitting near him, looking over his shoulder into his book, and wearing a sealskin belt with a yellow buckle, is another rich peasant of the village, not a bad villain, named Lubin, who also lives at home, and is called the little old man of the neighbourhood."

After this artistic sketch, the author dilates on the goodman Anselme. He says: "This good man possessed a moderate amount of knowledge, was a goodish grammarian, a musician, somewhat of a sophist, and rather given to picking holes in others." Some of Anselme's conversation is also given, and after beginning by describing in glowing terms the bygone days which he and his contemporaries had seen, and which he stated to be very different to the present, he goes on to say, "I must own, my good old friends, that I look back with pleasure on our young days; at all events the mode of doing things in those days was very superior and better in every way to that of the present.... O happy days! O fortunate times when our fathers and grandfathers, whom may God absolve, were still among us!" As he said this, he would raise the rim of his hat. He contented himself as to dress with a good coat of thick wool, well lined according to the fashion; and for feast days and other important occasions, one of thick cloth, lined with some old gabardine.

[Illustration: Fig. 70.—The Shepherds celebrating the Birth of the Messiah by Songs and Dances.—Fifteenth Century.—Fac–simile of an Engraving on Wood, from a Book of Hours, printed by Anthony Verard.]

"So we see," says M. Le Roux de Lincy, "at the end of the fifteenth century that the old peasants complained of the changes in the village customs, and of the luxury which every one wished to display in his furniture or apparel. On this point it seems that there has been little or no change. We read that, from the time of Homer down to that of the excellent author of 'Rustic Discourses,' and even later, the old people found fault with the manners of the present generation and extolled those of their forefathers, which they themselves had criticized in their own youth."

[Illustration: Fig. 71.—Purse or Leather Bag, with Knife or Dagger of the Fifteenth Century.]

Food and Cookery.

History of Bread.—Vegetables and Plants used in

Cooking.—Fruits.—Butchers' Meat.—Poultry, Game.—Milk, Butter,
Cheese, and Eggs.—Fish and Shellfish.—Beverages, Beer, Cider, Wine,
Sweet Wine, Refreshing Drinks, Brandy.—Cookery.—Soups, Boiled Food,
Pies, Stews, Salads, Roasts, Grills.—Seasoning, Truffles, Sugar,
Verjuice.—Sweets, Desserts, Pastry.—Meals and Feasts.—Rules of
Serving at Table from the Fifteenth to the Sixteenth Centuries.

"The private life of a people," says Legrand d'Aussy, who had studied that of the French
from a gastronomic point of view only, "from the foundation of monarchy down to the
eighteenth century, must, like that of mankind generally, commence with obtaining the
first and most pressing of its requirements. Not satisfied with providing food for his
support, man has endeavoured to add to his food something which pleased his taste. He
does not wait to be hungry, but he anticipates that feeling, and aggravates it by
condiments and seasonings. In a word his greediness has created on this score a very
complicated and wide–spread science, which, amongst nations which are considered
civilised, has become most important, and is designated the culinary art."

At all times the people of every country have strained the nature of the soil on which they
lived by forcing it to produce that which it seemed destined ever to refuse them. Such
food as human industry was unable to obtain from any particular soil or from any
particular climate, commerce undertook to bring from the country which produced it.
This caused Rabelais to say that the stomach was the father and master of industry.

We will rapidly glance over the alimentary matters which our forefathers obtained from
the animal and vegetable kingdom, and then trace the progress of culinary art, and
examine the rules of feasts and such matters as belong to the epicurean customs of the
Middle Ages.

Aliments.

Bread.—The Gauls, who principally inhabited deep and thick forests, fed on herbs and
fruits, and particularly on acorns. It is even possible that the veneration in which they
held the oak had no other origin. This primitive food continued in use, at least in times of
famine, up to the eighth century, and we find in the regulations of St. Chrodegand that if,
in consequence of a bad year, the acorn or beech–nut became scarce, it was the bishop's
duty to provide something to make up for it. Eight centuries later, when Rene du Bellay,

Bishop of Mans, came to report to Francis I. the fearful poverty of his diocese, he informed the king that the inhabitants in many places were reduced to subsisting on acorn bread.

[Illustration: Figs. 72 and 73.—Corn–threshing and Bread–making.—Miniatures from the Calendar of a Book of Hours.—Manuscript of the Sixteenth Century.]

In the earliest times bread was cooked under the embers. The use of ovens was introduced into Europe by the Romans, who had found them in Egypt. But, notwithstanding this importation, the old system of cooking was long after employed, for in the tenth century Raimbold, abbot of the monastery of St. Thierry, near Rheims, ordered in his will that on the day of his death bread cooked under the embers—*panes subcinericios*—should be given to his monks. By feudal law the lord was bound to bake the bread of his vassals, for which they were taxed, but the latter often preferred to cook their flour at home in the embers of their own hearths, rather than to carry it to the public oven.

[Illustration: Fig. 74.—The Miller.—From an Engraving of the Sixteenth Century, by J. Amman.]

It must be stated that the custom of leavening the dough by the addition of a ferment was not universally adopted amongst the ancients. For this reason, as the dough without leaven could only produce a heavy and indigestible bread, they were careful, in order to secure their loaves being thoroughly cooked, to make them very thin. These loaves served as plates for cutting up the other food upon, and when they thus became saturated with the sauce and gravy they were eaten as cakes. The use of the *tourteaux* (small crusty loaves), which were at first called *tranchoirs* and subsequently *tailloirs*, remained long in fashion even at the most splendid banquets. Thus, in 1336, the Dauphin of Vienna, Humbert II., had, besides the small white bread, four small loaves to serve as *tranchoirs* at table. The "Menagier de Paris" mentions "*des pains de tranchouers* half a foot in diameter, and four fingers deep," and Froissart the historian also speaks of *tailloirs*.

It would be difficult to point out the exact period at which leavening bread was adopted in Europe, but we can assert that in the Middle Ages it was anything but general. Yeast, which, according to Pliny, was already known to the Gauls, was reserved for pastry, and it was only at the end of the sixteenth century that the bakers of Paris used it for bread.

71

At first the trades of miller and baker were carried on by the same person (Figs. 74 and 75). The man who undertook the grinding of the grain had ovens near his mill, which he let to his lord to bake bread, when he did not confine his business to persons who sent him their corn to grind.

[Illustration: Fig. 75.—The Baker. From an Engraving of the Sixteenth Century, by J. Amman.]

At a later period public bakers established themselves, who not only baked the loaves which were brought to them already kneaded, but also made bread which they sold by weight; and this system was in existence until very recently in the provinces.

Charlemagne, in his "Capitulaires" (statutes), fixed the number of bakers in each city according to the population, and St. Louis relieved them, as well as the millers, from taking their turn at the watch, so that they might have no pretext for stopping or neglecting their work, which he considered of public utility. Nevertheless bakers as a body never became rich or powerful (Figs. 76 and 77). It is pretty generally believed that the name of *boulanger* (baker) originated from the fact that the shape of the loaves made at one time was very like that of a round ball. But loaves varied so much in form, quality, and consequently in name, that in his "Dictionary of Obscure Words" the learned Du Cange specifies at least twenty sorts made during the twelfth and thirteenth centuries, and amongst them may be mentioned the court loaf, the pope's loaf, the knight's loaf, the squire's loaf, the peer's loaf, the varlet's loaf, &c.

[Illustration: Fig. 76.—Banner of the Corporation of Bakers of Paris.]

[Illustration: Fig. 77.—Banner of the Corporation, of Bakers of Arras.]

The most celebrated bread was the white bread of Chailly or Chilly, a village four leagues (ten miles) south of Paris, which necessarily appeared at all the tables of the *elite* of the fourteenth century. The *pain mollet*, or soft bread made with milk and butter, although much in use before this, only became fashionable on the arrival of Marie de Medicis in France (1600), on account of this Tuscan princess finding it so much to her taste that she would eat no other.

The ordinary market bread of Paris comprised the *rousset bread*, made of meslin, and employed for soup; the *bourgeoisie bread*; and the *chaland* or *customer's bread*, which last was a general name given to all descriptions which were sent daily from the neighbouring villages to the capital. Amongst the best known varieties we will only mention the *Corbeil bread*, the *dog bread*, the *bread of two colours*, which last was composed of alternate layers of wheat and rye, and was used by persons of small means; there was also the *Gonesse bread*, which has maintained its reputation to this day.

The "table loaves," which in the provinces were served at the tables of the rich, were of such a convenient size that one of them would suffice for a man of ordinary appetite, even after the crust was cut off, which it was considered polite to offer to the ladies, who soaked it in their soup. For the servants an inferior bread was baked, called "common bread."

In many counties they sprinkled the bread, before putting it into the oven, with powdered linseed, a custom which still exists. They usually added salt to the flour, excepting in certain localities, especially in Paris, where, on account of its price, they only mixed it with the expensive qualities.

The wheats which were long most esteemed for baking purposes, were those of Brie, Champagne, and Bassigny; while those of the Dauphine were held of little value, because they were said to contain so many tares and worthless grains, that the bread made from them produced headache and other ailments.

An ancient chronicle of the time of Charlemagne makes mention of a bread twice baked, or biscuit. This bread was very hard, and easier to keep than any other description. It was also used, as now, for provisioning ships, or towns threatened with a siege, as well as in religious houses. At a later period, delicate biscuits were made of a sort of dry and crumbling pastry which retained the original name. As early as the sixteenth century, Rheims had earned a great renown for these articles of food.

Bread made with barley, oats, or millet was always ranked as coarse food, to which the poor only had recourse in years of want (Fig. 78). Barley bread was, besides, used as a kind of punishment, and monks who had committed any serious offence against discipline were condemned to live on it for a certain period.

Rye bread was held of very little value, although in certain provinces, such as Lyonnais, Forez, and Auvergne, it was very generally used among the country people, and contributed, says Bruyerin Champier in his treatise "De re Cibaria," to "preserve beauty and freshness amongst women." At a later period, the doctors of Paris frequently ordered the use of bread made half of wheat and half of rye as a means "of preserving the health." Black wheat, or buck wheat, which was introduced into Europe by the Moors and Saracens when they conquered Spain, quickly spread to the northern provinces, especially to Flanders, where, by its easy culture and almost certain yield, it averted much suffering from the inhabitants, who were continually being threatened with famine.

It was only later that maize, or Turkey wheat, was cultivated in the south, and that rice came into use; but these two kinds of grain, both equally useless for bread, were employed the one for fattening poultry, and the other for making cakes, which, however, were little appreciated.

[Illustration: Fig. 78.—Cultivation of Grain in use amongst the Peasants, and the Manufacture of Barley and Oat Bread.—Fac–simile of a Woodcut in an edition of Virgil published at Lyons in 1517.]

Vegetables and Plants Used in Cooking.—From the most ancient historical documents we find that at the very earliest period of the French monarchy, fresh and dried vegetables were the ordinary food of the population. Pliny and Columella attribute a Gallic origin to certain roots, and among them onions and parsnips, which the Romans cultivated in their gardens for use at their tables.

It is evident, however, that vegetables were never considered as being capable of forming solid nutriment, since they were almost exclusively used by monastic communities when under vows of extreme abstinence.

A statute of Charlemagne, in which the useful plants which the emperor desired should be cultivated in his domains are detailed, shows us that at that period the greater part of our cooking vegetables were in use, for we find mentioned in it, fennel, garlic, parsley, shallot, onions, watercress, endive, lettuce, beetroot, cabbage, leeks, carrots, artichokes; besides long–beans, broad–beans, peas or Italian vetches, and lentils.

In the thirteenth century, the plants fit for cooking went under the general appellation of *aigrun*, and amongst them, at a later date, were ranked oranges, lemons, and other acid fruits. St. Louis added to this category even fruits with hard rinds, such as walnuts, filberts, and chestnuts; and when the guild of the fruiterers of Paris received its statutes in 1608, they were still called "vendors of fruits and *aigrun*."

The vegetables and cooking–plants noticed in the "Menagier de Paris," which dates from the fourteenth century, and in the treatise "De Obsoniis," of Platina (the name adopted by the Italian Bartholomew Sacchi), which dates from the fifteenth century, do not lead us to suppose that alimentary horticulture had made much progress since the time of Charlemagne. Moreover, we are astonished to find the thistle placed amongst choice dishes; though it cannot be the common thistle that is meant, but probably this somewhat general appellation refers to the vegetable–marrow, which is still found on the tables of the higher classes, or perhaps the artichoke, which we know to be only a kind of thistle developed by cultivation, and which at that period had been recently imported.

About the same date melons begin to appear; but the management of this vegetable fruit was not much known. It was so imperfectly cultivated in the northern provinces, that, in the middle of the sixteenth century, Bruyerin Champier speaks of the Languedocians as alone knowing how to produce excellent *sucrins*—"thus called," say both Charles Estienne and Liebault in the "Maison Rustique," "because gardeners watered them with honeyed or sweetened water." The water–melons have never been cultivated but in the south.

Cabbages, the alimentary reputation of which dates from the remotest times, were already of several kinds, most of which have descended to us; amongst them may be mentioned the apple–headed, the Roman, the white, the common white head, the Easter cabbage, &c.; but the one held in the highest estimation was the famous cabbage of Senlis, whose leaves, says an ancient author, when opened, exhaled a smell more agreeable than musk or amber. This species no doubt fell into disuse when the plan of employing aromatic herbs in cooking, which was so much in repute by our ancestors, was abandoned.

[Illustration: Fig. 79.—Coat–of–arms of the Grain–measurers of Ghent, on their Ceremonial Banner, dated 1568.]

By a strange coincidence, at the same period as marjoram, carraway seed, sweet basil, coriander, lavender, and rosemary were used to add their pungent flavour to sauces and hashes, on the same tables might be found herbs of the coldest and most insipid kinds, such as mallows, some kinds of mosses, &c.

Cucumber, though rather in request, was supposed to be an unwholesome vegetable, because it was said that the inhabitants of Forez, who ate much of it, were subject to periodical fevers, which might really have been caused by noxious emanation from the ponds with which that country abounded. Lentils, now considered so wholesome, were also long looked upon as a doubtful vegetable; according to Liebault, they were difficult to digest and otherwise injurious; they inflamed the inside, affected the sight, and brought on the nightmare, &c. On the other hand, small fresh beans, especially those sold at Landit fair, were used in the most delicate repasts; peas passed as a royal dish in the sixteenth century, when the custom was to eat them with salt pork.

Turnips were also most esteemed by the Parisians. "This vegetable is to them," says Charles Estienne, "what large radishes are to the Limousins." The best were supposed to come from Maisons, Vaugirard, and Aubervilliers. Lastly, there were four kinds of lettuces grown in France, according to Liebault, in 1574: the small, the common, the curled, and the Roman: the seed of the last−named was sent to France by Francois Rabelais when he was in Rome with Cardinal du Bellay in 1537; and the salad made from it consequently received the name of Roman salad, which it has ever since retained. In fact, our ancestors much appreciated salads, for there was not a banquet without at least three or four different kinds.

Fruits.—Western Europe was originally very poor in fruits, and it only improved by foreign importations, mostly from Asia by the Romans. The apricot came from Armenia, the pistachio−nuts and plums from Syria, the peach and nut from Persia, the cherry from Cerasus, the lemon from Media, the filbert from the Hellespont, and chestnuts from Castana, a town of Magnesia. We are also indebted to Asia for almonds; the pomegranate, according to some, came from Africa, to others from Cyprus; the quince from Cydon in Crete; the olive, fig, pear, and apple, from Greece.

The statutes of Charlemagne show us that almost all these fruits were reared in his gardens, and that some of them were of several kinds or varieties.

A considerable period, however, elapsed before the finest and more luscious productions of the garden became as it were almost forced on nature by artificial means. Thus in the sixteenth century we find Rabelais, Charles Estienne, and La Framboisiere, physician to Henry IV., praising the Corbeil peach, which was only an inferior and almost wild sort, and describing it as having "*dry* and *solid* flesh, not adhering to the stone." The culture of this fruit, which was not larger than a damask plum, had then, according to Champier, only just been introduced into France. It must be remarked here that Jacques Coythier, physician to Louis XI., in order to curry favour with his master, who was very fond of new fruits, took as his crest an apricot–tree, from which he was jokingly called Abri–Coythier.

[Illustration: Fig. 80.—Cultivation of Fruit, from a Miniature of the "Proprietaire de Choses" (Manuscript of the Fifteenth Century, in the Library of the Arsenal of Paris).]

It must be owned that great progress has been made in the culture of the plum, the pear, and the apple. Champier says that the best plums are the *royale*, the *perdrigon*, and the *damas* of Tours; Olivier de Serres mentions eighteen kinds—amongst which, however, we do not find the celebrated Reine Claude (greengage), which owes its name to the daughter of Louis XII., first wife of Francis I.

Of pears, the most esteemed in the thirteenth century were the *hastiveau*, which was an early sort, and no doubt the golden pear now called St. Jean, the *caillou* or *chaillou*, a hard pear, which came from Cailloux in Burgundy and *l'angoisse* (agony), so called on account of its bitterness—which, however, totally disappeared in cooking. In the sixteenth century the palm is given to the *cuisse dame*, or *madame*; the *bon chretien*, brought, it is said, by St. Francois de Paule to Louis XI.; the *bergamote*, which came from Bergamo, in Lombardy; the *tant–bonne*, so named from its aroma; and the *caillou rosat*, our rosewater pear.

Amongst apples, the *blandureau* (hard white) of Auvergne, the *rouveau*, and the *paradis* of Provence, are of oldest repute. This reminds us of the couplet by the author of the "Street Cries of Paris," thirteenth century:—

"Primes ai pommes de rouviau,
Et d'Auvergne le blanc duriau."

77

("Give me first the russet apple,
And the hard white fruit of Auvergne.")

The quince, which was so generally cultivated in the Middle Ages, was looked upon as the most useful of all fruits. Not only did it form the basis of the farmers' dried preserves of Orleans, called *cotignac*, a sort of marmalade, but it was also used for seasoning meat. The Portugal quince was the most esteemed; and the cotignac of Orleans had such a reputation, that boxes of this fruit were always given to kings, queens, and princes on entering the towns of France. It was the first offering made to Joan of Arc on her bringing reinforcements into Orleans during the English siege.

Several sorts of cherries were known, but these did not prevent the small wild or wood cherry from being appreciated at the tables of the citizens; whilst the *cornouille*, or wild cornelian cherry, was hardly touched, excepting by the peasants; thence came the proverbial expression, more particularly in use at Orleans, when a person made a silly remark, "He has eaten cornelians," *i.e.*, he speaks like a rustic.

In the thirteenth century, chestnuts from Lombardy were hawked in the streets; but, in the sixteenth century, the chestnuts of the Lyonnais and Auvergne were substituted, and were to be found on the royal table. Four different sorts of figs, in equal estimation, were brought from Marseilles, Nismes, Saint–Andeol, and Pont Saint–Esprit; and in Provence, filberts were to be had in such profusion that they supplied from there all the tables of the kingdom.

The Portuguese claim the honour of having introduced oranges from China; however, in an account of the house of Humbert, Dauphin of Viennois, in 1333, that is, long before the expeditions of the Portuguese to India, mention is made of a sum of money being paid for transplanting orange–trees.

[Illustration: Figs. 81 and 82.—Culture of the Vine and Treading the Grape.—Miniatures taken from the Calendar of a Prayer–Book, in Manuscript, of the Sixteenth Century.]

In the time of Bruyerin Champier, physician to Henry II., raspberries were still completely wild; the same author states that wood strawberries had only just at that time been introduced into gardens, "by which," he says, "they had attained a larger size, though they at the same time lost their quality."

The vine, acclimatised and propagated by the Gauls, ever since the followers of Brennus had brought it from Italy, five hundred years before the Christian era, never ceased to be productive, and even to constitute the natural wealth of the country (Fig. 81 and 82). In the sixteenth century, Liebault enumerated nineteen sorts of grapes, and Olivier de Serres twenty–four, amongst which, notwithstanding the eccentricities of the ancient names, we believe that we can trace the greater part of those plants which are now cultivated in France. For instance, it is known that the excellent vines of Thomery, near Fontainebleau, which yield in abundance the most beautiful table grape which art and care can produce, were already in use in the reign of Henry IV. (Fig. 83).

[Illustration: Fig. 83.—The Winegrower, drawn and engraved in the Sixteenth Century, by J. Amman.]

In the time of the Gauls the custom of drying grapes by exposing them to the sun, or to a certain amount of artificial heat, was already known; and very soon after, the same means were adopted for preserving plums, an industry in which then, as now, the people of Tours and Rheims excelled. Drying apples in an oven was also the custom, and formed a delicacy which was reserved for winter and spring banquets. Dried fruits were also brought from abroad, as mentioned in the "Book of Street Cries in Paris:"—

"Figues de Melites sans fin,
 J'ai roisin d'outre mer, roisin."

("Figs from Malta without end,
 And grapes from over the sea.")

Butchers' Meat.—According to Strabo, the Gauls were great eaters of meat, especially of pork, whether fresh or salted. "Gaul," says he, "feeds so many flocks, and, above all, so many pigs, that it supplies not only Rome, but all Italy, with grease and salt meat." The second chapter of the Salic law, comprising nineteen articles, relates entirely to penalties for pig–stealing; and in the laws of the Visigoths we find four articles on the same subject.

[Illustration: Fig. 84.—Swineherd.

Illustration: Fig 85.—A Burgess at Meals.

Miniatures from the Calendar of a Book of Hours.—Manuscript of the Sixteenth Century.]

In those remote days, in which the land was still covered with enormous forests of oak, great facilities were offered for breeding pigs, whose special liking for acorns is well known. Thus the bishops, princes, and lords caused numerous droves of pigs to be fed on their domains, both for the purpose of supplying their own tables as well as for the fairs and markets. At a subsequent period, it became the custom for each household, whether in town or country, to rear and fatten a pig, which was killed and salted at a stated period of the year; and this custom still exists in many provinces. In Paris, for instance, there was scarcely a bourgeois who had not two or three young pigs. During the day these unsightly creatures were allowed to roam in the streets; which, however, they helped to keep clean by eating up the refuse of all sorts which was thrown out of the houses. One of the sons of Louis le Gros, while passing, on the 2nd of October, 1131, in the Rue du Martroi, between the Hotel de Ville and the church of St. Gervais, fractured his skull by a fall from his horse, caused by a pig running between that animal's legs. This accident led to the first order being issued by the provosts, to the effect that breeding pigs within the town was forbidden. Custom, however, deep-rooted for centuries, resisted this order, and many others on the same subject which followed it: for we find, under Francis I., a license was issued to the executioner, empowering him to capture all the stray pigs which he could find in Paris, and to take them to the Hotel Dieu, when he should receive either five sous in silver or the head of the animal.

It is said that the holy men of St. Antoine, in virtue of the privilege attached to the popular legend of their patron, who was generally represented with a pig, objected to this order, and long after maintained the exclusive right of allowing their pigs to roam in the streets of the capital.

The obstinate determination with which every one tried to evade the administrative laws on this subject, is explained, in fact, by the general taste of the French nation for pork. This taste appears somewhat strange at a time when this kind of food was supposed to engender leprosy, a disease with which France was at that time overrun.

[Illustration: Fig. 86.—Stall of Carved Wood (Fifteenth Century), representing the Proverb, "Margaritas ante Porcos," "Throwing Pearls before Swine," from Rouen Cathedral.]

Pigs' meat made up generally the greater part of the domestic banquets. There was no great feast at which hams, sausages, and black puddings were not served in profusion on all the tables; and as Easter Day, which brought to a close the prolonged fastings of Lent, was one of the great feasts, this food formed the most important dish on that occasion. It is possible that the necessity for providing for the consumption of that day originated the celebrated ham fair, which was and is still held annually on the Thursday of Passion Week in front of Notre–Dame, where the dealers from all parts of France, and especially from Normandy and Lower Brittany, assembled with their swine.

Sanitary measures were taken in Paris and in the various towns in order to prevent the evil effects likely to arise from the enormous consumption of pork; public officers, called *languayeurs*, were ordered to examine the animals to ensure that they had not white ulcers under the tongue, these being considered the signs that their flesh was in a condition to communicate leprosy to those who partook of it.

For a long time the retail sale of pork was confined to the butchers, like that of other meat. Salt or fresh pork was at one time always sold raw, though at a later period some retailers, who carried on business principally among the lowest orders of the people, took to selling cooked pork and sausages. They were named *charcuitiers* or *saucissiers*. This new trade, which was most lucrative, was adopted by so many people that parliament was forced to limit the number of *charcuitiers*, who at last formed a corporation, and received their statutes, which were confirmed by the King in 1475.

Amongst the privileges attached to their calling was that of selling red herrings and sea–fish in Lent, during which time the sale of pork was strictly forbidden. Although they had the exclusive monopoly of selling cooked pork, they were at first forbidden to buy their meat of any one but of the butchers, who alone had the right of killing pigs; and it was only in 1513 that the *charcuitiers* were allowed to purchase at market and sell the meat raw, in opposition to the butchers, who in consequence gradually gave up killing and selling pork (Fig. 87).

Although the consumption of butchers' meat was not so great in the Middle Ages as it is now, the trade of a butcher, to which extraordinary privileges were attached, was nevertheless one of the industries which realised the greatest profits.

We know what an important part the butchers played in the municipal history of France, as also of Belgium; and we also know how great their political influence was, especially in the fifteenth century.

[Illustration: Fig. 87.—The Pork–butcher (*Charcutier*).—Fac–simile of a Miniature in a Charter of the Abbey of Solignac (Fourteenth Century).]

The existence of the great slaughter–house of Paris dates back to the most remote period of monarchy. The parish church of the corporation of butchers, namely, that of St. Pierre aux Boeufs in the city, on the front of which were two sculptured oxen, existed before the tenth century. A Celtic monument was discovered on the site of the ancient part of Paris, with a bas–relief representing a wild bull carrying three cranes standing among oak branches. Archaeology has chosen to recognise in this sculpture a Druidical allegory, which has descended to us in the shape of the triumphal car of the Prize Ox (Fig. 88). The butchers who, for centuries at least in France, only killed sheep and pigs, proved themselves most jealous of their privileges, and admitted no strangers into their corporation. The proprietorship of stalls at the markets, and the right of being admitted as a master butcher at the age of seven years and a day, belonged exclusively to the male descendants of a few rich and powerful families. The Kings of France alone, on their accession, could create a new master butcher. Since the middle of the fourteenth century the "Grande Boucherie" was the seat of an important jurisdiction, composed of a mayor, a master, a proctor, and an attorney; it also had a judicial council before which the butchers could bring up all their cases, and an appeal from which could only be considered by Parliament. Besides this court, which had to decide cases of misbehaviour on the part of the apprentices, and all their appeals against their masters, the corporation had a counsel in Parliament, as also one at the Chatelet, who were specially attached to the interests of the butchers, and were in their pay.

[Illustration: Fig. 88.—The Holy Ox.—Celtic Monument found in Paris under the Choir of Notre–Dame in 1711, and preserved in the Musee de Cluny et des Thermes.]

Although bound, at all events with their money, to follow the calling of their fathers, we find many descendants of ancient butchers' families of Paris, in the fourteenth and fifteenth centuries, abandoning their stalls to fill high places in the state, and even at court. It must not be concluded that the rich butchers in those days occupied themselves with the minor details of their trade; the greater number employed servants who cut up and retailed the meat, and they themselves simply kept the accounts, and were engaged in dealing through factors or foremen for the purchase of beasts for their stalls (Fig. 89). One can form an opinion of the wealth of some of these tradesmen by reading the enumeration made by an old chronicler of the property and income of Guillaume de Saint–Yon, one of the principal master butchers in 1370. "He was proprietor of three stalls, in which meat was weekly sold to the amount of 200 *livres parisis* (the livre being equivalent to 24 francs at least), with an average profit of ten to fifteen per cent.; he had an income of 600 *livres parisis* ; he possessed besides his family house in Paris, four country–houses, well supplied with furniture and agricultural implements, drinking–cups, vases, cups of silver, and cups of onyx with silver feet, valued at 100 francs or more each. His wife had jewels, belts, purses, and trinkets, to the value of upwards of 1,000 gold francs (the gold franc was worth 24 livres); long and short gowns trimmed with fur; and three mantles of grey fur. Guillaume de Saint–Yon had generally in his storehouses 300 ox–hides, worth 24 francs each at least; 800 measures of fat, worth 3–1/2 sols each; in his sheds, he had 800 sheep worth 100 sols each; in his safes 500 or 600 silver florins of ready money (the florin was worth 12 francs, which must be multiplied five times to estimate its value in present currency), and his household furniture was valued at 12,000 florins. He gave a dowry of 2,000 florins to his two nieces, and spent 3,000 florins in rebuilding his Paris house; and lastly, as if he had been a noble, he used a silver seal."

[Illustration: Fig. 89.—The Butcher and his Servant, drawn and engraved by J. Amman (Sixteenth Century).]

We find in the "Menagier de Paris" curious statistics respecting the various butchers' shops of the capital, and the daily sale in each at the period referred to. This sale, without counting the households of the King, the Queen, and the royal family, which were specially provisioned, amounted to 26,624 oxen, 162,760 sheep, 27,456 pigs, and 15,912 calves per annum; to which must be added not only the smoked and salted flesh of 200 or 300 pigs, which were sold at the fair in Holy Week, but also 6,420 sheep, 823 oxen, 832 calves, and 624 pigs, which, according to the "Menagier," were used in the royal and princely households.

Sometimes the meat was sent to market already cut up, but the slaughter of beasts was more frequently done in the butchers' shops in the town; for they only killed from day to day, according to the demand. Besides the butchers' there were tripe shops, where the feet, kidneys, &c., were sold.

[Illustration: Figs. 90 and 91.—Seal and Counter–Seal of the Butchers of Bruges in 1356, from an impression on green wax, preserved in the archives of that town.]

According to Bruyerin Champier, during the sixteenth century the most celebrated sheep in France were those of Berri and Limousin; and of all butchers' meat, veal was reckoned the best. In fact, calves intended for the tables of the upper classes were fed in a special manner: they were allowed for six months, or even for a year, nothing but milk, which made their flesh most tender and delicate. Contrary to the present taste, kid was more appreciated than lamb, which caused the *rotisseurs* frequently to attach the tail of a kid to a lamb, so as to deceive the customer and sell him a less expensive meat at the higher price. This was the origin of the proverb which described a cheat as "a dealer in goat by halves."

In other places butchers were far from acquiring the same importance which they did in France and Belgium (Figs. 90 and 91), where much more meat was consumed than in Spain, Italy, or even in Germany. Nevertheless, in almost all countries there were certain regulations, sometimes eccentric, but almost always rigidly enforced, to ensure a supply of meat of the best quality and in a healthy state. In England, for instance, butchers were only allowed to kill bulls after they had been baited with dogs, no doubt with the view of making the flesh more tender. At Mans, it was laid down in the trade regulations, that "no butcher shall be so bold as to sell meat unless it shall have been previously seen alive by two or three persons, who will testify to it on oath; and, anyhow, they shall not sell it until the persons shall have declared it wholesome," &c.

To the many regulations affecting the interests of the public must be added that forbidding butchers to sell meat on days when abstinence from animal food was ordered by the Church. These regulations applied less to the vendors than to the consumers, who, by disobeying them, were liable to fine or imprisonment, or to severe corporal punishment by the whip or in the pillory. We find that Clement Marot was imprisoned and nearly burned alive for having eaten pork in Lent. In 1534, Guillaume des Moulins, Count of Brie, asked permission for his mother, who was then eighty years of age, to cease fasting; the Bishop of Paris only granted dispensation on condition that the old lady should take her meals in secret and out of sight of every one, and should still fast on Fridays. "In a certain town," says Brantome, "there had been a procession in Lent. A woman, who had assisted at it barefooted, went home to dine off a quarter of lamb and a ham. The smell got into the street; the house was entered. The fact being established, the woman was taken, and condemned to walk through the town with her quarter of lamb on the spit over her shoulder, and the ham hung round her neck." This species of severity increased during the times of religious dissensions. Erasmus says, "He who has eaten pork instead of fish is taken to the torture like a parricide." An edict of Henry II, 1549, forbade the sale of meat in Lent to persons who should not be furnished with a doctor's certificate. Charles IX forbade the sale of meat to the Huguenots; and it was ordered that the privilege of selling meat during the time of abstinence should belong exclusively to the hospitals. Orders were given to those who retailed meat to take the address of every purchaser, although he had presented a medical certificate, so that the necessity for his eating meat might be verified. Subsequently, the medical certificate required to be endorsed by the priest, specifying what quantity of meat was required. Even in these cases the use of butchers' meat alone was granted, pork, poultry, and game being strictly forbidden.

Poultry.—A monk of the Abbey of Cluny once went on a visit to his relations. On arriving he asked for food; but as it was a fast day he was told there was nothing in the house but fish. Perceiving some chickens in the yard, he took a stick and killed one, and brought it to his relations, saying, "This is the fish which I shall eat to–day." "Eh, but, my son," they said, "have you dispensation from fasting on a Friday?" "No," he answered; "but poultry is not flesh; fish and fowls were created at the same time; they have a common origin, as the hymn which I sing in the service teaches me."

This simple legend belongs to the tenth century; and notwithstanding that the opinion of this Benedictine monk may appear strange nowadays, yet it must be acknowledged that he was only conforming himself to the opinions laid down by certain theologians. In 817, the Council of Aix–la–Chapelle decided that such delicate nourishment could scarcely be called mortification as understood by the teaching of the Church. In consequence of this an order was issued forbidding the monks to eat poultry, except during four days at Easter and four at Christmas. But this prohibition in no way changed the established custom of certain parts of Christendom, and the faithful persisted in believing that poultry and fish were identical in the eyes of the Church, and accordingly continued to eat them indiscriminately. We also see, in the middle of the thirteenth century, St. Thomas Aquinas, who was considered an authority in questions of dogma and of faith, ranking poultry amongst species of aquatic origin.

Eventually, this palpable error was abandoned; but when the Church forbade Christians the use of poultry on fast days, it made an exception, out of consideration for the ancient prejudice, in favour of teal, widgeon, moor–hens, and also two or three kinds of small amphibious quadrupeds. Hence probably arose the general and absurd beliefs concerning the origin of teal, which some said sprung from the rotten wood of old ships, others from the fruits of a tree, or the gum on fir–trees, whilst others thought they came from a fresh–water shell analogous to that of the oyster and mussel.

As far back as modern history can be traced, we find that a similar mode of fattening poultry was employed then as now, and was one which the Gauls must have learnt from the Romans. Amongst the charges in the households of the kings of France one item was that which concerned the poultry–house, and which, according to an edict of St. Louis in 1261, bears the name of *poulaillier*. At a subsequent period this name was given to breeders and dealers in poultry (Fig. 92).

The "Menagier" tells as that, as is the present practice, chickens were fattened by depriving them of light and liberty, and gorging them with succulent food. Amongst the poultry yards in repute at that time, the author mentions that of Hesdin, a property of the Dukes of Luxemburg, in Artois; that of the King, at the Hotel Saint–Pol, Rue Saint–Antoine, Paris; that of Master Hugues Aubriot, provost of Paris; and that of Charlot, no doubt a bourgeois of that name, who also gave his name to an ancient street in that quarter called the Marais.

[Illustration: Fig. 92.—The Poulterer, drawn and engraved in the Sixteenth Century, by J. Amman.]

Capons are frequently mentioned in poems of the twelfth and thirteenth centuries; but the name of the *poularde* does not occur until the sixteenth.

We know that under the Roman rule, the Gauls carried on a considerable trade in fattened geese. This trade ceased when Gaul passed to new masters; but the breeding of geese continued to be carefully attended to. For many centuries geese were more highly prized than any other description of poultry, and Charlemagne ordered that his domains should be well stocked with flocks of geese, which were driven to feed in the fields, like flocks of sheep. There was an old proverb, "Who eats the king's goose returns the feathers in a hundred years." This bird was considered a great delicacy by the working classes and bourgeoisie. The *rotisseurs* (Fig. 94) had hardly anything in their shops but geese, and, therefore, when they were united in a company, they received the name of *oyers*, or *oyeurs*. The street in which they were established, with their spits always loaded with juicy roasts, was called Rue des *Oues* (geese), and this street, when it ceased to be frequented by the *oyers*, became by corruption Rue Auxours.

[Illustration: Fig. 93.—Barnacle Geese.—Fac-simile of an Engraving on Wood, from the "Cosmographie Universelle" of Munster, folio, Basle, 1552.]

There is every reason for believing that the domestication of the wild duck is of quite recent date. The attempt having succeeded, it was wished to follow it up by the naturalisation in the poultry-yard of two other sorts of aquatic birds, namely, the sheldrake (*tadorna*) and the moorhen, but without success. Some attribute the introduction of turkeys into France and Europe to Jacques Coeur, treasurer to Charles VII., whose commercial connections with the East were very extensive; others assert that it is due to King Rene, Count of Provence; but according to the best authorities these birds were first brought into France in the time of Francis I. by Admiral Philippe de Chabot, and Bruyerin Champier asserts that they were not known until even later. It was at about the same period that guinea-fowls were brought from the coast of Africa by Portuguese merchants; and the travelling naturalist, Pierre Belon, who wrote in the year 1555, asserts that in his time "they had already so multiplied in the houses of the nobles that they had become quite common."

[Illustration: Fig. 94.—The Poultry-dealer.—Fac-simile of an Engraving on Wood, after Cesare Vecellio.]

The pea-fowl played an important part in the chivalric banquets of the Middle Ages (Fig. 95). According to old poets the flesh of this noble bird is "food for the brave." A poet of the thirteenth century says, "that thieves have as much taste for falsehood as a hungry man has for the flesh of the peacock." In the fourteenth century poultry-yards were still stocked with these birds; but the turkey and the pheasant gradually replaced them, as their flesh was considered somewhat hard and stringy. This is proved by the fact that in 1581, "La Nouvelle Coutume du Bourbonnois" only reckons the value of these beautiful birds at two sous and a half, or about three francs of present currency.

[Illustration: Fig. 95.—State Banquet.—Serving the Peacock.—Fac–simile of a Woodcut in an edition of Virgil, folio, published at Lyons in 1517.]

Game.—Our forefathers included among the birds which now constitute feathered game the heron, the crane, the crow, the swan, the stork, the cormorant, and the bittern. These supplied the best tables, especially the first three, which were looked upon as exquisite food, fit even for royalty, and were reckoned as thorough French delicacies. There were at that time heronries, as at a later period there were pheasantries. People also ate birds of prey, and only rejected those which fed on carrion.

Swans, which were much appreciated, were very common on all the principal rivers of France, especially in the north; a small island below Paris had taken its name from these birds, and has maintained it ever since. It was proverbially said that the Charente was bordered with swans, and for this same reason Valenciennes was called *Val des Cygnes*, or the Swan Valley.

Some authors make it appear that for a long time young game was avoided owing to the little nourishment it contained and its indigestibility, and assert that it was only when some French ambassadors returned from Venice that the French learnt that young partridges and leverets were exquisite, and quite fit to appear at the most sumptuous banquets. The "Menagier" gives not only various receipts for cooking them, but also for dressing chickens, when game was out of season, so as to make them taste like young partridges.

There was a time when they fattened pheasants as they did capons; it was a secret, says Liebault, only known to the poultry dealers; but although they were much appreciated, the pullet was more so, and realised as much as two crowns each (this does not mean the gold crown, but a current coin worth three livres). Plovers, which sometimes came from Beauce in cart–loads, were much relished; they were roasted without being drawn, as also were turtle–doves and larks; "for," says an ancient author, "larks only eat small pebbles and sand, doves grains of juniper and scented herbs, and plovers feed on air." At a later period the same honour was conferred on woodcocks.

Thrushes, starlings, blackbirds, quail, and partridges were in equal repute according to the season. The *bec–figue*, a small bird like a nightingale, was so much esteemed in Provence that there were feasts at which that bird alone was served, prepared in various ways; but of all birds used for the table none could be compared to the young cuckoo taken just as it was full fledged.

As far as we can ascertain, the Gauls had a dislike to the flesh of rabbits, and they did not even hunt them, for according to Strabo, Southern Gaul was infested with these mischievous animals, which destroyed the growing crops, and even the barks of the trees. There was considerable change in this respect a few centuries later, for every one in town or country reared domesticated rabbits, and the wild ones formed an article of food which was much in request. In order to ascertain whether a rabbit is young, Strabo tells us we should feel the first joint of the fore–leg, when we shall find a small bone free and movable. This method is adopted in all kitchens in the present day. Hares were preferred to rabbits, provided they were young; for an old French proverb says, "An old hare and an old goose are food for the devil."

[Illustration: Fig. 96.—"The way to skin and cut up a Stag."—Fac–simile of a Miniature of "Phoebus, and his Staff for hunting Wild Animals" (Manuscript of the Fifteenth Century, National Library of Paris).]

The hedgehog and squirrel were also eaten. As for roe and red deer, they were, according to Dr. Bruyerin Ohampier, morsels fit for kings and rich people (Fig. 96). The doctor speaks of "fried slices of the young horn of the stag" as the daintiest of food, and the "Menagier de Paris" shows how, as early as the fourteenth century, beef was dished up like bear's–flesh venison, for the use of kitchens in countries where the black bear did not exist. This proves that bear's flesh was in those days considered good food.

Milk, Butter, Eggs, and Cheese.—These articles of food, the first which nature gave to man, were not always and everywhere uniformly permitted or prohibited by the Church on fast days. The faithful were for several centuries left to their own judgment on the subject. In fact, there is nothing extraordinary in eggs being eaten in Lent without scruple, considering that some theologians maintained that the hens which laid them were animals of aquatic extraction.

It appears, however, that butter, either from prejudice or mere custom, was only used on fast days in its fresh state, and was not allowed to be used for cooking purposes. At first, and especially amongst the monks, the dishes were prepared with oil; but as in some countries oil was apt to become very expensive, and the supply even to fail totally, animal fat or lard had to be substituted. At a subsequent period the Church authorised the use of butter and milk; but on this point, the discipline varied much. In the fourteenth century, Charles V., King of France, having asked Pope Gregory XI. for a dispensation to use milk and butter on fast days, in consequence of the bad state of his health, brought on owing to an attempt having been made to poison him, the supreme Pontiff required a certificate from a physician and from the King's confessor. He even then only granted the dispensation after imposing on that Christian king the repetition of a certain number of prayers and the performance of certain pious deeds. In defiance of the severity of ecclesiastical authority, we find, in the "Journal of a Bourgeois of Paris," that in the unhappy reign of Charles VI. (1420), "for want of oil, butter was eaten in Lent the same as on ordinary non–fast days."

In 1491, Queen Anne, Duchess of Brittany, in order to obtain permission from the Pope to eat butter in Lent, represented that Brittany did not produce oil, neither did it import it from southern countries. Many northern provinces adopted necessity as the law, and, having no oil, used butter; and thence originated that famous toast with slices of bread and butter, which formed such an important part of Flemish food. These papal dispensations were, however, only earned at the price of prayers and alms, and this was the origin of the *troncs pour le beurre*, that is, "alms–box for butter," which are still to be seen in some of the Flemish churches.

[Illustration: Fig. 97.—The Manufacture of Oil, drawn and engraved by J. Amman in the Sixteenth Century.]

It is not known when butter was first salted in order to preserve it or to send it to distant places; but this process, which is so simple and so natural, dates, no doubt, from very ancient times; it was particularly practised by the Normans and Bretons, who enclosed the butter in large earthenware jars, for in the statutes which were given to the fruiterers of Paris in 1412, mention is made of salt butter in earthenware jars. Lorraine only exported butter in such jars. The fresh butter most in request for the table in Paris, was that made at Vanvres, which in the month of May the people ate every morning mixed with garlic.

The consumption of butter was greatest in Flanders. "I am surprised," says Bruyerin Champier, speaking of that country, "that they have not yet tried to turn it into drink; in France it is mockingly called *beurriere; and when any one has to travel in that country,*

90

he is advised to take a knife with him if he wishes to taste the good rolls of butter."

[Illustration: Fig. 98.—A Dealer in Eggs.—Fac–simile of a Woodcut, after Cesare Vecellio, Sixteenth Century.]

It is not necessary to state that milk and cheese followed the fortunes of butter in the Catholic world, the same as eggs followed those of poultry. But butter having been declared lawful by the Church, a claim was put in for eggs (Fig. 98), and Pope Julius III. granted this dispensation to all Christendom, although certain private churches did not at once choose to profit by this favour. The Greeks had always been more rigid on these points of discipline than the people of the West. It is to the prohibition of eggs in Lent that the origin of "Easter eggs" must be traced. These were hardened by boiling them in a madder bath, and were brought to receive the blessing of the priest on Good Friday, and were then eaten on the following Sunday as a sign of rejoicing.

Ancient Gaul was celebrated for some of its home–made cheeses. Pliny praises those of Nismes, and of Mount Lozere, in Gevaudau; Martial mentions those of Toulouse, &c. A simple anecdote, handed down by the monk of St. Gall, who wrote in the ninth century, proves to us that the traditions with regard to cheeses were not lost in the time of Charlemagne: "The Emperor, in one of his travels, alighted suddenly, and without being expected, at the house of a bishop. It was on a Friday. The prelate had no fish, and did not dare to set meat before the prince. He therefore offered him what he had got, some boiled corn and green cheese. Charles ate of the cheese; but taking the green part to be bad, he took care to remove it with his knife. The Bishop, seeing this, took the liberty of telling his guest that this was the best part. The Emperor, tasting it, found that the bishop was right; and consequently ordered him to send him annually two cases of similar cheese to Aix–la–Chapelle. The Bishop answered, that he could easily send cheeses, but he could not be sure of sending them in proper condition, because it was only by opening them that you could be sure of the dealer not having deceived you in the quality of the cheese. 'Well,' said the Emperor, 'before sending them, cut them through the middle, so as to see if they are what I want; you will only have to join the two halves again by means of a wooden peg, and you can then put the whole into a case.'"

Under the kings of the third French dynasty, a cheese was made at the village of Chaillot, near Paris, which was much appreciated in the capital. In the twelfth and thirteenth centuries, the cheeses of Champagne and of Brie, which are still manufactured, were

91

equally popular, and were hawked in the streets, according to the "Book of Street–Cries in Paris,"—

"J'ai bon fromage de Champaigne;
Or i a fromage de Brie!"

("Buy my cheese from Champagne,
And my cheese from Brie!")

Eustache Deschamps went so far as to say that cheese was the only good thing which could possibly come from Brie.

The "Menagier de Paris" praises several kinds of cheeses, the names of which it would now be difficult to trace, owing to their frequent changes during four hundred years; but, according to the Gallic author of this collection, a cheese to be presentable at table, was required to possess certain qualities (in proverbial Latin, "Non Argus, nee Helena, nee Maria Magdalena," &c.), thus expressed in French rhyme:—

"Non mie (pas) blanc comme Helaine,
Non mie (pas) plourant comme Magdelaine,
Non Argus (a cent yeux), mais du tout avugle (aveugle)
Et aussi pesant comme un bugle (boeuf),
Contre le pouce soit rebelle,
Et qu'il ait ligneuse cotelle (epaisse croute)
Sans yeux, sans plourer, non pas blanc,
Tigneulx, rebelle, bien pesant."

("Neither–white like Helena,
Nor weeping as Magdelena,
Neither Argus, nor yet quite blind,
And having too a thickish rind,
Resisting somewhat to the touch,
And as a bull should weigh as much;
Not eyeless, weeping, nor quite white,
But firm, resisting, not too light.")

In 1509, Platina, although an Italian, in speaking of good cheeses, mentions those of Chauny, in Picardy, and of Brehemont, in Touraine; Charles Estienne praises those of Craponne, in Auvergne, the *angelots* of Normandy, and the cheeses made from fresh cream which the peasant–women of Montreuil and Vincennes brought to Paris in small wickerwork baskets, and which were eaten sprinkled with sugar. The same author names also the *rougerets* of Lyons, which were always much esteemed; but, above all the cheeses of Europe, he places the round or cylindrical ones of Auvergne, which were only made by very clean and healthy children of fourteen years of age. Olivier de Serres advises those who wish to have good cheeses to boil the milk before churning it, a plan which is in use at Lodi and Parma, "where cheeses are made which are acknowledged by all the world to be excellent."

The parmesan, which this celebrated agriculturist cites as an example, only became the fashion in France on the return of Charles VIII. from his expedition to Naples. Much was thought at that time of a cheese brought from Turkey in bladders, and of different varieties produced in Holland and Zetland. A few of these foreign products were eaten in stews and in pastry, others were toasted and sprinkled with sugar and powdered cinnamon.

"Le Roman de Claris," a manuscript which belongs to the commencement of the fourteenth century, says that in a town winch was taken by storm the following stores were found:—:

"Maint bon tonnel de vin,
Maint bon bacon (cochon), maint fromage a rostir."

("Many a ton of wine,
Many a slice of good bacon, plenty of good roasted cheese.")

[Illustration: Table Service of a Lady of Quality

Fac–simile of a miniature from the Romance of Renaud de Montauban, a ms. of fifteenth century Bibl. de l'Arsenal]

[Illustration: Ladies Hunting

Costumes of the fifteenth century. From a miniature in a ms. copy of *Ovid's Epistles*. No 7231 *bis.* Bibl. nat'le de Paris.]

Besides cheese and butter, the Normans, who had a great many cows in their rich pastures, made a sort of fermenting liquor from the butter–milk, which they called *serat*, by boiling the milk with onions and garlic, and letting it cool in closed vessels.

[Illustration: Fig. 99.—Manufacture of Cheeses in Switzerland.—Fac–simile of a Woodcut in the "Cosmographie Universelle" of Munster, folio, Basle, 1549.]

If the author of the "Menagier" is to be believed, the women who sold milk by retail in the towns were well acquainted with the method of increasing its quantity at the expense of its quality. He describes how his *froumentee*, which consists of a sort of soup, is made, and states that when he sends his cook to make her purchases at the milk market held in the neighbourhood of the Rues de la Savonnerie, des Ecrivains, and de la Vieille–Monnaie, he enjoins her particularly "to get very fresh cow's milk, and to tell the person who sells it not to do so if she has put water to it; for, unless it be quite fresh, or if there be water in it, it will turn."

Fish and Shellfish.—Freshwater fish, which was much more abundant in former days than now, was the ordinary food of those who lived on the borders of lakes, ponds, or rivers, or who, at all events, were not so far distant but that they could procure it fresh. There was of course much diversity at different periods and in different countries as regards the estimation in which the various kinds of fish were held. Thus Ausone, who was a native of Bordeaux, spoke highly of the delicacy of the perch, and asserted that shad, pike, and tench should be left to the lower orders; an opinion which was subsequently contradicted by the inhabitants of other parts of Gaul, and even by the countrymen of the Latin poet Gregory of Tours, who loudly praised the Geneva trout. But a time arrived when the higher classes preferred the freshwater fish of Orchies in Flanders, and even those of the Lyonnais. Thus we see in the thirteenth century the barbel of Saint–Florentin held in great estimation, whereas two hundred years later a man who was of no use, or a nonentity, was said to resemble a barbel, "which is neither good for roasting nor boiling."

[Illustration: Fig. 100.—The Pond Fisherman.—Fac–simile of a Woodcut of the "Cosmographie Universelle" of Munster, folio, Basle, 1549.]

In a collection of vulgar proverbs of the twelfth century mention is made, amongst the fish most in demand, besides the barbel of Saint—Florentin above referred to, of the eels of Maine, the pike of Chalons, the lampreys of Nantes, the trout of Andeli, and the dace of Aise. The "Menagier" adds several others to the above list, including blay, shad, roach, and gudgeon, but, above all, the carp, which was supposed to be a native of Southern Europe, and which must have been naturalised at a much later period in the northern waters (Figs. 100, 101, and 102).

[Illustration: Fig. 101.—The River Fisherman, designed and engraved, in the Sixteenth Century, by J. Amman.]

[Illustration: Fig. 102.—Conveyance of Fish by Water and Land.—Fac—simile of an Engraving in the Royal Statutes of the Provostship of Merchants, 1528.]

The most ancient documents bear witness that the natives of the sea—coasts of Europe, and particularly of the Mediterranean, fed on the same fish as at present: there were, however, a few other sea—fish, which were also used for food, but which have since been abandoned. Our ancestors were, not difficult to please: they had good teeth, and their palates, having become accustomed to the flesh of the cormorant, heron, and crane, without difficulty appreciated the delicacy of the nauseous sea—dog, the porpoise, and even the whale, which, when salted, furnished to a great extent all the markets of Europe.

The trade in salted sea—fish only began in Paris in the twelfth century, when a company of merchants was instituted, or rather re—established, on the principle of the ancient association of Nantes. This association had existed from the period of the foundation under the Gauls of Lutetia, the city of fluvial commerce (Fig. 103), and it is mentioned in the letters patent of Louis VII. (1170). One of the first cargoes which this company brought in its boats was that of salted herrings from the coast of Normandy. These herrings became a necessary food during Lent, and

"Sor et blanc harene fres pouldre (couvert de sel)!"

("Herrings smoked, fresh, and salted!")

was the cry of the retailers in the streets of Paris, where this fish became a permanent article of consumption to an extent which can be appreciated from the fact that Saint

95

Louis gave annually nearly seventy thousand herrings to the hospitals, plague–houses, and monasteries.

[Illustration: Fig. 103.—A Votive Altar of the Nantes Parisiens, or the Company for the Commercial Navigation of the Seine, erected in Lutelia during the reign of Tiberius.—Fragments of this Altar, which were discovered in 1711 under the Choir of the Church of Notre–Dame, are preserved in the Museums of Cluny and the Palais des Thermes.]

The profit derived from the sale of herrings at that time was so great that it soon became a special trade; it was, in fact, the regular practice of the Middle Ages for persons engaged in any branch of industry to unite together and form themselves into a corporation. Other speculators conceived the idea of bringing fresh fish to Paris by means of relays of posting conveyances placed along the road, and they called themselves *forains*. Laws were made to distinguish the rights of each of these trades, and to prevent any quarrel in the competition. In these laws, all sea–fish were comprised under three names, the fresh, the salted, and the smoked (*sor*). Louis IX. in an edict divides the dealers into two classes, namely, the sellers of fresh fish, and the sellers of salt or smoked fish. Besides salt and fresh herrings, an enormous amount of salted mackerel, which was almost as much used, was brought from the sea–coast, in addition to flat–fish, gurnets, skate, fresh and salted whiting and codfish.

In an old document of the thirteenth century about fifty kinds of fish are enumerated which were retailed in the markets of the kingdom; and a century later the "Menagier" gives receipts for cooking forty kinds, amongst which appears, under the name of *craspois*, the salted flesh of the whale, which was also called *le lard de careme*. This coarse food, which was sent from the northern seas in enormous slices, was only eaten by the lower orders, for, according to a writer of the sixteenth century, "were it cooked even for twenty–four hours it would still be very hard and indigestible."

The "Proverbes" of the thirteenth century, which mention the freshwater fish then in vogue, also names the sea–fish most preferred, and whence they came, namely, the shad from Bordeaux, the congers from La Rochelle, the sturgeon from Blaye, the fresh herrings from Fecamp, and the cuttle–fish from Coutances. At a later period the conger was not eaten from its being supposed to produce the plague. The turbot, John–dory, skate and sole, which were very dear, were reserved for the rich. The fishermen fed on the sea–dragon. A great quantity of the small sea crayfish were brought into market; and in certain countries these were called *sante*, because the doctors recommended them to invalids or those in consumption; on the other hand, freshwater crayfish were not much esteemed in the fifteenth and sixteenth centuries, excepting for their eggs, which were prepared with spice. It is well known that pond frogs were a favourite food of the Gauls and Franks; they were never out of fashion in the rural districts, and were served at the best tables, dressed with green sauce; at the same period, and especially during Lent, snails, which were served in pyramid–shaped dishes, were much appreciated; so much so that nobles and bourgeois cultivated snail beds, somewhat resembling our oyster beds of the present day.

The inhabitants of the coast at all periods ate various kinds of shell–fish, which were called in Italy sea–fruit; but it was only towards the twelfth century that the idea was entertained of bringing oysters to Paris, and mussels were not known there until much later. It is notorious that Henry IV. was a great oyster–eater. Sully relates that when he was created a duke "the king came, without being expected, to take his seat at the reception banquet, but as there was much delay in going to dinner, he began by eating some *huitres de chasse*, which he found very fresh."

By *huitres de chasse* were meant those oysters which were brought by the *chasse–marees*, carriers who brought the fresh fish from the coast to Paris at great speed.

Beverages.—Beer is not only one of the oldest fermenting beverages used by man, but it is also the one which was most in vogue in the Middle Ages. If we refer to the tales of the Greek historians, we find that the Gauls—who, like the Egyptians, attributed the discovery of this refreshing drink to their god Osiris—had two sorts of beer: one called *zythus*, made with honey and intended for the rich; the other called *corma*, in which there was no honey, and which was made for the poor. But Pliny asserts that beer in Gallie was called *cerevisia*, and the grain employed for making it *brasce*. This testimony seems true, as from *brasce* or *brasse* comes the name *brasseur* (brewer), and from *cerevisia*, *cervoise*, the generic name by which beer was known for centuries, and which only lately fell into disuse.

[Illustration: Fig. 104.—The Great Drinkers of the North.—Fac–simile of a Woodcut of the "Histoires des Pays Septentrionaux," by Olaus Magnus, 16mo., Antwerp, 1560.]

After a great famine, Domitian ordered all the vines in Gaul to be uprooted so as to make room for corn. This rigorous measure must have caused beer to become even more general, and, although two centuries later Probus allowed vines to be replanted, the use of beverages made from grain became an established custom; but in time, whilst the people still only drank *cervoise*, those who were able to afford it bought wine and drank it alternately with beer.

However, as by degrees the vineyards increased in all places having a suitable soil and climate, the use of beer was almost entirely given up, so that in central Gaul wine became so common and cheap that all could drink it. In the northern provinces, where the vine would not grow, beer naturally continued to be the national beverage (Fig. 104).

In the time of Charlemagne, for instance, we find the Emperor wisely ordered that persons knowing how to brew should be attached to each of his farms. Everywhere the monastic houses possessed breweries; but as early as the reign of St. Louis there were only a very few breweries in Paris itself, and, in spite of all the privileges granted to their corporation, even these were soon obliged to leave the capital, where there ceased to be any demand for the produce of their industry. They reappeared in 1428, probably in consequence of the political and commercial relations which had become established between Paris and the rich towns of the Flemish bourgeoisie; and then, either on account of the dearness of wine, or the caprice of fashion, the consumption of beer again became so general in France that, according to the "Journal d'un Bourgeois de Paris," it produced to the revenue two–thirds more than wine. It must be understood, however, that in times of scarcity, as in the years 1415 and 1482, brewing was temporarily stopped, and even forbidden altogether, on account of the quantity of grain which was thereby withdrawn from the food supply of the people (Fig. 105).

[Illustration: Fig. 105.—The Brewer, designed and engraved, in the Sixteenth. Century, by J. Amman.]

Under the Romans, the real *cervoise*, or beer, was made with barley; but, at a later period, all sorts of grain was indiscriminately used; and it was only towards the end of the sixteenth century that adding the flower or seed of hops to the oats or barley, which formed the basis of this beverage, was thought of.

Estienne Boileau's "Book of Trades," edited in the thirteenth century, shows us that, besides the *cervoise*, another sort of beer was known, which was called *godale*. This name, we should imagine, was derived from the two German words *god ael*, which mean "good beer," and was of a stronger description than the ordinary *cervoise*; this idea is proved by the Picards and Flemish people calling it "double beer." In any case, it is from the word *godale* that the familiar expression of *godailler* (to tipple) is derived.

In fact, there is hardly any sort of mixture or ingredient which has not been used in the making of beer, according to the fashions of the different periods. When, on the return from the Crusades, the use of spice had become the fashion, beverages as well as the food were loaded with it. Allspice, juniper, resin, apples, bread–crumbs, sage, lavender, gentian, cinnamon, and laurel were each thrown into it. The English sugared it, and the Germans salted it, and at times they even went so far as to put darnel into it, at the risk of rendering the mixture poisonous.

The object of these various mixtures was naturally to obtain high–flavoured beers, which became so much in fashion, that to describe the want of merit of persons, or the lack of value in anything, no simile was more common than to compare them to "small beer." Nevertheless, more delicate and less blunted palates were to be found which could appreciate beer sweetened simply with honey, or scented with ambergris or raspberries. It is possible, however, that these compositions refer to mixtures in which beer, the produce of fermented grain, was confounded with hydromel, or fermented honey. Both these primitive drinks claim an origin equally remote, which is buried in the most distant periods of history, and they have been used in all parts of the world, being mentioned in the oldest historical records, in the Bible, the Edda, and in the sacred books of India. In the thirteenth century, hydromel, which then bore the name of *borgerafre, borgeraste*, or *bochet*, was composed of one part of honey to twelve parts of water, scented with herbs, and allowed to ferment for a month or six weeks. This beverage, which in the customs and statutes of the order of Cluny is termed *potus dulcissimus* (the sweetest beverage), and which must have been both agreeable in taste and smell, was specially appreciated by the monks, who feasted on it on the great anniversaries of the Church. Besides this, an inferior quality of *bochet* was made for the consumption of the lower orders and peasants, out of the honeycomb after the honey had been drained away, or with the scum which rose during the fermentation of the better qualities.

[Illustration: Fig. 106.—The Vintagers, after a Miniature of the "Dialogues de Saint Gregoire" (Thirteenth Century).—Manuscript of the Royal Library of Brussels.]

Cider (in Latin *sicera*) and perry can also both claim a very ancient origin, since they are mentioned by Pliny. It does not appear, however, that the Gauls were acquainted with them. The first historical mention of them is made with reference to a repast which Thierry II., King of Burgundy and Orleans (596–613), son of Childebert, and grandson of Queen Brunehaut, gave to St. Colomban, in which both cider and wine were used. In the thirteenth century, a Latin poet (Guillaume le Breton) says that the inhabitants of the Auge and of Normandy made cider their daily drink; but it is not likely that this beverage was sent away from the localities where it was made; for, besides the fact that the "Menagier" only very curtly mentions a drink made of apples, we know that in the fifteenth century the Parisians were satisfied with pouring water on apples, and steeping them, so as to extract a sort of half–sour, half–sweet drink called *depense*. Besides this, Paulmier de Grandmesnil, a Norman by birth, a famous doctor, and the author of a Latin treatise on wine and cider (1588), asserts that half a century before, cider was very scarce at Rouen, and that in all the districts of Caux the people only drank beer. Duperron adds that the Normans brought cider from Biscay, when their crops of apples failed.

By whom and at what period the vine was naturalised in Gaul has been a long–disputed question, which, in spite of the most careful research, remains unsolved. The most plausible opinion is that which attributes the honour of having imported the vine to the Phoenician colony who founded Marseilles.

Pliny makes mention of several wines of the Gauls as being highly esteemed. He nevertheless reproaches the vine–growers of Marseilles, Beziers, and Narbonne with doctoring their wines, and with infusing various drugs into them, which rendered them disagreeable and even unwholesome (Fig. 106). Dioscorides, however, approved of the custom in use among the Allobroges, of mixing resin with their wines to preserve them and prevent them from turning sour, as the temperature of their country was not warm enough thoroughly to ripen the grape.

Rooted up by order of Domitian in 92, as stated above, the vine only reappeared in Gaul under Protus, who revoked, in 282, the imperial edict of his predecessor; after which period the Gallic wines soon recovered their ancient celebrity. Under the dominion of the Franks, who held wine in great favour, vineyard property was one of those which the barbaric laws protected with the greatest care. We find in the code of the Salians and in that of the Visigoths very severe penalties for uprooting a vine or stealing a bunch of grapes. The cultivation of the vine became general, and kings themselves planted them, even in the gardens of their city palaces. In 1160, there was still in Paris, near the Louvre, a vineyard of such an extent, that Louis VII. could annually present six hogsheads of wine made from it to the rector of St. Nicholas. Philip Augustus possessed about twenty vineyards of excellent quality in various parts of his kingdom.

The culture of the vine having thus developed, the wine trade acquired an enormous importance in France. Gascony, Aunis, and Saintonge sent their wines to Flanders; Guyenne sent hers to England. Froissart writes that, in 1372, a merchant fleet of quite two hundred sail came from London to Bordeaux for wine. This flourishing trade received a severe blow in the sixteenth century; for an awful famine having invaded France in 1566, Charles IX. did not hesitate to repeat the acts of Domitian, and to order all the vines to be uprooted and their place to be sown with corn; fortunately Henry III. soon after modified this edict by simply recommending the governors of the provinces to see that "the ploughs were not being neglected in their districts on account of the excessive cultivation of the vine."

[Illustration: Fig. 107.—Interior of an Hostelry.—Fac–simile of a Woodcut in a folio edition of Virgil, published at Lyons in 1517.]

Although the trade of a wine–merchant is one of the oldest established in Paris, it does not follow that the retail sale of wine was exclusively carried on by special tradesmen. On the contrary, for a long time the owner of the vineyard retailed the wine which he had not been able to sell in the cask. A broom, a laurel–wreath, or some other sign of the sort hung over a door, denoted that any one passing could purchase or drink wine within. When the wine–growers did not have the quality and price of their wine announced in the village or town by the public crier, they placed a man before the door of their cellar, who enticed the public to enter and taste the new wines. Other proprietors, instead of selling for people to take away in their own vessels, established a tavern in some room of their house, where they retailed drink (Fig. 107). The monks, who made wine extensively, also opened these taverns in the monasteries, as they only consumed part of their wine themselves; and this system was universally adopted by wine–growers, and even by the king and the nobles. The latter, however, had this advantage, that, whilst they were retailing their wines, no one in the district was allowed to enter into competition with

101

them. This prescriptive right, which was called *droit de ban–vin*, was still in force in the seventeenth century.

Saint Louis granted special statutes to the wine–merchants in 1264; but it was only three centuries later that they formed a society, which was divided into four classes, namely, hotel–keepers, publichouse–keepers, tavern proprietors, and dealers in wine *a pot*, that is, sold to people to take away with them. Hotel–keepers, also called *aubergistes*, accommodated travellers, and also put up horses and carriages. The dealers *a pot* sold wine which could not be drunk on their premises. There was generally a sort of window in their door through which the empty pot was passed, to be returned filled: hence the expression, still in use in the eighteenth century, *vente a huis coupe* (sale through a cut door). Publichouse–keepers supplied drink as well as *nappe et assiette* (tablecloth and plate), which meant that refreshments were also served. And lastly, the *taverniers* sold wine to be drunk on the premises, but without the right of supplying bread or meat to their customers (Figs 108 and 109).

[Illustration: Fig. 108.—Banner of the Corporation of the Publichouse–keepers of Montmedy.]

[Illustration: Fig. 109.—Banner of the Corporation of the Publichouse–keepers of Tonnerre.]

The wines of France in most request from the ninth to the thirteenth centuries were those of Macon, Cahors, Rheims, Choisy, Montargis, Marne, Meulan, and Orleanais. Amongst the latter there was one which was much appreciated by Henry I., and of which he kept a store, to stimulate his courage when he joined his army. The little fable of the Battle of Wines, composed in the thirteenth century by Henri d'Andelys, mentions a number of wines which have to this day maintained their reputation: for instance, the Beaune, in Burgundy; the Saint–Emilion, in Gruyenne; the Chablis, Epernay, Sezanne, in Champagne, &c. But he places above all, with good reason, according to the taste of those days, the Saint–Pourcain of Auvergne, which was then most expensive and in great request. Another French poet, in describing the luxurious habits of a young man of fashion, says that he drank nothing but Saint–Pourcain; and in a poem composed by Jean Bruyant, secretary of the Chatelet of Paris, in 1332, we find

"Du saint–pourcain
Que l'on met en son sein pour sain."

("Saint–Pourcain wine, which you imbibe for the good of your health.")

[Illustration: Fig. 110.—Banner of the Coopers of Bayonne.]

[Illustration: Fig. 111.—Banner of the Coopers of La Rochelle.]

Towards 1400, the vineyards of Ai became celebrated for Champagne as those of Beaune were for Burgundy; and it is then that we find, according to the testimony of the learned Paulmier de Grandmesnil, kings and queens making champagne their favourite beverage. Tradition has it that Francis I., Charles Quint, Henry VIII., and Pope Leon X. all possessed vineyards in Champagne at the same time. Burgundy, that pure and pleasant wine, was not despised, and it was in its honour that Erasmus said, "Happy province! she may well call herself the mother of men, since she produces such milk." Nevertheless, the above–mentioned physician, Paulmier, preferred to burgundy, "if not perhaps for their flavour, yet for their wholesomeness, the vines of the *Ile de France* or *vins francais*, which agree, he says, with scholars, invalids, the bourgeois, and all other persons who do not devote themselves to manual labour; for they do not parch the blood, like the wines of Gascony, nor fly to the head like those of Orleans and Chateau–Thierry; nor do they cause obstructions like those of Bordeaux." This is also the opinion of Baccius, who in his Latin treatise on the natural history of wines (1596) asserts that the wines of Paris "are in no way inferior to those of any other district of the kingdom." These thin and sour wines, so much esteemed in the first periods of monarchy and so long abandoned, first lost favour in the reign of Francis I., who preferred the strong and stimulating productions of the South.

Notwithstanding the great number of excellent wines made in their own country, the French imported from other lands. In the thirteenth century, in the "Battle of Wines" we find those of Aquila, Spain, and, above all, those of Cyprus, spoken of in high terms. A century later, Eustace Deschamps praised the Rhine wines, and those of Greece, Malmsey, and Grenache. In an edict of Charles VI. mention is also made of the muscatel, rosette, and the wine of Lieppe. Generally, the Malmsey which was drunk in France was an artificial preparation, which had neither the colour nor taste of the Cyprian wine. Olivier de Serres tells us that in his time it was made with water, honey, clary juice, beer grounds, and brandy. At first the same name was used for the natural wine, mulled and spiced, which was produced in the island of Madeira from the grapes which the Portuguese brought there from Cyprus in 1420.

The reputation which this wine acquired in Europe induced Francis I. to import some vines from Greece, and he planted fifty acres with them near Fontainebleau. It was at first considered that this plant was succeeding so well, that "there were hopes," says Olivier de Serres, "that France would soon be able to furnish her own Malmsey and Greek wines, instead of having to import them from abroad." It is evident, however, that they soon gave up this delusion, and that for want of the genuine wine they returned to artificial beverages, such as *vin cuit*, or cooked wine, which had at all times been cleverly prepared by boiling down new wine and adding various aromatic herbs to it.

Many wines were made under the name of *herbes*, which were merely infusions of wormwood, myrtle, hyssop, rosemary, &c., mixed with sweetened wine and flavoured with honey. The most celebrated of these beverages bore the pretentious name of "nectar;" those composed of spices, Asiatic aromatics, and honey, were generally called "white wine," a name indiscriminately applied to liquors having for their bases some slightly coloured wine, as well as to the hypocras, which was often composed of a mixture of foreign liqueurs. This hypocras plays a prominent part in the romances of chivalry, and was considered a drink of honour, being always offered to kings, princes, and nobles on their solemn entry into a town.

[Illustration: Fig. 112.—Butler at his Duties.—Fac-simile from a Woodcut in the "Cosmographie Universelle," of Munster, folio, Basle, 1549.]

The name of wine was also given to drinks composed of the juices of certain fruits, and in which grapes were in no way used. These were the cherry, the currant, the raspberry, and the pomegranate wines; also the *more*, made with the mulberry, which was so extolled by the poets of the thirteenth century. We must also mention the sour wines, which were made by pouring water on the refuse grapes after the wine had been extracted; also the drinks made from filberts, milk of almonds, the syrups of apricots and strawberries, and cherry and raspberry waters, all of which were refreshing, and were principally used in summer; and, lastly, *tisane*, sold by the confectioners of Paris, and made hot or cold, with prepared barley, dried grapes, plums, dates, gum, or liquorice. This *tisane* may be considered as the origin of that drink which is now sold to the poor at a sous a glass, and which most assuredly has not much improved since olden times.

It was about the thirteenth century that brandy first became known in France; but it does not appear that it was recognised as a liqueur before the sixteenth. The celebrated physician Arnauld de Villeneuve, who wrote at the end of the thirteenth century, to whom credit has wrongly been given for inventing brandy, employed it as one of his remedies, and thus expresses himself about it: "Who would have believed that we could have derived from wine a liquor which neither resembles it in nature, colour, or effect?.... This *eau de vin* is called by some *eau de vie*, and justly so, since it prolongs life.... It prolongs health, dissipates superfluous matters, revives the spirits, and preserves youth. Alone, or added to some other proper remedy, it cures colic, dropsy, paralysis, ague, gravel, &c."

At a period when so many doctors, alchemists, and other learned men made it their principal occupation to try to discover that marvellous golden fluid which was to free the human race of all its original infirmities, the discovery of such an elixir could not fail to attract the attention of all such manufacturers of panaceas. It was, therefore, under the name of *eau d'or* (*aqua auri*) that brandy first became known to the world; a name improperly given to it, implying as it did that it was of mineral origin, whereas its beautiful golden colour was caused by the addition of spices. At a later period, when it lost its repute as a medicine, they actually sprinkled it with pure gold leaves, and at the same time that it ceased to be exclusively considered as a remedy, it became a favourite beverage. It was also employed in distilleries, especially as the basis of various strengthening and exciting liqueurs, most of which have descended to us, some coming from monasteries and others from chateaux, where they had been manufactured.

The Kitchen.

Soups, broths, and stews, &c.—The French word *potage* must originally have signified a soup composed of vegetables and herbs from the kitchen garden, but from the remotest times it was applied to soups in general.

As the Gauls, according to Athenaeus, generally ate their meat boiled, we must presume that they made soup with the water in which it was cooked. It is related that one day Gregory of Tours was sitting at the table of King Chilperic, when the latter offered him a soup specially made in his honour from chicken. The poems of the twelfth and thirteenth centuries mention soups made of peas, of bacon, of vegetables, and of groats. In the southern provinces there were soups made of almonds, and of olive oil. When Du Gueselin went out to fight the English knight William of Blancbourg in single combat, he first ate three sorts of soup made with wine, "in honour of the three persons in the Holy Trinity."

[Illustration: Fig. 113.—Interior of a Kitchen of the Sixteenth Century.—Fac−simile from a Woodcut in the "Calendarium Romanum" of Jean Staeffler, folio, Tubingen, 1518.]

We find in the "Menagier," amongst a long list of the common soups the receipts for which are given, soup made of "dried peas and the water in which bacon has been boiled," and, in Lent, "salted−whale water;" watercress soup, cabbage soup, cheese soup, and *gramose* soup, which was prepared by adding stewed meat to the water in which meat had already been boiled, and adding beaten eggs and verjuice; and, lastly, the *souppe despourvue*, which was rapidly made at the hotels, for unexpected travellers, and was a sort of soup made from the odds and ends of the larder. In those days there is no doubt but that hot soup formed an indispensable part of the daily meals, and that each person took it at least twice a day, according to the old proverb:—

"Soupe la soir, soupe le matin,
C'est l'ordinaire du bon chretien."

("Soup in the evening, and soup in the morning,
Is the everyday food of a good Christian.")

The cooking apparatus of that period consisted of a whole glittering array of cauldrons, saucepans, kettles, and vessels of red and yellow copper, which hardly sufficed for all the rich soups for which France was so famous. Thence the old proverb, "En France sont les grands soupiers."

But besides these soups, which were in fact looked upon as "common, and without spice," a number of dishes were served under the generic name of soup, which constituted the principal luxuries at the great tables in the fourteenth century, but which do not altogether bear out the names under which we find them. For instance, there was haricot mutton, a sort of stew; thin chicken broth; veal broth with herbs; soup made of veal, roe, stag, wild boar, pork, hare and rabbit soup flavoured with green peas, &c.

The greater number of these soups were very rich, very expensive, several being served at the same time; and in order to please the eye as well as the taste they were generally made of various colours, sweetened with sugar, and sprinkled with pomegranate seeds and aromatic herbs, such as marjoram, sage, thyme, sweet basil, savoury, &c.

[Illustration: Fig. 114.—Coppersmith, designed and engraved in the Sixteenth Century by J. Amman.]

These descriptions of soups were perfect luxuries, and were taken instead of sweets. As a proof of this we must refer to the famous *soupe doree*, the description of which is given by Taillevent, head cook of Charles VII., in the following words, "Toast slices of bread, throw them into a jelly made of sugar, white wine, yolk of egg, and rosewater; when they are well soaked fry them, then throw them again into the rosewater and sprinkle them with sugar and saffron."

[Illustration: Fig. 115.—Kitchen and Table Uensils:—

1, Carving–knife (Sixteenth Century);
2, Chalice or Cup, with Cover (Fourteenth Century);
3, Doubled–handled Pot, in Copper (Ninth Century);
4, Metal Boiler, or Tin Pot, taken from "L'Histoire de la Belle Helaine" (Fifteenth Century);
5, Knife (Sixteenth Century);
6, Pot, with Handles (Fourteenth Century);
7, Copper Boiler, taken from "L'Histoire de la Belle Helaine" (Fifteenth Century);
8, Ewer, with Handle, in Oriental Fashion (Ninth Century);
9, Pitcher, sculptured, from among the Decorations of the Church of St. Benedict, Paris (Fifteenth Century);
10, Two–branched Candlestick (Sixteenth Century);
11, Cauldron (Fifteenth Century).]

It is possible that even now this kind of soup might find some favour; but we cannot say the same for those made with mustard, hemp–seed, millet, verjuice, and a number of others much in repute at that period; for we see in Rabelais that the French were the greatest soup eaters in the world, and boasted to be the inventors of seventy sorts.

107

We have already remarked that broths were in use at the remotest periods, for, from the time that the practice of boiling various meats was first adopted, it must have been discovered that the water in which they were so boiled became savoury and nourishing. "In the time of the great King Francis I.," says Noel du Fail, in his "Contes d'Eutrapel," "in many places the saucepan was put on to the table, on which there was only one other large dish, of beef, mutton, veal, and bacon, garnished with a large bunch of cooked herbs, the whole of which mixture composed a porridge, and a real restorer and elixir of life. From this came the adage, 'The soup in the great pot and the dainties in the hotch−potch.'"

At one time they made what they imagined to be strengthening broths for invalids, though their virtue must have been somewhat delusive, for, after having boiled down various materials in a close kettle and at a slow fire, they then distilled from this, and the water thus obtained was administered as a sovereign remedy. The common sense of Bernard Palissy did not fail to make him see this absurdity, and to protest against this ridiculous custom: "Take a capon," he says, "a partridge, or anything else, cook it well, and then if you smell the broth you will find it very good, and if you taste it you will find it has plenty of flavour; so much so that you will feel that it contains something to invigorate you. Distil this, on the contrary, and take the water then collected and taste it, and you will find it insipid, and without smell except that of burning. This should convince you that your restorer does not give that nourishment to the weak body for which you recommend it as a means of making good blood, and restoring and strengthening the spirits."

The taste for broths made of flour was formerly almost universal in France and over the whole of Europe; it is spoken of repeatedly in the histories and annals of monasteries; and we know that the Normans, who made it their principal nutriment, were surnamed *bouilleux*. They were indeed almost like the Romans who in olden times, before their wars with eastern nations, gave up making bread, and ate their corn simply boiled in water.

In the fourteenth century the broths and soups were made with millet−flour and mixed wheats. The pure wheat flour was steeped in milk seasoned with sugar, saffron, honey, sweet wine or aromatic herbs, and sometimes butter, fat, and yolks of eggs were added. It was on account of this that the bread of the ancients so much resembled cakes, and it was also from this fact that the art of the pastrycook took its rise.

Wheat made into gruel for a long time was an important ingredient in cooking, being the basis of a famous preparation called *fromentee*, which was a *bouillie* of milk, made creamy by the addition of yolks of eggs, and which served as a liquor in which to roast meats and fish. There were, besides, several sorts of *fromentee*, all equally esteemed, and Taillevent recommended the following receipt, which differs from the one above given:—"First boil your wheat in water, then put into it the juice or gravy of fat meat, or, if you like it better, milk of almonds, and by this means you will make a soup fit for fasts, because it dissolves slowly, is of slow digestion and nourishes much. In this way, too, you can make *ordiat*, or barley soup, which is more generally approved than the said *fromentee*."

[Illustration: Fig. 116.—Interior of a Kitchen.—Fac-simile from a Woodcut in the "Calendarium Romanum" of J. Staeffler, folio, Tubingen, 1518.]

Semolina, vermicelli, macaroni, &c., which were called Italian because they originally came from that country, have been in use in France longer than is generally supposed. They were first introduced after the expedition of Charles VIII. into Italy, and the conquest of the kingdom of Naples; that is, in the reign of Louis XII., or the first years of the sixteenth century.

Pies, Stews, Roasts, Salads, &c.—Pastry made with fat, which might be supposed to have been the invention of modern kitchens, was in great repute amongst our ancestors. The manufacture of sweet and savoury pastry was intrusted to the care of the good *menagiers* of all ranks and conditions, and to the corporation of pastrycooks, who obtained their statutes only in the middle of the sixteenth century; the united skill of these, both in Paris and in the provinces, multiplied the different sorts of tarts and meat pies to a very great extent. So much was this the case that these ingenious productions became a special art, worthy of rivalling even cookery itself (Figs. 117, 118, and 130). One of the earliest known receipts for making pies is that of Gaces de la Bigne, first chaplain of Kings John, Charles V., and Charles VI. We find it in a sporting poem, and it deserves to be quoted verbatim as a record of the royal kitchen of the fourteenth century. It will be observed on perusing it that nothing was spared either in pastry or in cookery, and that expense was not considered when it was a question of satisfying the appetite.

"Trois perdriaulx gros et reffais
Au milieu du pate me mets;

Manners, Custom and Dress During the Middle

Mais gardes bien que tu ne failles
A moi prendre six grosses cailles,
De quoi tu les apuyeras.
Et puis apres tu me prendras
Une douzaine d'alouetes
Qu'environ les cailles me mettes,
Et puis pendras de ces maches
Et de ces petits oiseles:
Selon ce que tu en auras,
Le pate m'en billeteras.
Or te fault faire pourveance
D'un pen de lart, sans point de rance,
Que tu tailleras comme de:
S'en sera le paste pouldre.
S tu le veux de bonne guise,
Du vertjus la grappe y soit mise,
D'un bien peu de sel soit pouldre ...
... Fay mettre des oeufs en la paste,
Les croutes un peu rudement
Faictes de flour de pur froment ...
... N'y mets espices ni fromaige ...
Au four bien a point chaud le met,
Qui de cendre ait l'atre bien net;
E quand sera bien a point cuit,
I n'est si bon mangier, ce cuit."

("Put me in the middle of the pie three young partridges large and fat;
But take good care not to fail to take six fine quail to put by their
  side.
After that you must take a dozen skylarks, which round the quail you must
  place;
And then you must take some thrushes and such other little birds as you
  can get to garnish the pie.
Further, you must provide yourself with a little bacon, which must not be
  in the least rank (reasty), and you must cut it into pieces of the size
  of a die, and sprinkle them into the pie.

If you want it to be in quite good form, you must put some sour grapes in
  and a very little salt ...
... Have eggs put into the paste, and the crust made rather hard of the
  flour of pure wheat.
Put in neither spice nor cheese ...
Put it into the oven just at the proper heat,
The bottom of which must be quite free from ashes;
And when it is baked enough, isn't that a dish to feast on!")

From this period all treatises on cookery are full of the same kind of receipts for making "pies of young chickens, of fresh venison, of veal, of eels, of bream and salmon, of young rabbits, of pigeons, of small birds, of geese, and of *narrois*" (a mixture of cod's liver and hashed fish). We may mention also the small pies, which were made of minced beef and raisins, similar to our mince pies, and which were hawked in the streets of Paris, until their sale was forbidden, because the trade encouraged greediness on the one hand and laziness on the other.

Ancient pastries, owing to their shapes, received the name of *tourte* or *tarte*, from the Latin *torta*, a large hunch of bread. This name was afterwards exclusively used for hot pies, whether they contained vegetables, meat, or fish. But towards the end of the fourteenth century *tourte* and *tarte* was applied to pastry containing, herbs, fruits, or preserves, and *pate* to those containing any kind of meat, game, or fish.

[Illustration: Fig. 117.—Banner of the Corporation of Pastrycooks of Caen.]

[Illustration: Fig. 118.—Banner of the Corporation of Pastrycooks of Bordeaux.]

It was only in the course of the sixteenth century that the name of *potage* ceased to be applied to stews, whose number equalled their variety, for on a bill of fare of a banquet of that period we find more than fifty different sorts of *potages* mentioned. The greater number of these dishes have disappeared from our books on cookery, having gone out of fashion; but there are two stews which were popular during many centuries, and which have maintained their reputation, although they do not now exactly represent what they formerly did. The *pot-pourri*, which was composed of veal, beef, mutton, bacon, and vegetables, and the *galimafree*, a fricassee of poultry, sprinkled with verjuice, flavoured with spices, and surrounded by a sauce composed of vinegar, bread crumbs, cinnamon,

111

ginger, &c. (Fig. 119).

The highest aim of the cooks of the Taillevent school was to make dishes not only palatable, but also pleasing to the eye. These masters in the art of cooking might be said to be both sculptors and painters, so much did they decorate their works, their object being to surprise or amuse the guests by concealing the real nature of the disbes. Froissart, speaking of a repast given in his time, says that there were a number of "dishes so curious and disguised that it was impossible to guess what they were." For instance, the bill of fare above referred to mentions a lion and a sun made of white chicken, a pink jelly, with diamond–shaped points; and, as if the object of cookery was to disguise food and deceive epicures, Taillevent facetiously gives us a receipt for making fried or roast butter and for cooking eggs on the spit.

[Illustration: Fig. 119.—Interior of Italian Kitchen.—Fac–simile of a Woodcut in the Book on Cookery of Christoforo di Messisburgo, "Banchetti compositioni di Vivende," 4to., Ferrara, 1549.]

The roasts were as numerous as the stews. A treatise of the fourteenth century names about thirty, beginning with a sirloin of beef, which must have been one of the most common, and ending with a swan, which appeared on table in full plumage. This last was the triumph of cookery, inasmuch as it presented this magnificent bird to the eyes of the astonished guests just as if he were living and swimming. His beak was gilt, his body silvered, resting 'on a mass of brown pastry, painted green in order to represent a grass field. Eight banners of silk were placed round, and a cloth of the same material served as a carpet for the whole dish, which towered above the other appointments of the table.

[Illustration: Fig. 120.—Hunting–Meal.—Fac–simile of a Miniature in the Manuscript of the "Livre du Roy Modus" (National Library of Paris).]

The peacock, which was as much thought of then as it is little valued now, was similarly arrayed, and was brought to table amidst a flourish of trumpets and the applause of all present. The modes of preparing other roasts much resembled the present system in their simplicity, with this difference, that strong meats were first boiled to render them tender, and no roast was ever handed over to the skill of the carver without first being thoroughly basted with orange juice and rose water, and covered with sugar and powdered spices.

We must not forget to mention the broiled dishes, the invention of which is attributed to hunters, and which Rabelais continually refers to as acting as stimulants and irresistibly exciting the thirst for wine at the sumptuous feasts of those voracious heroes (Fig. 120).

The custom of introducing salads after roasts was already established in the fifteenth century. However, a salad, of whatever sort, was never brought to table in its natural state; for, besides the raw herbs, dressed in the same manner as in our days, it contained several mixtures, such as cooked vegetables, and the crests, livers, or brains of poultry. After the salads fish was served; sometimes fried, sometimes sliced with eggs or reduced to a sort of pulp, which was called *carpee* or *charpie*, and sometimes it was boiled in water or wine, with strong seasoning. Near the salads, in the course of the dinner, dishes of eggs prepared in various ways were generally served. Many of these are now in use, such as the poached egg, the hard–boiled egg, egg sauce, &c.

[Illustration: Fig. 121.—Shop of a Grocer and Druggist, from a Stamp of Vriese (Seventeenth Century).]

Seasonings.—We have already stated that the taste for spices much increased in Europe after the Crusades; and in this rapid historical sketch of the food of the French people in the Middle Ages it must have been observed to what an extent this taste had become developed in France (Fig. 121). This was the origin of sauces, all, or almost all, of which were highly spiced, and were generally used with boiled, roast, or grilled meats. A few of these sauces, such as the yellow, the green, and the *cameline*, became so necessary in cooking that numerous persons took to manufacturing them by wholesale, and they were hawked in the streets of Paris.

These sauce–criers were first called *saulciers*, then *vinaigriers–moustardiers*, and when Louis XII. united them in a body, as their business had considerably increased, they were termed *sauciers–moutardiers–vinaigriers*, distillers of brandy and spirits of wine, and *buffetiers* (from *buffet*, a sideboard).

[Illustration: Fig. 122.—The Cook, drawn and engraved, in the Sixteenth Century, by J. Amman.]

But very soon the corporation became divided, no doubt from the force of circumstances; and on one side we find the distillers, and on the other the master–cooks and cooks, or *porte–chapes*, as they were called, because, when they carried on their business of cooking, they covered their dishes with a *chape*, that is, a cope or tin cover (Fig. 122), so as to keep them warm.

The list of sauces of the fourteenth century, given by the "Menagier de Paris," is most complicated; but, on examining the receipts, it becomes clear that the variety of those preparations, intended to sharpen the appetite, resulted principally from the spicy ingredients with which they were flavoured; and it is here worthy of remark that pepper, in these days exclusively obtained from America, was known and generally used long before the time of Columbus. It is mentioned in a document, of the time of Clotaire III. (660); and it is clear, therefore, that before the discovery of the New World pepper and spices were imported into Europe from the East.

Mustard, which was an ingredient in so many dishes, was cultivated and manufactured in the thirteenth century in the neighbourhood of Dijon and Angers.

According to a popular adage, garlic was the medicine (*theriaque*) of peasants; town–people for a long time greatly appreciated *aillee*, which was a sauce made of garlic, and sold ready prepared in the streets of Paris.

The custom of using anchovies as a flavouring is also very ancient. This was also done with *botargue* and *cavial*, two sorts of side–dishes, which consisted of fishes' eggs, chiefly mullet and sturgeon, properly salted or dried, and mixed with fresh or pickled olives. The olives for the use of the lower orders were brought from Languedoc and Provence, whereas those for the rich were imported from Spain and some from Syria. It was also from the south of France that the rest of the kingdom was supplied with olive oil, for which, to this day, those provinces have preserved their renown; but as early as the twelfth and thirteenth centuries oil of walnuts was brought from the centre of France to Paris, and this, although cheaper, was superseded by oil extracted from the poppy.

Truffles, though known and esteemed by the ancients, disappeared from the gastronomie collection of our forefathers. It was only in the fourteenth century that they were again introduced, but evidently without a knowledge of their culinary qualities, since, after being preserved in vinegar, they were soaked in hot water, and afterwards served up in butter. We may also here mention sorrel and the common mushroom, which were used in cooking during the Middle Ages.

On the strength of the old proverb, "Sugar has never spoiled sauce," sugar was put into all sauces which were not *piquantes*, and generally some perfumed water was added to them, such as rose–water. This was made in great quantities by exposing to the sun a basin full of water, covered over by another basin of glass, under which was a little vase containing rose–leaves. This rose–water was added to all stews, pastries, and beverages. It is very doubtful as to the period at which white lump sugar became known in the West. However, in an account of the house of the Dauphin Viennois (1333) mention is made of "white sugar;" and the author of the "Menagier de Paris" frequently speaks of this white sugar, which, before the discovery, or rather colonisation, of America, was brought, ready refined, from the Grecian islands, and especially from Candia.

[Illustration: Fig. 123.—The *Issue de Table*.—Fac–simile of a Woodcut in the Treatise of Christoforo di Messisburgo, "Banchetti compositioni di Vivende," 4to., Ferrara, 1549.]

Verjuice, or green juice, which, with vinegar, formed the essential basis of sauces, and is now extracted from a species of green grape, which never ripens, was originally the juice of sorrel; another sort was extracted by pounding the green blades of wheat. Vinegar was originally merely soured wine, as the word *vin–aigre* denotes. The mode of manufacturing it by artificial means, in order to render the taste more pungent and the quality better, is very ancient. It is needless to state that it was scented by the infusion of herbs or flowers—roses, elder, cloves, &c.; but it was not much before the sixteenth century that it was used for pickling herbs or fruits and vegetables, such as gherkins, onions, cucumber, purslain, &c.

Salt, which from the remotest periods was the condiment *par excellence*, and the trade in which had been free up to the fourteenth century, became, from that period, the subject of repeated taxation. The levying of these taxes was a frequent cause of tumult amongst the people, who saw with marked displeasure the exigencies of the excise gradually raising the price of an article of primary necessity. We have already mentioned times during which the price of salt was so exorbitant that the rich alone could put it in their bread. Thus, in the reign of Francis I., it was almost as dear as Indian spices.

Sweet Dishes, Desserts, &c.—In the fourteenth century, the first courses of a repast were called *mets* or *assiettes*; the last, "*entremets, dorures, issue de table, desserte,* and *boule–hors.*"

The dessert consisted generally of baked pears, medlars, pealed walnuts, figs, dates, peaches, grapes, filberts, spices, and white or red sugar–plums.

At the *issue de table* wafers or some other light pastry were introduced, which were eaten with the hypocras wine. The *boute–hors,* which was served when the guests, after having washed their hands and said grace, had passed into the drawing–room, consisted of spices, different from those which had appeared at dessert, and intended specially to assist the digestion; and for this object they must have been much needed, considering that a repast lasted several hours. Whilst eating these spices they drank Grenache, Malmsey, or aromatic wines (Fig. 123).

It was only at the banquets and great repeats that sweet dishes and *dorures* appeared, and they seem to have been introduced for the purpose of exhibiting the power of the imagination and the talent in execution of the master–cook.

The *dorures* consisted of jellies of all sorts and colours; swans, peacocks, bitterns, and herons, on gala feasts, were served in full feather on a raised platform in the middle of the table, and hence the name of "raised dishes." As for the side–dishes, properly so called, the long list collected in the "Menagier" shows us that they were served at table indiscriminately, for stuffed chickens at times followed hashed porpoise in sauce, lark pies succeeded lamb sausages, and pike's–eggs fritters appeared after orange preserve.

At a later period the luxury of side–dishes consisted in the quantity and in the variety of the pastry; Rabelais names sixteen different sorts at one repast; Taillevent mentions pastry called *covered pastry, Bourbonnaise pastry, double–faced pastry, pear pastry*, and *apple pastry*; Platina speaks of the *white pastry* with quince, elder flowers, rice, roses, chestnuts, &c. The fashion of having pastry is, however, of very ancient date, for in the book of the "Proverbs" of the thirteenth century, we find that the pies of Dourlens and the pastry of Chartres were then in great celebrity.

[Illustration: Fig. 124.—The Table of a Baron, as laid out in the Thirteenth Century.—Miniature from the "Histoire de St. Graal" (Manuscript from the Imperial Library, Paris).]

In a charter of Robert le Bouillon, Bishop of Amiens, in 1311, mention is made of a cake composed of puff flaky paste; these cakes, however, are less ancient than the firm pastry called bean cake, or king's cake, which, from the earliest days of monarchy, appeared on all the tables, not only at the feast of the Epiphany, but also on every festive occasion.

Amongst the dry and sweet pastries from the small oven which appeared at the *issue de table*, the first to be noticed were those made of almonds, nuts, &c., and such choice morsels, which were very expensive; then came the cream or cheesecakes, the *petits choux*, made of butter and eggs; the *echaudes*, of which the people were very fond, and St. Louis even allowed the bakers to cook them on Sundays and feast days for the poor; wafers, which are older than the thirteenth century; and lastly the *oublies*, which, under the names of *nieules, esterets*, and *supplications*, gave rise to such an extensive trade that a corporation was established in Paris, called the *oublayeurs, oublayers,* or *oublieux,* whose statutes directed that none should be admitted to exercise the trade unless he was able to make in one day 500 large *oublies*, 300 *supplications*, and 200 *esterets*.

Repasts and Feasts.

We have had to treat elsewhere of the rules and regulations of the repasts under the Merovingian and Carlovingian kings. We have also spoken of the table service of the thirteenth century (see chapter on "Private Life"). The earliest author who has left us any documents on this curious subject is that excellent bourgeois to whom we owe the "Menagier de Paris." He describes, for instance, in its fullest details, a repast which was given in the fourteenth century by the Abbe de Lagny, to the Bishop of Paris, the President of the Parliament, the King's attorney and advocate, and other members of his council, in all sixteen guests. We find from this account that "my lord of Paris, occupying the place of honour, was, in consequence of his rank, served on covered dishes by three of his squires, as was the custom for the King, the royal princes, the dukes, and peers; that Master President, who was seated by the side of the bishop, was also served by one of his own servants, but on uncovered dishes, and the other guests were seated at table according to the order indicated by their titles or charges."

The bill of fare of this feast, which was given on a fast–day, is the more worthy of attention, in that it proves to us what numerous resources cookery already possessed. This was especially the case as regards fish, notwithstanding that the transport of fresh sea–fish was so difficult, owing to the bad state of the roads.

First, a quarter of a pint of Grenache was given to each guest on sitting down, then "hot *eschaudes*, roast apples with white sugar–plums upon them, roasted figs, sorrel and watercress, and rosemary."

"Soups.—A rich soup, composed of six trout, six tenches, white herring, freshwater eels, salted twenty–four hours, and three whiting, soaked twelve hours; almonds, ginger, saffron, cinnamon powder and sweetmeats.

"Salt–Water Fish.—Soles, gurnets, congers, turbots, and salmon.

"Fresh–Water Fish.—*Lux faudis* (pike with roe), carps from the Marne, breams.

"Side–Dishes.—Lampreys *a la boee*, orange–apples (one for each guest), porpoise with sauce, mackerel, soles, bream, and shad *a la cameline*, with verjuice, rice and fried almonds upon them; sugar and apples.

[Illustration: Fig. 125.—Officers of the Table and of the Chamber of the Imperial Court: Cup–bearer, Cook, Barber, and Tailor, from a Picture in the "Triomphe de Maximilien T.," engraved by J. Resch, Burgmayer, and others (1512), from Drawings by Albert Durer.]

"Dessert.—Stewed fruit with white and vermilion sugar–plums; figs, dates, grapes, and filberts.

"Hypocras for *issue de table*, with *oublies* and *supplications*.

"Wines and spices compose the *baute–hors*."

To this fasting repast we give by way of contrast the bill of fare at the nuptial feast of Master Helye, "to which forty guests were bidden on a Tuesday in May, a 'day of flesh.'"

"Soups.—Capons with white sauce, ornamented with pomegranate and crimson sweetmeats.

"Roasts.—Quarter of roe–deer, goslings, young chickens, and sauces of orange, cameline, and verjuice.

"Side–Dishes.—Jellies of crayfish and loach; young rabbits and pork.

"Dessert.—*Froumentee* and venison.

"Issue.—Hypocras.

"Boute–Hors.—Wine and spices."

The clever editor of the "Menagier de Paris," M. le Baron Jerome Pichon, after giving us this curious account of the mode of living of the citizens of that day, thus sums up the whole arrangements for the table in the fourteenth century: "The different provisions necessary for food are usually entrusted to the squires of the kitchen, and were chosen, purchased, and paid for by one or more of these officials, assisted by the cooks. The dishes prepared by the cooks were placed, by the help of the esquires, on dressers in the kitchen until the moment of serving. Thence they were carried to the tables. Let us imagine a vast hall hung with tapestries and other brilliant stuffs. The tables are covered with fringed table–cloths, and strewn with odoriferous herbs; one of them, called the Great Table, is reserved for the persons of distinction. The guests are taken to their seats by two butlers, who bring them water to wash. The Great Table is laid out by a butler, with silver salt–cellars (Figs. 126 and 127), golden goblets with lids for the high personages, spoons and silver drinking cups. The guests eat at least certain dishes on *tranchoirs*, or large slices of thick bread, afterwards thrown into vases called *couloueres* (drainers). For the other tables the salt is placed on pieces of bread, scooped out for that purpose by the intendants, who are called *porte–chappes*. In the hall is a dresser covered with plate and various kinds of wine. Two squires standing near this dresser give the guests clean spoons, pour out what wine they ask for, and remove the silver when used; two other squires superintend the conveyance of wine to the dresser; a varlet placed under their orders is occupied with nothing but drawing wine from the casks." At that time wine was not bottled, and they drew directly from the cask the amount necessary for the day's consumption. "The dishes, consisting of three, four, five, and even six courses, called *mets* or *assiettes*, are brought in by varlets and two of the principal squires, and in certain wedding–feasts the bridegroom walked in front of them. The dishes are placed on the table by an *asseeur* (placer), assisted by two servants. The latter take away the remains at the conclusion of the course, and hand them over to the squires of the kitchen who have charge of them. After the *mets* or *assiettes* the table–cloths are changed, and the *entremets* are then brought in. This course is the most brilliant of the repast, and at some of the princely banquets the dishes are made to imitate a sort of theatrical representation. It is composed of sweet dishes, of coloured jellies of swans, of peacocks, or of pheasants adorned with their feathers, having the beak and feet gilt, and placed on the middle of the table on a sort of pedestal. To the *entremets*, a course which does not appear on all bills of fare, succeeds the dessert. The *issue*, or exit from table, is mostly composed of hypocras and a sort of *oublie* called *mestier*; or, in summer, when hypocras is out of season on account of its strength, of apples, cheeses, and sometimes of pastries and sweetmeats. The *boute–hors* (wines and spices) end the repast. The guests then wash their hands, say grace, and pass into the *chambre de parement* or drawing–room. The servants then sit down and dine after their masters. They subsequently bring the guests wine and *epices de chambre*, after which each retires home."

[Illustration: Figs. 126 and 127.—Sides of an Enamelled Salt–cellar, with six facings representing the Labours of Hercules, made at Limoges, by Pierre Raymond, for Francis I.]

But all the pomp and magnificence of the feasts of this period would have appeared paltry a century later, when royal banquets were managed by Taillevent, head cook to Charles VII. The historian of French cookery, Legrand d'Aussy, thus desoribes a great feast given in 1455 by the Count of Anjou, third son of Louis II., King of Sicily:—

"On the table was placed a centre–piece, which represented a green lawn, surrounded with large peacocks' feathers and green branches, to which were tied violets and other sweet–smelling flowers. In the middle of this lawn a fortress was placed, covered with silver. This was hollow, and formed a sort of cage, in which several live birds were shut up, their tufts and feet being gilt. On its tower, which was gilt, three banners were placed, one bearing the arms of the count, the two others those of Mesdemoiselles de Chateaubrun and de Villequier, in whose honour the feast was given.

"The first course consisted of a civet of hare, a quarter of stag which had been a night in salt, a stuffed chicken, and a loin of veal. The two last dishes were covered with a German sauce, with gilt sugar–plums, and pomegranate seeds.... At each end, outside the green lawn, was an enormous pie, surmounted with smaller pies, which formed a crown. The crust of the large ones was silvered all round and gilt at the top; each contained a whole roe–deer, a gosling, three capons, six chickens, ten pigeons, one young rabbit, and, no doubt to serve as seasoning or stuffing, a minced loin of veal, two pounds of fat, and twenty-six hard-boiled eggs, covered with saffron and flavoured with cloves. For the three following courses, there was a roe-deer, a pig, a sturgeon cooked in parsley and vinegar, and covered with powdered ginger; a kid, two goslings, twelve chickens, as many pigeons, six young rabbits, two herons, a leveret, a fat capon stuffed, four chickens covered with yolks of eggs and sprinkled with powder *de Duc* (spice), a wild boar, some wafers (*darioles*), and stars; a jelly, part white and part red, representing the crests of the three above-mentioned persons; cream with *Duc* powder, covered with fennel seeds preserved in sugar; a white cream, cheese in slices, and strawberries; and, lastly, plums stewed in rose-water. Besides these four courses, there was a fifth, entirely composed of the prepared wines then in vogue, and of preserves. These consisted of fruits and various sweet pastries. The pastries represented stags and swans, to the necks of which were suspended the arms of the Count of Anjou and those of the two young ladies."

In great houses, dinner was announced by the sound of the hunting-horn; this is what Froissard calls *corner l'assiette,* but which was at an earlier period called *corner l'eau,* because it was the custom to wash the hands before sitting down to table as well as on leaving the dining-room.

[Illustration: Fig. 128.—Knife-handles in Sculptured Ivory, Sixteenth Century (Collection of M. Becker, of Frankfort).]

[Illustration: Fig. 129.—Nut-crackers, in Boxwood, Sixteenth Century (Collection of M. Achille Jubinal).]

For these ablutions scented water, and especially rose-water, was used, brought in ewers of precious and delicately wrought metals, by pages or squires, who handed them to the ladies in silver basins. It was at about this period, that is, in the times of chivalry, that the custom of placing the guests by couples was introduced, generally a gentleman and lady, each couple having but one cup and one plate; hence the expression, to eat from the same plate.

Historians relate that in the thirteenth and fourteenth centuries, at certain gala feasts, the dishes were brought in by servants in full armour, mounted on caparisoned horses; but this is a custom exclusively attached to chivalry. As early as those days, powerful and ingenious machines were in use, which lowered from the story above, or raised from that below, ready-served tables, which were made to disappear after use as if by enchantment.

At that period the table service of the wealthy required a considerable staff of retainers and varlets; and, at a later period, this number was much increased. Thus, for instance, when Louis of Orleans went on a diplomatic mission to Germany from his brother Charles VI., this prince, in order that France might be worthily represented abroad, raised the number of his household to more than two hundred and fifty persons, of whom about one hundred were retainers and table attendants. Olivier de la Marche, who, in his "Memoires," gives the most minute details of the ceremonial of the court of Charles the Bold, Duke of Burgundy, tells us that the table service was as extensive as in the other great princely houses.

This extravagant and ruinous pomp fell into disuse during the reigns of Louis XI., Charles VIII., and Louis XII., but reappeared in that of Francis I. This prince, after his first wars in Italy, imported the cookery and the gastronomic luxury of that country, where the art of good living, especially in Venice, Florence, and Rome, had reached the highest degree of refinement and magnificence. Henry II. and Francis II. maintained the magnificence of their royal tables; but after them, notwithstanding the soft effeminacy of the manners at court, the continued wars which Henry III. and Charles IX. had to sustain in their own states against the Protestants and the League necessitated a considerable economy in the households and tables of those kings.

"It was only by fits and starts," says Brantome, "that one was well fed during this reign, for very often circumstances prevented the proper preparation of the repasts; a thing much disliked by the courtiers, who prefer open table to be kept at both court and with the army, because it then costs them nothing." Henry IV. was neither fastidious nor greedy; we must therefore come down to the reign of Louis XIII. to find a vestige of the splendour of the banquets of Francis I.

[Illustration: Fig. 130.—Grand Ceremonial Banquet at the Court of France in the Fourteenth Century, archaeological Restoration from Miniatures and Narratives of the Period.

From the "Dictionnaire du Mobilier Francais" of M. Viollet–Leduc.]

From the establishment of the Franks in Gaul down to the fifteenth century inclusive, there were but two meals a day; people dined at ten o'clock in the morning, and supped at four in the afternoon. In the sixteenth century they put back dinner one hour and supper three hours, to which many people objected. Hence the old proverb:—

"Lever a six, diner a dix,
Souper a six, coucher a dix,
Fait vivre l'homme dix fois dix."

("To rise at six, dine at ten,
Sup at six, to bed at ten,
Makes man live ten times ten.")

[Illustration: Fig. 131.—Banner of the Corporation of Pastrycooks of Tonnerre.]

Hunting.

Venery and Hawking.—Origin of Aix–la–Chapelle.—Gaston Phoebus and his Book.—The Presiding Deities of Sportsmen.—Sporting Societies and Brotherhoods.—Sporting Kings: Charlemagne, Louis IX., Louis XI., Charles VIII., Louis XII., Francis I., &c.—Treatise on Venery.—Sporting Popes.—Origin of Hawking.—Training Birds.—Hawking Retinues.—Book of King Modus.—Technical Terms used in Hawking.—Persons who have excelled in this kind of Sport.—Fowling.

By the general term hunting is included the three distinct branches of an art, or it may be called a science, which dates its origin from the earliest times, but which was particularly esteemed in the Middle Ages, and was especially cultivated in the glorious days of chivalry.

Venery, which is the earliest, is defined by M. Elzear Blaze as "the science of snaring, taking, or killing one particular animal from amongst a herd." *Hawking* came next. This was not only the art of hunting with the falcon, but that of training birds of prey to hunt feathered game. Lastly, *l'oisellerie* (fowling), which, according to the author of several well–known works on the subject we are discussing, had originally no other object than

123

that of protecting the crops and fruits from birds and other animals whose nature it was to feed on them.

Venery will be first considered. Sportsmen always pride themselves in placing Xenophon, the general, philosopher, and historian, at the head of sporting writers, although his treatise on the chase (translated from the Greek into Latin under the title of "De Venatione"), which gives excellent advice respecting the training of dogs, only speaks of traps and nets for capturing wild animals. Amongst the Greeks Arrian and Oppian, and amongst the Romans, Gratius Faliscus and Nemesianus, wrote on the same subject. Their works, however, except in a few isolated or scattered passages, do not contain anything about venery properly so called, and the first historical information on the subject is to be found in the records of the seventh century.

Long after that period, however, they still hunted, as it were, at random, attacking the first animal they met. The sports of Charlemagne, for instance, were almost always of this description. On some occasions they killed animals of all sorts by thousands, after having tracked and driven them into an enclosure composed of cloths or nets.

This illustrious Emperor, although usually at war in all parts of Europe, never missed an opportunity of hunting: so much so that it might be said that he rested himself by galloping through the forests. He was on these occasions not only followed by a large number of huntsmen and attendants of his household, but he was accompanied by his wife and daughters, mounted on magnificent coursers, and surrounded by a numerous and elegant court, who vied with each other in displaying their skill and courage in attacking the fiercest animals.

It is even stated that Aix–la–Chapelle owes its origin to a hunting adventure of Charlemagne. The Emperor one day while chasing a stag required to cross a brook which came in his path, but immediately his horse had set his foot in the water he pulled it out again and began to limp as if it were hurt. His noble rider dismounted, and on feeling the foot found it was quite hot. This induced him to put his hand into the water, which he found to be almost boiling. On that very spot therefore he caused a chapel to be erected, in the shape of a horse's hoof. The town was afterwards built, and to this day the spring of hot mineral water is enclosed under a rotunda, the shape of which reminds one of the old legend of Charlemagne and his horse.

The sons of Charlemagne also held hunting in much esteem, and by degrees the art of venery was introduced and carried to great perfection. It was not, however, until the end of the thirteenth century that an anonymous author conceived the idea of writing its principal precepts in an instructive poem, called "Le Dict de la Chace du Cerf." In 1328 another anonymous writer composed the "Livre du Roy Modus," which contains the rules for hunting all furred animals, from the stag to the hare. Then followed other poets and writers of French prose, such as Gace de la Vigne (1359), Gaston Phoebus (1387), and Hardouin, lord of Fontaine–Guerin (1394). None of these, however, wrote exclusively on venery, but described the different sports known in their day. Towards 1340, Alphonse XI., king of Castile, caused a book on hunting to be compiled for his use; but it was not so popular as the instruction of Gaston Phoebus (Fig. 132). If hunting with hounds is known everywhere by the French name of the chase, it is because the honour of having organized it into a system, if not of having originated it, is due to the early French sporting authors, who were able to form a code of rules for it. This also accounts for so many of the technical terms now in use in venery being of French origin, as they are no others than those adopted by these ancient authors, whose works, so to speak, have perpetuated them.

[Illustration: Fig. 132.—Gaston Phoebus teaching the Art of Venery.—Fac–simile of a Miniature of "Phoebus and his Staff for Hunting Wild Animals and Birds of Prey" (Manuscript, Fifteenth Century, National Library of Paris)]

[Illustration: Fig. 133.—"How to carry a Cloth to approach Beasts."—Fac–simile of a Miniature in the Manuscript of Phoebus (Fifteenth Century).]

The curious miniatures which accompany the text in the original manuscript of Gaston Phoebus, and which have been reproduced in nearly all the ancient copies of this celebrated manuscript, give most distinct and graphic ideas of the various modes of hunting. We find, for instance, that the use of an artificial cow for approaching wild–fowl was understood at that time, the only difference being that a model was used more like a horse than a cow (Fig. 133); we also see sportsmen shooting at bears, wild boars, stags, and such live animals with arrows having sharp iron points, intended to enter deep into the flesh, notwithstanding the thickness of the fur and the creature's hard skin. In the case of the hare, however, the missile had a heavy, massive end, probably made of lead, which stunned him without piercing his body (Fig. 134). In other cases the sportsman is represented with a crossbow seated in a cart, all covered up with boughs, by which plan he was supposed to approach the prey without alarming it any more than a swinging branch would do (Fig. 135).

Gaston Phoebus is known to have been one of the bravest knights of his time; and, after fighting, he considered hunting as his greatest delight. Somewhat ingenuously he writes of himself as a hunter, "that he doubts having any superior." Like all his contemporaries, he is eloquent as to the moral effect of his favourite pastime. "By hunting," he says, "one avoids the sin of indolence; and, according to our faith, he who avoids the seven mortal sins will be saved; therefore the good sportsman will be saved."

[Illustration: Fig. 134.—"How to allure the Hare."—Fac-simile of a Miniature in the Manuscript of Phoebus (Fifteenth Century).]

From the earliest ages sportsmen placed themselves under the protection of some special deity. Among the Greeks and Romans it was Diana and Phoebe. The Gauls, who had adopted the greater number of the gods and goddesses of Rome, invoked the moon when they sallied forth to war or to the chase; but, as soon as they penetrated the sacred obscurity of the forests, they appealed more particularly to the goddess *Ardhuina*, whose name, of unknown origin, has probably since been applied to the immense well-stocked forests of Ardenne or Ardennes. They erected in the depths of the woods monstrous stone figures in honour of this goddess, such as the heads of stags on the bodies of men or women; and, to propitiate her during the chase, they hung round these idols the feet, the skins, and the horns of the beasts they killed. Cernunnos, who was always represented with a human head surmounted by stags' horns, had an altar even in Lutetia, which was, no doubt, in consequence of the great woods which skirted the banks of the Seine.

[Illustration: Fig. 135.—"How to take a Cart to allure Beasts."—Fac-simile of a Miniature in the Manuscript of Phoebus (Fifteenth Century).]

The Gallic Cernunnos, which we also find among the Romans, since Ovid mentions the votary stags' horns, continued to be worshipped to a certain extent after the establishment of the Christian religion. In the fifth century, Germain, an intrepid hunter, who afterwards became Bishop of Auxerre, possessed not far from his residence an oak of enormous diameter, a thorough Cernunnos, which he hung with the skins and other portions of animals he had killed in the chase. In some countries, where the Cernunnos remained an object of veneration, everybody bedecked it in the same way. The largest oak to be found

126

in the district was chosen on which to suspend the trophies both of warriors and of hunters; and, at a more recent period, sportsmen used to hang outside their doors stags' heads, boars' feet, birds of prey, and other trophies, a custom which evidently was a relic of the one referred to.

On pagan idolatry being abandoned, hunters used to have a presiding genius or protector, whom they selected from amongst the saints most in renown. Some chose St. Germain d'Auxerre, who had himself been a sportsman; others St. Martin, who had been a soldier before he became Bishop of Tours. Eventually they all agreed to place themselves under the patronage of St. Hubert, Bishop of Liege, a renowned hunter of the eighth century. This saint devoted himself to a religious life, after one day haying encountered a miraculous stag whilst hunting in the woods, which appeared to him as bearing between his horns a luminous image of our Saviour. At first the feast of St. Hubert was celebrated four times a year, namely, at the anniversaries of his conversion and death, and on the two occasions on which his relics were exhibited. At the celebration of each of these feasts a large number of sportsmen in "fine apparel" came from great distances with their horses and dogs. There was, in fact, no magnificence or pomp deemed too imposing to be displayed, both by the kings and nobles, in honour of the patron–saint of hunting (Fig. 136).

[Illustration: Fig. 136.—"How to shout and blow Horns."—Fac–simile of a Miniature in the Manuscript of Phoebus (Fifteenth Century).]

[Illustration: Ladies Hunting

Costumes of the fifteenth century. From a miniature in a ms. copy of *Ovid's Epistles* No 7234 *bis*. Bibl. nat'le de Paris.]

[Illustration: Fig. 137.—German Sportsman, drawn and engraved by J. Amman in the Sixteenth Century.]

Hunters and sportsmen in those days formed brotherhoods, which had their rank defined at public ceremonials, and especially in processions. In 1455, Gerard, Duke of Cleves and Burgrave of Ravensberg, created the order of the Knights of St. Hubert, into which those of noble blood only were admitted. The insignia consisted of a gold or silver chain formed of hunting horns, to which was hung a small likeness of the patron–saint in the act of doing homage to our Saviour's image as it shone on the head of a stag. It was popularly believed that the Knights of St. Hubert had the power of curing madness, which, for some unknown reason, never showed itself in a pack of hounds. This, however, was not the only superstitious belief attached to the noble and adventurous occupations of the followers of St. Hubert. Amongst a number of old legends, which mostly belong to Germany (Fig. 137), mention is made of hunters who sold their souls to the devil in exchange for some enchanted arrow which never missed its aim, and which reached game at extraordinary distances. Mention is also made in these legends of various animals which, on being pursued by the hunters, were miraculously saved by throwing themselves into the arms of some saint, or by running into some holy sanctuary. There were besides knights who, having hunted all their lives, believed that they were to continue the same occupation in another world. An account is given in history of the apparition of a fiery phantom to Charles IX. in the forest of Lyons, and also the ominous meeting of Henry IV. with the terrible *grand–veneur* in the forest of Fontainebleau. We may account for these strange tales from the fact that hunting formerly constituted a sort of freemasonry, with its mysterious rites and its secret language. The initiated used particular signs of recognition amongst themselves, and they also had lucky and unlucky numbers, emblematical colours, &c.

The more dangerous the sport the more it was indulged in by military men. The Chronicles of the Monk of Saint–Gall describe an adventure which befell Charlemagne on the occasion of his setting out with his huntsmen and hounds in order to chase an enormous bear which was the terror of the Vosges. The bear, after having disabled numerous dogs and hunters, found himself face to face with the Emperor, who alone dared to stand up before him. A fierce combat ensued on the summit of a rock, in which both were locked together in a fatal embrace. The contest ended by the death of the bear, Charles striking him with his dagger and hurling him down the precipice. On this the hills resounded with the cry of "Vive Charles le Grand!" from the numerous huntsmen and others who had assembled; and it is said that this was the first occasion on which the companions of the intrepid monarch gave him the title of *Grand* (Magnus), so from that time King Charles became King *Charlemagne.*

This prince was most jealous of his rights of hunting, which he would waive to no one. For a long time he refused permission to the monks of the Abbey of St. Denis, whom he nevertheless held in great esteem, to have some stags killed which were destroying their forests. It was only on condition that the flesh of these animals would serve as food to the monks of inferior order, and that their hides should be used for binding the missals, that he eventually granted them permission to kill the offending animals (Fig. 138).

If we pass from the ninth to the thirteenth century, we find that Louis IX., king of France, was as keen a sportsman and as brave a warrior as any of his ancestors. He was, indeed, as fond of hunting as of war, and during his first crusade an opportunity occurred to him of hunting the lion. "As soon as he began to know the country of Cesarea," says Joinville, "the King set to work with his people to hunt lions, so that they captured many; but in doing so they incurred great bodily danger. The mode of taking them was this: They pursued them on the swiftest horses. When they came near one they shot a bolt or arrow at him, and the animal, feeling himself wounded, ran at the first person he could see, who immediately turned his horse's head and fled as fast as he could. During his flight he dropped a portion of his clothing, which the lion caught up and tore, thinking it was the person who had injured him; and whilst the lion was thus engaged the hunters again approached the infuriated animal and shot more bolts and arrows at him. Soon the lion left the cloth and madly rushed at some other hunter, who adopted the same strategy as before. This was repeated until the animal succumbed, becoming exhausted by the wounds he had received."

[Illustration: Fig. 138.—"Nature and Appearance of Deer, and how they can be hunted with Dogs."—Fac–simile of a Miniature in the "Livre du Roy Modus"—Manuscript of the Fourteenth Century (National Library of Paris)]

Notwithstanding the passion which this king had for hunting, he was the first to grant leave to the bourgeoisie to enjoy the sport. The condition he made with them was that they should always give a haunch of any animal killed to the lord of the soil. It is to this that we must trace the origin of giving the animal's foot to the huntsman or to the person who has the lead of the hunting party.

Louis XI., however, did not at all act in this liberal manner, and although it might have been supposed that the incessant wars and political intrigues in which he was constantly engaged would have given him no time for amusements of this kind, yet he was, nevertheless, the keenest sportsman of his day. This tyrant of the Castle of Plessis–les–Tours, who was always miserly, except in matters of hunting, in which he was most lavish, forbade even the higher classes to hunt under penalty of hanging. To ensure the execution of his severe orders, he had all the castles as well as the cottages searched, and any net, engine, or sporting arm found was immediately destroyed. His only son, the heir to the throne, was not exempted from these laws. Shut up in the Castle of Amboise, he had no permission to leave it, for it was the will of the King that the young prince should remain ignorant of the noble exercises of chivalry. One day the Dauphin prayed his governor, M. du Bouchage, with so much earnestness to give him an idea of hunting, that this noble consented to make an excursion into the neighbouring wood with him. The King, however, managed to find it out, and Du Bouchage had great difficulty in keeping his head on his shoulders.

One of the best ways of pleasing Louis XI. was to offer him some present relating to his favourite pastime, either pointers, hounds, falcons, or varlets who were adepts in the art of venery or hawking (Figs. 139 and 140). When the cunning monarch became old and infirm, in order to make his enemies believe that he was still young and vigorous, he sent messengers everywhere, even to the most remote countries, to purchase horses, dogs, and falcons, for which, according to Comines, he paid large sums (Fig. 141).

On his death, the young prince, Charles VIII., succeeded him, and he seems to have had an innate taste for hunting, and soon made up for lost time and the privation to which his father had subjected him. He hunted daily, and generously allowed the nobles to do the same. It is scarcely necessary to say that these were not slow in indulging in the privilege thus restored to them, and which was one of their most ancient pastimes and occupations; for it must be remembered that, in those days of small intellectual culture, hunting must have been a great, if not at times the only, resource against idleness and the monotony of country life.

Everything which related to sport again became the fashion amongst the youth of the nobility, and their chief occupation when not engaged in war. They continued as formerly to invent every sort of sporting device. For example, they obtained from other countries traps, engines, and hunting–weapons; they introduced into France at great expense foreign animals, which they took great pains in naturalising as game or in training as auxiliaries in hunting. After having imported the reindeer from Lapland, which did not succeed in their temperate climate, and the pheasant from Tartary, with which they stocked the woods, they imported with greater success the panther and the leopard from Africa, which were used for furred game as the hawk was for feathered game. The mode of hunting with these animals was as follows: The sportsmen, preceded by their dogs, rode across country, each with a leopard sitting behind him on his saddle. When the dogs had started the game the leopard jumped off the saddle and sprang after it, and as soon as it was caught the hunters threw the leopard a piece of raw flesh, for which he gave up the prey and remounted behind his master (Fig. 142)

Louis XI., Charles VIII., and Louis XII. often hunted thus. The leopards, which formed a part of the royal venery, were kept in an enclosure of the Castle of Amboise, which still exists near the gate *des Lions*, so called, no doubt, on account of these sporting and carnivorous animals being mistaken for lions by the common people. There, were, however, always lions in the menageries of the kings of France.

[Illustration: Fig. 139.—"The Way to catch Squirrels on the Ground in the Woods"—Fac-simile of a Miniature in the Manuscript of the "Livre du Roy Modus" (Fourteenth Century)]

Francis I. was quite as fond of hunting as any of his predecessors. His innate taste for sport was increased during his travels in Italy, where he lived with princes who displayed great splendour in their hunting equipages. He even acquired the name of the *Father of Sportsmen*. His *netting* establishment alone, consisted of one captain, one lieutenant, twelve mounted huntsmen, six varlets to attend the bloodhounds; six whips, who had under their charge sixty hounds; and one hundred bowmen on foot, carrying large stakes for fixing the nets and tents, which were carried by fifty six-horsed chariots. He was much pleased when ladies followed the chase; and amongst those who were most inclined to share its pleasures, its toils, and even its perils, was Catherine de Medicis, then Dauphine, who was distinguished for her agility and her graceful appearance on horseback, and who became a thorough sportswoman.

[Illustration: Fig. 140.-"The Way of catching Partridges with an Osier Net-Work Apparatus"—Fac-simile of a Miniature in "Livre du Roy Modus."]

The taste for hunting having become very general, and the art being considered as the most noble occupation to which persons could devote themselves, it is not surprising to find sporting works composed by writers of the greatest renown and of the highest rank. The learned William Bude, whom Erasmus called the *wonder of France*, dedicated to the children of Francis I. the second book of his "Philologie," which contains a treatise on stag-hunting. This treatise, originally written in Latin, was afterwards translated into French by order of Charles IX., who was acknowledged to be one of the boldest and most

131

scientific hunters of his time. An extraordinary feat, which has never been imitated by any one, is recorded of him, and that was, that alone, on horseback and without dogs, he hunted down a stag. The "Chasse Royale," the authorship of which is attributed to him, is replete with scientific information. "Wolf–hunting," a work by the celebrated Clamorgan, and "Yenery," by Du Fouilloux, were dedicated to Charles IX., and a great number of special treatises on such subjects appeared in his reign.

[Illustration: Fig. 141.—"Kennel in which Dogs should live, and how they should be kept."—Fac–simile of a Miniature in Manuscript of Phoebus (Fifteenth Century).]

His brother, the effeminate Henry III., disliked hunting, as he considered it too fatiguing and too dangerous.

On the other hand, according to Sully, Henry IV., *le Bearnais*, who learned hunting in early youth in the Pyrenees, "loved all kinds of sport, and, above all, the most fatiguing and adventurous pursuits, such as those after wolves, bears, and boars." He never missed a chance of hunting, "even when in face of an enemy. If he knew a stag to be near, he found time to hunt it," and we find in the "Memoirs of Sully " that the King hunted the day after the famous battle of Ivry.

One day, when he was only King of Navarre, he invited the ladies of Pau to come and see a bear–hunt. Happily they refused, for on that occasion their nerves would have been put to a serious test. Two bears killed two of the horses, and several bowmen were hugged to death by the ferocious animals. Another bear, although pierced in several places, and having six or seven pike–heads in his body, charged eight men who were stationed on the top of a rock, and the whole of them with the bear were all dashed to pieces down the precipice. The only point in which Louis XIII. resembled his father was his love of the chase, for during his reign hunting continued in France, as well as in other countries, to be a favourite royal pastime.

We have remarked that St. Germain d'Auxerre, who at a certain period was the patron of sportsmen, made hunting his habitual relaxation. He devoted himself to it with great keenness in his youth, before he became bishop, that is, when he was Duke of Auxerre and general of the troops of the provinces. Subsequently, when against his will he was raised to the episcopal dignity, not only did he give up all pleasures, but he devoted himself to the strictest religious life. Unfortunately, in those days, all church–men did not understand, as he did, that the duties of their holy vocation were not consistent with these pastimes, for, in the year 507, we find that councils and synods forbade priests to hunt. In spite of this, however, the ancient historians relate that several noble prelates, yielding to the customs of the times, indulged in hunting the stag and flying the falcon.

[Illustration: Fig. 142.—Hunting with the Leopard, from a Stamp of Jean Stradan (Sixteenth Century).]

It is related in history that some of the most illustrious popes were also great lovers of the chase, namely, Julius II, Leo X., and, previously to them, Pius II, who, before becoming Pope, amongst other literary and scientific works, wrote a Latin treatise on venery under his Christian names, AEneas Silvius. It is easy to understand how it happened that sports formerly possessed such attractions for ecclesiastical dignitaries. In early life they acquired the tastes and habits of people of their rank, and they were accordingly extremely jealous of the rights of chase in their domains. Although Pope Clement V., in his celebrated "Institutions," called "Clementines," had formally forbidden the monks to hunt, there were few who did not evade the canonical prohibition by pursuing furred game, and that without considering that they were violating the laws of the Church. The papal edict permitted the monks and priests to hunt under certain circumstances, and especially where rabbits or beasts of prey increased so much as to damage the crops. It can easily be imagined that such would always be the case at a period when the people were so strictly forbidden to destroy game; and therefore hunting was practised at all seasons in the woods and fields in the vicinity of each abbey. The jealous peasants, not themselves having the right of hunting, and who continually saw *Master Abbot* passing on his hunting excursions, said, with malice, that "the monks never forgot to pray for the success of the litters and nests (*pro pullis et nidis*), in order that game might always be abundant."

[Illustration: Fig. 143.—"How Wolves may be caught with a Snare."—Fac-simile of a Miniature in the Manuscript of Phoebus (Fifteenth Century).]

If venery, as a regular science, dates from a comparatively recent period, it is not so with falconry, the first traces of which are lost in obscure antiquity. This kind of sport, which had become a most learned and complicated art, was the delight of the nobles of the Middle Ages and during the Renaissance period. It was in such esteem that a nobleman or his lady never appeared in public without a hawk on the wrist as a mark of dignity (Fig.

147). Even bishops and abbots entered the churches with their hunting birds, which they placed on the steps of the altar itself during the service.

[Illustration: Fig. 144.—"How Bears and other Beasts may be caught with a Dart."—Fac-simile of a Miniature in the Manuscript of Phoebus (Fifteenth Century).]

The bird, like the sword, was a distinctive mark which was inseparable from the person of gentle birth, who frequently even went to war with the falcon on his wrist. During the battle he would make his squire hold the bird, which he replaced on his gauntlet when the fight was over. In fact, it was forbidden by the laws of chivalry for persons to give up their birds, even as a ransom, should they be made prisoners; in which case they had to let the noble birds fly, in order that they might not share their captivity.

The falcon to a certain degree partook of his owner's nobility; he was, moreover, considered a noble bird by the laws of falconry, as were all birds of prey which could be trained for purposes of sport. All other birds, without distinction, were declared *ignoble*, and no exception was made to this rule by the naturalists of the Middle Ages, even in favour of the strongest and most magnificent, such as the eagle and vulture. According to this capricious classification, they considered the sparrow-hawk, which was the smallest of the hunting-birds, to rank higher than the eagle. The nickname of this diminutive sporting bird was often applied to a country-gentleman, who, not being able to afford to keep falcons, used the sparrow-hawk to capture partridges and quail.

[Illustration: Fig. 145.—Olifant, or Hunting-horn, in Ivory (Fourteenth Century).—From an Original existing in England.]

It was customary for gentlemen of all classes, whether sportsmen or not, to possess birds of some kind, "to keep up their rank," as the saying then was. Only the richest nobles, however, were expected to keep a regular falconry, that is, a collection of birds suited for taking all kinds of game, such as the hare, the kite, the heron, &c., as each sport not only required special birds, but a particular and distinctive retinue and establishment.

[Illustration: Fig. 146.—Details Hunting-horn of the Fourteenth Century.—From the Original in an English Collection.]

Besides the cost of falcons, which was often very great (for they were brought from the most distant countries, such as Sweden, Iceland, Turkey, and Morocco), their rearing and training involved considerable outlay, as may be more readily understood from the illustrations (Figs. 148 to 155), showing some of the principal details of the long and difficult education which had to be given them.

To succeed in making the falcon obey the whistle, the voice, and the signs of the falconer was the highest aim of the art, and it was only by the exercise of much patience that the desired resuit was obtained. All birds of prey, when used for sport, received the generic name of *falcon*; and amongst them were to be found the gerfalcon, the saker–hawk, the lanner, the merlin, and the sparrow–hawk. The male birds were smaller than the females, and were called *tiercelet* —this name, however, more particularly applied to the gosshawk or the largest kind of male hawk, whereas the males of the above mentioned were called *laneret, sacret, emouchet.* Generally the male birds were used for partridges and quail, and the female birds for the hare, the heron, and crane. *Oiseaux de poing,* or *hand–birds,* was the name given to the gosshawk, common hawk, the gerfalcon, and the merlin, because they returned to the hand of their master after having pursued game. The lanner, sparrow–hawk, and saker–hawk were called *oiseaux de leure*, from the fact that it was always necessary to entice them back again.

[Illustration: Fig. 147.—A Noble of Provence (Fifteenth Century).—Bonnart's "Costumes from the Tenth to the Sixteenth Century."]

The lure was an imitation of a bird, made of red cloth, that it might be more easily seen from a distance. It was stuffed so that the falcon could settle easily on it, and furnished with the wings of a partridge, duck, or heron, according to circumstances. The falconer swung his mock bird like a sling, and whistled as he did so, and the falcon, accustomed to find a piece of flesh attached to the lure, flew down in order to obtain it, and was thus secured.

[Illustration: Fig. 148.—King Modus teaching the Art of Falconry.—Fac–simile of a Miniature in the Manuscript of "Livre du Roy Modus" (Fourteenth Century).]

The trainers of birds divided them into two kinds, namely, the *niais* or simple bird, which had been taken from the nest, and the wild bird (*hagard*) captured when full–grown. The education of the former was naturally very much the easier, but they succeeded in taming

135

both classes, and even the most rebellious were at last subdued by depriving them of sleep, by keeping away the light from them, by coaxing them with the voice, by patting them, by giving them choice food, &c.

Regardless of his original habits, the bird was first accustomed to have no fear of men, horses, and dogs. He was afterwards fastened to a string by one leg, and, being allowed to fly a short distance, was recalled to the lure, where he always found a dainty bit of food. After he had been thus exercised for several months, a wounded partridge was let loose that he might catch it near the falconer, who immediately took it from him before he could tear it to pieces. When he appeared sufficiently tame, a quail or partridge, previously stripped of a few feathers so as to prevent it flying properly, was put in his way as before. If he was wanted for hunting hares, a stuffed hare was dragged before him, inside of which was a live chicken, whose head and liver was his reward if he did his work well. Then they tried him with a hare whose fore–leg was broken in order to ensure his being quickly caught. For the kite, they placed two hawks together on the same perch, so as to accustom them peaceably to live and hunt together, for if they fought with one another, as strange birds were apt to do, instead of attacking the kite, the sport would of course have failed. At first a hen of the colour of a kite was given them to fight with. When they had mastered this, a real kite was used, which was tied to a string and his claws and beak were filed so as to prevent him from wounding the young untrained falcons. The moment they had secured their prey, they were called off it and given chickens' flesh to eat on the lure. The same System was adopted for hunting the heron or crane (Fig. 159).

[Illustration: Fig. 149.—Falconers dressing their Birds.—Fac–simile of a Miniature in the Manuscript of "Livre du Roy Modus" (Fourteenth Century).]

It will be seen that, in order to train birds, it was necessary for a large number of the various kinds of game to be kept on the premises, and for each branch of sport a regular establishment was required. In falconry, as in venery, great care was taken to secure that a bird should continue at one object of prey until he had secured it, that is to say, it was most essential to teach it not to leave the game he was after in order to pursue another which might come in his way.

To establish a falconry, therefore, not only was a very large poultry–yard required, but also a considerable staff of huntsmen, falconers, and whips, besides a number of horses and dogs of all sorts, which were either used for starting the game for the hawks, or for running it down when it was forced to ground by the birds.

[Illustration: Fig. 150.—Varlets of Falconry.—Fac–simile of a Miniature in the Manuscript of "Livre du Roy Modus" (Fourteenth Century).]

A well–trained falcon was a bird of great value, and was the finest present that could be made to a lady, to a nobleman, or to the King himself, by any one who had received a favour. For instance, the King of France received six birds from the Abbot of St. Hubert as a token of gratitude for the protection granted by him to the abbey. The King of Denmark sent him several as a gracious offering in the month of April; the Grand Master of Malta in the month of May. At court, in those days, the reception of falcons either in public or in private was a great business, and the first trial of any new birds formed a topic of conversation among the courtiers for some time after.

The arrival at court of a hawk–dealer from some distant country was also a great event. It is said that Louis XI. gave orders that watch should be kept night and day to seize any falcons consigned to the Duke of Brittany from Turkey. The plan succeeded, and the birds thus stolen were brought to the King, who exclaimed, "By our holy Lady of Clery! what will the Duke Francis and his Bretons do? They will be very angry at the good trick I have played them."

European princes vied with each other in extravagance as regards falconry; but this was nothing in comparison to the magnificence displayed in oriental establishments. The Count de Nevers, son of Philip the Bold, Duke of Burgundy, having been made prisoner at the battle of Nicopolis, was presented to the Sultan Bajazet, who showed him his hunting establishment consisting of seven thousand falconers and as many huntsmen. The Duke of Burgundy, on hearing this, sent twelve white hawks, which were very scarce birds, as a present to Bajazet. The Sultan was so pleased with them that he sent him back his son in exchange.

[Illustration: Fig. 151.—"How to train a New Falcon."—Fac–simile of a Miniature in the Manuscript of "Livre du Roy Modus" (Fourteenth Century).]

The "Livre du Roy Modus" gives the most minute and curious details on the noble science of hawking. For instance, it tells us that the *nobility* of the falcon was held in such respect that their utensils, trappings, or feeding–dishes were never used for other birds. The glove on which they were accustomed to alight was frequently elaborately embroidered in gold, and was never used except for birds of their own species. In the private establishments the leather hoods, which were put on their heads to prevent them seeing, were embroidered with gold and pearls and surmounted with the feathers of birds of paradise. Each bird wore on his legs two little bells with his owner's crest upon them; the noise made by these was very distinct, and could be heard even when the bird was too high in the air to be seen, for they were not made to sound in unison; they generally came from Italy, Milan especially being celebrated for their manufacture. Straps were also fastened to the falcon's legs, by means of which he was attached to the perch; at the end of this strap was a brass or gold ring with the owner's name engraved upon it. In the royal establishments each ring bore on one side, "I belong to the king," and on the other the name of the Grand Falconer. This was a necessary precaution, for the birds frequently strayed, and, if captured, they could thus be recognised and returned. The ownership of a falcon was considered sacred, and, by an ancient barbaric law, the stealer of a falcon was condemned to a very curious punishment. The unfortunate thief was obliged to allow the falcon to eat six ounces of the flesh of his breast, unless he could pay a heavy fine to the owner and another to the king.

[Illustration: Fig. 152.—Falconers.—Fac–simile from a Miniature in Manuscript of the Thirteenth Century, which treats of the "Cour de Jaime, Roi de Maiorque."]

A man thoroughly acquainted with the mode of training hawks was in high esteem everywhere. If he was a freeman, the nobles outbid each other as to who should secure his services; if he was a serf, his master kept him as a rare treasure, only parted with him as a most magnificent present, or sold him for a considerable sum. Like the clever huntsman, a good falconer (Fig. 156) was bound to be a man of varied information on natural history, the veterinary art, and the chase; but the profession generally ran in families, and the son added his own experience to the lessons of his father. There were also special schools of venery and falconry, the most renowned being of course in the royal household.

The office of Grand Falconer of France, the origin of which dates from 1250, was one of the highest in the kingdom. The Marechal de Fleuranges says, in his curious "Memoirs"—"The Grand Falconer, whose salary is four thousand florins" (the golden florin was worth then twelve or fifteen francs, and this amount must represent upwards of eighty thousand francs of present currency), "has fifty gentlemen under him, the salary of each being from five to six thousand livres. He has also fifty assistant falconers at two hundred livres each, all chosen by himself. His establishment consists of three hundred birds; he has the right to hunt wherever he pleases in the kingdom; he levies a tax on all bird–dealers, who are forbidden, under penalty of the confiscation of their stock, from selling a single bird in any town or at court without his sanction." The Grand Falconer was chief at all the hunts or hawking meetings; in public ceremonies he always appeared with the bird on his wrist, as an emblem of his rank; and the King, whilst hawking, could not let loose his bird until after the Grand Falconer had slipped his.

[Illustration: Fig. 153.—"How to bathe a New Falcon."—Fac–simile of a Miniature in the Manuscript of "Livre du Roy Modus" (Fourteenth Century).]

Falconry, like venery, had a distinctive and professional vocabulary, which it was necessary for every one who joined in hawking to understand, unless he wished to be looked upon as an ignorant yeoman. "Flying the hawk is a royal pastime," says the Jesuit Claude Binet, "and it is to talk royally to talk of the flight of birds. Every one speaks of it, but few speak well. Many speak so ignorantly as to excite pity among their hearers. Sometimes one says the *hand* of the bird instead of saying the *talon*, sometimes the *talon* instead of the *claw*, sometimes the *claw* instead of the *nail*" &c.

The fourteenth century was the great epoch of falconry. There were then so many nobles who hawked, that in the rooms of inns there were perches made under the large mantel–pieces on which to place the birds while the sportsmen were at dinner. Histories of the period are full of characteristic anecdotes, which prove the enthusiasm which was created by hawking in those who devoted themselves to it.

[Illustration: Fig. 154.—"How to make Young Hawks fly."—Fac–simile of a Miniature in the Manuscript of "Livre du Roy Modus" (Fourteenth Century).]

Emperors and kings were as keen as others for this kind of sport. As early as the tenth century the Emperor Henry I. had acquired the soubriquet of "the Bird–catcher," from the fact of his giving much more attention to his birds than to his subjects. His example was followed by one of his successors, the Emperor Henry VI., who was reckoned the first falconer of his time. When his father, the Emperor Frederick Barbarossa (Red–beard), died in the Holy Land, in 1189, the Archdukes, Electors of the Empire, went out to meet the prince so as to proclaim him Emperor of Germany. They found him, surrounded by dogs, horses, and birds, ready to go hunting. "The day is fine," he said; "allow us to put off serious affairs until to−morrow."

Two centuries later we find at the court of France the same ardour for hawking and the same admiration for the performances of falcons. The Constable Bertrand du Guesclin gave two hawks to King Charles VI.; and the Count de Tancarville, whilst witnessing a combat between these noble birds and a crane which had been powerful enough to keep two greyhounds at bay, exclaimed, "I would not give up the pleasure which I feel for a thousand florins!"

The court−poet, William Cretin, although he was Canon of the holy chapel of Vincennes, was as passionately fond of hawking as his good master Louis XII. He thus describes the pleasure he felt in seeing a heron succumb to the vigorous attack of the falcons:—

"Qui auroit la mort aux dents,
Il revivroit d'avour un tel passe−temps!"

("He who is about to die
Would live again with such amusement.")

[Illustration: Fig. 155.—Lady setting out Hawking.—Fac−simile of a Miniature in the Manuscript of "Livre du Roy Modus" (Fourteenth. Century).]

At a hunting party given by Louis XII. to the Archduke Maximilian, Mary of Burgundy, the Archduke's wife, was killed by a fall from her horse. The King presented his best falcons to the Archduke with a view to divert his mind and to turn his attention from the sad event, and one of the historians tells us that the bereaved husband was soon consoled: "The partridges, herons, wild ducks, and quails which he was enabled to take on his journey home by means of the King's present, materially lessening his sorrow."

Falconry, after having been in much esteem for centuries, at last became amenable to the same law which affects all great institutions, and, having reached the height of its glory, it was destined to decay. Although the art disappeared completely under Louis the Great, who only liked stag−kunting, and who, by drawing all the nobility to court, disorganized country life, no greater adept had ever been known than King Louis XIII. His first favourite and Grand Falconer was Albert de Luynes, whom he made prime minister and constable. Even in the Tuileries gardens, on his way to mass at the convent of the Feuillants, this prince amused himself by catching linnets and wrens with noisy magpies trained to pursue small birds.

It was during this reign that some ingenious person discovered that the words LOUIS TREIZIEME, ROY DE FRANCE ET DE NAVARRE, exactly gave this anagram, ROY TRES−RARE, ESTIME DIEU DE LA FAUCONNERIE. It was also at this time that Charles d'Arcussia, the last author who wrote a technical work on falconry, after praising his majesty for devoting himself so thoroughly to the divine sport, compared the King's birds to domestic angels, and the carnivorous birds which they destroyed he likened to the devil. From this he argued that the sport was like the angel Gabriel destroying the demon Asmodeus. He also added, in his dedication to the King, "As the nature of angels is above that of men, so is that of these birds above all other animals."

[Illustration: Fig. 156.—Dress of the Falconer (Thirteenth Century).—Sculpture of the Cathedral of Rouen.]

At that time certain religious or rather superstitious ceremonies were in use for blessing the water with which the falcons were sprinkled before hunting, and supplications were addressed to the eagles that they might not molest them. The following words were used: "I adjure you, O eagles! by the true God, by the holy God, by the most blessed Virgin Mary, by the nine orders of angels, by the holy prophets, by the twelve apostles, &c.... to leave the field clear to our birds, and not to molest them: in the name of the Father, and of the Son, and of the Holy Ghost." It was at this time that, in order to recover a lost bird, the Sire de la Brizardiere, a professional necromancer, proposed beating the owner of the bird with birch−rods until he bled, and of making a charm with the blood, which was reckoned infallible.

[Illustration: Fig. 157.—Diseases of Dogs and their Cure.—Fac−simile of a Miniature in the Manuscript of Phoebus (Fourteenth Century).]

Elzear Blaze expressed his astonishment that the ladies should not have used their influence to prevent falconry from falling into disuse. The chase, he considered, gave them an active part in an interesting and animated scene, which only required easy and graceful movements on their part, and to which no danger was attached. "The ladies knowing," he says, "how to fly a bird, how to call him back, and how to encourage him with their voice, being familiar with him from having continually carried him on their wrist, and often even from having broken him in themselves, the honour of hunting belongs to them by right. Besides, it brings out to advantage their grace and dexterity as they gallop amongst the sportsmen, followed by their pages and varlets and a whole herd of horses and dogs."

The question of precedence and of superiority had, at every period, been pretty evenly balanced between venery and falconry, each having its own staunch supporters. Thus, in the "Livre du Roy Modus," two ladies contend in verse (for the subject was considered too exalted to be treated of in simple prose), the one for the superiority of the birds, the other for the superiority of dogs. Their controversy is at length terminated by a celebrated huntsman and falconer, who decides in favour of venery, for the somewhat remarkable reason that those who pursue it enjoy oral and ocular pleasure at the same time. In an ancient Treatise by Gace de la Vigne, in which the same question occupies no fewer than ten thousand verses, the King (unnamed) ends the dispute by ordering that in future they shall be termed pleasures of dogs and pleasures of birds, so that there may be no superiority on one side or the other (Fig. 160). The court–poet, William Cretin, who was in great renown during the reigns of Louis XII. and Francis I., having asked two ladies to discuss the same subject in verse, does not hesitate, on the contrary, to place falconry above venery.

[Illustration: Fig. 158.—German Falconer, designed and engraved, in the Sixteenth Century, by J. Amman.]

It may fairly be asserted that venery and falconry have taken a position of some importance in history; and in support of this theory it will suffice to mention a few facts borrowed from the annals of the chase.

The King of Navarre, Charles the Bad, had sworn to be faithful to the alliance made between himself and King Edward III. of England; but the English troops having been beaten by Du Guesclin, Charles saw that it was to his advantage to turn to the side of the King of France. In order not to appear to break his oath, he managed to be taken prisoner by the French whilst out hunting, and thus he sacrificed his honour to his personal interests. It was also due to a hunting party that Henry III., another King of Navarre, who was afterwards Henry IV., escaped from Paris, on the 3rd February, 1576, and fled to

Senlis, where his friends of the Reformed religion came to join him.

[Illustration: Fig. 159.—Heron—hawking.—Fac—simile of a Miniature in the Manuscript of the "Livre du Roy Modus" (Fourteenth Century).]

Hunting formed a principal entertainment when public festivals were celebrated, and it was frequently accompanied with great magnificence. At the entry of Isabel of Bavaria into Paris, a sort of stag hunt was performed, when "the streets," according to a popular story of the time, "were full to profusion of hares, rabbits, and goslings." Again, at the solemn entry of Louis XI. into Paris, a representation of a doe hunt took place near the fountain St. Innocent; "after which the queen received a present of a magnificent stag, made of confectionery, and having the royal arms hung round its neck." At the memorable festival given at Lille, in 1453, by the Duke of Burgundy, a very curious performance took place. "At one end of the table," says the historian Mathieu de Coucy, "a heron was started, which was hunted as if by falconers and sportsmen; and presently from the other end of the table a falcon was slipped, which hovered over the heron. In a few minutes another falcon was started from the other side of the table, which attacked the heron so fiercely that he brought him down in the middle of the hall. After the performance was over and the heron was killed, it was served up at the dinner—table."

[Illustration: Fig. 160.—Sport with Dogs.—"How the Wild Boar is hunted by means of Dogs."—Fac—simile of a Miniature in the Manuscript of the "Livre du Roy Modus" (Fourteenth Century).]

We shall conclude this chapter with a few words on bird—fowling, a kind of sport which was almost disdained in the Middle Ages. The anonymous author of the "Livre du Roy Modus" called it, in the fourteenth century, the pastime of the poor, "because the poor, who can neither keep hounds nor falcons to hunt or to fly, take much pleasure in it, particularly as it serves at the same time as a means of subsistence to many of them."

In this book, which was for a long time the authority in matters of sport generally, we find that nearly all the methods and contrivances now employed for bird—fowling were known and in use in the Middle Ages, in addition to some which have since fallen into disuse. We accordingly read in the "Roy Modus" a description of the drag—net, the mirror, the screech—owl, the bird—pipe (Fig. 161), the traps, the springs, &c., the use of all of which is now well understood. At that time, when falcons were so much required, it was necessary that people should be employed to catch them when young; and the author of this book speaks of nets of various sorts, and the pronged piece of wood in the middle of which a screech-owl or some other bird was placed in order to attract the falcons (Fig. 162).

[Illustration: Fig. 161.—Bird-piping.—"The Manner of Catching Birds by piping."—Fac-simile of Miniature in the Manuscript of the "Livre du Roy Modus" (Fourteenth Century).]

Two methods were in use in those days for catching the woodcook and pheasant, which deserve to be mentioned. "The pheasants," says "King Modus," "are of such a nature that the male bird cannot bear the company of another." Taking advantage of this weakness, the plan of placing a mirror, which balanced a sort of wicker cage or coop, was adopted. The pheasant, thinking he saw his fellow, attacked him, struck against the glass and brought down the coop, in which he had leisure to reflect on his jealousy (Fig. 163).

Woodcocks, which are, says the author, "the most silly birds," were caught in this way. The bird-fowler was covered from head to foot with clothes of the colour of dead leaves, only having two little holes for his eyes. When he saw one he knelt down noiselessly, and supported his arms on two sticks, so as to keep perfectly still. When the bird was not looking towards him he cautiously approached it on his knees, holding in his hands two little dry sticks covered with red cloth, which he gently waved so as to divert the bird's attention from himself. In this way he gradually got near enough to pass a noose, which he kept ready at the end of a stick, round the bird's neck (Fig. 164).

However ingenious these tricks may appear, they are eclipsed by one we find recorded in the "Ixeuticon," a very elegant Latin poem, by Angelis de Barga, written two centuries later. In order to catch a large number of starlings, this author assures us, it is only necessary to have two or three in a cage, and, when a flight of these birds is seen passing, to liberate them with a very long twine attached to their claws. The twine must be covered with bird-lime, and, as the released birds instantly join their friends, all those they come near get glued to the twine and fall together to the ground.

[Illustration: Fig. 162.—Bird-catching with a Machine like a Long Arm.—Fac-simile of Miniature in the Manuscript of the "Livre du Roy Modus" (Fourteenth Century).]

As at the present time, the object of bird–fowling was twofold, namely, to procure game for food and to capture birds to be kept either for their voice or for fancy as pets. The trade in the latter was so important, at least in Paris, that the bird–catchers formed a numerous corporation having its statutes and privileges.

The Pont au Change (then covered on each side with houses and shops occupied by goldsmiths and money–changers) was the place where these people carried on their trade; and they had the privilege of hanging their cages against the houses, even without the sanction of the proprietors. This curious right was granted to them by Charles VI. in 1402, in return for which they were bound to "provide four hundred birds" whenever a king was crowned, "and an equal number when the queen made her first entry into her good town of Paris." The goldsmiths and money–changers, however, finding that this became a nuisance, and that it injured their trade, tried to get it abolished. They applied to the authorities to protect their rights, urging that the approaches to their shops, the rents of which they paid regularly, were continually obstructed by a crowd of purchasers and dealers in birds. The case was brought several times before parliament, which only confirmed the orders of the kings of France and the ancient privileges of the bird–catchers. At the end of the sixteenth century the quarrel became so bitter that the goldsmiths and changers took to "throwing down the cages and birds and trampling them under foot," and even assaulted and openly ill–treated the poor bird–dealers. But a degree of parliament again justified the sale of birds on the Pont an Change, by condemning the ring–leader,

[Illustration: Fig. 163.—Pheasant Fowling.—"Showing how to catch Pheasants."—Fac–simile of a Miniature in the Manuscript of the "Livre du Roy Modus" (Fourteenth Century).]

Pierre Filacier, the master goldsmith who had commenced the proceedings against the bird–catchers, to pay a double fine, namely, twenty crowns to the plaintiffs and ten to the King.

[Illustration: Fig. 164.—The Mode of catching a Woodcock.—Fac–simile of a Miniature in the Manuscript of the "Livre du Roy Modus" (Fourteenth Century).]

It is satisfactory to observe that at that period measures were taken to preserve nests and to prevent bird–fowling from the 15th of March to the 15th of August. Besides this, it was necessary to have an express permission from the King himself to give persons the right of catching birds on the King's domains. Before any one could sell birds it was required for him to have been received as a master bird-catcher. The recognised bird-catchers, therefore, had no opponents except dealers from other countries, who brought canary-birds, parrots, and other foreign specimens into Paris. These dealers were, however, obliged to conform to strict rules. They were required on their arrival to exhibit their birds from ten to twelve o'clock on the marble stone in the palace yard on the days when parliament sat, in order that the masters and governors of the King's aviary, and, after them, the presidents and councillors, might have the first choice before other people of anything they wished to buy. They were, besides, bound to part the male and female birds in separate cages with tickets on them, so that purchasers might not be deceived; and, in case of dispute on this point, some sworn inspectors were appointed as arbitrators.

No doubt, emboldened by the victory which they had achieved over the goldsmiths of the Pont an Change, the bird-dealers of Paris attempted to forbid any bourgeois of the town from breeding canaries or any sort of cage birds. The bourgeois resented this, and brought their case before the Marshals of France. They urged that it was easy for them to breed canaries, and it was also a pleasure for their wives and daughters to teach them, whereas those bought on the Pont an Change were old and difficult to educate. This appeal was favourably received, and an order from the tribunal of the Marshals of France permitted the bourgeois to breed canaries, but it forbade the sale of them, which it was considered would interfere with the trade of the master-fowlers of the town, faubourgs, and suburbs of Paris.

[Illustration: Fig. 165.—Powder-horn.—Work of the Sixteenth Century (Artillery Museum of Brussels).]

Games and Pastimes.

Games of the Ancient Greeks and Romans.—Games of the Circus.—Animal Combats.—Daring of King Pepin.—The King's Lions.—Blind Men's Fights.—Cockneys of Paris.—Champ de Mars.—Cours Plenieres and Cours Couronnees.—Jugglers, Tumblers, and Minstrels.—Rope-dancers.—Fireworks.—Gymnastics.—Cards and

Dice.—Chess, Marbles, and Billiards.—La Soule, La Pirouette,
&c.—Small Games for Private Society.—History of Dancing.—Ballet des
Ardents.—The "Orchesographie" (Art of Dancing) of Thoinot Arbeau.—List
of Dances.

People of all countries and at all periods have been fond of public amusements, and have indulged in games and pastimes with a view to make time pass agreeably. These amusements have continually varied, according to the character of each nation, and according to the capricious changes of fashion. Since the learned antiquarian, J. Meursius, has devoted a large volume to describing the games of the ancient Greeks ("De Ludis Graecorum"), and Rabelais has collected a list of two hundred and twenty games which were in fashion at different times at the court of his gay master, it will be easily understood that a description of all the games and pastimes which have ever been in use by different nations, and particularly by the French, would form an encyclopaedia of some size.

We shall give a rapid sketch of the different kinds of games and pastimes which were most in fashion during the Middle Ages and to the end of the sixteenth century—omitting, however, the religious festivals, which belong to a different category; the public festivals, which will come under the chapter on Ceremonials; the tournaments and tilting matches and other sports of warriors, which belong to Chivalry; and, lastly, the scenic and literary representations, which specially belong to the history of the stage.

We shall, therefore, limit ourselves here to giving in a condensed form a few historical details of certain court amusements, and a short description of the games of skill and of chance, and also of dancing.

The Romans, especially during the times of the emperors, had a passionate love for performances in the circus and amphitheatre, as well as for chariot races, horse races, foot races, combats of animals, and feats of strength and agility. The daily life of the Roman people may be summed up as consisting of taking their food and enjoying games in the circus (*panem et circenses*). A taste for similar amusements was common to the Gauls as well as to the whole Roman Empire; and, were historians silent on the subject, we need no further information than that which is to be gathered from the ruins of the numerous amphitheatres, which are to be found at every centre of Roman occupation. The circus disappeared on the establishment of the Christian religion, for the bishops condemned it as a profane and sanguinary vestige of Paganism, and, no doubt, this led to the cessation of combats between man and beast. They continued, however, to pit wild or savage animals against one another, and to train dogs to fight with lions, tigers, bears, and bulls; otherwise it would be difficult to explain the restoration by King Chilperic (A.D. 577) of the circuses and arenas at Paris and Soissons. The remains of one of these circuses was not long ago discovered in Paris whilst they were engaged in laying the foundations for a new street, on the west side of the hill of St. Genevieve, a short distance from the old palace of the Caesars, known by the name of the Thermes of Julian.

Gregory of Tours states that Chilperic revived the ancient games of the circus, but that Gaul had ceased to be famous for good athletes and race-horses, although animal combats continued to take place for the amusement of the kings. One day King Pepin halted, with the principal officers of his army, at the Abbey of Ferrieres, and witnessed a fight between a lion and a bull. The bull was of enormous size and extraordinary strength, but nevertheless the lion overcame him; whereupon Pepin, who was surnamed the Short, turned to his officers, who used to joke him about his short stature, and said to them, "Make the lion loose his hold of the bull, or kill him." No one dared to undertake so perilous a task, and some said aloud that the man who would measure his strength with a lion must be mad. Upon this, Pepin sprang into the arena sword in hand, and with two blows cut off the heads of the lion and the bull. "What do you think of that?" he said to his astonished officers. "Am I not fit to be your master? Size cannot compare with courage. Remember what little David did to the Giant Goliath."

Eight hundred years later there were occasional animal combats at the court of Francis I. "A fine lady," says Brantome, "went to see the King's lions, in company with a gentleman who much admired her. She suddenly let her glove drop, and it fell into the lions' den. 'I beg of you,' she said, in the calmest way, to her admirer, 'to go amongst the lions and bring me back my glove.' The gentleman made no remark, but, without even drawing his sword, went into the den and gave himself up silently to death to please the lady. The lions did not move, and he was able to leave their den without a scratch and return the lady her missing glove. 'Here is your glove, madam,' he coldly said to her who evidently valued his life at so small a price; 'see if you can find any one else who would do the same as I have done for you.' So saying he left her, and never afterwards looked at or even spoke to her."

to them, and they had a place assigned to them at all feasts. They were the principal attraction at the *Cours Plenieres*, and, according to the testimony of one of their poets, they frequently retired from business loaded with presents, such as riding–horses, carriage–horses, jewels, cloaks, fur robes, clothing of violet or scarlet cloth, and, above all, with large sums of money. They loved to recall with pride the heroic memory of one of their own calling, the brave Norman, Taillefer, who, before the battle of Hastings, advanced alone on horseback between the two armies about to commence the engagement, and drew off the attention of the English by singing them the song of Roland. He then began juggling, and taking his lance by the hilt, he threw it into the air and caught it by the point as it fell; then, drawing his sword, he spun it several times over his head, and caught it in a similar way as it fell. After these skilful exercises, during which the enemy were gaping in mute astonishment, he forced his charger through the English ranks, and caused great havoc before he fell, positively riddled with wounds.

Notwithstanding this noble instance, not to belie the old proverb, jugglers were never received into the order of knighthood. They were, after a time, as much abused as they had before been extolled. Their licentious lives reflected itself in their obscene language. Their pantomimes, like their songs, showed that they were the votaries of the lowest vices. The lower orders laughed at their coarseness, and were amused at their juggleries; but the nobility were disgusted with them, and they were absolutely excluded from the presence of ladies and girls in the chateaux and houses of the bourgeoisie. We see in the tale of "Le Jugleor" that they acquired ill fame everywhere, inasmuch as they were addicted to every sort of vice. The clergy, and St. Bernard especially, denounced them and held them up to public contempt. St. Bernard spoke thus of them in one of his sermons written in the middle of the twelfth century: "A man fond of jugglers will soon enough possess a wife whose name is Poverty. If it happens that the tricks of jugglers are forced upon your notice, endeavour to avoid them, and think of other things. The tricks of jugglers never please God."

[Illustration: Fig. 172.—Equestrian Performances.—Fac–simile of a Miniature in an English Manuscript of the Thirteenth Century.]

From this remark we may understand their fall as well as the disrepute in which they were held at that time, and we are not surprised to find in an old edition of the "Memoires du Sire de Joinville" this passage, which is, perhaps, an interpolation from a contemporary document: "St. Louis drove from his kingdom all tumblers and players of sleight of hand, through whom many evil habits and tastes had become engendered in the people." A troubadour's story of this period shows that the jugglers wandered about the country with their trained animals nearly starved; they were half naked, and were often without anything on their heads, without coats, without shoes, and always without money. The lower orders welcomed them, and continued to admire and idolize them for their clever tricks (Fig. 173), but the bourgeois class, following the example of the nobility, turned their backs upon them. In 1345 Guillaume de Gourmont, Provost of Paris, forbad their singing or relating obscene stories, under penalty of fine and imprisonment.

[Illustration: Fig. 173.—Jugglers performing in public.—From a Miniature of the Manuscript of "Guarin de Loherane" (Thirteenth Century).—Library of the Arsenal, Paris.]

Having been associated together as a confraternity since 1331, they lived huddled together in one street of Paris, which took the name of *Rue des Jougleurs*. It was at this period that the Church and Hospital of St. Julian were founded through the exertions of Jacques Goure, a native of Pistoia, and of Huet le Lorrain, who were both jugglers. The newly formed brotherhood at once undertook to subscribe to this good work, and each member did so according to his means. Their aid to the cost of the two buildings was sixty livres, and they were both erected in the Rue St. Martin, and placed under the protection of St. Julian the Martyr. The chapel was consecrated on the last Sunday in September, 1335, and on the front of it there were three figures, one representing a troubadour, one a minstrel, and one a juggler, each with his various instruments.

The bad repute into which jugglers had fallen did not prevent the kings of France from attaching buffoons, or fools, as they were generally called, to their households, who were often more or less deformed dwarfs, and who, to all intents and purposes, were jugglers. They were allowed to indulge in every sort of impertinence and waggery in order to excite the risibility of their masters (Figs. 174 and 175). These buffoons or fools were an institution at court until the time of Louis XIV., and several, such as Caillette, Triboulet, and Brusquet, are better known in history than many of the statesmen and soldiers who were their contemporaries.

[Illustration: Fig. 174.—Dance of Fools.—Fac–simile of a Miniature in Manuscript of the Thirteenth Century in the Bodleian Library of Oxford.]

At the end of the fourteenth century the brotherhood of jugglers divided itself into two distinct classes, the jugglers proper and the tumblers. The former continued to recite serious or amusing poetry, to sing love–songs, to play comic interludes, either singly or in concert, in the streets or in the houses, accompanying themselves or being accompanied by all sorts of musical instruments. The tumblers, on the other hand, devoted themselves exclusively to feats of agility or of skill, the exhibition of trained animals, the making of comic grimaces, and tight–rope dancing.

[Illustration: A Court–Fool, of the 15th Century.

Fac–simile of a miniature from a ms. in the Bibl. de l'Arsenal, Th. lat., no 125.]

The art of rope dancing is very ancient; it was patronised by the Franks, who looked upon it as a marvellous effort of human genius. The most remarkable rope–dancers of that time were of Indian origin. All performers in this art came originally from the East, although they afterwards trained pupils in the countries through which they passed, recruiting themselves chiefly from the mixed tribe of jugglers. According to a document quoted by the learned Foncemagne, rope–dancers appeared as early as 1327 at the entertainments given at state banquets by the kings of France. But long before that time they are mentioned in the poems of troubadours as the necessary auxiliaries of any feast given by the nobility, or even by the monasteries. From the fourteenth to the end of the sixteenth century they were never absent from any public ceremonial, and it was at the state entries of kings and queens, princes and princesses, that they were especially called upon to display their talents.

[Illustration: Fig. 175.—Court Fool.—Fac–simile of a Woodcut in the "Cosmographie Universelle" of Munster: folio (Basle, 1552).]

One of the most extraordinary examples of the daring of these tumblers is to be found in the records of the entry of Queen Isabel of Bavaria into Paris, in 1385 (see chapter on Ceremonials); and, indeed, all the chronicles of the fifteenth century are full of anecdotes of their doings. Mathieu de Coucy, who wrote a history of the time of Charles VII., relates some very curious details respecting a show which took place at Milan, and which astonished the whole of Europe:—"The Duke of Milan ordered a rope to be stretched across his palace, about one hundred and fifty feet from the ground, and of equal length. On to this a Portuguese mounted, walked straight along, going backwards and forwards, and dancing to the sound of the tambourine. He also hung from the rope with his head downwards, and went through all sorts of tricks. The ladies who were looking on could not help hiding their eyes in their handkerchiefs, from fear lest they should see him overbalance and fall and kill himself." The chronicler of Charles XII., Jean d'Arton, tells us of a not less remarkable feat, performed on the occasion of the obsequies of Duke Pierre de Bourbon, which were celebrated at Moulins, in the month of October, 1503, in the presence of the king and the court. "Amongst other performances was that of a German tight–rope dancer, named Georges Menustre, a very young man, who had a thick rope stretched across from the highest part of the tower of the Castle of Macon to the windows of the steeple of the Church of the Jacobites. The height of this from the ground was twenty–five fathoms, and the distance from the castle to the steeple some two hundred and fifty paces. On two evenings in succession he walked along this rope, and on the second occasion when he started from the tower of the castle his feat was witnessed by the king and upwards of thirty thousand persons. He performed all sorts of graceful tricks, such as dancing grotesque dances to music and hanging to the rope by his feet and by his teeth. Although so strange and marvellous, these feats were nevertheless actually performed, unless human sight had been deceived by magic. A female dancer also performed in a novel way, cutting capers, throwing somersaults, and performing graceful Moorish and other remarkable and peculiar dances." Such was their manner of celebrating a funeral.

In the sixteenth century these dancers and tumblers became so numerous that they were to be met with everywhere, in the provinces as well as in the towns. Many of them were Bohemians or Zingari. They travelled in companies, sometimes on foot, sometimes on horseback, and sometimes with some sort of a conveyance containing the accessories of their craft and a travelling theatre. But people began to tire of these sorts of entertainments, the more so as they were required to pay for them, and they naturally preferred the public rejoicings, which cost them nothing. They were particularly fond of illuminations and fireworks, which are of much later origin than the invention of gunpowder; although the Saracens, at the time of the Crusades, used a Greek fire for illuminations, which considerably alarmed the Crusaders when they first witnessed its effects. Regular fireworks appear to have been invented in Italy, where the pyrotechnic art has retained its superiority to this day, and where the inhabitants are as enthusiastic as ever for this sort of amusement, and consider it, in fact, inseparable from every religious, private, or public festival. This Italian invention was first introduced into the Low Countries by the Spaniards, where it found many admirers, and it made its appearance in

France with the Italian artists who established themselves in that country in the reigns of Charles VIII., Louis XII., and Francis I. Fireworks could not fail to be attractive at the Court of the Valois, to which Catherine de Medicis had introduced the manners and customs of Italy. The French, who up to that time had only been accustomed to the illuminations of St. John's Day and of the first Sunday in Lent, received those fireworks with great enthusiasm, and they soon became a regular part of the programme for public festivals (Fig. 176).

[Illustration: Fig. 176.—Fireworks on the Water, with an Imitation of a Naval Combat.—Fac-simile of an Engraving on Copper of the "Pyrotechnie" of Hanzelet le Lorrain: 4to (Pont-a-Mousson, 1630).]

We have hitherto only described the sports engaged in for the amusement of the spectators; we have still to describe those in which the actors took greater pleasure than even the spectators themselves. These were specially the games of strength and skill as well as dancing, with a notice of which we shall conclude this chapter. There were, besides, the various games of chance and the games of fun and humour. Most of the bourgeois and the villagers played a variety of games of agility, many of which have descended to our times, and are still to be found at our schools and colleges. Wrestling, running races, the game of bars, high and wide jumping, leap-frog, blind-man's buff, games of ball of all sorts, gymnastics, and all exercises which strengthened the body or added to the suppleness of the limbs, were long in use among the youth of the nobility (Figs. 177 and 178). The Lord of Fleuranges, in his memoirs written at the court of Francis I., recounts numerous exercises to which he devoted himself during his childhood and youth, and which were then looked upon as a necessary part of the education of chivalry. The nobles in this way acquired a taste for physical exercises, and took naturally to combats, tournaments, and hunting, and subsequently their services in the battle-field gave them plenty of opportunities to gratify the taste thus developed in them. These were not, however, sufficient for their insatiable activity; when they could not do anything else, they played at tennis and such games at all hours of the day; and these pastimes had so much attraction for nobles of all ages that they not unfrequently sacrificed their health in consequence of overtaxing their strength. In 1506 the King of Castile, Philippe le Beau, died of pleurisy, from a severe cold which he caught while playing tennis.

[Illustration: Fig. 177.—Somersaults.—Fac-simile of a Woodcut in "Exercises in Leaping and Vaulting," by A. Tuccaro: 4to (Paris, 1599).]

Tennis also became the favourite game amongst the bourgeois in the towns, and tennis–courts were built in all parts, of such spacious proportions and so well adapted for spectators, that they were often converted into theatres. Their game of billiards resembled the modern one only in name, for it was played on a level piece of ground with wooden balls which were struck with hooked sticks and mallets. It was in great repute in the fourteenth century, for in 1396 Marshal de Boucicault, who was considered one of the best players of his time, won at it six hundred francs (or more than twenty–eight thousand francs of present currency). At the beginning of the following century the Duke Louis d'Orleans ordered *billes et billars* to be bought for the sum of eleven sols six deniers tournois (about fifteen francs of our money), that he might amuse himself with them. There were several games of the same sort, which were not less popular. Skittles; *la Soule* or *Soulette*, which consisted of a large ball of hay covered over with leather, the possession of which was contested for by two opposing sides of players; Football; open Tennis; Shuttlecock, &c. It was Charles V. who first thought of giving a more serious and useful character to the games of the people, and who, in a celebrated edict forbidding games of chance, encouraged the establishment of companies of archers and bowmen. These companies, to which was subsequently added that of the arquebusiers, outlived political revolutions, and are still extant, especially in the northern provinces of France.

[Illustration: Fig. 178.—The Spring–board.—Fac–simile of a Woodcut in "Exercises in Leaping and Vaulting," by A. Tuccaro: 4to (Paris, 1599).]

At all times and in all countries the games of chance were the most popular, although they were forbidden both by ecclesiastical and royal authority. New laws were continually being enacted against them, and especially against those in which dice were used, though with little avail. "Dice shall not be made in the kingdom," says the law of 1256; and "those who are discovered using them, and frequenting taverns and bad places, will be looked upon as suspicions characters." A law of 1291 repeats, "That games with dice be forbidden." Nevertheless, though these prohibitions were frequently renewed, people continued to disregard them and to lose much money at such games. The law of 1396 is aimed particularly against loaded dice, which must have been contemporary with the origin of dice themselves, for no games ever gave rise to a greater amount of roguery than those of this description. They were, however, publicly sold in spite of all the laws to the contrary; for, in the "Dit du Mercier," the dealer offers his merchandise thus:—

"J'ay dez de plus, j'ay dez de moins,
De Paris, de Chartres, de Rains."

("I have heavy dice, I have light dice,
From Paris, from Chartres, and from Rains.")

It has been said that the game of dice was at first called the *game of God*, because the regulation of lottery was one of God's prerogatives; but this derivation is purely imaginary. What appears more likely is, that dice were first forbidden by the Church, and then by the civil authorities, on account of the fearful oaths which were so apt to be uttered by those players who had a run of ill luck. Nothing was commoner than for people to ruin themselves at this game. The poems of troubadours are full of imprecations against the fatal chance of dice; many troubadours, such as Guillaume Magret and Gaucelm Faydit, lost their fortunes at it, and their lives in consequence. Rutebeuf exclaims, in one of his satires, "Dice rob me of all my clothes, dice kill me, dice watch me, dice track me, dice attack me, and dice defy me." The blasphemies of the gamblers did not always remain unpunished. "Philip Augustus," says Bigord, in his Latin history of this king, "carried his aversion for oaths to such an extent, that if any one, whether knight or of any other rank, let one slip from his lips in the presence of the sovereign, even by mistake, he was ordered to be immediately thrown into the river." Louis XII., who was somewhat less severe, contented himself with having a hole bored with a hot iron through the blasphemer's tongue.

[Illustration: Figs. 179 and 180.—French Cards for a Game of Piquet, early Sixteenth Century.—Collection of the National Library of Paris.]

The work "On the Manner of playing with Dice," has handed down to us the technical terms used in these games, which varied as much in practice as in name. They sometimes played with three dice, sometimes with six; different games were also in fashion, and in some the cast of the dice alone decided. The games of cards were also most numerous, but it is not our intention to give the origin of them here. It is sufficient to name a few of the most popular ones in France, which were, Flux, Prime, Sequence, Triomphe, Piquet, Trente–et–un, Passe–dix, Condemnade, Lansquenet, Marriage, Gay, or J'ai, Malcontent, Here, &c. (Figs. 179 and 180). All these games, which were as much forbidden as dice, were played in taverns as well as at court; and, just as there were loaded dice, so were there also false cards, prepared by rogues for cheating. The greater number of the games

159

of cards formerly did not require the least skill on the part of the players, chance alone deciding. The game of *Tables*, however, required skill and calculation, for under this head were comprised all the games which were played on a board, and particularly chess, draughts, and backgammon. The invention of the game of chess has been attributed to the Assyrians, and there can be no doubt but that it came from the East, and reached Gaul about the beginning of the ninth century, although it was not extensively known till about the twelfth. The annals of chivalry continually speak of the barons playing at these games, and especially at chess. Historians also mention chess, and show that it was played with the same zest in the camp of the Saracens as in that of the Crusaders. We must not be surprised if chess shared the prohibition laid upon dice, for those who were ignorant of its ingenious combinations ranked it amongst games of chance. The Council of Paris, in 1212, therefore condemned chess for the same reasons as dice, and it was specially forbidden to church people, who had begun to make it their habitual pastime. The royal edict of 1254 was equally unjust with regard to this game. "We strictly forbid," says Louis IX., "any person to play at dice, tables, or chess." This pious king set himself against these games, which he looked upon as inventions of the devil. After the fatal day of Mansorah, in 1249, the King, who was still in Egypt with the remnants of his army, asked what his brother, the Comte d'Anjou, was doing. "He was told," says Joinville, "that he was playing at tables with his Royal Highness Gaultier de Nemours. The King was highly incensed against his brother, and, though most feeble from the effects of his illness, went to him, and taking the dice and the tables, had them thrown into the sea." Nevertheless Louis IX. received as a present from the *Vieux de la Montagne*, chief of the Ismalians, a chessboard made of gold and rock crystal, the pieces being of precious metals beautifully worked. It has been asserted, but incorrectly, that this chessboard was the one preserved in the Musee de Cluny, after having long formed part of the treasures of the Kings of France.

Amongst the games comprised under the name of *tables*, it is sufficient to mention that of draughts, which was formerly played with dice and with the same men as were used for chess; also the game of *honchet*, or *jonchees*, that is, bones or spillikins, games which required pieces or men in the same way as chess, but which required more quickness of hand than of intelligence; and *epingles*, or push–pin, which was played in a similar manner to the *honchets*, and was the great amusement of the small pages in the houses of the nobility. When they had not epingles, honchets, or draughtsmen to play with, they used their fingers instead, and played a game which is still most popular amongst the Italian people, called the *morra*, and which was as much in vogue with the ancient

Romans as it is among the modern Italians. It consisted of suddenly raising as many fingers as had been shown by one's adversary, and gave rise to a great amount of amusement among the players and lookers-on. The games played by girls were, of course, different from those in use among boys. The latter played at marbles, *luettes*, peg or humming tops, quoits, *fouquet, merelles*, and a number of other games, many of which are now unknown. The girls, it is almost needless to say, from the earliest times played with dolls. *Briche*, a game in which a brick and a small stick was used, were also a favourite. *Martiaus*, or small quoits, wolf or fox, blind man's buff, hide and seek, quoits, &c., were all girls' games. The greater part of these amusements were enlivened by a chorus, which all the girls sang together, or by dialogues sung or chanted in unison.

[Illustration: Fig. 181.—Allegorical Scene of one of the Courts of Love in Provence—In the First Compartment, the God of Love, Cupid, is sitting on the Stump of a Laurel-tree, wounding with his Darts those who do him homage, the Second Compartment represents the Love Vows of Men and Women.—From the Cover of a Looking-glass, carved in Ivory, of the end of the Thirteenth Century.]

[Illustration: The Chess-Players.

After a miniature of "*The Three Ages of Man*", a ms. of the fifteenth century attributed to Estienne Porchier. (Bibl. of M. Ambroise Firmin-Didot.)

The scene is laid in one of the saloons of the castle of Plessis-les-Tours, the residence of Louis XI; in the player to the right, the features of the king are recognisable.]

If children had their games, which for many generations continued comparatively unchanged, so the dames and the young ladies had theirs, consisting of gallantry and politeness, which only disappeared with those harmless assemblies in which the two sexes vied with each other in urbanity, friendly roguishness, and wit. It would require long antiquarian researches to discover the origin and mode of playing many of these pastimes, such as *des oes, des trois anes, des accords bigarres, du jardin madame, de la fricade, du feiseau, de la mick*, and a number of others which are named but not described in the records of the times. The game *a l'oreille*, the invention of which is attributed to the troubadour Guillaume Adhemar, the *jeu des Valentines,* or the game of lovers, and the numerous games of forfeits, which have come down to us from the Courts of Love of the Middle Ages, we find to be somewhat deprived of their original simplicity in the way they are now played in country–houses in the winter and at village festivals in the summer. But the Courts of Love are no longer in existence gravely to superintend all these diversions (Fig. 181).

Amongst the amusements which time has not obliterated, but which, on the contrary, seem destined to be of longer duration than monuments of stone and brass, we must name dancing, which was certainly one of the principal amusements of society, and which has come down to us through all religions, all customs, all people, and all ages, preserving at the same time much of its original character. Dancing appears, at each period of the world's history, to have been alternately religions and profane, lively and solemn, frivolous and severe. Though dancing was as common an amusement formerly as it is now, there was this essential difference between the two periods, namely, that certain people, such as the Romans, were very fond of seeing dancing, but did not join in it themselves. Tiberius drove the dancers out of Rome, and Domitian dismissed certain senators from their seats in the senate who had degraded themselves by dancing; and there seems to be no doubt that the Romans, from the conquest of Julius Caesar, did not themselves patronise the art. There were a number of professional dancers in Gaul, as well as in the other provinces of the Roman Empire, who were hired to dance at feasts, and who endeavoured to do their best to make their art as popular as possible. The lightheartedness of the Gauls, their natural gaiety, their love for violent exercise and for pleasures of all sorts, made them delight in dancing, and indulge in it with great energy; and thus, notwithstanding the repugnance of the Roman aristocracy and the prohibitions and anathemas of councils and synods, dancing has always been one of the favourite pastimes of the Gauls and the French.

[Illustration: Fig. 182.—Dancers on Christmas Night punished for their Impiety, and condemned to dance for a whole Year (Legend of the Fifteenth Century).—Fac–simile of a Woodcut by P. Wohlgemuth, in the "Liber Chronicorum Mundi:" folio (Nuremberg, 1493).]

Leuce Carin, a writer of doubtful authority, states that in the early history of Christianity the faithful danced, or rather stamped, in measured time during religions ceremonials, gesticulating and distorting themselves. This is, however, a mistake. The only thing approaching to it was the slight trace of the ancient Pagan dances which remained in the feast of the first Sunday in Lent, and which probably belonged to the religious ceremonies of the Druids. At nightfall fires were lighted in public places, and numbers of people danced madly round them. Rioting and disorderly conduct often resulted from this popular feast, and the magistrates were obliged to interfere in order to suppress it. The church, too, did not close her eyes to the abuses which this feast engendered, although episcopal admonitions were not always listened to (Fig. 182). We see, in the records of one of the most recent Councils of Narbonne, that the custom of dancing in the churches and in the cemeteries on certain feasts had not been abolished in some parts of the Languedoc at the end of the sixteenth century.

Dancing was at all times forbidden by the Catholic Church on account of its tendency to corrupt the morals, and for centuries ecclesiastical authority was strenuously opposed to it; but, on the other hand, it could not complain of want of encouragement from the civil power. When King Childebert, in 554, forbade all dances in his domains, he was only induced to do so by the influence of the bishops. We have but little information respecting the dances of this period, and it would be impossible accurately to determine as to the justice of their being forbidden. They were certainly no longer those war–dances which the Franks had brought with them, and which antiquarians have mentioned under the name of *Pyrrhichienne* dances. In any case, war–dances reappeared at the commencement of chivalry; for, when a new knight was elected, all the knights in full armour performed evolutions, either on foot or on horseback, to the sound of military music, and the populace danced round them. It has been said that this was the origin of court ballets, and La Colombiere, in his "Theatre d'Honneur et de Chevalerie," relates that this ancient dance of the knights was kept up by the Spaniards, who called it the *Moresque*.

The Middle Ages was the great epoch for dancing, especially in France. There were an endless number of dancing festivals, and, from reading the old poets and romancers, one might imagine that the French had never anything better to do than to dance, and that at all hours of the day and night. A curious argument in favour of the practical utility of dancing is suggested by Jean Tabourot in his "Orchesographie," published at Langres in 1588, under the name of Thoinot Arbeau. He says, "Dancing is practised in order to see whether lovers are healthy and suitable for one another: at the end of a dance the gentlemen are permitted to kiss their mistresses, in order that they may ascertain if they have an agreeable breath. In this matter, besides many other good results which follow from dancing, it becomes necessary for the good governing of society." Such was the doctrine of the Courts of Love, which stoutly took up the defence of dancing against the clergy. In those days, as soon as the two sexes were assembled in sufficient numbers, before or after the feasts, the balls began, and men and women took each other by the hand and commenced the performance in regular steps (Fig. 183). The author of the poem of Provence, called "Flamenca," thus allegorically describes these amusements: "Youth and Gaiety opened the ball, accompanied by their sister Bravery; Cowardice, confused, went of her own accord and hid herself." The troubadours mention a great number of dances, without describing them; no doubt they were so familiar that they thought a description of them needless. They often speak of the *danse au virlet*, a kind of round dance, during the performance of which each person in turn sang a verse, the chorus being repeated by all. In the code of the Courts of Love, entitled "Arresta Amorum," that is, the decrees of love, the *pas de Brabant* is mentioned, in which each gentleman bent his knee before his lady; and also the *danse au chapelet*, at the end of which each dancer kissed his lady. Romances of chivalry frequently mention that knights used to dance with the dames and young ladies without taking off their helmets and coats of mail. Although this costume was hardly fitted for the purpose, we find, in the romance of "Perceforet," that, after a repast, whilst the tables were being removed, everything was prepared for a ball, and that although the knights made no change in their accoutrements, yet the ladies went and made fresh toilettes. "Then," says the old novelist, "the young knights and the young ladies began to play their instruments and to have the dance." From this custom may be traced the origin of the ancient Gallic proverb, *"Apres la panse vient la danse"* ("After the feast comes the dance"). Sometimes a minstrel sang songs to the accompaniment of the harp, and the young ladies danced in couples and repeated at intervals the minstrel's songs. Sometimes the torch–dance was performed; in this each performer bore in his hand a long lighted taper, and endeavoured to prevent his neighbours from blowing it out, which each one tried to do if possible (Fig. 184). This dance, which was in use up to the end of the sixteenth century at court, was generally reserved for weddings.

[Illustration: Fig. 183.—Peasant Dances at the May Feasts.—Fac–simile of a Miniature in a Prayer–book of the Fifteenth Century, in the National Library of Paris.]

[Illustration: Fig. 184.—Dance by Torchlight, a Scene at the Court of Burgundy.—From a Painting on Wood of 1463, belonging to M. H. Casterman, of Tournai (Belgium).]

Dancing lost much of its simplicity and harmlessness when masquerades were introduced, these being the first examples of the ballet. These masquerades, which soon after their introduction became passionately indulged in at court under Charles VI., were, at first, only allowed during Carnival, and on particular occasions called *Charivaris*, and they were usually made the pretext for the practice of the most licentious follies. These masquerades had a most unfortunate inauguration by the catastrophe which rendered the madness of Charles VI. incurable, and which is described in history under the name of the *Burning Ballet*. It was on the 29th of January, 1393, that this ballet made famous the festival held in the Royal Palace of St. Paul in Paris, on the occasion of the marriage of one of the maids of honour of Queen Isabel of Bavaria with a gentleman of Vermandois. The bride was a widow, and the second nuptials were deemed a fitting occasion for the Charivaris.

[Illustration: Fig. 185.—The Burning Ballet.—Fac-simile of a Miniature in the Manuscript of the "Chroniques" of Froissart (Fifteenth Century), in the National Library of Paris.]

A gentleman from Normandy, named Hugonin de Grensay, thought he could create a sensation by having a dance of wild men to please the ladies. "He admitted to his plot," says Froissart, "the king and four of the principal nobles of the court. These all had themselves sewn up in close-fitting linen garments covered with resin on which a quantity of tow was glued, and in this guise they appeared in the middle of the ball. The king was alone, but the other four were chained together. They jumped about like madmen, uttered wild cries, and made all sorts of eccentric gestures. No one knew who these hideous objects were, but the Duke of Orleans determined to find out, so he took a candle and imprudently approached too near one of the men. The tow caught fire, and the flames enveloped him and the other three who were chained to him in a moment." "They were burning for nearly an hour like torches," says a chronicler. "The king had the good fortune to escape the peril, because the Duchesse de Berry, his aunt, recognised him, and had the presence of mind to envelop him in her train" (Fig. 185). Such a calamity, one would have thought, might have been sufficient to disgust people with masquerades, but they were none the less in favour at court for many years afterwards; and, two centuries later, the author of the "Orchesographie" thus writes on the subject: "Kings and princes give dances and masquerades for amusement and in order to afford a joyful welcome to foreign nobles; we also practise the same amusements on the celebration of marriages." In no country in the world was dancing practised with more grace and elegance than in France. Foreign dances of every kind were introduced, and, after being remodelled and brought to as great perfection as possible, they were often returned to the countries from which they had been imported under almost a new character.

[Illustration: Fig. 186.—Musicians accompanying the Dancing.—Fac–simile of a Wood Engraving in the "Orchesographie" of Thoinot Arbeau (Jehan Tabourot): 4to (Langres, 1588).]

In 1548, the dances of the Bearnais, which were much admired at the court of the Comtes de Foix, especially those called the *danse mauresque* and the *danse des sauvages*, were introduced at the court of France, and excited great merriment. So popular did they become, that with a little modification they soon were considered essentially French. The German dances, which were distinguished by the rapidity of their movements, were also thoroughly established at the court of France. Italian, Milanese, Spanish, and Piedmontese dances were in fashion in France before the expedition of Charles VIII. into Italy: and when this king, followed by his youthful nobility, passed over the mountains to march to the conquest of Naples, he found everywhere in the towns that welcomed him, and in which balls and masquerades were given in honour of his visit, the dance *a la mode de France*, which consisted of a sort of medley of the dances of all countries. Some hundreds of these dances have been enumerated in the fifth book of the "Pantagruel" of Rabelais, and in various humorous works of those who succeeded him. They owed their success to the singing with which they were generally accompanied, or to the postures, pantomimes, or drolleries with which they were supplemented for the amusement of the spectators. A few, and amongst others that of the *five steps* and that of the *three faces*, are mentioned in the "History of the Queen of Navarre."

[Illustration: Fig. 187.—The Dance called "La Gaillarde."—Fac–simile of Wood Engravings from the "Orchesographie" of Thoinot Arbeau (Jehan Tabourot): 4to (Langres, 1588).]

Dances were divided into two distinct classes—*danses basses*, or common and regular dances, which did not admit of jumping, violent movements, or extraordinary contortions—and the *danses par haut*, which were irregular, and comprised all sorts of antics and buffoonery. The regular French dance was a *basse* dance, called the *gaillarde*; it was accompanied by the sound of the hautbois and tambourine, and originally it was danced with great form and state. This is the dance which Jean Tabouret has described; it began with the two performers standing opposite to each other, advancing, bowing, and retiring. "These advancings and retirings were done in steps to the time of the music, and continued until the instrumental accompaniment stopped; then the gentleman made his bow to the lady, took her by the hand, thanked her, and led her to her seat." The *tourdion* was similar to the *gaillarde*, only faster, and was accompanied with more action. Each province of France had its national dance, such as the *bourree* of Auvergne, the *trioris* of Brittany, the *branles* of Poitou, and the *valses* of Lorraine, which constituted a very agreeable pastime, and one in which the French excelled all other nations. This art, "so ancient, so honourable, and so profitable," to use the words of Jean Tabourot, was long in esteem in the highest social circles, and the old men liked to display their agility, and the dames and young ladies to find a temperate exercise calculated to contribute to their health as well as to their amusement.

The sixteenth century was the great era of dancing in all the courts of Europe; but under the Valois, the art had more charm and prestige at the court of France than anywhere else. The Queen–mother, Catherine, surrounded by a crowd of pretty young ladies, who composed what she called her *flying squadron*, presided at these exciting dances. A certain Balthazar de Beaujoyeux was master of her ballets, and they danced at the Castle of Blois the night before the Duc de Guise was assassinated under the eyes of Henry III., just as they had danced at the Chateau of the Tuileries the day after St. Bartholomew's Day.

[Illustration: Fig. 188.—The Game of Bob Apple, or Swinging Apple.—Manuscript of the Fourteenth Century, in the British Museum.]

Commerce.

State of Commerce after the Fall of the Roman. Empire.—Its Revival under the Frankish Kings.—Its Prosperity under Charlemagne.—Its Decline down to the Time of the Crusaders.—The Levant Trade of the East.—Flourishing State of the Towns of Provence and Languedoc.—Establishment of Fairs.—Fairs of Landit, Champagne, Beaucaire, and Lyons.—Weights and Measures.—Commercial Flanders. Laws of Maritime Commerce.—Consular Laws.—Banks and Bills of Exchange.—French. Settlements on the Coast of Africa.—Consequences of the Discovery of America.

"Commerce in the Middle Ages," says M. Charles Grandmaison, "differed but little from that of a more remote period. It was essentially a local and limited traffic, rather inland than maritime, for long and perilous sea voyages only commenced towards the end of the fifteenth century, or about the time when Columbus discovered America."

On the fall of the Roman Empire, commerce was rendered insecure, and, indeed, it was almost completely put a stop to by the barbarian invasions, and all facility of communication between different nations, and even between towns of the same country, was interrupted. In those times of social confusion, there were periods of such poverty and distress, that for want of money commerce was reduced to the simple exchange of the positive necessaries of life. When order was a little restored, and society and the minds of people became more composed, we see commerce recovering its position; and France was, perhaps, the first country in Europe in which this happy change took place. Those famous cities of Gaul, which ancient authors describe to us as so rich and so industrious, quickly recovered their former prosperity, and the friendly relations which were established between the kings of the Franks and the Eastern Empire encouraged the Gallic cities in cultivating a commerce, which was at that time the most important and most extensive in the world.

Marseilles, the ancient Phoenician colony, once the rival and then the successor to Carthage, was undoubtedly at the head of the commercial cities of France. Next to her came Arles, which supplied ship–builders and seamen to the fleet of Provence; and Narbonne, which admitted into its harbour ships from Spain, Sicily, and Africa, until, in consequence of the Aude having changed its course, it was obliged to relinquish the greater part of its maritime commerce in favour of Montpellier.

[Illustration: Fig. 189.—View of Alexandria in Egypt, in the Sixteenth Century.—Fac–simile of a Woodcut in the Travels of P. Belon, "Observations de Plusieurs Singularitez," &c.: 4to (Paris, 1588).]

Commerce maintained frequent communications with the East; it sought its supplies on the coast of Syria, and especially at Alexandria, in Egypt, which was a kind of depot for goods obtained from the rich countries lying beyond the Red Sea (Figs. 189 and 190). The Frank navigators imported from these countries, groceries, linen, Egyptian paper, pearls, perfumes, and a thousand other rare and choice articles. In exchange they offered chiefly the precious metals in bars rather than coined, and it is probable that at this period they also exported iron, wines, oil, and wax. The agricultural produce and manufactures of Gaul had not sufficiently developed to provide anything more than what was required for the producers themselves. Industry was as yet, if not purely domestic, confined to monasteries and to the houses of the nobility; and even the kings employed women or serf workmen to manufacture the coarse stuffs with which they clothed themselves and their households. We may add, that the bad state of the roads, the little security they offered to travellers, the extortions of all kinds to which foreign merchants were subjected, and above all the iniquitous System of fines and tolls which each landowner thought right to exact, before letting merchandise pass through his domains, all created insuperable obstacles to the development of commerce.

[Illustration: Fig. 190.—Transport of Merchandise on the Backs of Camels.—Fac−simile of a Woodcut in the "Cosmographie Universelle," of Thevet: folio, 1575.]

The Frank kings on several occasions evinced a desire that communications favourable to trade should be re−established in their dominions. We find, for instance, Chilperic making treaties with Eastern emperors in favour of the merchants of Agde and Marseilles, Queen Brunehaut making viaducts worthy of the Romans, and which still bear her name, and Dagobert opening at St. Denis free fairs—that is to say, free, or nearly so, from all tolls and taxes—to which goods, both agricultural and manufactured, were sent from every corner of Europe and the known world, to be afterwards distributed through the towns and provinces by the enterprise of internal commerce.

After the reign of Dagobert, commerce again declined without positively ceasing, for the revolution, which transferred the power of the kings to the mayors of the palace was not of a nature to exhaust the resources of public prosperity; and a charter of 710 proves that the merchants of Saxony, England, Normandy, and even Hungary, still flocked to the fairs of St. Denis.

Under the powerful and administrative hand of Charlemagne, the roads being better kept up, and the rivers being made more navigable, commerce became safe and more general; the coasts were protected from piratical incursions; lighthouses were erected at dangerous points, to prevent shipwrecks; and treaties of commerce with foreign nations, including even the most distant, guaranteed the liberty and security of French traders abroad.

Under the weak successors of this monarch, notwithstanding their many efforts, commerce was again subjected to all sorts of injustice and extortions, and all its safeguards were rapidly destroyed. The Moors in the south, and the Normans in the north, appeared to desire to destroy everything which came in their way, and already Marseilles, in 838, was taken and pillaged by the Greeks. The constant altercations between the sons of Louis le Debonnaire and their unfortunate father, their jealousies amongst themselves, and their fratricidal wars, increased the measure of public calamity, so that soon, overrun by foreign enemies and destroyed by her own sons, France became a vast field of disorder and desolation.

The Church, which alone possessed some social influence, never ceased to use its authority in endeavouring to remedy this miserable state of things; but episcopal edicts, papal anathemas, and decrees of councils, had only a partial effect at this unhappy period. At any moment agricultural and commercial operations were liable to be interrupted, if not completely ruined, by the violence of a wild and rapacious soldiery; at every step the roads, often impassable, were intercepted by toll–bars for some due of a vexatious nature, besides being continually infested by bands of brigands, who carried off the merchandise and murdered those few merchants who were so bold as to attempt to continue their business. It was the Church, occupied as she was with the interests of civilisation, who again assisted commerce to emerge from the state of annihilation into which it had fallen; and the "Peace or Truce of God," established in 1041, endeavoured to stop at least the internal wars of feudalism, and it succeeded, at any rate for a time, in arresting these disorders. This was all that could be done at that period, and the Church accomplished it, by taking the high hand; and with as much unselfishness as energy and courage, she regulated society, which had been abandoned by the civil power from sheer impotence and want of administrative capability.

[Illustration: Fig. 191.—Trade on the Seaports of the Levant.—After a Miniature in a Manuscript of the Travels of Marco Polo (Fifteenth Century), Library of the Arsenal of Paris.]

At all events, thanks to ecclesiastical foresight, which increased the number of fairs and markets at the gates of abbeys and convents, the first step was made towards the general resuscitation of commerce. Indeed, the Church may be said to have largely contributed to develop the spirit of progress and liberty, whence were to spring societies and nationalities, and, in a word, modern organization.

The Eastern commerce furnished the first elements of that trading activity which showed itself on the borders of the Mediterranean, and we find the ancient towns of Provence and

Languedoc springing up again by the aide of the republics of Amalfi, Venice, Genoa, and Pisa, which had become the rich depots of all maritime trade.

At first, as we have already stated, the wares of India came to Europe through the Greek port of Alexandria, or through Constantinople. The Crusades, which had facilitated the relations with Eastern countries, developed a taste in the West for their indigenous productions, gave a fresh vigour to this foreign commerce, and rendered it more productive by removing the stumbling blocks which had arrested its progress (Fig. 191).

The conquest of Palestine by the Crusaders had first opened all the towns and harbours of this wealthy region to Western traders, and many of them were able permanently to establish themselves there, with all sorts of privileges and exemptions from taxes, which were gladly offered to them by the nobles who had transferred feudal power to Mussulman territories.

Ocean commerce assumed from this moment proportions hitherto unknown. Notwithstanding the papal bulls and decrees, which forbade Christians from having any connection with infidels, the voice of interest was more listened to than that of the Church (Fig. 192), and traders did not fear to disobey the political and religions orders which forbade them to carry arms and slaves to the enemies of the faith.

It was easy to foretell, from the very first, that the military occupation of the Holy Land would not be permanent. In consequence of this, therefore, the nearer the loss of this fine conquest seemed to be, the greater were the efforts made by the maritime towns of the West to re–establish, on a more solid and lasting basis, a commercial alliance with Egypt, the country which they selected to replace Palestine, in a mercantile point of view. Marseilles was the greatest supporter of this intercourse with Egypt; and in the twelfth and thirteenth centuries she reached a very high position, which she owed to her shipowners and traders. In the fourteenth century, however, the princes of the house of Anjou ruined her like the rest of Provence, in the great and fruitless efforts which they made to recover the kingdom of Naples; and it was not until the reign of Louis XI. that the old Phoenician city recovered its maritime and commercial prosperity (Fig. 193).

[Illustration: Fig. 192.—Merchant Vessel in a Storm.—Fac–simile of a Woodcut in the "Grand Kalendrier et Compost des Bergers," in folio: printed at Troyes, about 1490, by Nicolas de Rouge.[*]

[Footnote *: "Mortal man, living in the world, is compared to a vessel on perilous seas, bearing rich merchandise, by which, if it can come to harbour, the merchant will be rendered rich and happy. The ship from the commencement to the end of its voyage is in great peril of being lost or taken by an enemy, for the seas are always beset with perils. So is the body of man during its sojourn in the world. The merchandise he bears is his soul, his virtues, and his good deeds. The harbour is paradise, and he who reaches that haven is made supremely rich. The sea is the world, full of vices and sins, and in which all, during their passage through life, are in peril and danger of losing body and soul and of being drowned in the infernal sea, from which God in His grace keep us! Amen."]]

[Illustration: Fig. 193.—View and Plan of Marseilles and its Harbour, in the Sixteenth Century.—From a Copper-plate in the Collection of G. Bruin, in folio: "Theatre des Citez du Monde."]

Languedoc, depressed, and for a time nearly ruined in the thirteenth century by the effect of the wars of the Albigenses, was enabled, subsequently, to recover itself. Beziers, Agde, Narbonne, and especially Montpellier, so quickly established important trading connections with all the ports of the Mediterranean, that at the end of the fourteenth century consuls were appointed at each of these towns, in order to protect and direct their transmarine commerce. A traveller of the twelfth century, Benjamin de Tudele, relates that in these ports, which were afterwards called the stepping stones to the Levant, every language in the world might be heard.

Toulouse was soon on a par with the towns of Lower Languedoc, and the Garonne poured into the markets, not only the produce of Guienne, and of the western parts of France, but also those of Flanders, Normandy, and England. We may observe, however, that Bordeaux, although placed in a most advantageous position, at the mouth of the river, only possessed, when under the English dominion, a very limited commerce, principally confined to the export of wines to Great Britain in exchange for corn, oil, &c.

La Rochelle, on the same coast, was much more flourishing at this period, owing to the numerous coasters which carried the wines of Aunis and Saintonge, and the salt of Brouage to Flanders, the Netherlands, and the north of Germany. Vitre already had its silk manufactories in the fifteenth century, and Nantes gave promise of her future greatness as a depot of maritime commerce. It was about this time also that the fisheries became a new industry, in which Bayonne and a few villages on the sea-coast took the lead, some being especially engaged in whaling, and others in the cod and herring fisheries (Fig. 194).

Long before this, Normandy had depended on other branches of trade for its commercial prosperity. Its fabrics of woollen stuffs, its arms and cutlery, besides the agricultural productions of its fertile and well-cultivated soil, each furnished material for export on a large scale.

The towns of Rouen and Caen were especially manufacturing cities, and were very rich. This was the case with Rouen particularly, which was situated on the Seine, and was at that time an extensive depot for provisions and other merchandise which was sent down the river for export, or was imported for future internal consumption. Already Paris, the abode of kings, and the metropolis of government, began to foreshadow the immense development which it was destined to undergo, by becoming the centre of commercial affairs, and by daily adding to its labouring and mercantile population (Figs. 195 and 196).

It was, however, outside the walls of Paris that commerce, which needed liberty as well as protection, at first progressed most rapidly. The northern provinces had early united manufacturing industry with traffic, and this double source of local prosperity was the origin of their enormous wealth. Ghent and Bruges in the Low Countries, and Beauvais and Arras, were celebrated for their manufacture of cloths, carpets, and serge, and Cambrai for its fine cloths. The artizans and merchants of these industrious cities then established their powerful corporations, whose unwearied energy gave rise to that commercial freedom so favourable to trade.

[Illustration: Fig. 194. Whale-Fishing. Fac-simile of a Woodcut in the "Cosmographie Universelle" of Thevet, in folio: Paris, 1574.]

More important than the woollen manufactures—for the greater part of the wool used was brought from England—was the manufacture of flax, inasmuch as it encouraged agriculture, the raw material being produced in France. This first flourished in the north-east of France, and spread slowly to Picardy, to Beauvois, and Brittany. The central countries, with the exception of Bruges, whose cloth manufactories were already celebrated in the fifteenth century, remained essentially agricultural; and their principal towns were merely depots for imported goods. The institution of fairs, however, rendered, it is true, this commerce of some of the towns as wide-spread as it was productive. In the Middle Ages religious feasts and ceremonials almost always gave rise to fairs, which commerce was not slow in multiplying as much as possible. The merchants naturally came to exhibit their goods where the largest concourse of people afforded the greatest promise of their readily disposing of them. As early as the first dynasty of Merovingian kings, temporary and periodical markets of this kind existed; but, except at St. Denis, articles of local consumption only were brought to them. The reasons for this were, the heavy taxes which were levied by the feudal lords on all merchandise exhibited for sale, and the danger which foreign merchants ran of being plundered on their way, or even at the fair itself. These causes for a long time delayed the progress of an institution which was afterwards destined to become so useful and beneficial to all classes of the community.

We have several times mentioned the famous fair of Landit, which is supposed to have been established by Charlemagne, but which no doubt was a sort of revival of the fairs of St. Denis, founded by Dagobert, and which for a time had fallen into disuse in the midst of the general ruin which preceded that emperor's reign. This fair of Landit was renowned over the whole of Europe, and attracted merchants from all countries. It was held in the month of June, and only lasted fifteen days. Goods of all sorts, both of home and foreign manufacture, were sold, but the sale of parchment was the principal object of the fair, to purchase a supply of which the University of Paris regularly went in procession. On account of its special character, this fair was of less general importance than the six others, which from the twelfth century were held at Troyes, Provins, Lagny-sur-Marne, Rheims, and Bar-sur-Aube. These infused so much commercial vitality into the province of Champagne, that the nobles for the most part shook off the prejudice which forbad their entering into any sort of trading association.

Fairs multiplied in the centre and in the south of France simultaneously. Those of Puy-en-Velay, now the capital of the Haute-Loire, are looked upon as the most ancient, and they preserved their old reputation and attracted a considerable concourse of people, which was also increased by the pilgrimages then made to Notre-Dame du Puy. These fairs, which were more of a religious than of a commercial character, were then of less importance as regards trade than those held at Beaucaire. This town rose to great repute in the thirteenth century, and, with the Lyons market, became at that time the largest centre of commerce in the southern provinces. Placed at the junction of the Saone and the Rhone, Lyons owed its commercial development to the proximity of Marseilles and the towns of Italy. Its four annual fairs were always much frequented, and when the kings of France transferred to it the privileges of the fairs of Champagne, and transplanted to within its walls the silk manufactories formerly established at Tours, Lyons really became the second city of France.

[Illustration: Fig. 195.—Measurers of Corn in Paris.

Fig. 196.—Hay Carriers.

Fac–simile of Woodcuts from the "Royal Orders concerning the Jurisdiction of the Company of Merchants and Shrievalty in the City of Paris," in small folio goth.: Jacques Nyverd, 1528.]

It may be asserted as an established fact that the gradual extension of the power of the king, produced by the fall of feudalism, was favourable to the extension of commerce. As early as the reign of Louis IX. many laws and regulations prove that the kings were alive to the importance of trade. Among the chief enactments was one which led to the formation of the harbour of Aigues–Mortes on the Mediterranean; another to the publication of the book of "Weights and Measures," by Etienne Boileau, a work in which the ancient statutes of the various trades were arranged and codified; and a third to the enactment made in the very year of this king's death, to guarantee the security of vendors, and, at the same time, to ensure purchasers against fraud. All these bear undoubted witness that an enlightened policy in favour of commerce had already sprung up.

Philippe le Bel issued several prohibitory enactments also in the interest of home commerce and local industry, which Louis X. confirmed. Philippe le Long attempted even to outdo the judicious efforts of Louis XI., and tried, though unsuccessfully, to establish a uniformity in the weights and measures throughout the kingdom; a reform, however, which was never accomplished until the revolution of 1789. It is difficult to credit how many different weights and measures were in use at that time, each one varying according to local custom or the choice of the lord of the soil, who probably in some way profited by the confusion which this uncertain state of things must have produced. The fraud and errors to which this led may easily be imagined, particularly in the intercourse between one part of the country and another. The feudal stamp is here thoroughly exhibited; as M. Charles de Grandmaison remarks, "Nothing is fixed, nothing is uniform, everything is special and arbitrary, settled by the lord of the soil by virtue of his right of *justesse*, by which he undertook the regulation and superintendence of the weights and measures in use in his lordship."

Measures of length and contents often differed much from one another, although they might be similarly named, and it would require very complicated comparative tables approximately to fix their value. The *pied de roi* was from ten to twelve inches, and was the least varying measure. The fathom differed much in different parts, and in the attempt to determine the relations between the innumerable measures of contents which we find recorded—a knowledge of which must have been necessary for the commerce of the period—we are stopped by a labyrinth of incomprehensible calculations, which it is impossible to determine with any degree of certainty.

The weights were more uniform and less uncertain. The pound was everywhere in use, but it was not everywhere of the same standard (Fig. 201). For instance, at Paris it weighed sixteen ounces, whereas at Lyons it only weighed fourteen; and in weighing silk fifteen ounces to the pound was the rule. At Toulouse and in Upper Languedoc the pound was only thirteen and a half ounces; at Marseilles, thirteen ounces; and at other places it even fell to twelve ounces. There was in Paris a public scale called *poids du roi*; but this scale, though a most important means of revenue, was a great hindrance to retail trade.

In spite of these petty and irritating impediments, the commerce of France extended throughout the whole world.

[Illustration: Fig. 197.—View of Lubeck and its Harbour (Sixteenth Century).—From a Copper–plate in the Work of P. Bertius, "Commentaria Rerum Germanicarum," in 4to: Amsterdam, 1616.]

The compass—known in Italy as early as the twelfth century, but little used until the fourteenth—enabled the mercantile navy to discover new routes, and it was thus that true maritime commerce may be said regularly to have begun. The sailors of the Mediterranean, with the help of this little instrument, dared to pass the Straits of Gibraltar, and to venture on the ocean. From that moment commercial intercourse, which had previously only existed by land, and that with great difficulty, was permanently established between the northern and southern harbours of Europe.

Flanders was the central port for merchant vessels, which arrived in great numbers from the Mediterranean, and Bruges became the principal depot. The Teutonic league, the origin of which dates from the thirteenth century, and which formed the most powerful confederacy recorded in history, also sent innumerable vessels from its harbours of Lubeck (Fig. 197) and Hamburg. These carried the merchandise of the northern countries into Flanders, and this rich province, which excelled in every branch of industry, and especially in those relating to metals and weaving, became the great market of Europe (Fig. 198).

The commercial movement, formerly limited to the shores of the Mediterranean, extended to all parts, and gradually became universal. The northern states shared in it, and England, which for a long time kept aloof from a stage on which it was destined to play the first part, began to give indications of its future commercial greatness. The number of transactions increased as the facility for carrying them on became greater. Consumption being extended, production progressively followed, and so commerce went on gaining strength as it widened its sphere. Everything, in fact, seemed to contribute to its expansion. The downfall of the feudal system and the establishment in each country of a central power, more or less strong and respected, enabled it to extend its operations by land with a degree of security hitherto unknown; and, at the same time, international legislation came in to protect maritime trade, which was still exposed to great dangers. The sea, which was open freely to the whole human race, gave robbers comparatively easy means of following their nefarious practices, and with less fear of punishment than they could obtain on the shore of civilised countries. For this reason piracy continued its depredations long after the enactment of severe laws for its suppression.

This maritime legislation did not wait for the sixteenth century to come into existence. Maritime law was promulgated more or less in the twelfth century, but the troubles and agitations which weakened and disorganized empires during that period of the Middle Ages, deprived it of its power and efficiency. The *Code des Rhodiens* dates as far back as 1167; the *Code de la Mer*, which became a sort of recognised text–book, dates from the same period; the *Lois d'Oleron* is anterior to the twelfth century, and ruled the western coasts of France, being also adopted in Flanders and in England; Venice dated her most ancient law on maritime rights from 1255, and the Statutes of Marseilles date from 1254.

177

[Illustration: Fig. 198.—Execution of the celebrated pirate Stoertebeck and his seventy accomplices, in 1402, at Hamburg.—From a popular Picture of the end of the Sixteenth Century (Hamburg Library).]

The period of the establishment of commercial law and justice corresponds with that of the introduction of national and universal codes of law and consular jurisdiction. These may be said to have originated in the sixth century in the laws of the Visigoths, which empowered foreign traders to be judged by delegates from their own countries. The Venetians had consuls in the Greek empire as early as the tenth century, and we may fairly presume that the French had consuls in Palestine during the reign of Charlemagne. In the thirteenth century the towns of Italy had consular agents in France; and Marseilles had them in Savoy, in Arles, and in Genoa. Thus traders of each country were always sure of finding justice, assistance, and protection in all the centres of European commerce.

Numerous facilities for barter were added to these advantages. Merchants, who at first travelled with their merchandise, and who afterwards merely sent a factor as their representative, finally consigned it to foreign agents. Communication by correspondence in this way became more general, and paper replaced parchment as being less rare and less expensive. The introduction of Arabic figures, which were more convenient than the Roman numerals for making calculations, the establishment of banks, of which the most ancient was in operation in Venice as early as the twelfth century, the invention of bills of exchange, attributed to the Jews, and generally in use in the thirteenth century, the establishment of insurance against the risks and perils of sea and land, and lastly, the formation of trading companies, or what are now called partnerships, all tended to give expansion and activity to commerce, whereby public and private wealth was increased in spite of obstacles which routine, envy, and ill–will persistently raised against great commercial enterprises.

For a long time the French, through indolence or antipathy—for it was more to their liking to be occupied with arms and chivalry than with matters of interest and profit—took but a feeble part in the trade which was carried on so successfully on their own territory. The nobles were ashamed to mix in commerce, considering it unworthy of them, and the bourgeois, for want of liberal feeling and expansiveness in their ideas, were satisfied with appropriating merely local trade. Foreign commerce, even of the most lucrative description, was handed over to foreigners, and especially to Jews, who were often banished from the kingdom and as frequently ransomed, though universally despised and hated. Notwithstanding this, they succeeded in rising to wealth under the stigma of shame and infamy, and the immense gains which they realised by means of usury reconciled them to, and consoled them for, the ill-treatment to which they were subjected.

[Illustration: Fig. 199.—Discovery of America, 12th of May, 1492.—Columbus erects the Cross and baptizes the Isle of Guanahani (now Cat Island, one of the Bahamas) by the Christian Name of St. Salvador.—From a Stamp engraved on Copper by Th. de Bry, in the Collection of "Grands Voyages," in folio, 1590.]

At a very early period, and especially when the Jews had been absolutely expelled, the advantage of exclusively trading with and securing the rich profits from France had attracted the Italians, who were frequently only Jews in disguise, concealing themselves as to their character under the generic name of Lombards. It was under this name that the French kings gave them on different occasions various privileges, when they frequented the fairs of Champagne and came to establish themselves in the inland and seaport towns. These Italians constituted the great corporation of money-changers in Paris, and hoarded in their coffers all the coin of the kingdom, and in this way caused a perpetual variation in the value of money, by which they themselves benefited.

In the sixteenth century the wars of Italy rather changed matters, and we find royal and important concessions increasing in favour of Castilians and other Spaniards, whom the people maliciously called *negroes*, and who had emigrated in order to engage in commerce and manufactures in Saintonge, Normandy, Burgundy, Agenois, and Languedoc.

About the time of Louis XI., the French, becoming more alive to their true interests, began to manage their own affairs, following the suggestions and advice of the King, whose democratic instincts prompted him to encourage and favour the bourgeois. This result was also attributable to the state of peace and security which then began to exist in the kingdom, impoverished and distracted as it had been by a hundred years of domestic and foreign warfare.

From 1365 to 1382 factories and warehouses were founded by Norman navigators on the western coast of Africa, in Senegal and Guinea. Numerous fleets of merchantmen, of

179

great size for those days, were employed in transporting cloth, grain of all kinds, knives, brandy, salt, and other merchandise, which were bartered for leather, ivory, gum, amber, and gold dust. Considerable profits were realised by the shipowners and merchants, who, like Jacques Coeur, employed ships for the purpose of carrying on these large and lucrative commercial operations. These facts sufficiently testify the condition of France at this period, and prove that this, like other branches of human industry, was arrested in its expansion by the political troubles which followed in the fourteenth and fifteenth centuries.

Fortunately these social troubles were not universal, and it was just at the period when France was struggling and had become exhausted and impoverished that the Portuguese extended their discoveries on the same coast of Africa, and soon after succeeded in rounding the Cape of Good Hope, and opening a new maritime road to India, a country which was always attractive from the commercial advantages which it offered.

Some years after, Christopher Columbus, the Genoese, more daring and more fortunate still, guided by the compass and impelled by his own genius, discovered a new continent, the fourth continent of the world (Fig. 199). This unexpected event, the greatest and most remarkable of the age, necessarily enlarged the field for produce as well as for consumption to an enormous extent, and naturally added, not only to the variety and quantity of exchangeable wares, but also to the production of the precious metals, and brought about a complete revolution in the laws of the whole civilised world.

Maritime commerce immediately acquired an extraordinary development, and merchants, forsaking the harbours of the Mediterranean, and even those of the Levant, which then seemed to them scarcely worthy of notice, sent their vessels by thousands upon the ocean in pursuit of the wonderful riches of the New World. The day of caravans and coasting had passed; Venice had lost its splendour; the sway of the Mediterranean was over; the commerce of the world was suddenly transferred from the active and industrious towns of that sea, which had so long monopolized it, to the Western nations, to the Portuguese and Spaniards first, and then to the Dutch and English.

France, absorbed in, and almost ruined by civil war, and above all by religious dissensions, only played a subordinate part in this commercial and pacific revolution, although it has been said that the sailors of Dieppe and Honfleur really discovered America before Columbus. Nevertheless the kings of France, Louis XII., Francis I., and

Henry II., tried to establish and encourage transatlantic voyages, and to create, in the interest of French commerce, colonies on the coasts of the New World, from Florida and Virginia to Canada.

But these colonies had but a precarious and transitory existence; fisheries alone succeeded, and French commerce continued insignificant, circumscribed, and domestic, notwithstanding the increasing requirements of luxury at court. This luxury contented itself with the use of the merchandise which arrived from the Low Countries, Spain, and Italy. National industry did all in its power to surmount this ignominious condition; she specially turned her attention to the manufacture of silks and of stuffs tissued with gold and silver. The only practical attempt of the government in the sixteenth century to protect commerce and manufactures was to forbid the import of foreign merchandise, and to endeavour to oppose the progress of luxury by rigid enactments.

Certainly the government of that time little understood the advantages which a country derived from commerce when it forbade the higher classes from engaging in mercantile pursuits under penalty of having their privileges of nobility withdrawn from them. In the face of the examples of Italy, Genoa, Venice, and especially of Florence, where the nobles were all traders or sons of traders, the kings of the line of Valois thought proper to make this enactment. The desire seemed to be to make the merchant class a separate class, stationary, and consisting exclusively of bourgeois, shut up in their counting–houses, and prevented in every way from participating in public life. The merchants became indignant at this banishment, and, in order to employ their leisure, they plunged with all their energy into the sanguinary struggles of Reform and of the League.

[Illustration: Fig. 200.—Medal to commemorate the Association of the Merchants of the City of Rouen.]

It was not until the reign of Henry IV. that they again confined themselves to their occupations as merchants, when Sully published the political suggestions of his master for renewing commercial prosperity. From this time a new era commenced in the commercial destiny of France. Commerce, fostered and protected by statesmen, sought to extend its operations with greater freedom and power. Companies were formed at Paris, Marseilles, Lyons, and Rouen to carry French merchandise all over the world, and the rules of the mercantile associations, in spite of the routine and jealousies which guided the trade corporations, became the code which afterwards regulated commerce (Fig. 200).

[Illustration: Fig. 201.—Standard Weight in Brass of the Fish–market at Mans: Sign of the Syren (End of the Sixteenth Century).]

Guilds and Trade Corporations.

Uncertain Origin of Corporations.—Ancient Industrial Associations.—The Germanic Guild.—Colleges.—Teutonic Associations.—The Paris Company for the Transit of Merchandise by Water.—Corporations properly so called.—Etienne Boileau's "Book of Trades," or the First Code of Regulations.—The Laws governing Trades.—Public and Private Organization of Trade Corporations and other Communities.—Energy of the Corporations.—Masters, Journeymen, Supernumeraries, and Apprentices.—Religious Festivals and Trade Societies.—Trade Unions.

Learned authorities have frequently discussed, without agreeing, on the question of the origin of the Corporations of the Middle Ages. It may be admitted, we think *a priori*, that associations of artisans were as ancient as the trades themselves. It may readily be imagined that the numerous members of the industrial classes, having to maintain and defend their common rights and common interests, would have sought to establish mutual fraternal associations among themselves. The deeper we dive into ancient history the clearer we perceive traces, more or less distinct, of these kinds of associations. To cite only two examples, which may serve to some extent as an historical parallel to the analogous institutions of the present day, we may mention the Roman *Colleges*, which were really leagues of artisans following the same calling; and the Scandinavian guilds, whose object was to assimilate the different branches of industry and trade, either of a city or of some particular district.

Indeed, brotherhoods amongst the labouring classes always existed under the German conquerors from the moment when Europe, so long divided into Roman provinces, shook off the yoke of subjection to Rome, although she still adhered to the laws and customs of the nation which had held her in subjection for so many generations. We can, however, only regard the few traces which remain of these brotherhoods as evidence of their having once existed, and not as indicative of their having been in a flourishing state. In the fifth century, the Hermit Ampelius, in his "Legends of the Saints," mentions *Consuls* or Chiefs of Locksmiths. The Corporation of Goldsmiths is spoken of as existing in the first dynasty of the French kings. Bakers are named collectively in 630 in the laws of Dagobert, which seems to show that they formed a sort of trade union at that remote period. We also see Charlemagne, in several of his statutes, taking steps in order that the number of persons engaged in providing food of different kinds should everywhere be adequate to provide for the necessities of consumption, which would tend to show a general organization of that most important branch of industry. In Lombardy colleges of artisans were established at an early period, and were, no doubt, on the model of the Roman ones. Ravenna, in 943, possessed a College of Fishermen; and ten years later the records of that town mention a *Chief of the Corporation of Traders*, and, in 1001, a *Chief of the Corporation of Butchers*. France at the same time kept up a remembrance of the institutions of Roman Gaul, and the ancient colleges of trades still formed associations and companies in Paris and in the larger towns. In 1061 King Philip I. granted certain privileges to Master Chandlers and Oilmen. The ancient customs of the butchers are mentioned as early as the time of Louis VII., 1162. The same king granted to the wife of Ives Laccobre and her heirs the collectorship of the dues which were payable by tanners, purse–makers, curriers, and shoemakers. Under Philip Augustus similar concessions became more frequent, and it is evident that at that time trade was beginning to take root and to require special and particular administration. This led to regulations being drawn up for each trade, to which Philip Augustus gave his sanction. In 1182 he confirmed the statutes of the butchers, and the furriers and drapers also obtained favourable concessions from him.

According to the learned Augustin Thierry, corporations, like civic communities, were engrafted on previously existing guilds, such as on the colleges or corporations of workmen, which were of Roman origin. In the *guild*, which signifies a banquet at common expense, there was a mutual assurance against misfortunes and injuries of all sorts, such as fire and shipwreck, and also against all lawsuits incurred for offences and crimes, even though they were proved against the accused. Each of these associations was placed under the patronage of a god or of a hero, and had its compulsory statutes; each had its chief or president chosen from among the members, and a common treasury supplied by annual contributions. Roman colleges, as we have already stated, were established with a more special purpose, and were more exclusively confined to the peculiar trade to which they belonged; but these, equally with the guilds, possessed a common exchequer, enjoyed equal rights and privileges, elected their own presidents, and celebrated in common their sacrifices, festivals, and banquets. We have, therefore, good reason for agreeing in the opinion of the celebrated historian, who considers that in the establishment of a corporation "the guild should be to a certain degree the motive power, and the Roman college, with its organization, the material which should be used to bring it into existence."

[Illustration: Fig. 202.—Craftsmen in the Fourteenth Century—Fac–simile of a Miniature of a Manuscript in the Library of Brussels.]

It is certain, however, that during several centuries corporations were either dissolved or hidden from public notice, for they almost entirely disappeared from the historic records during the partial return to barbarism, when the production of objects of daily necessity and the preparation of food were entrusted to slaves under the eye of their master. Not till the twelfth century did they again begin to flourish, and, as might be supposed, it was Italy which gave the signal for the resuscitation of the institutions whose birthplace had been Rome, and which barbarism had allowed to fall into decay. Brotherhoods of artisans were also founded at an early period in the north of Gaul, whence they rapidly spread beyond the Rhine. Under the Emperor Henry I., that is, during the tenth century, the ordinary condition of artisans in Germany was still serfdom; but two centuries later the greater number of trades in most of the large towns of the empire had congregated together in colleges or bodies under the name of unions (*Einnungen* or *Innungen*) (Fig. 202), as, for example, at Gozlar, at Wuerzburg, at Brunswick, &c. These colleges, however, were not established without much difficulty and without the energetic resistance of the ruling powers, inasmuch as they often raised their pretensions so high as to wish to substitute their authority for the senatorial law, and thus to grasp the government of the cities. The thirteenth century witnessed obstinate and sanguinary feuds between these two parties, each of which was alternately victorious. Whichever had the upper hand took advantage of the opportunity to carry out the most cruel reprisals against its defeated opponents. The Emperors Frederick II. and Henry VII. tried to put an end to these strifes by abolishing the corporations of workmen, but these powerful associations fearlessly opposed the imperial authority. In France the organization of communities of artisans, an organization which in many ways was connected with the commercial movement, but which must not be confounded with it, did not give rise to any political difficulty. It seems not even to have met with any opposition from the feudal powers, who no doubt found it an easy pretext for levying additional rates and taxes.

The most ancient of these corporations was the Parisian *Hanse*, or corporation of the bourgeois for canal navigation, which probably dates its origin back to the college of Parisian *Nautes*, existing before the Roman conquest. This mercantile association held its meetings in the island of Lutetia, on the very spot where the church of Notre–Dame was afterwards built. From the earliest days of monarchy tradesmen constituted entirely the bourgeois of the towns (Fig. 203). Above them were the nobility or clergy, beneath them the artisans. Hence we can understand how the bourgeois, who during the twelfth and thirteenth centuries were a distinct section of the community, became at last the important commercial body itself. The kings invariably treated them with favour. Louis VI. granted them new rights, Louis VII. confirmed their ancient privileges, and Philip Augustus increased them. The Parisian Hanse succeeded in monopolising all the commerce which was carried on by water on the Seine and the Yonne between Mantes and Auxerre. No merchandise coming up or down the stream in boats could be disembarked in the interior of Paris without becoming, as it were, the property of the corporation, which, through its agents, superintended its measurement and its sale in bulk, and, up to a certain point, its sale by retail. No foreign merchant was permitted to send his goods to Paris without first obtaining *lettres de Hanse*, whereby he had associated with him a bourgeois of the town, who acted as his guarantee, and who shared in his profits.

[Illustration: Fig. 203.—Merchants or Tradesmen of the Fourteenth Century.—Fac–simile of a Miniature in a Manuscript of the Library at Brussels.]

There were associations of the same kind in most of the commercial towns situated on the banks of rivers and on the sea–coast, as, for example, at Rouen, Arles, Marseilles, Narbonne, Toulouse, Ratisbon, Augsburg, and Utrecht. Sometimes neighbouring towns, such as the great manufacturing cities of Flanders, agreed together and entered into a leagued bond, which gave them greater power, and constituted an offensive and defensive compact (Fig. 204). A typical example of this last institution is that of the commercial association of the *Hanseatic Towns* of Germany, which were grouped together to the number of eighty around their four capitals, viz., Lubeck, Cologne, Dantzic, and Brunswick.

[Illustration: Fig. 204.—Seal of the United Trades of Ghent (End of the Fifteenth Century).]

Although, as we have already seen, previous to the thirteenth century many of the corporations of artisans had been authorised by several of the kings of France to make special laws whereby they might govern themselves, it was really only from the reign of St. Louis that the first general measures of administration and police relating to these communities can be dated. The King appointed Etienne Boileau, a rich bourgeois, provost of the capital in 1261, to set to work to establish order, wise administration, and "good faith" in the commerce of Paris. To this end he ascertained from the verbal testimony of the senior members of each corporation the customs and usages of the various crafts, which for the most part up to that time had not been committed to writing. He arranged and probably amended them in many ways, and thus composed the famous "Book of Trades," which, as M. Depping, the able editor of this valuable compilation, first published in 1837, says, "has the advantage of being to a great extent the genuine production of the corporations themselves, and not a list of rules established and framed by the municipal or judicial authorities." From that time corporations gradually introduced themselves into the order of society. The royal decrees in their favour were multiplied, and the regulations with regard to mechanical trades daily improved, not only in Paris and in the provinces, and also abroad, both in the south and in the north of Europe, especially in Italy, Germany, England, and the Low Countries (Figs. 205 to 213).

Etienne Boileau's "Book of Trades" contained the rules of one hundred different trade associations. It must be observed, however, that several of the most important trades, such as the butchers, tanners, glaziers, &c., were omitted, either because they neglected to be registered at the Chatelet, where the inquiry superintended by Boileau was made, or because some private interest induced them to keep aloof from this registration, which probably imposed some sort of fine and a tax upon them. In the following century the number of trade associations considerably increased, and wonderfully so during the reigns of the last of the Valois and the first of the Bourbons.

The historian of the antiquities of Paris, Henry Sauval, enumerated no fewer than fifteen hundred and fifty–one trade associations in the capital alone in the middle of the seventeenth century. It must be remarked, however, that the societies of artisans were much subdivided owing to the simple fact that each craft could only practise its own special work. Thus, in Boileau's book, we find four different corporations of *patenotriers*, or makers of chaplets, six of hatters, six of weavers, &c.

Besides these societies of artisans, there were in Paris a few privileged corporations, which occupied a more important position, and were known under the name of *Corps des Marchands*. Their number at first frequently varied, but finally it was settled at six, and they were termed *les Six Corps*. They comprised the drapers, which always took precedence of the five others, the grocers, the mercers, the furriers, the hatters, and the goldsmiths. These five for a long time disputed the question of precedence, and finally they decided the matter by lot, as they were not able to agree in any other way.

[Illustration: Fig. 205.—Seal of the Corporation of Carpenters of St. Trond (Belgium)—From an Impression preserved in the Archives of that Town (1481).]

[Illustration: Fig. 206.—Seal of the Corporation of Shoemakers of St. Trond, from a Map of 1481, preserved in the Archives of that Town.]

[Illustration: Fig. 207.—Seal of the Corporation of Wool–weavers of Hasselt (Belgium), from a Parchment Title–deed of June 25, 1574.]

[Illustration: Fig. 208.—Seal of the Corporation of Clothworkers of Bruges (1356).—From an Impression preserved in the Archives of that Town.]

[Illustration: Fig. 209.—Seal of the Corporation of Fullers of St. Trond (about 1350).—From an Impression preserved in the Archives of that Town.]

[Illustration: Fig. 210.—Seal of the Corporation of Joiners of Bruges (1356).—From an Impression preserved in the Archives of that Town.]

[Illustration: Fig. 211.—Token of the Corporation of Carpenters of Maestricht.]

[Illustration: Fig. 212.—Token of the Corporation of Carpenters of Antwerp.]

[Illustration: Fig. 213.—Funeral Token of the Corporation of Carpenters of Maestricht.]

Trades.

Fac–simile of Engravings on Wood, designed and engraved by J. Amman, in the Sixteenth Century.

[Illustration: Fig. 214.—Cloth-worker.]

[Illustration: Fig. 215.—Tailor.]

[Illustration: Fig. 216.—Hatter.]

[Illustration: Fig. 217.—Dyer.]

[Illustration: Fig. 218.—Druggist]

[Illustration: Fig. 219.—Barber]

[Illustration: Fig. 220.—Goldsmith]

[Illustration: Fig. 221.—Goldbeater]

[Illustration: Fig. 222.—Pin and Needle Maker.]

[Illustration: Fig. 223.—Clasp-maker.]

[Illustration: Fig. 224.—Wire-worker.]

[Illustration: Fig. 225.—Dice-maker.]

[Illustration: Fig. 226.—Sword-maker.]

[Illustration: Fig. 227.—Armourer.]

[Illustration: Fig. 228.—Spur-maker.]

[Illustration: Fig. 229.—Shoemaker.]

[Illustration: Fig. 230.—Basin-maker.]

[Illustration: Fig. 231.—Tinman.]

[Illustration: Fig. 232.—Coppersmith.]

[Illustration: Fig. 233.—Bell and Cannon Caster.]

Apart from the privilege which these six bodies of merchants exclusively enjoyed of being called upon to appear, though at their own expense, in the civic processions and at the public ceremonials, and to carry the canopy over the heads of kings, queens, or princes on their state entry into the capital (Fig. 234), it would be difficult to specify the nature of the privileges which were granted to them, and of which they were so jealous. It is clear, however, that these six bodies were imbued with a kind of aristocratic spirit which made them place trading much above handicraft in their own class, and set a high value on their calling as merchants. Thus contemporary historians tell us that any merchant who compromised the dignity of the company "fell into the class of the lower orders;" that mercers boasted of excluding from their body the upholsterers, "who were but artisans;" that hatters, who were admitted into the *Six Corps* to replace one of the other trades, became in consequence "merchants instead of artisans, which they had been up to that time."

Notwithstanding the statutes so carefully compiled and revised by Etienne Boileau and his successors, and in spite of the numerous arbitrary rules which the sovereigns, the magistrates, and the corporations themselves strenuously endeavoured to frame, order and unity were far from governing the commerce and industry of Paris during the Middle Ages, and what took place in Paris generally repeated itself elsewhere. Serious disputes continually arose between the authorities and those amenable to their jurisdiction, and between the various crafts themselves, notwithstanding the relation which they bore to each other from the similarity of their employments.

In fact in this, as in many other matters, social disorder often emanated from the powers whose duty it was in the first instance to have repressed it. Thus, at the time when Philip Augustus extended the boundaries of his capital so as to include the boroughs in it, which until then had been separated from the city, the lay and clerical lords, under whose feudal dominion those districts had hitherto been placed, naturally insisted upon preserving all their rights. So forcibly did they do this that the King was obliged to recognise their claims; and in several boroughs, including the Bourg l'Abbe, the Beau Bourg, the Bourg St. Germain, and the Bourg Auxerrois, &c., there were trade associations completely distinct from and independent of those of ancient Paris. If we simply limit our

189

examination to that of the condition of the trade associations which held their authority immediately from royalty, we still see that the causes of confusion were by no means trifling; for the majority of the high officers of the crown, acting as delegates of the royal authority, were always disputing amongst themselves the right of superintending, protecting, judging, punishing, and, above all, of exacting tribute from the members of the various trades. The King granted to various officers the privilege of arbitrarily disposing of the freedom of each trade for their own profit, and thereby gave them power over all the merchants and craftsmen who were officially connected with them, not only in Paris, but also throughout the whole kingdom. Thus the lord chamberlain had jurisdiction over the drapers, mercers, furriers, shoemakers, tailors, and other dealers in articles of wearing apparel; the barbers were governed by the king's varlet and barber; the head baker was governor over the bakers; and the head butler over the wine merchants.

[Illustration: Fig. 234.—Group of Goldsmiths preceding the *Chasse de St. Marcel* in the Reign of Louis XIII.—From a Copper–plate of the Period (Cabinet of Stamps in the National Library of Paris).]

These state officers granted freedoms to artisans, or, in other words, they gave them the right to exercise such and such a craft with assistants or companions, exacting for the performance of this trifling act a very considerable tax. And, as they preferred receiving their revenues without the annoyance of having direct communication with their humble subjects, they appointed deputies, who were authorised to collect them in their names.

The most celebrated of these deputies were the *rois des merciers*, who lived on the fat of the land in complete idleness, and who were surrounded by a mercantile court, which appeared in all its splendour at the trade festivals.

[Illustration: Fig. 235.—Banner of the Corporation of the United Boot and Shoe Makers of Issoudun.]

The great officers of the crown exercised in their own interests, and without a thought for the public advantage, a complete magisterial jurisdiction over all crafts; they adjudicated in disputes arising between masters and men, decided quarrels, visited, either personally or through their deputies, the houses of the merchants, in order to discover frauds or infractions in the rules of the trade, and levied fines accordingly. We must remember that the collectors of court dues had always to contend for the free exercise of their jurisdiction against the provost of Paris, who considered their acquisitions of authority as interfering with his personal prerogatives, and who therefore persistently opposed them on all occasions. For instance, if the head baker ordered an artisan of the same trade to be imprisoned in the Chatelet, the high provost, who was governor of the prison, released him immediately; and, in retaliation, if the high provost punished a baker, the chief baker warmly espoused his subordinate's cause. At other times the artisans, if they were dissatisfied with the deputy appointed by the great officer of the crown, whose dependents they were, would refuse to recognise his authority. In this way constant quarrels and interminable lawsuits occurred, and it is easy to understand the disorder which must have arisen from such a state of things. By degrees, however, and in consequence of the new tendencies of royalty, which were simply directed to the diminution of feudal power, the numerous jurisdictions relating to the various trades gradually returned to the hand of the municipal provostship; and this concentration of power had the best results, as well for the public good as for that of the corporations themselves.

Having examined into corporations collectively and also into their general administration, we will now turn to consider their internal organization. It was only after long and difficult struggles that these trade associations succeeded in taking a definite and established position; without, however, succeeding at any time in organizing themselves as one body on the same basis and with the same privileges. Therefore, in pointing out the influential character of these institutions generally, we must omit various matters specially connected with individual associations, which it would be impossible to mention in this brief sketch.

In the fourteenth century, the period when the communities of crafts were at the height of their development and power, no association of artisans could legally exist without a license either from the king, the lord, the prince, the abbot, the bailiff, or the mayor of the district in which it proposed to establish itself.

[Illustration: Fig. 236.—Banner of the Tilers of Paris, with the Armorial Bearings of the Corporation.]

[Illustration: Fig. 237.—Banner of the Nail-makers of Paris, with Armorial Bearings of the Corporation.]

[Illustration: Fig. 238.—Banner of the Harness–makers of Paris, with the Armorial Bearings of the Corporation.]

[Illustration: Fig. 239.—Banner of the Wheelwrights of Paris, with the Armoral Bearings of the Corporation.]

[Illustration: Fig. 240.—Banner of the Tanners of Vie, with the Patron Saint of the Corporation.]

[Illustration: Fig. 241.—Banner of the Weavers of Poulon, with the Patron Saint of the Corporation.]

These communities had their statutes and privileges; they were distinguished at public ceremonials by their *liveries* or special dress, as well as by their arms and banners (Figs. 235 to 241). They possessed the right freely to discuss their general interests, and at meetings composed of all their members they might modify their statutes, provided that such changes were confirmed by the King or by the authorities. It was also necessary that these meetings, at which the royal delegates were present, should be duly authorised; and, lastly, so as to render the communication between members more easy, and to facilitate everything which concerned the interests of the craft, artisans of the same trade usually resided in the same quarter of the town, and even in the same street. The names of many streets in Paris and other towns of France testify to this custom, which still partially exists in the towns of Germany and Italy.

[Illustration: Fig. 242.—Ceremonial Dress of an Elder and a Juror of the Corporation of Old Shoemakers of Ghent.]

The communities of artisans had, to a certain extent, the character and position of private individuals. They had the power in their corporate capacity of holding and administrating property, of defending or bringing actions at law, of accepting inheritances, &c.; they disbursed from a common treasury, which was supplied by legacies, donations, fines, and periodical subscriptions.

These communities exercised in addition, through their jurors, a magisterial authority, and even, under some circumstances, a criminal jurisdiction over their members. For a long time they strove to extend this last power or to keep it independent of municipal control and the supreme courts, by which it was curtailed to that of exercising a simple police authority strictly confined to persons or things relating to the craft. They carefully watched for any infractions of the rules of the trade. They acted as arbitrators between master and man, particularly in quarrels when the parties had had recourse to violence. The functions of this kind of domestic magistracy were exercised by officers known under various names, such as *kings, masters, elders, guards, syndics*, and *jurors*, who were besides charged to visit the workshops at any hour they pleased in order to see that the laws concerning the articles of workmanship were observed. They also received the taxes for the benefit of the association; and, lastly, they examined the apprentices and installed masters into their office (Fig. 242).

The jurors, or syndics, as they were more usually called, and whose number varied according to the importance of numerical force of the corporation, were generally elected by the majority of votes of their fellow–workmen, though sometimes the choice of these was entirely in the hands of the great officers of state. It was not unfrequent to find women amongst the dignitaries of the arts and crafts; and the professional tribunals, which decided every question relative to the community and its members, were often held by an equal number of masters and associate craftsmen. The jealous, exclusive, and inflexible spirit of caste, which in the Middle Ages is to be seen almost everywhere, formed one of the principal features of industrial associations. The admission of new members was surrounded with conditions calculated to restrict the number of associates and to discourage candidates. The sons of masters alone enjoyed hereditary privileges, in consequence of which they were always allowed to be admitted without being subjected to the tyrannical yoke of the association.

[Illustration: Martyrdom of SS. Crispin and Crepinien.

From a window in the Hopital des Quinze–Vingts (Fifteenth Century).]

Generally the members of a corporation were divided into three distinct classes—the masters, the paid assistants or companions, and the apprentices. Apprenticeship, from which the sons of masters were often exempted, began between the ages of twelve and seventeen years, and lasted from two to five years. In most of the trades the master could only receive one apprentice in his house besides his own son. Tanners, dyers, and goldsmiths were allowed one of their relatives in addition, or a second apprentice if they had no relation willing to learn their trade; and although some commoner trades, such as butchers and bakers, were allowed an unlimited number of apprentices, the custom of restriction had become a sort of general law, with the object of limiting the number of masters and workmen to the requirements of the public. The position of paid assistant or companion was required to be held in many trades for a certain length of time before promotion to mastership could be obtained.

[Illustration: Fig. 243.—Bootmaker's Apprentice working at a Trial—piece.—From a Window of the Thirteenth Century, published by Messrs. Cahier and Martin]

When apprentices or companions wished to become masters, they were called *aspirants*, and were subjected to successive examinations. They were particularly required to prove their ability by executing what was termed a *chef—d'oeuvre*, which consisted in fabricating a perfect specimen of whatever craft they practised. The execution of the *chef—d'oeuvre* gave rise to many technical formalities, which were at times most frivolous. The aspirant in certain cases had to pass a technical examination, as, for instance, the barber in forging and polishing lancets; the wool—weaver in making and adjusting the different parts of his loom; and during the period of executing the *chef—d'oeuvre,* which often extended over several months, the aspirant was deprived of all communication with his fellows. He had to work at the office of the association, which was called the *bureau,* under the eyes of the jurors or syndics, who, often after an angry debate, issued their judgment upon the merits of the work and the capability of the workman (Figs. 243 and 244).

[Illustration: Fig. 244.—Carpenter's Apprentice working at a Trial—piece.—From one of the Stalls called *Misericordes*, in Rouen Cathedral (Fifteenth Century).]

On his admission the aspirant had first to take again the oath of allegiance to the King before the provost or civil deputy, although he had already done so on commencing his apprenticeship. He then had to pay a duty or fee, which was divided between the sovereign or lord and the brotherhood, from which fee the sons of masters always obtained a considerable abatement. Often, too, the husbands of the daughters of masters were exempted from paying the duties. A few masters, such as the goldsmiths and the cloth—workers, had besides to pay a sum of money by way of guarantee, which remained in the funds of the craft as long as they carried on the trade. After these forms had been complied with, the masters acquired the exclusive privilege of freely exercising their profession. There were, however, certain exceptions to this rule, for a king on his coronation, a prince or princess of the royal blood at the time of his or her marriage, and, in certain towns, the bishop on his installation, had the right of creating one or more masters in each trade, and these received their licence without going through any of the usual formalities.

[Illustration: Fig. 245.—Staircase of the Office of the Goldsmiths of Rouen (Fifteenth Century). The Shield which the Lion holds with his Paw shows the Arms of the Goldsmiths of Rouen. (Present Condition).]

A widower or widow might generally continue the craft of the deceased wife or husband who had acquired the freedom, and which thus became the inheritance of the survivor. The condition, however, was that he or she did not contract a second marriage with any one who did not belong to the craft. Masters lost their rights directly they worked for any other master and received wages. Certain freedoms, too, were only available in the towns in which they had been obtained. In more than one craft, when a family holding the freedom became extinct, their premises and tools became the property of the corporation, subject to an indemnity payable to the next of kin.

[Illustration: Fig. 246.—Shops under Covered Market (Goldsmith, Dealer in Stuffs, and Shoemaker).—From a Miniature in Aristotle's "Ethics and Politics," translated by Nicholas Oresme (Manuscript of the Fifteenth Century, Library of Rouen).]

At times, and particularly in those trades where the aspirants were not required to produce a *chef–d'oeuvre*, the installation of masters was accompanied with extraordinary ceremonies, which no doubt originally possessed some symbolical meaning, but which, having lost their true signification, became singular, and appeared even ludicrous. Thus with the bakers, after four years' apprenticeship, the candidate on purchasing the freedom from the King, issued from his door, escorted by all the other bakers of the town, bearing a new pot filled with walnuts and wafers. On arriving before the chief of the corporation, he said to him, "Master, I have accomplished my four years; here is my pot filled with walnuts and wafers." The assistants in the ceremony having vouched for the truth of this statement, the candidate broke the pot against the wall, and the chief solemnly pronounced his admission, which was inaugurated by the older masters emptying a number of tankards of wine or beer at the expense of their new brother. The ceremony was also of a jovial character in the case of the millwrights, who only admitted the candidate after he had received a caning on the shoulders from the last–elected brother.

[Illustration: Fig. 247.—Fac–simile of the first six Lines on the Copper Tablet on which was engraved, from the year 1470, the Names and Titles of those who were elected Members of the Corporation of Goldsmiths of Ghent.]

The statutes of the corporations, which had the force of law on account of being approved and accepted by royal authority, almost always detailed with the greatest precision the conditions of labour. They fixed the hours and days for working, the size of the articles to be made, the quality of the stuffs used in their manufacture, and even the price at which they were to be sold (Fig. 246). Night labour was pretty generally forbidden, as likely to produce only imperfect work. We nevertheless find that carpenters were permitted to make coffins and other funeral articles by night. On the eve of religious feasts the shops were shut earlier than usual, that is to say, at three o'clock, and were not opened on the next day, with the exception of those of pastrycooks, whose assistance was especially required on feast days, and who sold curious varieties of cakes and sweetmeats. Notwithstanding the strictness of the rules and the administrative laws of each trade, which were intended to secure good faith and loyalty between the various members, it is unnecessary to state that they were frequently violated. The fines which were then imposed on delinquents constituted an important source of revenue, not only to the corporations themselves, but also to the town treasury. The penally, however, was not always a pecuniary one, for as late as the fifteenth century we have instances of artisans being condemned to death simply for having adulterated their articles of trade.

[Illustration: Fig. 248.—Elder and Jurors of the Tanners of the Town of Ghent in Ceremonial Dress.—Fac–simile of a Miniature in a Manuscript of the Fifteenth Century.]

This deception was looked upon as of the nature of robbery, which we know to have been for a long time punishable by death. Robbery on the part of merchants found no indulgence nor pardon in those days, and the whole corporation demanded immediate and exemplary justice.

According to the statutes, which generally tended to prevent frauds and falsifications, in most crafts the masters were bound to put their trade–mark on their goods, or some particular sign which was to be a guarantee for the purchaser and one means of identifying the culprit in the event of complaints arising on account of the bad quality or bad workmanship of the articles sold.

[Illustration: Fig. 249.—Companion Carpenter.—Fragment of a Woodcut of the Fifteenth Century, after a Drawing by Wohlgemueth for the "Chronique de Nuremberg."]

Besides taking various steps to maintain professional integrity, the framers of the various statutes, as a safeguard to the public interests, undertook also to inculcate morality and good feeling amongst their members. A youth could not be admitted unless he could prove his legitimacy of birth by his baptismal register; and, to obtain the freedom, he was bound to bear an irreproachable character. Artisans exposed themselves to a reprimand, and even to bodily chastisement, from the corporation, for even associating with, and certainly for working or drinking with those who had been expelled. Licentiousness and misconduct of any kind rendered them liable to be deprived of their mastership. In some trade associations all the members were bound to solemnize the day of the decease of a brother, to assist at his funeral, and to follow him to the grave. In another community the slightest indecent or discourteous word was punishable by a fine. A new master could not establish himself in the same street as his former master, except at a distance, which was determined by the statutes; and, further, no member was allowed to ask for or attract customers when the latter were nearer the shop of his neighbour than of his own.

In the Middle Ages religion placed its stamp on every occupation and calling, and corporations were careful to maintain this characteristic feature. Each was under the patronage of some saint, who was considered the special protector of the craft; each possessed a shrine or chapel in some church of the quarter where the trade was located, and some even kept chaplains at their own expense for the celebration of masses which were daily said for the souls of the good deceased members of the craft. These associations, animated by Christian charity, took upon them to invoke the blessings of heaven on all members of the fraternity, and to assist those who were either laid by through sickness or want of work, and to take care of the widows and to help the orphans of the less prosperous craftsmen. They also gave alms to the poor, and presented the broken meat left at their banquets to the hospitals.

Under the name of *garcons*, or *compagnons de devoir* (this surname was at first specially applied to carpenters and masons, who from a very ancient date formed an important association, which was partly secret, and from which Freemasonry traces its origin) (Fig. 250), the companions, notwithstanding that they belonged to the community of their own special craft, also formed distinct corporations among themselves with a view to mutual assistance. They made a point of visiting any foreign workman on his arrival in their town, supplied his first requirements, found him work, and, when work was wanting, the oldest companion gave up his place to him. These associations of companionship, however, soon failed to carry out the noble object for which they were instituted. After a time the meeting together of the fraternity was but a pretext for intemperance and debauchery, and at times their tumultuous processions and indecent masquerades occasioned much disorder in the cities. The facilities which these numerous associations possessed of extending and mutually co–operating with one another also led to coalitions among them for the purpose of securing any advantage which they desired to possess. Sometimes open violence was resorted to to obtain their exorbitant and unjust demands, which greatly excited the industrious classes, and eventually induced the authorities to interfere. Lastly, these brotherhoods gave rise to many violent quarrels, which ended in blows and too often in bloodshed, between workmen of the same craft, who took different views on debateable points. The decrees of parliament, the edicts of sovereigns, and the decisions of councils, as early as at the end of the fifteenth century and throughout the whole of the sixteenth, severely proscribed the doings of these brotherhoods, but these interdictions were never duly and rigidly enforced, and the authorities themselves often tolerated infractions of the law, and thus license was given to every kind of abuse.

[Illustration: Fig. 250.—Carpenters.—Fac–simile of a Miniature in the "Chroniques de Hainaut," Manuscript of the Fifteenth Century, in the Burgundy Library, Brussels.]

We have frequently mentioned in the course of this volume the political part played by the corporations during the Middle Ages. We know the active and important part taken by trades of all descriptions, in France in the great movement of the formation of communities. The spirit of fraternal association which constituted the strength of the corporations (Fig. 251), and which exhibited itself so conspicuously in every act of their public and private life, resisted during several centuries the individual and collective attacks made on it by craftsmen themselves. These rich and powerful corporations began to decline from the moment they ceased to be united, and they were dissolved by law at the beginning of the revolution of 1789, an act which necessarily dealt a heavy blow to industry and commerce.

[Illustration: Fig. 251.—Painting commemorative of the Union of the Merchants of Rouen at the End of the Seventeenth Century.]

[Illustration: Fig. 252.—Banner of the Drapers of Caen.]

Taxes, Money, and Finance.

Taxes under the Roman Rule.—Money Exactions of the Merovingian Kings.—Varieties of Money.—Financial Laws under Charlemagne.—Missi Dominici.—Increase of Taxes owing to the Crusades.—Organization of Finances by Louis IX.—Extortions of Philip le Bel.—Pecuniary Embarrassaient of his Successors.—Charles V. re−establishes Order in Finances.—Disasters of France under Charles VI., Charles VII., and Jacques Coeur.—Changes in Taxation from Louis XI. to Francis I.—The great Financiers.—Florimond Robertet.

If we believe Caesar's Commentaries on the Gallic War, the Gauls were groaning in his time under the pressure of taxation, and struggled hard to remove it. Rome lightened their burden; but the fiscal system of the metropolis imperceptibly took root in all the Roman provinces. There was an arbitrary personal tax, called the poll tax, and a land tax which was named *cens*, calculated according to the area of the holding. Besides these, there were taxes on articles of consumption, on salt, on the import and export of all articles of merchandise, on sales by auction; also on marriages, on burials, and on houses. There were also legacy and succession duties, and taxes on slaves, according to their number. Tolls on highways were also created; and the treasury went so far as to tax the hearth. Hence the origin of the name, *feu*, which was afterwards applied to each household or family group assembled in the same house or sitting before the same fire. A number of other taxes sprung up, called *sordides*, from which the nobility and the government functionaries were exempt.

This ruinous system of taxation, rendered still more insupportable by the exactions of the proconsuls, and the violence of their subordinates, went on increasing down to the time of the fall of the Roman Empire. The Middle Ages gave birth to a new order of things. The municipal administration, composed in great part of Gallo−Roman citizens, did not perceptibly deviate from the customs established for five centuries, but each invading nation by degrees introduced new habits and ideas into the countries they subdued. The Germans and Franks, having become masters of part of Gaul, established themselves on the lands which they had divided between them. The great domains, with their revenues which had belonged to the emperors, naturally became the property of the barbarian chiefs, and served to defray the expenses of their houses or their courts. These chiefs, at each general assembly of the *Leudes*, or great vassals, received presents of money, of arms, of horses, and of various objects of home or of foreign manufacture. For a long time these gifts were voluntary. The territorial fief, which was given to those soldiers who had deserved it by their military services, involved from the holders a personal service to the King. They had to attend him on his journeys, to follow him to war, and to defend him under all circumstances. The fief was entirely exempt from taxes. Many misdeeds—even robberies and other crimes, which were ordinarily punishable by death—were pardonable on payment of a proportionate fine, and oaths, in many cases, might be absolved in the same way. Thus a large revenue was received, which was generally divided equally between the State, the procurator fiscal, and the King.

[Illustration: Fig. 253.—The Extraction of Metals.—Fac-simile of a Woodcut in the "Cosmographie Universelle" of Munster, folio: Basle, 1552.]

War, which was almost constant in those turbulent times, furnished the barbarian kings with occasional resources, which were usually much more important than the ordinary supplies from taxation. The first chiefs of the Visigoths, the Ostrogoths, and the Franks, sought means of replenishing their treasuries by their victorious arms. Alaric, Totila, and Clovis thus amassed enormous wealth, without troubling themselves to place the government finances on a satisfactory basis. We see, however, a semblance of financial organization in the institutions of Alaric and his successors. Subsequently, the great Theodoric, who had studied the administrative theories of the Byzantine Court, exercised his genius in endeavouring to work out an accurate system of finance, which was adopted in Italy.

Gregory of Tours, a writer of the sixteenth century, relates in several passages of his "History of the Franks," that they exhibited the same repugnance to compulsory taxation as the Germans of the time of Tacitus. The *Leudes* considered that they owed nothing to the treasury, and to force them to submit to taxation was not an easy matter. About the year 465, Childeric I., father of Clovis, lost his crown for wishing all classes to submit to taxation equally. In 673, Childeric II., King of Austrasia, had one of these *Leudes*, named Bodillon, flogged with rods for daring to reproach him with the injustice of certain taxes. He, however, was afterwards assassinated by this same Bodillon, and the *Leudes* maintained their right of immunity. A century before the *Leudes* were already quarrelling with royalty on account of the taxes, which they refused to pay, and they sacrificed Queen Brunehaut because she attempted to enrich the treasury with the confiscated property of a few nobles who had rebelled against her authority. The wealth of the Frank kings, which was always very great, was a continual object of envy, and on one occasion Chilperic I., King of Soissons, having the *Leudes* in league with him, laid his hands on the wealth amassed by his father, Clotaire I., which was kept in the Palace of Braine. He was, nevertheless, obliged to share his spoil with his brothers and their followers, who came in arms to force him to refund what he had taken. Chilperic (Fig. 254) was so much in awe of these *Leudes* that he did not ask them for money. His wife, the much–feared Fredegonde, did not, however, exempt them more than Brunehaut had done; and her judges or ministers, Audon and Mummius, having met with an insurmountable resistance in endeavouring to force taxation on the nobles, nearly lost their lives in consequence.

[Illustration: Fig. 254.—Tomb of Chilperic.—Sculpture of the Eleventh Century, in the Abbey of St. Denis.]

The custom of numbering the population, such as was carried on in Rome through the censors, appears to have been observed under the Merovingian kings. At the request of the Bishop of Poitiers, Childebert gave orders to amend the census taken under Sigebert, King of Austrasia. It is a most curious document mentioned by Gregory of Tours. "The ancient division," he says, "had been one so unequal, owing to the subdivision of properties and other changes which time had made in the condition of the taxpayers, that the poor, the orphans, and the helpless classes generally alone bore the real burden of taxation." Florentius, comptroller of the King's household, and Romulfus, count of the palace, remedied this abuse. After a closer examination of the changes which had taken place, they relieved the taxpayers who were too heavily rated and placed the burden on those who could better afford it.

This direct taxation continued on this plan until the time of the kings of the second dynasty. The Franks, who had not the privilege of exemption, paid a poll tax and a house tax; about a tenth was charged on the produce of highly cultivated lands, a little more on that of lands of an inferior description, and a certain measure, a *cruche*, of wine on the produce of every half acre of vineyard. There were assessors and royal agents charged with levying such taxes and regulating the farming of them. In spite of this precaution, however, an edict of Clovis II., in the year 615, censures the mode of imposing rates and taxes; it orders that they shall only be levied in the places where they have been authorised, and forbade their being used under any pretext whatever for any other object than that for which they were imposed.

[Illustration: Fig. 255.—Signature of St. Eloy (Eligius), Financier and Minister to Dagobert I.; from the Charter of Foundation of the Abbey of Solignac (Mabillon, "Da Re Diplomatica").]

Under the Merovingians specie was not in common use, although the precious metals were abundant among the Gauls, as their mines of gold and silver were not yet exhausted. Money was rarely coined, except on great occasions, such as a coronation, the birth of an heir to the throne, the marriage of a prince, or the commemoration of a decisive victory. It is even probable that each time that money was used in large sums the pound or the *sou* of gold was represented more by ingots of metal than by stamped coin. The third of the *sou* of gold, which was coined on state occasions, seems to have been used only as a commemorative medal, to be distributed amongst the great officers of state, and this circumstance explains their extreme rarity. The general character of the coinage, whether of gold, silver, or of the baser metals, of the Burgundian, Austrasian, and Frank kings, differs little from what it had been at the time of the last of the Roman emperors, though the *Angel bearing the cross* gradually replaced the *Renommee victorieuse* formerly stamped on the coins. Christian monograms and symbols of the Trinity were often intermingled with the initials of the sovereign. It also became common to combine in a monogram letters thought to be sacred or lucky, such as C, M, S, T, &c.; also to introduce the names of places, which, perhaps, have since disappeared, as well as some particular mark or sign special to each mint. Some of these are very difficult to understand, and present a number of problems which have yet to be solved (Figs. 256 to 259). Unfortunately, the names of places on Merovingian coins to the number of about nine hundred, have rarely been studied by coin collectors, expert both as geographers and linguists. We find, for example, one hundred distinct mints, and, up to the present time, have not been able to determine where the greater number of them were situated.

[Illustration: Merovingian Gold Coins, Struck by St. Eloy, Moneyer to Dagobert I. (628–638).

Fig. 256.—Parisinna Ceve Fit.. Head of Dagobert with double diadem of pearls, hair hanging down the back of the neck. *Rev.*, Dagobertvs Rex. Cross; above, omega; under the arms of the cross, Eligi.

Fig. 257.—Parissin. Civ. Head of Clovis II., with diadem of pearls, hair braided and hanging down the back of the neck. *Rev.*, Chlodovevs Rex. Cross with anchor; under the arms of the cross, Eligi.

Fig. 258.—Parisivs Fit. Head of King. *Rev.*, Eligivs Mone. Cross; above, omega; under, a ball.

Fig. 259.—Mon. Palati. Head of King. *Rev.*, Scolare. I. A. Cross with anchor; under the arms of the cross, Eligi.]

From the time that Clovis became a Christian, he loaded the Church with favours, and it soon possessed considerable revenues, and enjoyed many valuable immunities. The sons of Clovis contested these privileges; but the Church resisted for a time, though she was eventually obliged to give way to the iron hand of Charles Martel. In 732 this great military chieftain, after his struggle with Rainfroy, and after his brilliant victories over the Saxons, the Bavarians, the Swiss, and the Saracens, stripped the clergy of their landed possessions, in order to distribute them amongst his *Leudes*, who by this means he secured as his creatures, and who were, therefore, ever willing and eager to serve him in arms.

On ascending the throne, King Pepin, who wanted to pacify the Church, endeavoured as far as possible to obliterate the recollection of the wrongs of which his father had been guilty towards her; he ordered the *dimes* and the *nones* (tenth and ninth denier levied on the value of lands) to be placed to the account of the possessors of each ecclesiastical domain, on their under–taking to repair the buildings (churches, chateaux, abbeys, and presbyteries), and to restore to the owners the properties on which they held mortgages. The nobles long resented this, and it required the authority and the example of Charlemagne to soothe the contending parties, and to make Church and State act in harmony.

Charlemagne renounced the arbitrary rights established by the Mayors of the Palace, and retained only those which long usage had legitimatised. He registered them clearly in a code called the *Capitulaires*, into which he introduced the ancient laws of the Ripuaires, the Burgundians, and the Franks, arranging them so as to suit the organization and requirements of his vast empire. From that time each freeman subscribed to the military service according to the amount of his possessions. The great vassal, or fiscal judge, was no longer allowed to practise extortion on those citizens appointed to defend the State. Freemen could legally refuse all servile or obligatory work imposed on them by the nobles, and the amount of labour to be performed by the serfs was lessened. Without absolutely abolishing the authority of local customs in matters of finance, or penalties which had been illegally exacted, they were suspended by laws decided at the *Champs de Mai*, by the Counts and by the *Leudes*, in presence of the Emperor. Arbitrary taxes were abolished, as they were no longer required. Food, and any articles of consumption, and military munitions, were exempted from taxation; and the revenues derived from tolls on road gates, on bridges, and on city gates, &c., were applied to the purposes for which they were imposed, namely, to the repair of the roads, the bridges, and the fortified enclosures. The *heriban*, a fine of sixty sols—which in those days would amount to more than 6,000 francs—was imposed on any holder of a fief who refused military service, and each noble was obliged to pay this for every one of his vassals who was absent when summoned to the King's banner. These fines must have produced considerable sums. A special law exempted ecclesiastics from bearing arms, and Charlemagne decreed that their possessions should be sacred and untouched, and everything was done to ensure the payment of the indemnity—*dime* and *none*—which was due to them.

[Illustration: Fig. 260.—Toll on Markets levied by a Cleric.—From one of the Painted Windows of the Cathedral of Tournay (Fifteenth Century).]

Charlemagne also superintended the coining and circulation of money. He directed that the silver sou should exactly contain the twenty–second part by weight of the pound. He also directed that money should only be coined in the Imperial palaces. He forbade the circulation of spurious coin; he ordered base coiners to be severely punished, and imposed heavy fines upon those who refused to accept the coin in legal circulation. The tithe due to the Church (Fig. 260), which was imposed at the National Assembly in 779, and disbursed by the diocesan bishops, gave rise to many complaints and much opposition. This tithe was in addition to that paid to the King, which was of itself sufficiently heavy. The right of claiming the two tithes, however, had a common origin, so that the sovereign defended his own rights in protecting those of the Church. This is set forth in the text of the *Capitulaires*, from the year 794 to 829. "What had originally been only a voluntary and pious offering of a few of the faithful," says the author of the "Histoire Financiere de la France," "became thus a perpetual tax upon agriculture, custom rather than law enforcing its payment; and a tithe which was at first limited to the produce of the soil, soon extended itself to cattle and other live stock."

Royal delegates (*missi dominici*), who were invested with complex functions, and with very extensive power, travelled through the empire exercising legal jurisdiction over all matters of importance. They assembled all the *placites*, or provincial authorities, and inquired particularly into the collection of the public revenue. During their tours, which took place four times a year, they either personally annulled unjust sentences, or submitted them to the Emperor. They denounced any irregularities on the part of the Counts, punished the negligences of their assessors, and often, in order to replace unworthy judges, they had to resort to a system of election of assessors, chosen from among the people. They verified the returns for the census; superintended the keeping up of the royal domains; corrected frauds in matters of taxation; and punished usurers as much as base coiners, for at that time money was not considered a commercial article, nor was it thought right that a money–lender should be allowed to carry on a trade which required a remuneration proportionate to the risk which he incurred.

[Illustration: Fig. 261.—Sale by Town–Crier. *Preco*, the Crier, blowing a trumpet; *Subhastator*, public officer charged with the sale. In the background is seen another sale, by the Bellman.—Fac–simile of a Woodcut in the Work of Josse Damhoudere, "Praxis Rerum Civilium," 4to: Antwerp, 1557.]

These *missi dominici* were too much hated by the great vassals to outlive the introduction of the feudal system. Their royal masters, as they themselves gradually lost a part of their own privileges and power, could not sustain the authority of these officers. Dukes, counts, and barons, having become magistrates, arbitrarily levied new taxes, imposed new fines, and appropriated the King's tributes to such an extent that, towards the end of the tenth century, the laws of Charlemagne had no longer any weight. We then find a number of new taxes levied for the benefit of the nobles, the very names of which have fallen into disuse with the feudal claims which they represented. Among these new taxes were those of *escorte* and *entree*, of *mortmain*, of *lods et ventes*, of *relief*, the *champarts*, the *taille*, the *fouage*, and the various fees for wine–pressing, grinding, baking, &c., all of which were payable without prejudice to the tithes due to the King and the Church. However, as the royal tithe was hardly ever paid, the kings were obliged to look to other means for replenishing their treasuries; and coining false money was a common practice. Unfortunately each great vassal vied with the kings in this, and to such an extent, that the enormous quantity of bad money coined during the ninth century completed the public ruin, and made this a sad period of social chaos. The freeman was no longer distinguishable from the villain, nor the villain from the serf. Serfdom was general; men

205

found themselves, as it were, slaves, in possession of land which they laboured at with the sweat of their brow, only to cultivate for the benefit of others. The towns even—with the exception of a few privileged cities, as Florence, Paris, Lyons, Rheims, Metz, Strasburg, Marseilles, Hamburg, Frankfort, and Milan—were under the dominion of some ecclesiastical or lay lord, and only enjoyed liberty of a more or less limited character.

Towards the end of the eleventh century, under Philip I., the enthusiasm for Crusades became general, and, as all the nobles joined in the holy mission of freeing the tomb of Jesus Christ from the hands of the infidels, large sums of money were required to defray the costs. New taxes were accordingly imposed; but, as these did not produce enough at once, large sums were raised by the sale of some of the feudal rights. Certain franchises were in this way sold by the nobles to the boroughs, towns, and abbeys, though, in not a few instances, these very privileges had been formerly plundered from the places to which they were now sold. Fines were exacted from any person declining to go to Palestine; and foreign merchants—especially the Jews—were required to subscribe large sums. A number of the nobles holding fiefs were reduced to the lowest expedients with a view to raising money, and even sold their estates at a low price, or mortgaged them to the very Jews whom they taxed so heavily. Every town in which the spirit of Gallo–Roman municipality was preserved took advantage of these circumstances to extend its liberties. Each monarch, too, found this a favourable opportunity to add new fiefs to the crown, and to recall as many great vassals as possible under his dominion. It was at this period that communities arose, and that the first charters of freedom which were obligatory and binding contracts between the King and the people, date their origin. Besides the annual fines due to the King and the feudal lords, and in addition to the general subsidies, such as the quit–rent and the tithes, these communities had to provide for the repair of the walls or ramparts, for the paving of the streets, the cleaning of the pits, the watch on the city gates, and the various expenses of local administration.

Louis le Gros endeavoured to make a re–arrangement of the taxes, and to establish them on a definite basis. By his orders a new register of the lands throughout the kingdom was commenced, but various calamities caused this useful measure to be suspended. In 1149, Louis le Jeune, in consequence of a disaster which had befallen the Crusaders, did what none of his predecessors had dared to attempt: he exacted from all his subjects a sol per pound on their income. This tax, which amounted to a twentieth part of income, was paid even by the Church, which, for example's sake, did not take advantage of its immunities.

Forty years later, at a council, or *great parliament*, called by Philip Augustus, a new crusade was decided upon; and, under the name of Saladin's tithe, an annual tax was imposed on all property, whether landed or personal, of all who did not take up the cross to go to the Holy Land. The nobility, however, so violently resisted this, that the King was obliged to substitute for it a general tax, which, although it was still more productive, was less offensive in its mode of collection.

On returning to France in 1191, Philip Augustus rated and taxed every one—nobility, bourgeois, and clergy—in order to prosecute the great wars in which he was engaged, and to provide for the first paid troops ever known in France. He began by confirming the enormous confiscations of the properties of the Jews, who had been banished from the kingdom, and afterwards sold a temporary permission to some of the richest of them to return.

The Jews at that time were the only possessors of available funds, as they were the only people who trafficked, and who lent money on interest. On this account the Government were glad to recall them, so as to have at hand a valuable resource which it could always make use of. As the King could not on his own authority levy taxes upon the vassals of feudal lords, on emergencies he convoked the barons, who discussed financial matters with the King, and, when the sum required was settled, an order of assessment was issued, and the barons undertook the collection of the taxes. The assessment was always fixed higher than was required for the King's wants, and the barons, having paid the King what was due to him, retained the surplus, which they divided amongst themselves.

The creation of a public revenue, raised by the contributions of all classes of society, with a definite sum to be kept in reserve, thus dates from the reign of Philip Augustus. The annual income of the State at that time amounted to 36,000 marks, or 72,000 pounds' weight of silver—about sixteen or seventeen million francs of present currency. The treasury, which was kept in the great tower of the temple (Fig. 262), was under the custody of seven bourgeois of Paris, and a king's clerk kept a register of receipts and disbursements. This treasury must have been well filled at the death of Philip Augustus, for that monarch's legacies were very considerable. One of his last wishes deserves to be mentioned: and this was a formal order, which he gave to Louis VIII., to employ a certain sum, left him for that purpose, solely and entirely for the defence of the kingdom.

[Illustration: Fig. 262.—The Tower of the Temple, in Paris.—From an Engraving of the Topography of Paris, in the Cabinet des Estampes, of the National Library.]

[Illustration: Gold Coins of the Sixth and Seventh Centuries.

Fig. 263.—Merovee, Son of Chilperic I.

Fig. 264.—Dagobert I.

Fig. 265.—Clotaire III.]

[Illustration: Silver Coins from the Eighth to the Eleventh Centures.

Fig 266.—Pepin the Short.

Fig. 267.—Charlemagne.

Fig. 268.—Henri I.]

[Illustration: Gold and Silver Coins of the Thirteenth Century.

Fig. 269.—Gold Florin of Louis IX.

Fig. 270.—Silver Gros of Tours.—Philip III.]

When Louis IX., in 1242, at Taillebourg and at Saintes, had defeated the great vassals who had rebelled against him, he hastened to regulate the taxes by means of a special code which bore the name of the *Etablissements*. The taxes thus imposed fell upon the whole population, and even lands belonging to the Church, houses which the nobles did not themselves occupy, rural properties and leased holdings, were all subjected to them. There were, however, two different kinds of rates, one called the *occupation* rate, and the other the rate of *exploitation*; and they were both collected according to a register, kept in the most regular and systematic manner possible. Ancient custom had maintained a tax exceptionally in the following cases: when a noble dubbed his son a knight, or gave his daughter in marriage, when he had to pay a ransom, and when he set out on a campaign against the enemies of the Church, or for the defence of the country. These taxes were

208

called *l'aide aux quatre cas*. At this period despotism too often overruled custom, and the good King Louis IX., by granting legal power to custom, tried to bring it back to the true principles of justice and humanity. He was, however, none the less jealous of his own personal privileges, especially as regarded coining (Figs. 263 to 270). He insisted that coining should be exclusively carried on in his palace, as in the times of the Carlovingian kings, and he required every coin to be made of a definite standard of weight, which he himself fixed. In this way he secured the exclusive control over the mint. For the various localities, towns, or counties directly under the crown, Louis IX. settled the mode of levying taxes. Men of integrity were elected by the vote of the General Assembly, consisting of the three orders—namely, of the nobility, the clergy, and the *tiers etat* —to assess the taxation of each individual; and these assessors themselves were taxed by four of their own number. The custom of levying proprietary subsidies in each small feudal jurisdiction could not be abolished, notwithstanding the King's desire to do so, owing to the power still held by the nobles. Nobles were forbidden to levy a rate under any consideration, without previously holding a meeting of the vassals and their tenants. The tolls on roads, bridges (Fig. 271), fairs, and markets, and the harbour dues were kept up, notwithstanding their obstruction to commerce, with the exception that free passage was given to corn passing from one province to another. The exemptions from taxes which had been dearly bought were removed; and the nobles were bound not to divert the revenue received from tolls for any purposes other than those for which they were legitimately intended. The nobles were also required to guard the roads "from sunrise to sunset," and they were made responsible for robberies committed upon travellers within their domains.

Louis IX., by refunding the value of goods which had been stolen through the carelessness of his officers, himself showed an example of the respect due to the law. Those charged with collecting the King's dues, as well as the mayors whose duty it was to take custody of the money contributed, and to receive the taxes on various articles of consumption, worked under the eye of officials appointed by the King, who exercised a financial jurisdiction which developed later into the department or office called the Chamber of Accounts. A tax, somewhat similar to the tithe on funds, was imposed for the benefit of the nobles on property held by corporations or under charter, in order to compensate the treasury for the loss of the succession duties. This tax represented about the fifth part of the value of the estate. To cover the enormous expenses of the two crusades, Louis IX., however, was obliged to levy two new taxes, called *decimes*, from his already overburdened people. It does not, however, appear that this excessive taxation alienated the affection of his subjects. Their minds were entirely taken up with the pilgrimages to the East, and the pious monarch, notwithstanding his fruitless sacrifices and his disastrous expeditions, earned for himself the title of *Prince of Peace and of Justice*.

[Illustration: Fig. 271.—Paying Toll on passing a Bridge.—From a Painted Window in the Cathedral of Tournay (Fifteenth Century).]

From the time of Louis IX. down to that of Philippe le Bel, who was the most extravagant of kings, and at the same time the most ingenious in raising funds for the State treasury, the financial movement of Europe took root, and eventually became centralised in Italy. In Florence was presented an example of the concentration of the most complete municipal privileges which a great flourishing city could desire. Pisa, Genoa, and Venice attracted a part of the European commerce towards the Adriatic and the Mediterranean. Everywhere the Jews and Lombards—already well initiated into the mysterious System of credit, and accustomed to lend money—started banks and pawn establishments, where jewels, diamonds, glittering arms, and paraphernalia of all kinds were deposited by princes and nobles as security for loans (Fig. 272).

[Illustration: Fig. 272.—View of the ancient Pont aux Changeurs.—From an Engraving of the Topography of Paris, in the Cabinet des Estampes, of the National Library.]

The tax collectors (*maltotiers*, a name derived from the Italian *mala tolta*, unjust tax), receivers, or farmers of taxes, paid dearly for exercising their calling, which was always a dishonourable one, and was at times exercised with a great amount of harshness and even of cruelty. The treasury required a certain number of *deniers, oboles*, or *pittes* (a small coin varying in value in each province) to be paid by these men for each bank operation they effected, and for every pound in value of merchandise they sold, for they and the Jews were permitted to carry on trades of all kinds without being subject to any kind of rates, taxes, work, military service, or municipal dues.

Philippe le Bel, owing to his interminable wars against the King of Castille, and against England, Germany, and Flanders, was frequently so embarrassed as to be obliged to resort to extraordinary subsidies in order to carry them on. In 1295, he called upon his subjects for a forced loan, and soon after he shamelessly required them to pay the one–hundredth part of their incomes, and after but a short interval he demanded another fiftieth part. The king assumed the exclusive right to debase the value of the coinage, which caused him to be commonly called the *base coiner*, and no sovereign ever coined a greater quantity of base money. He changed the standard or name of current coin with a view to counterbalance the mischief arising from the illicit coinage of the nobles, and especially to baffle the base traffic of the Jews and Lombards, who occasionally would obtain possession of a great part of the coin, and mutilate each piece before restoring it to circulation; in this way they upset the whole monetary economy of the realm, and secured immense profits to themselves (Figs. 273 to 278).

In 1303, the *aide au leur,* which was afterwards called the *aide de l'ost,* or the army tax, was invented by Philippe le Bel for raising an army without opening his purse. It was levied without distinction upon dukes, counts, barons, ladies, damsels, archbishops, bishops, abbots, chapters, colleges, and, in fact, upon all classes, whether noble or not. Nobles were bound to furnish one knight mounted, equipped, and in full armour, for every five hundred marks of land which they possessed; those who were not nobles had to furnish six foot–soldiers for every hundred households. By another enactment of this king the privilege was granted of paying money instead of complying with these demands for men, and a sum of 100 livres—about 10,000 francs of present currency—was exacted for each armed knight; and two sols—about ten francs per diem—for each soldier which any one failed to furnish. An outcry was raised throughout France at this proceeding, and rebellions broke out in several provinces: in Paris the mob destroyed the house of Stephen Barbette, master of the mint, and insulted the King in his palace. It was necessary to enforce the royal authority with vigour, and, after considerable difficulty, peace was at last restored, and Philip learned, though too late, that in matters of taxation the people should first be consulted. In 1313, for the first time, the bourgeoisie, syndics, or deputies of communities, under the name of *tiers etat*—third order of the state—were called to exercise the right of freely voting the assistance or subsidy which it pleased the King to ask of them. After this memorable occasion an edict was issued ordering a levy of six deniers in the pound on every sort of merchandise sold in the kingdom. Paris paid this without hesitation, whereas in the provinces there was much discontented murmuring. But the following year, the King having tried to raise the six deniers voted by the assembly of 1313 to twelve, the clergy, nobility, and *tiers etat* combined to resist the extortions of the government. Philippe le Bel died, after having yielded to the opposition of his indignant subjects, and in his last moments he recommended his son to exercise moderation in taxing and honesty in coining.

[Illustration: Gold Coins of the Fourteenth and Fifteenth Centuries.

Fig. 273.—Masse d'Or. Philip IV.

Fig. 274.—Small Aignel d'Or. Charles IV.

Fig. 275.—Large Aignel d'Or. John the Good.

Fig. 276.—Franc a Cheval d'Or. Charles V.

Fig. 277.—Ecu d'Or. Philip VI.

Fig. 278.—Salut d'Or. Charles VI.]

On the accession of Louis X., in 1315, war against the Flemish was imminent, although the royal treasury was absolutely empty. The King unfortunately, in spite of his father's advice, attempted systematically to tamper with the coinage, and he also commenced the exaction of fresh taxes, to the great exasperation of his subjects. He was obliged, through fear of a general rebellion, to do away with the tithe established for the support of the army, and to sacrifice the superintendent of finances, Enguerrand de Marigny, to the public indignation which was felt against him. This man, without being allowed to defend himself, was tried by an extraordinary commission of parliament for embezzling the public money, was condemned to death, and was hung on the gibbet of Montfaucon. Not daring to risk a convocation of the States–General of the kingdom, Louis X. ordered the seneschals to convoke the provincial assemblies, and thus obtained a few subsidies, which he promised to refund out of the revenues of his domains. The clergy even allowed themselves to be taxed, and closed their eyes to the misappropriation of the funds, which were supposed to be held in reserve for a new crusade. Taxes giving commercial franchise and of exchange were levied, which were paid by the Jews, Lombards, Tuscans, and other Italians; judiciary offices were sold by auction; the trading class purchased letters of nobility, as they had already done under Philippe le Bel; and, more than this, the enfranchisement of serfs, which had commenced in 1298, was continued on the payment of a tax, which varied according to the means of each individual. In consequence of this system, personal servitude was almost entirely abolished under Philippe de Long, brother of Louis X.

Each province, under the reign of this rapacious and necessitous monarch, demanded some concession from the crown, and almost always obtained it at a money value. Normandy and Burgundy, which were dreaded more than any other province on account of their turbulence, received remarkable concessions. The base coin was withdrawn from circulation, and Louis X. attempted to forbid the right of coinage to those who broke the wise laws of St. Louis. The idea of bills of exchange arose at this period.

Thanks to the peace concluded with Flanders, on which occasion that country paid into the hands of the sovereign thirty thousand florins in gold for arrears of taxes, and, above all, owing to the rules of economy and order, from which Philip V., surnamed the Long, never deviated, the attitude of France became completely altered. We find the King initiating reform by reducing the expenses of his household. He convened round his person a great council, which met monthly to examine and discuss matters of public interest; he allowed only one national treasury for the reception of the State revenues; he required the treasurers to make a half–yearly statement of their accounts, and a daily journal of receipts and disbursements; he forbad clerks of the treasury to make entries either of receipts or expenditure, however trifling, without the authority and supervision of accountants, whom he also compelled to assist at the checking of sums received or paid by the money–changers (Fig. 279). The farming of the crown lands, the King's taxes, the stamp registration, and the gaol duties were sold by auction, subject to certain regulations with regard to guarantee. The bailiffs and seneschals sent in their accounts to Paris annually, they were not allowed to absent themselves without the King's permission, and they were formally forbidden, under pain of confiscation, or even a severer penalty, to speculate with the public money. The operations of the treasury were at this period always involved in the greatest mystery.

[Illustration: Fig. 279.—Hotel of the Chamber of Accounts in the Courtyard of the Palace in Paris. From a Woodcut of the "Cosmographie Universelle" of Munster, in folio: Basle, 1552.]

[Illustration: Fig. 280.—Measuring Salt.—Fac–simile of a Woodcut of the "Ordonnances de la Prevoste des Marchands de Paris," in folio: 1500.]

[Illustration: Fig. 281.—Toll under the Bridges of Paris.—Fac–simile of a Woodcut of the "Ordonnances de la Prevoste des Marchands de Paris," in folio: 1500.]

The establishment of a central mint for the whole kingdom, the expulsion of the money–dealers, who were mostly of Italian origin, and the confiscation of their goods if it was discovered that they had acted falsely, signalised the accession of Charles le Bel in 1332. This beginning was welcomed as most auspicious, but before long the export duties, especially on grain, wine, hay, cattle, leather, and salt, became a source of legitimate complaint (Figs. 280 and 281).

Philip VI., surnamed *de Valois*, a more astute politician than his predecessor, felt the necessity of gaining the affections of the people by sparing their private fortunes. In order to establish the public revenue on a firm basis, he assembled, in 1330, the States–General, composed of barons, prelates, and deputies from the principal towns, and then, hoping to awe the financial agents, he authorised the arrest of the overseer, Pierre de Montigny, whose property was confiscated and sold, producing to the treasury the enormous sum of 1,200,000 livres, or upwards of 100,000,000 francs of present currency. The long and terrible war which the King was forced to carry on against the English, and which ended in the treaty of Bretigny in 1361, gave rise to the introduction of taxation of extreme severity. The dues on ecclesiastical properties were renewed and maintained for several years; all beverages sold in towns were taxed, and from four to six deniers in the pound were levied upon the value of all merchandise sold in any part of the kingdom. The salt tax, which Philippe le Bel had established, and which his successor, Louis X., immediately abolished at the unanimous wish of the people, was again levied by Philip VI., and this king, having caused the salt produced in his domains to be sold, "gave great offence to all classes of the community." It was on account of this that Edward III., King of England, facetiously called him the author of the *Salic* law. Philippe de Valois, when he first ascended the throne, coined his money according to the standard weight of St. Louis, but in a short time he more or less alloyed it. This he did secretly, in order to be able to withdraw the pieces of full weight from circulation and to replace them with others having less pure metal in them, and whose weight was made up by an extra amount of alloy. In this dishonest way a considerable sum was added to the coffers of the state.

King John, on succeeding his father in 1350, found the treasury empty and the resources of the kingdom exhausted. He was nevertheless obliged to provide means to continue the war against the English, who continually harassed the French on their own territory. The tax on merchandise not being sufficient for this war, the payment of public debts contracted by the government was suspended, and the State was thus obliged to admit its insolvency. The mint taxes, called *seigneuriage*, were pushed to the utmost limits, and the King levied them on the new coin, which he increased at will by largely alloying the gold with base metals. The duties on exported and imported goods were increased, notwithstanding the complaints that commerce was declining. These financial expedients would not have been tolerated by the people had not the King taken the precaution to have them approved by the States–General of the provincial states, which he annually assembled. In 1355 the States–General were convoked, and the King, who had to maintain thirty thousand soldiers, asked them to provide for this annual expenditure, estimated at 5,000,000 *livres parisis*, about 300,000,000 francs of present currency. The States–General, animated by a generous feeling of patriotism, "ordered a tax of eight deniers in the pound on the sale and transfer of all goods and articles of merchandise, with the exception of inheritances, which was to be payable by the vendors, of whatever rank they might be, whether ecclesiastics, nobles, or others, and also a salt tax to be levied throughout the whole kingdom of France." The King promised as long as this assistance lasted to levy no other subsidy and to coin good and sterling money—i.e., *deniers* of fine gold, *white*, or silver coin, coin of *billon*, or mixed metal, and *deniers* and *mailles* of copper. The assembly appointed travelling agents and three inspectors or superintendents, who had under them two receivers and a considerable number of sub–collectors, whose duties were defined with scrupulous minuteness. The King at this time renounced the right of seizin, his dues over property, inherited or conveyed by sale, exchange, gift, or will, his right of demanding war levies by proclamation, and of issuing forced loans, the despotic character of which offended everybody. The following year, the tax of eight deniers having been found insufficient and expensive in its collection, the assembly substituted for it a property and income tax, varying according to the property and income of each individual.

[Illustration: Fig. 282.—The Courtiers amassing Riches at the Expense of the Poor.—From a Miniature in the 'Tresor of Brunetto Latini, Manuscript of the Fourteenth Century, in the Library of the Arsenal, Paris.]

The finances were, notwithstanding these additions, in a low and unsatisfactory condition, which became worse and worse from the fatal day of Poitiers, when King John fell into the hands of the English. The States–General were summoned by the Dauphin, and, seeing the desperate condition in which the country was placed, all classes freely opened their purses. The nobility, who had already given their blood, gave the produce of all their feudal dues besides. The church paid a tenth and a half, and the bourgeois showed the most noble unselfishness, and rose as one man to find means to resist the common enemy. The ransom of the King had been fixed at three millions of *ecus d'or,* nearly a thousand million francs, payable in six years, and the peace of Bretigny was concluded by the cession of a third of the territory of France. There was, however, cause for congratulation in this result, for "France was reduced to its utmost extremity," says a chronicler, "and had not something led to a reaction, she must have perished irretrievably."

King John, grateful for the love and devotion shown to him by his subjects under these trying circumstances, returned from captivity with the solemn intention of lightening the burdens which pressed upon them, and in consequence be began by spontaneously reducing the enormous wages which the tax-gatherers had hitherto received, and by abolishing the tolls on highways. He also sold to the Jews, at a very high price, the right of remaining in the kingdom and of exercising any trade in it, and by this means he obtained a large sum of money. He solemnly promised never again to debase the coin, and he endeavoured to make an equitable division of the taxes. Unfortunately it was impossible to do without a public revenue, and it was necessary that the royal ransom should be paid off within six years. The people, from whom taxes might be always extorted at pleasure, paid a good share of this, for the fifth of the three millions of *ecus d'or* was realised from the tax on salt, the thirteenth part from the duty on the sale of fermented liquors, and twelve deniers per pound from the tax on the value of all provisions sold and resold within the kingdom. Commerce was subjected to a new tax called *imposition foraine*, a measure most detrimental to the trade and manufactures of the country, which were continually struggling under the pitiless oppression of the treasury. Royal despotism was not always able to shelter itself under the sanction of the general and provincial councils, and a few provinces, which forcibly protested against this excise duty, were treated on the same footing as foreign states with relation to the transit of merchandise from them. Other provinces compounded for this tax, and in this way, owing to the different arrangements in different places, a complicated system of exemptions and prohibitions existed which although most prejudicial to all industry, remained in force to a great extent until 1789.

When Charles V.—surnamed the Wise—ascended the throne in 1364, France, ruined by the disasters of the war, by the weight of taxation, by the reduction in her commerce, and by the want of internal security, exhibited everywhere a picture of misery and desolation; in addition to which, famine and various epidemics were constantly breaking out in various parts of the kingdom. Besides this, the country was incessantly overrun by gangs of plunderers, who called themselves *ecorcheurs, routiers, tardvenus*, &c., and who were more dreaded by the country people even than the English had been. Charles V., who was celebrated for his justice and for his economical and provident habits, was alone capable of establishing order in the midst of such general confusion. Supported by the vote of the Assembly held at Compiegne in 1367, he remitted a moiety of the salt tax and diminished the number of the treasury agents, reduced their wages, and curtailed their privileges. He inquired into all cases of embezzlement, so as to put a stop to fraud; and he insisted that the accounts of the public expenditure in its several departments should be annually audited. He protected commerce, facilitated exchanges, and reduced, as far as possible, the rates and taxes on woven articles and manufactured goods. He permitted Jews to hold funded property, and invited foreign merchants to trade with the country. For the first time he required all gold and silver articles to be stamped, and called in all the old gold and silver coins, in order that by a new and uniform issue the value of money might no longer be fictitious or variable. For more than a century coins had so often changed in name, value, and standard weight, that in an edict of King John we read, "It was difficult for a man when paying money in the ordinary course to know what he was about from one day to another."

The recommencement of hostilities between England and France in 1370 unfortunately interrupted the progressive and regular course of these financial improvements. The States–General, to whom the King was obliged to appeal for assistance in order to carry on the war, decided that salt should be taxed one sol per pound, wine by wholesale a thirteenth of its value, and by retail a fourth; that a *fouage*, or hearth tax, of six francs should be established in towns, and of two francs in the country,[*] and that a duty should be levied in walled towns on the entrance of all wine. The produce of the salt tax was devoted to the special use of the King. Each district farmed its excise and its salt tax, under the superintendence of clerks appointed by the King, who regulated the assessment and the fines, and who adjudicated in the first instance in all cases of dispute. Tax–gatherers were chosen by the inhabitants of each locality, but the chief officers of finance, four in number, were appointed by the King. This administrative organization, created on a sound basis, marked the establishment of a complete financial system. The Assembly, which thus transferred the administration of all matters of taxation from the people at large to the King, did not consist of a combination of the three estates, but simply of persons of position—namely, prelates, nobles, and bourgeois of Paris, in addition to the leading magistrates of the kingdom.

[Footnote *: This is the origin of the saying "smoke farthing."]

The following extract from the accounts of the 15th November, 1372, is interesting, inasmuch as it represents the actual budget of France under Charles V.:—

Article 18. Assigned for the payment of men at arms ...... 50,000 francs.
" 19. For payment of men at arms and crossbowmen
     newly formed .... 42,000 "
" " For sea purposes .... 8,000 "
" 20. For the King's palace .... 6,000 "
" " To place in the King's coffers............... 5,000 "
" 21. It pleases the King that the receiver–general
     should have monthly for matters that daily
     arise in the chamber .... 10,000 "
" " For the payment of debts .... 10,000 "

        Total .... 131,000 "

[Illustration: Settlement of Accounts by the Brothers of Cherite–Dieu of the Recovery of Roles

A miniature from the "*Livre des Comptes*" of the Society (Fifteenth Century).]

Thus, for the year, 131,000 francs in *ecus d'or* representing in present money about 12,000,000 francs, were appropriated to the expenses of the State, out of which the sum of 5,000 francs, equal to 275,000 francs of present money, was devoted to what we may call the *Civil List*.

On the death of Charles V., in 1380, his eldest son Charles, who was a minor, was put under the guardianship of his uncles, and one of these, the Duke d'Anjou, assumed the regency by force. He seized upon the royal treasury, which was concealed in the Castle of Melun, and also upon all the savings of the deceased king; and, instead of applying them to alleviate the general burden of taxation, he levied a duty for the first time on the common food of the people. Immediately there arose a general outcry of indignation, and a formidable expression of resistance was made in Paris and in the large towns. Mob orators loudly proclaimed the public rights thus trampled upon by the regent and the

King's uncles; the expression of the feelings of the masses began to take the shape of open revolt, when the council of the regency made an appearance of giving way, and the new taxes were suppressed, or, at all events, partially abandoned. The success of the insurrectionary movement, however, caused increased concessions to be demanded by the people. The Jews and tax−collectors were attacked. Some of the latter were hung or assassinated, and their registers torn up; and many of the former were ill−treated and banished, notwithstanding the price they had paid for living in the kingdom.

The assembly of the States, which was summoned by the King's uncles to meet in Paris, sided with the people, and, in consequence, the regent and his brother pretended to acknowledge the justice of the claims which were made upon them in the name of the people, and, on their withdrawing the taxes, order was for a time restored. No sooner, however, was this the case than, in spite of the solemn promises made by the council of regency, the taxes were suddenly reimposed, and the right of farming them was sold to persons who exacted them in the most brutal manner. A sanguinary revolt, called that of the *Maillotins*, burst forth in Paris; and the capital remained for some time in the power of the people, or rather of the bourgeois, who led the mob on to act for them (1381−1382). The towns of Rouen, Rheims, Troyes, Orleans, and Blois, many places in Beauvoise, in Champagne, and in Normandy, followed the example of the Parisians, and it is impossible to say to what a length the revolt would have reached had it not been for the victory over the Flemish at Rosebecque. This victory enabled the King's uncles to re−enter Paris in 1383, and to re−establish the royal authority, at the same time making the *Maillotins* and their accomplices pay dearly for their conduct. The excise duties, the hearth tax, the salt tax, and various other imposts which had been abolished or suspended, were re−established; the taxes on wine, beer, and other fermented liquors was lowered; bread was taxed twelve deniers per pound, and the duty on salt was fixed at the excessive rate of twenty francs in gold—about 1,200 francs of present money—per hogshead of sixty hundredweight. Certain concessions and compromises were made exceptionally in favour of Artois, Dauphine, Poitou, and Saintonge, in consideration of the voluntary contributions which those provinces had made.

[Illustration: Fig. 283.—Assassination of the Duke of Burgundy, John the Fearless, on the Bridge of Montereau, in 1419.—Fac−simile of a Miniature in the "Chronicles" of Monstrelet, Manuscript of the Fifteenth Century, in the Library of the Arsenal of Paris.]

Emboldened by the success of their exacting and arbitrary rule, the Dukes of Anjou, Burgundy, and Berry, under pretext of requiring money for war expenses, again increased the taxes from the year 1385 to 1388; and the salt tax was raised to forty golden francs, about 24,000 francs of present money, per hogshead. The ecclesiastics paid a half decime to the King, and several decimes to the Pope, but these did not prevent a forced loan being ordered. Happily, Charles VI. about this period attained his majority, and assumed his position as king; and his uncle, the Duke of Bourbon, who was called to the direction of affairs, re-established comparative order in financial matters; but soon after the King's brother, the Duke of Orleans, seized the reins of government, and, jointly with his sister-in-law, Isabel of Bavaria, increased the taxation far beyond that imposed by the Duke d'Anjou. The Duke of Burgundy, called John the Fearless, in order to gratify his personal hatred to his cousin, Louis of Orleans, made himself the instrument of the strong popular feeling by assassinating that prince as he was returning from an entertainment. The tragical death of the Duke of Orleans no more alleviated the ills of France than did that of the Duke of Burgundy sixteen years later—for he in his turn was the victim of a conspiracy, and was assassinated on the bridge of Montereau in the presence of the Dauphin (Fig. 283). The marriage of Isabel of France with the young king Richard of England, the ransom of the Christian prisoners in the East, the money required by the Emperor of Constantinople to stop the invasions of the Turks into Europe, the pay of the French army, which was now permanent, each necessarily required fresh subsidies, and money had to be raised in some way or other from the French people. Distress was at its height, and though the people were groaning under oppression, they continued to pay not only the increased taxes on provisions and merchandise, and an additional general tax, but to submit to the most outrageous confiscations and robbery of the public money from the public treasuries. The State Assemblies held at Auxerre and Paris in 1412 and 1413, denounced the extravagance and maladministration of the treasurers, the generals, the excisemen, the receivers of royal dues, and of all those who took part in the direction of the finances; though they nevertheless voted the taxes, and promulgated most severe regulations with respect to their collection. To meet emergencies, which were now becoming chronic, extraordinary taxes were established, the non-payment of which involved the immediate imprisonment of the defaulter; and the debasement of the coinage, and the alienation of certain parts of the kingdom, were authorised in the name of the King, who had been insane for more than fifteen years. The incessant revolts of the bourgeois, the reappearance of the English on the soil of France, the ambitious rivalry of Queen Isabel of Bavaria leagued with the Duke of Burgundy against the Dauphin, who had been made regent, at last, in 1420, brought about the humiliating treaty of Troyes, by which Henry V., king of England, was to become king of France on the death of Charles VI.

This treaty of Troyes became the cause of, and the pretext for, a vast amount of extortion being practised upon the unfortunate inhabitants of the conquered country. Henry V., who had already made several exactions from Normandy before he had obtained by force the throne of France, did not spare the other provinces, and, whilst proclaiming his good intentions towards his future subjects, he added a new general impost, in the shape of a forced loan, to the taxes which already weighed so heavily on the people. He also issued a new coinage, maintained many of the taxes, especially those on salt and on liquors, even after he had announced his intention of abolishing them.

At the same time the Dauphin Charles, surnamed *Roi de Bourges*, because he had retired with his court and retinue into the centre of the kingdom (1422), was sadly in want of money. He alienated the State revenues, he levied excise duties and subsidies in the provinces which remained faithful to his cause, and he borrowed largely from those members of the Church and the nobility who manifested a generous pity for the sad destiny of the King and the monarchy. Many persons, however, instead of sacrificing themselves for their king and country, made conditions with him, taking advantage of his position. The heir to the throne was obliged in many points to give way, either to a noble whose services he bargained for, or to a town or an abbey whose aid he sought. At times he bought over influential bodies, such as universities and other corporation, by granting exemptions from, or privileges in, matters of taxation, &c. So much was this the case that it may be said that Charles VII. treated by private contract for the recovery of the inheritances of his fathers. The towns of Paris and Rouen, as well as the provinces of Brittany, Languedoc, Normandy, and Guyenne, only returned to their allegiance to the King on conditions more or less advantageous to themselves. Burgundy, Picardy, and Flanders—which were removed from the kingdom of Charles VII. at the treaty of peace of Arras in 1435—cordially adopted the financial system inaugurated by the Duke of Burgundy, Philip the Good.

[Illustration: Fig. 284.—The House of Jacques Coeur at Bourges, now converted into the Hotel de Ville.]

Charles VII. reconquered his kingdom by a good and wise policy as much as by arms. He, doubtless, had cause to be thankful for the valeur and devotion of his officers, but he principally owed the success of his cause to one man, namely, his treasurer, the famous Jacques Coeur, who possessed the faculty of always supplying money to his master, and at the same time of enriching himself (Fig. 284). Thus it was that Charles VII., whose finances had been restored by the genius of Jacques Coeur, was at last able to re–enter his capital triumphantly, to emancipate Guyenne, Normandy, and the banks of the Loire from the English yoke, to reattach to the crown a portion of its former possessions, or to open the way for their early return, to remove bold usurpers from high places in the State, and to bring about a real alleviation of those evils which his subjects had so courageously borne. He suppressed the fraud and extortion carried on under the name of justice, put a stop to the sale of offices, abolished a number of rates illegally levied, required that the receivers' accounts should be sent in biennially, and whilst regulating the taxation, he devoted its proceeds entirely to the maintenance and pay of the army. From that time taxation, once feudal and arbitrary, became a fixed royal due, which was the surest means of preventing the pillage and the excesses of the soldiery to which the country people had been subjected for many years. Important triumphs of freedom were thus obtained over the tyrannical supremacy of the great vassals; but in the midst of all this improvement we cannot but regret that the assessors, who, from the time of their creation by St. Louis, had been elected by the towns or the corporations, now became the nominees of the crown.

[Illustration: Fig. 285.—*Amende honorable* of Jacques Coeur before Charles VII.—Fac–simile of a Miniature of the "Chroniques" of Monstrelet, Manuscript of the Fifteenth Century, in the National Library of Paris.]

Philip the Good, Duke of Burgundy, taxed his subjects but little: "Therefore," says Philippe de Commines, "they became very wealthy, and lived in much comfort." But Louis XI did not imitate him. His first care was to reinstate that great merchant, that clever financier, Jacques Coeur, to whom, as much as to Joan of Arc, the kingdom owed its freedom, and whom Charles VII., for the most contemptible reasons, had had the weakness to allow to be judicially condemned Louis XI. would have been very glad to entrust the care of his finances to another Jacques Coeur; for being sadly in want of money, he ran through his father's earnings, and, to refill his coffers, he increased taxation, imposed a duty on the importation of wines, and levied a tax on those holding offices, &c. A revolution broke out in consequence, which was only quenched in the blood of the insurgents. In this manner he continued, by force of arms, to increase and strengthen his own regal power at the expense of feudalism.

He soon found himself opposed by the *Ligue du Bien Public*, formed by the great vassals ostensibly to get rid of the pecuniary burden which oppressed the people, but really with the secret intention of restoring feudalism and lessening the King's power. He was not powerful enough openly to resist this, and appeared to give way by allowing the leagued nobles immense privileges, and himself consenting to the control of a sort of council of "thirty−six notables appointed to superintend matters of finance." Far from acknowledging himself vanquished, however, he immediately set to work to cause division among his enemies, so as to be able to overcome them. He accordingly showed favour towards the bourgeois, whom he had already flattered, by granting new privileges, and abolishing or reducing certain vexatious taxes of which they complained. The thirty−six notables appointed to control his financial management reformed nothing. They were timid and docile under the cunning eye of the King, and practically assisted him in his designs; for in a very few years the taxes were increased from 1,800,000 ecus—about 45,000,000 francs of present money—to 3,600,000 ecus—about 95,000,000 francs. Towards the end of the reign they exceeded 4,700,000 ecus—130,000,000 francs of present money. Louis XI. wasted nothing on luxury and pleasure; he lived parsimoniously, but he maintained 110,000 men under arms, and was ready to make the greatest sacrifices whenever there was a necessity for augmenting the territory of the kingdom, or for establishing national unity. At his death, on the 25th of August, 1483, he left a kingdom considerably increased in area, but financialty almost ruined.

When Anne de Beaujeu, eldest sister of the King, who was a minor, assumed the reins of government as regent, an immediate demand was made for reparation of the evils to which the finance ministers had subjected the unfortunate people. The treasurer−general Olivier le Dain, and the attorney−general Jean Doyat, were almost immediately sacrificed to popular resentment, six thousand Swiss were subsidised, the pensions granted during the previous reign were cancelled, and a fourth part of the taxes was removed. Public opinion being thus satisfied, the States−General assembled. The bourgeois here showed great practical good sense, especially in matters of finance; they proved clearly that the assessment was illegal, and that the accounts were fictitious, inasmuch as the latter only showed 1,650,000 livres of subsidies, whereas they amounted to three times as much. It was satisfactorily established that the excise, the salt tax, and the revenues of the public lands amply sufficed for the wants of the country and the crown. The young King Charles was only allowed 1,200,000 livres for his private purse for two years, and 300,000 livres for the expenses of the festivities of his coronation. On the Assembly being dissolved, the Queen Regent found ample means of pleasing the bourgeois and the people generally by breaking through the engagements she had entered into in the King's name, by remitting taxation, and finally by force of arms destroying the power of the last remaining vassals of the crown.

[Illustration: Fig. 286.—The Mint.—Fac–simile of a Woodcut in the Translation of the Latin Work of Francis Patricius, "De l'Institution et Administration de la Chose Politique:" folio, 1520.]

[Illustration: Fig. 287.—The receiver of Taxes.—Fac–simile of a Woodcut in Damhoudere's "Praxis Rerum Civilium."]

Charles VIII., during a reign of fourteen years, continued to waste the public money. His disastrous expedition for the conquest of the kingdom of Naples forced him to borrow at the rate of forty–two per cent. A short time previous to his death he acknowledged his errors, but continued to spend money, without consideration or restraint, in all kinds of extravagances, but especially in buildings. During his reign the annual expenditure almost invariably doubled the revenue. In 1492 it reached 7,300,000 francs, about 244,000,000 francs of present money. The deficit was made up each year by a general tax, "which was paid neither by the nobles nor the Church, but was obtained entirely from the people" (letters from the ambassadors of Venice).

When the Duke of Orleans ascended the throne as Louis XII., the people were again treated with some consideration. Having chosen George d'Amboise as premier and Florimond Robertet as first secretary of the treasury, he resolutely pursued a course of strict economy; he refused to demand of his subjects the usual tax for celebrating the joyous accession, the taxes fell by successive reductions to the sum of 2,600,000 livres, about 76,000,000 francs of present money, the salt tax was entirely abolished, and the question as to what should be the standard measure of this important article was legislated upon. The tax–gatherers were forced to reside in their respective districts, and to submit their registers to the royal commissioners before beginning to collect the tax. By strict discipline pillage by soldiers was put a stop to (Fig. 288).

Notwithstanding the resources obtained by the King through mortgaging a part of the royal domains, and in spite of the excellent administration of Robertet, who almost always managed to pay the public deficit without any additional tax, it was necessary in 1513, after several disastrous expeditions to Italy, to borrow, on the security of the royal domains, 400,000 livres, 10,000,000 francs of present money, and to raise from the excise and from other dues and taxes the sum of 3,300,000 livres, about 80,000,000 francs of present money. This caused the nation some distress, but it was only temporary, and was not much felt, for commerce, both domestic and foreign, much extended at the same time, and the sale of collectorships, of titles of nobility, of places in parliament, and of nominations to numerous judicial offices, brought in considerable sums to the treasury. The higher classes surnamed the king *Le Roitelet*, because he was sickly and of small stature, parsimonious and economical. The people called him their "father and master," and he has always been styled the father of the people ever since.

[Illustration: Fig. 288.—A Village pillaged by Soldiers.—Fac-simile of a Woodcut in Hamelmann's "Oldenburgisches Chronicon." in folio, 1599.]

In an administrative and financial point of view, the reign of Francis I. was not at all a period of revival or of progress. The commencement of a sounder System of finance is rather to be dated from that of Charles V.; and good financial organization is associated with the names of Jacques Coeur, Philip the Good, Charles XI., and Florimond Robertet. As an example of this, it may be stated that financiers of that time established taxes on registration of all kinds, also on stamps, and on sales, which did not before exist in France, and which were borrowed from the Roman emperors. We must also give them the credit of having first commenced a public debt, under the name of *rentes perpetuelles*, which at that time realised eight per cent. During this brilliant and yet disastrous reign the additional taxes were enormous, and the sale of offices produced such a large revenue that the post of parliamentary counsel realised the sum of 2,000 golden ecus, or nearly a million francs of present currency. It was necessary to obtain money at any price, and from any one who would lend it. The ecclesiastics, the nobility, the bourgeois, all gave up their plate and their jewels to furnish the mint, which continued to coin money of every description, and, in consequence of the discovery of America, and the working of the gold and silver mines in that country, the precious metals poured into the hands of the money-changers. The country, however, was none the more prosperous, and the people often were in want of even the commonest necessaries of life. The King and the court swallowed up everything, and consumed all the resources of the country on their luxury and their wars. The towns, the monasteries, and the corporations, were bound to furnish a certain number of troops, either infantry or cavalry. By the establishment of a lottery and a bank of deposit, by the monopoly of the mines and by the taxes on imports, exports, and manufactured articles, enormous sums were realised to the treasury, which, as it was being continually drained, required to be as continually replenished. Francis I. exhausted every source of credit by his luxury, his caprices, and his wars. Jean de Beaune, Baron de Semblancay, the old minister of finance, died a victim to false accusations of having misappropriated the public funds. Robertet, who was in office with him, and William Bochetel, who succeeded him, were more fortunate: they so managed the treasury business that, without meeting with any legal difficulty, they were enabled to centralise the responsibility in themselves instead of having it distributed over sixteen branches in all parts of the kingdom, a system which has continued to our day. In those days the office of superintendent of finance was usually only a short and rapid road to the gibbet of Montfaucon.

[Illustrations: Gold and Silver Coins of the Fifteenth and Sixteenth Centuries.

Fig. 289.—Royal d'Or. Charles VII Fig. 290.—Ecu d'Argent a la Couronne. Louis XI. Fig. 291.—Ecu d'Or a la Couronne. Charles VIII. Fig. 292.—Ecu d'Or au Porc–epic. Louis XII. Fig. 293.—Teston d'Argent. Francis I. Fig. 294.—Teston d'Argent au Croissant. Henry II.]

[Illustration: Fig. 295.—Silver Franc. Henry IV.]

Law and the Administration of Justice.

The Family the Origin of Government.—Origin of Supreme Power amongst the Franks.—The Legislation of Barbarism humanised by Christianity.—Right of Justice inherent to the Bight of Property.—The Laws under Charlemagne.—Judicial Forms.—Witnesses.—Duels, &c.— Organization of Royal Justice under St. Louis.—The Chatelet and the Provost of Paris.—Jurisdiction of Parliament, its Duties and its Responsibilities.—The Bailiwicks. Struggles between Parliament and the Chatelet.—Codification of the Customs and Usages.—Official Cupidity.—Comparison between the Parliament and the Chatelet.

Amongst the ancient Celtic and German population, before any Greek or Roman innovations had become engrafted on to their customs, everything, even political power as well as the rightful possession of lands, appears to have been dependent on families.

Julius Caesar, in his "Commentaries," tells us that "each year the magistrates and princes assigned portions of land to families as well as to associations of individuals having a common object whenever they thought proper, and to any extent they chose, though in the following year the same authorities compelled them to go and establish themselves elsewhere." We again find families (*familiae*) and associations of men (*cognationes hominum*) spoken of by Caesar, in the barbaric laws, and referred to in the histories of the Middle Ages under the names of *genealogiae, faramanni, farae*, &c.; but the extent of the relationship (*parentela*) included under the general appellation of *families* varied amongst the Franks, Lombards, Visigoths, and Bavarians. Generally, amongst all the people of German origin, the relationship only extended to the seventh degree; amongst the Celts it was determined merely by a common ancestry, with endless subdivisions of the tribe into distinct families. Amongst the Germans, from whom modern Europe has its origin, we find only three primary groups; namely, first, the family proper, comprising the father, mother, and children, and the collateral relatives of all degrees; secondly, the vassals (*ministeriales*) or servants of the free class; and, thirdly, the servants (*mansionarii, coloni, liti, servi*) of the servile class attached to the family proper (Fig. 296).

Domestic authority was represented by the *mund*, or head of the family, also called *rex* (the king), who exercised a special power over the persons and goods of his dependents, a guardianship, in fact, with certain rights and prerogatives, and a sort of civil and political responsibility attached to it. Thus the head of the family, who was responsible for his wife and for those of his children who lived with him, was also responsible for his slaves and domestic animals. To such a pitch did these primitive people carry their desire that justice should be done in all cases of infringement of the law, that the head was held legally responsible for any injury which might be done by the bow or the sword of any of his dependents, without it being necessary that he should himself have handled either of these weapons.

Long before the commencement of the Merovingian era, the family, whose sphere of action had at first been an isolated and individual one, became incorporated into one great national association, which held official meetings at stated periods on the *Malberg* (Parliament hill). These assemblies alone possessed supreme power in its full signification. The titles given to certain chiefs of *rex* (king), *dux* (duke), *graff* (count), *brenn* (general of the army), only defined the subdivisions of that power, and were applied, the last exclusively, to those engaged in war, and the others to those possessing judicial and administrative functions. The duty of dispensing justice was specially assigned to the counts, who had to ascertain the cause of quarrels between parties and to inflict penalties. There was a count in each district and in each important town; there were, besides, several counts attached to the sovereign, under the title of counts of the palace (*comites palatii*), an honourable position, which was much sought after and much coveted on account of its pecuniary and other contingent advantages. The counts of the palace deliberated with the sovereign on all matters and all questions of State, and at the same time they were his companions in hunting, feasting, and religious exercises; they acted as arbitrators in questions of inheritance of the crown; during the minority of princes they exercised the same authority as that which the constitution gave to sovereigns who were of full age; they confirmed the nominations of the principal functionaries and even those of the bishops; they gave their advice on the occasion of a proposed alliance between one nation and another, on matters connected with treaties of peace or of commerce, on military expeditions, or on exchanges of territory, as well as in reference to the marriage of a prince, and they incurred no responsibility beyond that naturally attached to persons in so distinguished a position among a semi—barbarous community. At first the legates (*legati*), and afterwards the King's ambassadors (*missi dominici*), the bishops and the dukes or commanders of the army were usually selected from the higher court officials, such as the counts of the palace, whereas the *ministeriales*, forming the second class of the royal officials, filled inferior though very honourable and lucrative posts of an administrative and magisterial character.

[Illustration: Fig. 296.—The Familles and the Barbarians.—Fac—simile of a Woodcut in the "Cosmographie Universelle" of Munster: in folio, Basle, 1552.]

Under the Merovingians the legal principle of power was closely bound up with the possession of landed property. The subdivision of that power, however, closely followed this union, and the constant ruin of some of the nobles rapidly increased the power of others, who absorbed to themselves the lost authority of their more unfortunate brethren, so much so that the Frank kings perceived that society would soon escape their rule unless they speedily found a remedy for this state of things. It was then that the *lois Salique* and *Ripuaire* appeared, which were subjected to successive revisions and gradual or sudden modifications, necessitated by political changes or by the increasing exigencies of the prelates and nobles. But, far from lessening the supremacy of the King, the national customs which were collected in a code extended the limits of the royal authority and facilitated its exercise.

In 596, Childebert, in concert with his *leudes*, decided that in future the crime of rape should be punished with death, and that the judge of the district (*pagus*) in which it had been committed should kill the ravisher, and leave his body on the public road. He also enacted that the homicide should have the same fate. "It is just," to quote the words of the law, "that he who knows how to kill should learn how to die." Robbery, attested by seven witnesses, also involved capital punishment, and a judge convicted of having let a noble escape, underwent the same punishment that would have been inflicted on the criminal. The punishment, however, differed according to the station of the delinquent. Thus, for the non–observance of Sunday, a Salian paid a fine of fifteen sols, a Roman seven and a half sols, a slave three sols, or "his back paid the penalty for him." At this early period some important changes in the barbaric code had been made: the sentence of death when once given had to be carried out, and no arrangements between the interested parties could avert it. A crime could no longer be condoned by the payment of money; robbery even, which was still leniently regarded at that time, and beyond the Rhine even honoured, was pitilessly punished by death. We therefore cannot have more striking testimony than this of the abridgment of the privileges of the Frankish aristocracy, and of the progress which the sovereign power was making towards absolute and uncontrolled authority over cases of life and death. By almost imperceptible steps Roman legislation became more humane and perfect, Christianity engrafted itself into barbarism, licentiousness was considered a crime, crime became an offence against the King and society, and it was in one sense by the King's hand that the criminals received punishment.

From the time of the baptism of Clovis, the Church had much to do with the re–arrangement of the penal code; for instance, marriage with a sister–in–law, a mother–in–law, an aunt, or a niece, was forbidden; the travelling shows, nocturnal dances, public orgies, formerly permitted at feasts, were forbidden as being profane. In the time of Clotaire, the prelates sat as members of the supreme council, which was strictly speaking the highest court of the land, having the power of reversing the decisions of the judges of the lower courts. It pronounced sentence in conjunction with the King, and from these decisions there was no appeal. The nation had no longer a voice in the election of the magistrates, for the assemblies of *Malberg* did not meet except on extraordinary occasions, and all government and judicial business was removed to the supreme and often capricious arbitration of the King and his council.

As long as the mayors of the palace of Austrasia, and of that of Burgundy, were only temporarily appointed, royal authority never wavered, and the sovereign remained supreme judge over his subjects. Suddenly, however, after the execution of Brunehaut, who was sacrificed to the hatred of the feudal lords, the mayoralty of the palace became a life appointment, and, in consequence, the person holding the office became possessed almost of supreme power, and the rightful sovereigns from that time practically became subject to the authority of the future usurpers of the crown. The edict of 615, to which the ecclesiastical and State nobility were parties, was in its laws and customs completely at variance with former edicts. In resuming their places in the French constitution, the Merovingian kings, who had been deprived both of influence and authority, were compelled by the Germanic institutions to return to the passive position which their predecessors had held in the forests of Germany, but they no longer had, like the latter, the prestige of military authority to enable them to keep the position of judges or arbitrators. The canons of the Council of Paris, which were confirmed by an edict of the King bearing date the 15th of the calends of November, 615, upset the political and legal system so firmly established in Europe since the fifth century. The royal power was shorn of some of its most valuable prerogatives, one of which was that of selecting the bishops; lay judges were forbidden to bring an ecclesiastic before the tribunals; and the treasury was prohibited from seizing intestate estates, with a view to increasing the rates and taxes; and it was decreed that Jews should not be employed in collecting the public taxes. By these canons the judges and other officers of State were made responsible, the benefices which had been withdrawn from the *leudes* were restored, the King was forbidden from granting written orders (*praecepta*) for carrying off rich widows, young virgins, and nuns; and the penalty of death was ordered to be enforced against those who disobeyed the canons of the council. Thence sprung two new species of legislation, one ecclesiastical, the other civil, between which royalty, more and more curtailed of its authority, was compelled for many centuries to struggle.

Amongst the Germanic nations the right of justice was inherent to landed property from the earliest times, and this right had reference to things as well as to persons. It was the patronage (*patrocinium*) of the proprietor, and this patronage eventually gave origin to feudal jurisdictions and to lordly and customary rights in each domain. We may infer from this that under the two first dynasties laws were made by individuals, and that each lord, so to speak, made his own.

The right of jurisdiction seems to have been so inherent to the right of property, that a landed proprietor could always put an end to feuds and personal quarrels, could temporarily bring any lawsuit to a close, and, by issuing his *ban*, stop the course of the law in his own immediate neighbourhood—at least, within a given circumference of his residence. This was often done during any family festival, or any civil or religious public ceremony. On these occasions, whoever infringed the *ban* of the master, was liable to be brought before his *court*, and to have to pay a fine. The lord who was too poor to create a court of sufficient power and importance obtained assistance from his lord paramount or relinquished the right of justice to him; whence originated the saying, "The fief is one thing, and justice another."

The law of the Visigoths speaks of nobles holding local courts, similar to those of the official judge, count, or bishop. King Dagobert required the public and the private judges to act together. In the law of Lombardy landlords are mentioned who, in virtue of the double title of nobles and judges, assumed the right of protecting fugitive slaves taking shelter in their domains. By an article of the Salie law, the noble is made to answer for his vassal before the court of the count. We must hence conclude that the landlord's judgment was exercised indiscriminately on the serfs, the colons, and the vassals, and a statute of 855 places under his authority even the freemen who resided with other persons.

From these various sources we discover a curious fact, which has hitherto remained unnoticed by historians—namely, that there existed an intermediate legislation between the official court of the count and his subordinates and the private courts, which was a kind of court of arbitration exercised by the neighbours (*vicini*) without the assistance of the judges of the county, and this was invested with a sort of authority which rendered its decisions binding.

[Illustration: Fig. 297.—The Emperor Charlemagne holding in one hand the Globe and in the other the Sword.—After a Miniature in the Registers of the University of Paris (Archives of the Minister of Public Instruction of the University). The Motto, *In scelus exurgo, sceleris discrimina purgo,* is written on a Scroll round the Sword.]

Private courts, however, were limited in their power. They were neither absolutely independent, nor supreme and without appeal. All conducted their business much in the same way as the high, middle, and lower courts of the Middle Ages; and above all these authorities towered the King's jurisdiction. The usurpation of ecclesiastical bishops and abbots—who, having become temporal lords, assumed a domestic jurisdiction—was curtailed by the authority of the counts, and they were even more obliged to give way before that of the *missi dominici*, or the official delegates of the monarch. Charles the Bald, notwithstanding his enormous concessions to feudalism and to the Church, never gave up his right of final appeal.

During the whole of the Merovingian epoch, the *mahl* (*mallus*), the general and regular assembly of the nation, was held in the month of March. Persons of every class met there clad in armour; political, commercial, and judicial interests were discussed under the presidency of the monarch; but this did not prevent other special assemblies of the King's court (*curia regalis*) being held on urgent occasions. This court formed a parliament (*parlamentum*), which at first was exclusively military, but from the time of Clovis was composed of Franks, Burgundians, Gallo–Romans, as well as of feudal lords and ecclesiastics. As, by degrees, the feudal System became organized, the convocation of national assemblies became more necessary, and the administration of justice more complicated. Charlemagne decided that two *mahls* should be held annually, one in the month of May, the other in the autumn, and, in addition, that in each county two annual *plaids* should meet independently of any special *mahls* and *plaids* which it should please him to convoke. In 788, the emperor found it necessary to call three general *plaids*, and, besides these, he was pleased to summon his great vassals, both clerical and lay, to the four principal feasts of the year. It may be asserted that the idea of royalty being the central authority in matters of common law dates from the reign of Charlemagne (Fig. 297).

The authority of royalty based on law took such deep root from that time forth, that it maintained itself erect, notwithstanding the weakness of the successors of the great Charles, and the repeated infractions of it by the Church and the great vassals of the crown (Fig. 298).

[Illustration: Fig. 298.—Carlovingian King in his Palace personifying Wisdom appealing to the whole Human Race.—After a Miniature in a Manuscript of the Ninth Century in the Burgundian Library of Brussels, from a Drawing by Count Horace de Vielcastel.]

The authoritative and responsible action of a tribunal which represented society (Fig. 299) thus took the place of the unchecked animosity of private feuds and family quarrels, which were often avenged by the use of the gibbet, a monument to be found erected at almost every corner. Not unfrequently, in those early times, the unchecked passions of a chief of a party would be the only reason for inflicting a penalty; often such a person would constitute himself sole judge, and, without the advice of any one, he would pass sentence, and even, with his own sword or any other available instrument, he would act as his own executioner. The tribunal thus formed denounced duelling, the pitiless warfare between man and man, and between family and family, and its first care was to protect, not each individual man's life, which was impossible in those days of blind barbarism, but at least his dwelling. Imperceptibly, the sanctuary of a man's house extended, first to towns of refuge, and then to certain public places, such as the church, the *mahlum*, or place of national assemblies, the market, the tavern, &c. It was next required that the accused, whether guilty or not, should remain unharmed from the time of the crime being committed until the day on which judgment was passed.

[Illustration: Fig. 299.—The Court of the Nobles.—Fac–simile of a Miniature in an old Poetical Romance of Chivalry, Manuscript of the Thirteenth Century, in the Library of the Arsenal of Paris.]

This right of revenge, besides being thus circumscribed as to locality, was also subject to certain rules as to time. Sunday and the principal feasts of the year, such as Advent, Christmas week, and from that time to the Epiphany, from the Ascension to the Day of Pentecost, certain vigils, &c., were all occasions upon which the right of revenge could not be exercised. "The power of the King," says a clever and learned writer, "partook to a certain degree of that of God and of the Saints; it was his province to calm human passions; by the moral power of his seal and his hand he extended peace over all the great lines of communication, through the forests, along the principal rivers, the highways and the byways, &c. The *Treve du Dieu* in 1035, was the logical application of these humane principles."

We must not suppose that justice in those days was dispensed without formalities, and that there were no regular intervals between the various steps to be gone through before final judgment was given, and in consequence of which some guarantee was afforded that the decisions arrived at were carefully considered. No one was tried without having been previously summoned to appear before the tribunal. Under the Carlovingians, as in previous times, the periods when judicial courts were held were regulated by the moon. Preference was given to the day on which it entered the first quarter, or during the full moon; the summonses were returnable by moons or quarter moons—that is, every seventh day. The summons was issued four times, after which, if the accused did not appear, he lost the right of counterplea, or was nonsuited. The Salic law allowed but two summonses before a count, which had to be issued at an interval of forty nights the one from the other. The third, which summoned the accused before the King, was issued fourteen nights later, and if he had not put in an appearance before sunset on the fourteenth day, he was placed *hors de sa parole*, his goods were confiscated, and he forfeited the privilege of any kind of refuge.

Among the Visigoths justice was equally absolute from the count to the tithe–gatherer. Each magistrate had his tribunal and his special jurisdiction. These judges called to their assistance assessors or colleagues, either *rachimbourgs*, who were selected from freemen; or provosts, or *echevins* (*scabini*), whose appointment was of an official and permanent character. The scabins created by Charlemagne were the first elected magistrates. They numbered seven for each bench. They alone prepared the cases and arranged as to the sentence. The count or his delegate alone presided at the tribunal, and pronounced the judgment. Every vassal enjoyed the right of appeal to the sovereign, who, with his court, alone decided the quarrels between ecclesiastics and nobles, and between private individuals who were specially under the royal protection. Criminal business was specially referred to the sovereign, the *missi*, or the Count Palatine. Final appeal lay with the Count Palatine in all cases in which the public peace was endangered, such as in revolts or in armed encounters.

As early as the time of the invasion, the Franks, Bavarians, and Visigoths, when investigating cases, began by an inquiry, and, previously to having recourse to trials before a judge, they examined witnesses on oath. Then, he who swore to the matter was believed, and acquitted accordingly. This system was no doubt flattering to human veracity, but, unfortunately, it gave rise to abuses; which it was thought would be avoided by calling the family and friends of the accused to take an oath, and it was then administered by requiring them to place their hands on the crucifix, on some relics, or on the consecrated Host. These witnesses, who were called *conjuratores*, came to attest before the judges not the fact itself, but the veracity of the person who invoked their testimony.

[Illustration: Fig. 300.—The Judicial Duel. The Plaintiff opening his Case before the Judge.—Fac–simile of a Miniature in the "Ceremonies des Gages des Batailles," Manuscript of the Fifteenth Century in the National Library of Paris.]

The number and respectability of the *conjuratores* varied according to the importance of the case in dispute. Gregory of Tours relates, that King Gontran being suspicious as to the legitimacy of the child who afterwards became Clotaire II., his mother, Fredegonde, called in the impartial testimony of certain nobles. These, to the number of three hundred, with three bishops at their head (*tribus episcopis et trecentis viris optimis*), swore, or, as we say, made an affidavit, and the queen was declared innocent.

The laws of the Burgundians and of the Anglians were more severe than those of the Germanic race, for they granted to the disputants trial by combat. After having employed the ordeal of red–hot iron, and of scalding water, the Franks adopted the judicial duel (Fig. 300). This was imposed first upon the disputing parties, then on the witnesses, and sometimes even on the judges themselves. Dating from the reign of the Emperor Otho the Great in 967, the judicial duel, which had been at first restricted to the most serious cases, was had recourse to in almost all suits that were brought before the courts. Neither women, old men, children, nor infirm persons were exempted. When a person could not himself fight he had to provide a champion, whose sole business was to take in hand the quarrels of others.

[Illustration: Fig. 301.—Judicial Duel.—Combat of a Knight with a Dog.—Fac–simile of a Miniature in the Romance of "Macaire," of the Thirteenth Century (Library of the Arsenal of Paris).]

Ecclesiastics were obliged, in the same maimer, to fight by deputy. The champion or substitute required, of course, to be paid beforehand. If the legend of the Dog of Montargis is to be believed, the judicial duel seems to have been resorted to even against an animal (Fig. 301).

In the twelfth century Europe was divided, so to speak, into two vast judicial zones: the one, Southern, Gallo–Roman, and Visigoth; the other, Northern and Western, half Germanic and half Scandinavian, Anglian, or Saxon. Christianity established common ties between these different legislations, and imperceptibly softened their native coarseness, although they retained the elements of their pagan and barbaric origin. Sentences were not as yet given in writing: they were entrusted to the memory of the judges who had issued them; and when a question or dispute arose between the interested parties as to the terms of the decision which had been pronounced, an inquiry was held, and the court issued a second decision, called a *recordatum*.

As long as the King's court was a movable one, the King carried about with him the original text of the law in rolls (*rotuli*). It was in consequence of the seizure of a number of these by the English, during the reign of Philip Augustus in 1194, that the idea was suggested of preserving the text of all the laws as state archives, and of opening authentic registers of decisions in civil and criminal cases. As early as the time of Charles the Bald, the inconvenience was felt of the high court of the count being movable from place to place, and having no special locality where instructions might be given as to modes of procedure, for the hearing of witnesses, and for keeping the accused in custody, &c. A former statute provided for this probable difficulty, but there seems to be no proof that previous to the twelfth century any fixed courts of justice had been established. The Kings, and likewise the counts, held courts in the open air at the entrance to the palace (Fig. 302), or in some other public place—under a large tree, for instance, as St. Louis did in the wood of Vincennes.

M. Desmaze, in his valuable researches on the history of the Parliament of Paris, says—"In 1191, Philip Augustus, before starting for Palestine, established bailiwicks, which held their assizes once a month; during their sitting they heard all those who had complaints to make, and gave summary judgment. The bailiff's assize was held at stated periods from time to time, and at a fixed place; it was composed of five judges, the King deciding the number and quality of the persons who were to take part in the deliberations of the court for each session. The royal court only sat when it pleased the King to order it; it accompanied the King wherever he went, so that it had no settled place of residence."

Louis IX. ordered that the courts of the nobles should be consolidated with the King's court, and succeeded in carrying out this reform. The bailiffs who were the direct delegates of the sovereign power, assumed an authority before which even the feudal lord was obliged to bend, because this authority was supported by the people, who were at that time organized in corporations, and these corporations were again bound together in communes. Under the bailiffs a system was developed, the principles of which more nearly resembled the Roman legislation than the right of custom, which it nevertheless respected, and the judicial trial by duel completely disappeared. Inquiries and appeals were much resorted to in all kinds of proceedings, and Louis IX. succeeded in controlling the power of ecclesiastical courts, which had been much abused in reference to excommunication. He also suppressed the arbitrary and ruinous confiscations which the nobles had unjustly made on their vassals.

[Illustration: Fig. 302.—The Palace as it was in the Sixteenth Century.—After an Engraving of that Period, National Library of Paris (Cabinet des Estampes).]

The edict of 1276 very clearly established the jurisdiction of parliaments and bailiwicks; it defined the important duties of the bailiffs, and at the same time specified the mode in which proceedings should be taken; it also regulated the duties of counsel, *maitres des requetes*, auditors, and advocates.

To the bailiwicks already in existence Louis IX. added the four great assizes of Vermandois, of Sens, of Saint-Pierre-le-Moustier, and of Macon, "to act as courts of final appeal from the judgment of the nobles." Philippe le Bel went still further, for, in 1287, he invited "all those who possess temporal authority in the kingdom of France to appoint, for the purpose of exercising civil jurisdiction, a bailiff, a provost, and some serjeants, who were to be laymen, and not ecclesiastics, and if there should be ecclesiastics in the said offices, to remove them." He ordered, besides, that all those who had cases pending before the court of the King and the secular judges of the kingdom should be furnished with lay attorneys; though the chapters, as well as the abbeys and convents, were allowed to be represented by canons. M. Desmaze adds, "This really amounted to excluding ecclesiastics from judicial offices, not only from the courts of the King, but also from those of the nobles, and from every place in which any temporal jurisdiction existed."

At the time of his accession, Hugh Capet was Count of Paris, and as such was invested with judicial powers, which he resigned in 987, on the understanding that his county of Paris, after the decease of the male heirs of his brother Eudes, should return to the crown. In 1032, a new magistrate was created, called the Provost of Paris, whose duty it was to give assistance to the bourgeois in arresting persons for debt. This functionary combined in his own person the financial and political chief of the capital, he was also the head of the nobility of the county, he was independent of the governor, and was placed above the bailiffs and seneschals. He was the senior of the urban magistracy and police, leader of the municipal troops, and, in a word, the prefect (*praefectus urbis*), as he was called under the Emperor Aurelian, or the first magistrate of Lutetia, as he was still called under Clotaire in 663. Assessors were associated with the provost, and together they formed a tribunal, which was afterwards known as the Chatelet (Fig. 303), because they assembled in that fortress, the building of which is attributed to Julius Caesar. The functions of this tribunal did not differ much from those of the royal *chatellenies:* its jurisdiction embraced quarrels between individuals, assaults, revolts, disputes between the universities and the students, and improper conduct generally (*ribaudailles*), in consequence of which the provost acquired the popular surname of *Roi des Ribauds*. At first his judgment was final, but very soon those under his jurisdiction were allowed to appeal to Parliament, and that court was obliged to have certain cases sent back for judgment from the Chatelet. This was, however, done only in a few very important instances, notwithstanding frequent appeals being made to its supreme arbitration.

[Illustration: Fig. 303.—The Great Chatelet of Paris.—Principal Front opposite the Pont–au–Change.—Fac–simile of an Engraving on Copper by Merian, in the "Topographia Galliae" of Zeller.]

In addition to the courts of the counts and bailiffs established in certain of the large towns, aldermanic or magisterial courts existed, which rather resembled the Chatelet of Paris. Thus the *capiloulat* of Toulouse, the senior alderman of Metz, and the burgomaster of Strasburg and Brussels, possessed in each of these towns a tribunal, which judged without appeal, and united the several functions of a civil, criminal, and simple police court. Several places in the north of France had provosts who held courts whose duties were various, but who were principally charged with the maintenance of public order, and with suppressing disputes and conflicts arising from the privileges granted to the trade corporations, whose importance, especially in Flanders, had much increased since the twelfth century.

"On his return from abroad, Louis IX. took his seat upon the bench, and administered justice, by the side of the good provost of Paris." This provost was no other than the learned Estienne Boileau, out of respect to whom the provostship was declared a *charge de magistrature*. The increase of business which fell to the provost's office, especially after the boundaries of Paris were extended by Philip Augustus, caused him to be released from the duty of collecting the public taxes. He was authorised to furnish himself with competent assistants, who were employed with matters of minor detail, and he was allowed the assistance of *juges auditeurs*. "We order that they shall be eight in number," says an edict of Philippe le Bel, of February, 1324, "four of them being ecclesiastics and four laymen, and that they shall assemble at the Chatelet two days in the week, to take into consideration the suits and causes in concert with our provost...." In 1343, the provost's court was composed of one King's attorney, one civil commissioner, two King's counsel, eight councillors, and one criminal commissioner, whose sittings took place daily at the Chatelet.

From the year 1340 this tribunal had to adjudicate in reference to all the affairs of the university, and from the 6th of October, 1380, to all those of the salt–fish market, which were no less numerous, so that its importance increased considerably. Unfortunately, numerous abuses were introduced into this municipal jurisdiction. In 1313 and 1320, the officers of the Chatelet were suspended, on account of the extortions which they were guilty of, and the King ordered an inquiry to be made into the matter. The provost and two councillors of the Parliament sat upon it, and Philip de Valois, adopting its decisions, prescribed fresh statutes, which were naturally framed in such a way as to show the distrust in which the Chatelet was then held. To these the officers of the Chatelet promised on oath to submit. The ignorance and immorality of the lay officers, who had been substituted for the clerical, caused much disturbance. Parliament authorised two of its principal members to examine the officers of the Chatelet. Twenty years later, on the receipt of fresh complaints, Parliament decided that three qualified councillors, chosen from its own body, should proceed with the King's attorney to the Chatelet, so as to reform the abuses and informalities of that court.

[Illustration: Fig. 304.—The King's Court, or Grand Council.—Fac–simile of a Miniature in the "Chroniques" of Froissart, Manuscript of the Fifteenth Century (formerly in the possession of Charles V), in the Library of the Arsenal, Paris.]

In the time of Philippe le Bel there existed in reality but one Parliament, and that was the *King's Court*. Its action was at once political, administrative, financial, and judicial, and was necessarily, therefore, of a most complicated character. Philippe le Bel made it exclusively a judicial court, defined the territorial limit of its power, and gave it as a judicial body privileges tending to strengthen its independence and to raise its dignity. He assigned political functions to the Great Council (*Conseil d'Etat*); financial matters to the chamber of accounts; and the hearing of cases of heresy, wills, legacies, and dowries to the prelates. But in opposition to the wise edict of 1295, he determined that Jews should be excluded from Parliament, and prelates from the palace of justice; by which latter proceeding he was depriving justice of the abilities of the most worthy representatives of the Gallican Church. But Philippe le Bel and his successors, while incessantly quarrelling either with the aristocracy or with the clergy, wanted the great judicial bodies which issued the edicts, and the urban or municipal magistrates—which, being subject to re–election, were principally recruited from among the bourgeois—to be a common centre of opposition to any attempt at usurpation of power, whether on the part of the Church, the nobility, or the crown.

The Great Days of Troyes (*dies magni Trecenses*), the assizes of the ancient counts of Champagne, and the exchequer of Normandy, were also organized by Philipe le Bel; and, further, he authorised the maintenance of a Parliament at Toulouse, a court which he solemnly opened in person on the 10th of January, 1302. In times of war the Parliament of Paris sat once a year, in times of peace twice. There were, according to circumstances, during the year two, three, or four sittings of the exchequer of Normandy, and two of the Great Days of Troyes, tribunals which were annexed to the Parliament of Paris, and generally presided over by one of its delegates, and sometimes even by the supreme head of that high court. At the King's council (Fig. 304) it was decided whether a case should be reserved for the Parliament of Paris, or passed on either to the exchequer or to the Great Days of Troyes.

As that advanced reformer, Philippe le Bel, died before the institutions he had established had taken root, for many years, even down to the time of Louis XI., a continual conflict for supremacy was waged between the Parliament of Paris and the various courts of the kingdom—between the counts and the Parliament, and between the latter and the King, which, without lessening the dignity of the crown, gradually tended to increase the influence which the judges possessed. Immediately on the accession of Louis le Hutin, in 1314, a reaction commenced—the higher clergy re-entered Parliament; but Philippe le Long took care that the laity should be in a majority, and did not allow that in his council of State the titled councillors should be more numerous than the lawyers. The latter succeeded in completely carrying the day on account of the services they rendered, and the influence which their knowledge of the laws of the country gave them. As for centuries the sword had ruled the gown, so, since the emancipation of the bourgeois, the lawyers had become masters of the administrative and judicial world; and, notwithstanding the fact that they were still kept in a somewhat inferior position to the peers and barons, their opinion alone predominated, and their decision frequently at once settled the most important questions.

An edict issued at Val Notre-Dame on the 11th of March, 1344, increased the number of members of Parliament, which from that time consisted of three presidents, fifteen clerical councillors, fifteen lay councillors, twenty-four clergymen and sixteen laymen of the Court of Inquiry, and five clergymen and sixteen laymen of the Court of Petitions.

The King filled up the vacant seats on the recommendation of the Chancellor and of the Parliament. The reporters were enjoined to write the decisions and sentences which were given by the court "in large letters, and far apart, so that they might be more easily read." The duties of police in the courts, the keeping of the doors, and the internal arrangements generally for those attending the courts and the Parliament, were entrusted to the ushers, "who divided among themselves the gratuities which were given them by virtue of their office." Before an advocate was admitted to plead he was required to take oath and to be inscribed on the register.

The Parliament as then established was somewhat similar in its character to that of the old national representative government under the Germans and Franks. For centuries it protected the King against the undue interference of the spiritual power, it defended the people against despotism, but it often lacked independence and political wisdom, and it was not always remarkable for its correct appreciation of men and things. This tribunal, although supreme over all public affairs, sometimes wavered before the threats of a minister or of a court favourite, succumbed to the influence of intrigues, and adapted itself to the prejudices of the times. We see it, in moments of error and of blindness, both condemning eminent statesmen and leading citizens, such as Jacques Coeur and Robertet, and handing over to the executioner distinguished men of learning and science in advance of the times in which they lived, because they were falsely accused of witchcraft, and also doing the same towards unfortunate maniacs who fancied they had dealings with the devil.

[Illustration: Fig. 305.—Trial of the Constable de Bourbon before the Peers of France (1523).—From an Engraving in "La Monarchie Francoise" of Montfaucon.]

In the fourteenth and fifteenth centuries all the members of Parliament formed part of the council of State, which was divided into the Smaller Council and the Greater Council. The Greater Council only assembled in cases of urgency and for extraordinary and very important purposes, the Smaller Council assembled every month, and its decisions were registered. From this arose the custom of making a similar registration in Parliament, confirming the decisions after they had been formally arrived at. The most ancient edict placed on the register of the Parliament of Paris dates from the year 1334, and is of a very important character. It concerns a question of royal authority, and decides that in spiritual matters the right of supremacy does not belong more to the Pope than to the King. Consequently Philippe de Valois ordered "his friends and vassals who shall attend the next Parliament and the keepers of the accounts, that for the perpetual record of so memorable a decision, it shall be registered in the Chambers of Parliament and kept for reference in the Treasury of the Charters." From that time "cases of complaint and other matters relating to benefices have no longer been discussed before the ecclesiastical judges, but before Parliament or some other secular court."

During the captivity of King John in England, royal authority having considerably declined, the powers of Parliament and other bodies of the magistracy so increased, that under Charles VI. the Parliament of Paris was bold enough to assert that a royal edict should not become law until it had been registered in Parliament. This bold and certainly novel proceeding the kings nevertheless did not altogether oppose, as they foresaw that the time would come when it might afford them the means of repudiating a treaty extorted from them under difficult circumstances (Fig. 306).

The close connection which existed between the various Parliaments and their political functions—for they had occasion incessantly to interfere between the acts of the government and the respective pretensions of the provinces or of the three orders—naturally increased the importance of this supreme magistracy. More than once the kings had cause to repent having rendered it so powerful, and this was the case especially with the Parliament of Paris. In this difficulty it is interesting to note how the kings acted. They imperceptibly curtailed the various powers of the other courts of justice, they circumscribed the power of the Parliament of Paris, and proportionately enlarged the jurisdiction of the great bailiwicks, as also that of the Chatelet. The provost of Paris was an auxiliary as well as a support to the royal power, which nevertheless held him in its grasp. The Chatelet was also a centre of action and of strength, which counteracted in certain cases parliamentary opposition. Thence arose the most implacable rivalries and dissensions between these various parties.

[Illustration: Fig. 306.—Promulgation of an Edict.—Fac-simile of a Miniature in "Anciennetes des Juifs," (French Translation from Josephus), Manuscript of the Fifteenth Century, executed for the Duke of Burgundy (Library of the Arsenal of Paris.)]

It is curious to notice with what ingenuity and how readily Parliament took advantage of the most trifling circumstances or of charges based upon the very slightest grounds to summon the officers of the Chatelet before its bar on suspicion of prevarication or of outrages against religion, morals, or the laws. Often were these officers and the provost himself summoned to appear and make *amende honourable* before the assembly, notwithstanding which they retained their offices. More than once an officer of the Chatelet was condemned to death and executed, but the King always annulled that part of the sentence which had reference to the confiscation of the goods of the condemned, thus proving that in reality the condemnation had been unjust, although for grave reasons the royal authority had been unable to save the victim from the avenging power of Parliament. Hugues Aubriot, the provost, was thus condemned to imprisonment for life on the most trivial grounds, and he would have undergone capital punishment if Charles V. had abandoned him at the time of his trial. During the English occupation, in the disastrous reign of Charles VI., the Chatelet of Paris, which took part with the people, gave proof of extraordinary energy and of great force of character. The blood of many of its members was shed on the scaffold, and this circumstance must ever remain a reproach to the judges and to those who executed their cruel sentences, and a lasting crown of glory to the martyrs themselves.

An edict of King John, issued after his return from London in 1363, a short time before his death, clearly defined the duties of Parliament. They were to try cases which concerned peers of France, and such prelates, chapters, barons, corporations, and councils as had the privilege of appealing to the supreme court; and to hear cases relating to estates, and appeals from the provost of Paris, the bailiffs, seneschals, and other judges (Fig. 307). It disregarded minor matters, but took cognizance of all judicial debates which concerned religion, the King, or the State. We must remark here that advocates were only allowed to speak twice in the same cause, and that they were subjected to fine, or at least to remonstrance, if they were tedious or indulged in needless repetition in their replies, and especially if they did not keep carefully to the facts of the case. After pleading they were permitted to give a summary in writing of "the principal points of importance as well as their clients' grounds of defence." Charles V. confirmed these orders and regulations with respect to advocates, and added others which were no less important, among which we find a provision for giving "legal assistance to poor and destitute persons who go to law." These regulations of Charles also limited the time in which officers of justice were to get through their business under a certain penalty; they also proclaimed that the King should no longer hear minor causes, and that, whatever might be the rules of the court, they forbad the presidents from deferring their judgment or from retarding the regular course of justice. Charles VI., before he became insane, contributed no less than his father to the establishment on a better footing of the supreme court of the kingdom, as well as that of the Chatelet and the bailiwicks.

243

Manners, Custom and Dress During the Middle

[Illustration: Fig. 307.—Bailiwick.—Fac–simile of a Woodcut in the "Cosmographie Universelle" of Munster: in folio, Basle, 1552.]

In the fifteenth century, the Parliament of Paris was so organized as not to require material change till 1789. There were noble, clerical, and lay councillors, honorary members, and *maitres de requete*, only four of whom sat; a first president, who was supreme head of the Parliament, a master of the great chamber of pleas, and three presidents of the chamber, all of whom were nominated for life. There were fifteen masters (*maistres*) or clerical councillors, and fifteen who were laymen, and these were annually approved by the King on the opening of the session. An attorney–general, several advocates–general, and deputies, who formed a committee or college, constituted the active part of this court, round which were grouped consulting advocates (*consiliarii*), pleading advocates (*proponentes*), advocates who were mere listeners (*audientes*), ushers and serjeants, whose chief, on his appointment, became a member of the nobility.

The official costume of the first president resembled that of the ancient barons and knights. He wore a scarlet gown lined with ermine, and a black silk cap ornamented with tassels. In winter he wore a scarlet mantle lined with ermine over his gown, on which his crest was worked on a shield. This mantle was fastened to the left shoulder by three gold cords, in order to leave the sword–side free, because the ancient knights and barons always sat in court wearing their swords. Amongst the archives of the mayoralty of London, we find in the "account of the entry of Henry V., King of England, into Paris" (on the 1st of December, 1420), that "the first president was in royal dress (*estoit en habit roial*), the first usher preceding him, and wearing a fur cap; the church dignitaries wore blue robes and hoods, and all the others in the procession scarlet robes and hoods." This imposing dress, in perfect harmony with the dignity of the office of those who wore them, degenerated towards the fifteenth century. So much was this the case, that an order of Francis I. forbad the judges from wearing pink "slashed hose" or other "rakish garments."

In the early times of monarchy, the judicial functions were performed gratuitously; but it was the custom to give presents to the judges, consisting of sweetmeats, spices, sugar–plums, and preserves, until at a subsequent period, 1498, when, as the judges "preferred money to sweetmeats," says the Chancellor Etienne Pasquier, the money value of the spices, &c., was fixed by law and made compulsory. In the bills of expenses preserved among the national archives, we find that the first president of the Parliament of Paris received a thousand *livres parisis* annually, representing upwards of one hundred thousand francs at the present rate of money; the three presidents of the chamber five hundred livres, equal to fifty thousand francs; and the other nobles of the said Parliament five *sols parisis*, or six sols three deniers—about twenty–five francs—per day for the days only on which they sat. They received, besides, two mantles annually. The prelates, princes, and barons who were chosen by the King received no salaries—*ils ne prennent nuls guaiges* (law of 27th January, 1367). The seneschals and high bailiffs, like the presidents of the chambers, received five hundred livres—fifty thousand francs. They and the bailiffs of inferior rank were expressly forbidden from receiving money or fees from the parties in any suit, but they were allowed to accept on one day refreshment and bottles of wine. The salaries were paid monthly; but this was not always done regularly; sometimes the King was to blame for this, and sometimes it was owing to the ill–nature of the chiefs of finance, or of the receivers and payers. When the blame rested with the King, the Parliament humbly remonstrated or closed the court. When, on the contrary, an officer of finance did not pay the salaries, Parliament sent him the bailiff's usher, and put him under certain penalties until he had done so. The question of salaries was frequently arising. On the 9th of February, 1369, "the court having been requested to serve without any remuneration for one Parliament, on the understanding that the King would make up for it another time, the nobles of the court replied, after private deliberation, that they were ready to do the King's pleasure, but could not do so properly without receiving their salaries" (Register of the Parliament of Paris).

At the commencement of the fifteenth century, the scale of remuneration was not increased. In 1411 it was raised for the whole Parliament to twenty–five thousand livres, which, calculated according to the present rate, amounted to nearly a million francs. In consequence of financial difficulties and the general distress, the unpleasant question in reference to claims for payment of salaries was renewed, with threats that the course of justice would be interrupted if they were not paid or not promised. On the 2nd of October, 1419, two councillors and one usher were sent to the house of one of the chiefs of finance, with orders to demand payment of the salaries of the court. In October, 1430, the government owed the magistrates two years of arrears. After useless appeals to the Regent, and to the Bishop of Therouanne, the then Chancellor of France, the Parliament sent two of its members to the King at Rouen, who obtained, after much difficulty, "one month's pay, on the understanding that the Parliament should hold its sittings in the month of April." In the month of July, 1431, there was another deputation to the King, "in order to lay before him the necessities of the court, and that it had for some time been

245

prorogued, and was still prorogued, on account of the non–payment of salaries." After two months of repeated remonstrance, the deputies only bringing back promises, the court assumed a menacing aspect; and on the 11th of January, 1437, it pointed out to the chancellor the evil which would arise if Parliament ceased to hold its sittings; and this time the chancellor announced that the salaries would be paid, though six months passed without any resuit or any practical step being taken in the matter. This state of affairs grew worse until the year 1443, when the King was obliged to plead with the Parliament in the character of an insolvent debtor, and, in order to obtain remission of part of his debt to the members, to guarantee to them a part of the salt duties.

Charles VII, after having reconquered his states, hastened to restore order. He first occupied himself with the System of justice, the Parliament, the Chatelet, and the bailiwicks; and in April, 1453, in concert with the princes, the prelates, the council of State, the judges, and others in authority, he framed a general law, in one hundred and twenty–five articles, which was considered as the great charter of Parliament (Fig. 308). According to the terms of these articles, "the councillors are to sit after dinner, to get through the minor causes. Prisoners are to be examined without delay, and to hold no communication with any one, unless by special permission. The cases are to be carefully gone through in their proper order; for courts are instructed to do justice as promptly for the poor as for the rich, as it is a greater hardship for the poor to be kept waiting than the rich." The fees of attorneys were taxed and reduced in amount. Those of advocates were reduced "to such moderation and fairness, that there should be no cause for complaint." The judgments by commissary were forbidden. The bailiffs and seneschals were directed to reside within their districts. The councillors were ordered to abstain from all communication with the parties in private, and consultations between themselves were to be held in secret. The judgments given in lawsuits were inscribed in a register, and submitted every two months to the presidents, who, if necessary, called the reporters to account for any neglect of duty. The reporter was ordered to draw attention to any point of difficulty arising in a suit, and the execution of sentences or judgments was entrusted to the ushers of the court.

In 1454 the King, in consequence of a difficulty in paying the regular instalments of the usual salaries of the Parliament, created "after–dinner fees" (*des gages d'apres dinees*) of five sols parisis—more than ten francs of our money—per day, payable to those councillors who should hold a second hearing. Matters did not improve much, however; nothing seemed to proceed satisfactorily, and members of Parliament, deprived of their salaries, were compelled to contract a loan, in order to commence proceedings against the treasury for the non–payment of the amount due to them. In 1493, the annual salaries of Parliament were raised to the sum of 40,630 livres, equal to about 1,100,000 francs.

[Illustration: Fig. 308.—Supreme Court, presided over by the King, who is in the act of issuing a Decree which is being registered by the Usher.—Fac–simile of a Miniature in Camareu of the "Information des Rois," Manuscript of the Fifteenth Century, in the Library of the Arsenal of Paris.]

The first president received 4 livres, 22 solis parisis—about 140 francs—per day; a clerical councillor 25 sols parisis—about 40 francs—and a lay councillor 20 sols—about 32 francs. This was an increase of a fifth on the preceding year. Charles VIII., in thus improving the remuneration of the members of the first court of the kingdom, reminded them of their duties, which had been too long neglected; he told them "that of all the cardinal virtues justice was the most noble and most important;" and he pointed out to them the line of conduct they were to pursue. The councillors were to be present daily in their respective chambers, from St. Martin's day to Easter, before seven o'clock in the morning; and from Easter to the closing of Parliament, immediately after six o'clock, without intermission, under penalty of punishment. Strict silence was enforced upon them during the debates; and they were forbidden to occupy themselves with anything which did not concern the case under discussion. Amidst a mass of other points upon which directions are given, we notice the following: the necessity of keeping secret the matters in course of deliberation; the prohibition to councillors from receiving, either directly or indirectly, anything in the shape of a douceur from the parties in any suit; and the forbidding all attorneys from receiving any bribe or claiming more than the actual expenses of a journey and other just charges.

The great charter of the Parliament, promulgated in April, 1453, was thus amended, confirmed, and completed, by this code of Charles VIII., with a wisdom which cannot be too highly extolled.

The magistrature of the supreme courts had been less favoured during the preceding reign. Louis XI., that cautious and crafty reformer, after having forbidden ecclesiastical judges to examine cases referring to the revenues of vacant benefices, remodelled the secular courts, but he ruthlessly destroyed anything which offended him personally. For this reason, as he himself said, he limited the power of the Parliaments of Paris and

Toulouse, by establishing, to their prejudice, several other courts of justice, and by favouring the Chatelet, where he was sure always to find those who would act with him against the aristocracy. The Parliament would not give way willingly, nor without the most determined opposition. It was obliged, however, at last to succumb, and to pass certain edicts which were most repugnant to it. On the death of Louis XI., however, it took its revenge, and called those who had been his favourites and principal agents to answer a criminal charge, for no other reason than that they had exposed themselves to the resentment of the supreme court.

The Chatelet, in its judicial functions, was inferior to the Parliament, nevertheless it acquired, through its provost, who represented the bourgeois of Paris, considerable importance in the eyes of the supreme court. In fact, for two centuries the provost held the privilege of ruling the capital, both politically and financially, of commanding the citizen militia, and of being chief magistrate of the city. In the court of audiences, a canopy was erected, under which he sat, a distinction which no other magistrate enjoyed, and which appears to have been exclusively granted to him because he sat in the place of *Monsieur Saint Loys* (Saint Louis), *dispensing justice to the good people of the City of Paris*. When the provost was installed, he was solemnly escorted, wearing his cap, to the great chamber of Parliament, accompanied by four councillors.

[Illustration: Fig. 309.—The Court of a Baron.—Fac–simile of a Woodcut in the "Cosmographie Universelle" of Munster: in folio, Basle, 1552.]

After the ceremony of installation he gave his horse to the president, who had come to receive him. His dress consisted of a short robe, with mantle, collar turned down, sword, and hat with feathers; he also carried a staff of office, profusely ornamented with silver. Thus attired he attended Parliament, and assisted at the levees of the sovereign, where he took up his position on the lowest step of the throne, below the great Chamberlain. Every day, excepting at the vintage time, he was required to be present at the Chatelet, either personally or by deputy, punctually at nine in the morning. There he received the list of the prisoners who had been arrested the day before; after that he visited the prisons, settled business of various kinds, and then inspected the town. His jurisdiction extended to several courts, which were presided over by eight deputies or judges appointed by him, and who were created officers of the Chatelet by Louis XII. in 1498. Subsequently, these received their appointments direct from the King. Two auditing judges, one king's attorney, one registrar, and some bailiffs, completed the provost's staff.

[Illustration: Fig. 310.—Sergeants–at–Arms of the Fourteenth Century, carved in Stone.—From the Church of St. Catherine du Val des Ecoliers, in Paris.]

The bailiffs at the Chatelet were divided into five classes: the *king's sergeant–at–arms,* the *sergeants de la douzaine,* the *sergeants of the mace,* or *foot sergeants,* the *sergeants fieffes,* and the *mounted sergeants.* The establishment of these officers dated from the beginning of the fourteenth century, and they were originally appointed by the provost, but afterwards by the King himself. The King's sergeants–at–arms (Fig. 310) formed his body–guard; they were not under the jurisdiction of the high constable, but of the ordinary judges, which proves that they were in civil employ. The sergeants *de la douzaine* were twelve in number, as their name implies, all of whom were in the service of the provost; the foot sergeants, who were civilians, were gradually increased to the number of two hundred and twenty as early as the middle of the fifteenth century. They acted only in the interior of the capital, and guarded the city, the suburbs, and the surrounding districts, whereas the mounted sergeants had "to watch over the safety of the rural parishes, and to act throughout the whole extent of the provost's jurisdiction, and of that of the viscount of Paris."

In the midst of the changes of the Middle Ages, especially after the communes became free, all those kings who felt the importance of a strict system of justice, particularly St. Louis, Philippe le Bel, and Charles VIII., had seen the necessity of compiling a record of local customs. An edict of 1453 orders that "the custom shall be registered in writing, so as to be examined by the members of the great council of the Parliament." Nevertheless, this important work was never properly carried out, and to Louis XII. is due the honour of introducing a customary or usage law, and at the same time of correcting the various modes of procedure, upon which customs and usages had been based, and which had become singularly antiquated since the edict of 1302.

No monarch showed more favour to Parliament than Louis XII. During his reign of seventeen years we never find complaints from the magistracy for not having been paid punctually. But in contrast with this, on the accession of Francis I., the court complained of not having been paid its first quarter's salary. From that moment claims were perpetually being made; there were continually delays, or absolute refusals; the members were expecting "remuneration for their services, in order absolutely to enable them to support their families and households." We can thus judge of the state of the various minor courts, which, being less powerful than the supreme tribunals, and especially than that of Paris, were quite unable to get their murmurings even listened to by the proper authorities. This sad state of things continued, and, in fact, grew worse, until the assembly of the League, when Mayenne, the chief of the leaguers, in order to gratify the Parliament, promised to double the salaries, although he was unable to fulfil his promise.

[Illustration: Fig. 311.—Inferior Court in the Great Bailiwick. Adoption of Orphan Children.—Fac–simile of a Woodcut in J. Damhoudere's "Refuge et Garand des Pupilles, Orphelins:" Antwerp, J. Bellere, 1557.]

Towards the end of the sixteenth century the highest French tribunal was represented by nine superior courts—namely, the Parliament of Bordeaux, created on the 9th of June, 1642; the Parliament of Brittany, which replaced the ancient *Grands–Jours,* in March, 1553, and sat alternately at Nantes and at Rennes; the Parliament of the Dauphine, established at Grenoble in 1451 to replace the Delphinal Council; the Parliament of Burgundy, established at Dijon in 1477, which took the place of the *Grands–Jours* at Beaune; the movable Parliament of Dombes, created in 1528, and consisting at the same time of a court of excise and a chamber of accounts; the Parliament of Normandy, established by Louis XII. in April, 1504, intended to replace the Exchequer of Rouen, and the ancient ducal council of the province; the Parliament of Provence, founded at Aix in July, 1501; the Parliament of Toulouse, created in 1301; and the Parliament of Paris, which took precedence of all the others, both on account of its origin, its antiquity, the extent of its jurisdiction, the number of its prerogatives, and the importance of its decrees. In 1551, Henry II. created, besides these, an inferior court in each bailiwick, the duties of which were to hear, on appeal, all matters in which sums of less than two hundred livres were involved (Fig. 311). There existed, besides, a branch of the *Grands–Jours,* occasionally sitting at Poitiers, Bayeux, and at some other central towns, in order to suppress the excesses which at times arose from religious dissensions and political controversy.

The Parliament of Paris—or *Great French Parliament,* as it was called by Philip V. and Charles V., in edicts of the 17th of November, 1318, and of the 8th of October, 1371—was divided into four principal chambers: the Grand Chamber, the Chamber of Inquiry, the Criminal Chamber, and the Chamber of Appeal. It was composed of ordinary councillors, both clerical and lay; of honorary councillors, some of whom were ecclesiastics, and others members of the nobility; of masters of inquiry; and of a considerable number of officers of all ranks (Figs. 312 to 314). It had at times as many as twenty–four presidents, one hundred and eighty–two councillors, four knights of honour, four masters of records; a public prosecutor's office was also attached, consisting of the king's counsel, an attorney–general and deputies, thus forming an assembly of from fifteen to twenty persons, called a *college*. Amongst the inferior officers we may mention twenty–six ushers, four receivers–general of trust money, three commissioners for the receipt of goods which had been seized under distress, one treasurer and paymaster, three controllers, one physician, two surgeons, two apothecaries, one matron, one receiver of fines, one inspector of estates, several keepers of refreshment establishments, who resided within the precincts of the palace, sixty or eighty notaries, four or five hundred advocates, two hundred attorneys, besides registers and deputy registers. Down to the reign of Charles VI. (1380—1422) members of Parliament held their appointment by commissions granted by the King, and renewed eaeh session. From Charles VI. to Francis I. these appointments became royal charges; but from that time, owing to the office being so often prostituted for reward, it got more and more into disrepute.

[Illustration: Fig. 312.—Judge.—From a Drawing in "Proverbes, Adages, &c.," Manuscript of the Fifteenth Century, in the Imperial Library of Paris.]

Louis XI. made the office of member of the Parliament of Paris a permanent one, and Francis I. continued this privilege. In 1580 the supreme magistracy poured 140,000,000 francs, which now would be worth fifteen or twenty times as much, into the State treasury, so as to enable members to sit permanently *sur les fleurs de lis*, and to obtain hereditary privileges. The hereditary transmission of office from father to son dealt a heavy blow at the popularity of the parliamentary body, which had already deeply suffered through shameful abuses, the enormity of the fees, the ignorance of some of the members, and the dissolute habits of many others.

[Illustration: Fig. 313.—Lawyer.—From the "Danse des Morts" of Basle, engraved by Merian: in 4to, Frankfort, 1596.]

[Illustration: Fig. 314.—Barrister.—From a Woodout in the "Danse Macabre:" Guyot's edition, 1490.]

[Illustration: Fig. 315.—Assembly of the Provostship of the Merchants of Paris.—Fac–simile of a Woodcut in "Ordonnances Royaux de la Jurisdiction de la Prevote des Marchands et Eschevinage de la Ville de Paris:" in small folio, goth. edition of Paris, Jacques Nyverd, 1528.]

The Chatelet, on the contrary, was less involved in intrigue, less occupied with politics, and was daily engaged in adjudicating in cases of litigation, and thus it rendered innumerable services in promoting the public welfare, and maintained, and even increased, the respect which it had enjoyed from the commencement of its existence. In 1498, Louis XII. required that the provost should possess the title of doctor *in utroque jure,* and that his officers, whom he made to hold their appointments for life, should be chosen from amongst the most distinguished counsellors at law. This excellent arrangement bore its fruits. As early as 1510, the "Usages of the City, Provosty, and Viscounty of Paris," were published *in extenso,* and were then received with much ceremony at a solemn audience held on the 8th of March in the episcopal palace, and were deposited among the archives of the Chatelet (Fig. 315).

The Parliament held a very different line of policy from that adopted by the Chatelet, which only took a political part in the religious troubles of Protestantism and the League with a view to serve and defend the cause of the people. In spite of its fits of personal animosity, and its rebellious freaks, Parliament remained almost invariably attached to the side of the King and the court. It always leaned to the absolute maintenance of things as they were, instead of following progress and changes which time necessitated. It was for severe measures, for intimidation more than for gentleness and toleration, and it yielded sooner or later to the injunctions and admonitions of the King, although, at the same time, it often disapproved the acts which it was asked to sanction.

[Illustration: Fig. 316.—Seal of King Chilperic, found in his Tomb at Tournay in 1654.]

Secret Tribunals.

The Old Man of the Mountain and his Followers in Syria.—The Castle of Alamond, Paradise of Assassins.—Charlemagne the Founder of Secret Tribunals amongst the Saxons.—The Holy Vehme.—Organization of the Tribunal of the *Terre Rouge,* and Modes adopted in its Procedures.—Condemnations and Execution of Sentences.—The Truth respecting the Free Judges of Westphalia.—Duration and Fall of the Vehmic Tribunal.—Council of Ten in Venice; its Code and Secret

Decisions.—End of the Council of Ten.

During the Middle Ages, human life was generally held in small respect; various judicial institutions—if not altogether secret, at least more or less enveloped in mystery—were remarkable for being founded on the monstrous right of issuing the most severe sentences with closed doors, and of executing these sentences with inflexible rigour on individuals who had not been allowed the slightest chance of defending themselves.

While passing judgment in secret, they often openly dealt blows as unexpected and terrible as they were fatal. Therefore, the most innocent and the most daring trembled at the very name of the *Free Judges of the Terre–Rouge,* an institution which adopted Westphalia as the special, or rather as the central, region of its authority; the *Council of Ten* exercised their power in Venice and the states of the republic; and the *Assassins* of Syria, in the time of St. Louis, made more than one invasion into Christian Europe. We must nevertheless acknowledge that, terrible as these mysterious institutions were, the general credulity, the gross ignorance of the masses, and the love of the marvellous, helped not a little to render them even more outrageous and alarming than they really were.

Marco Polo, the celebrated Venetian traveller of the thirteenth century, says, "We will speak of the Old Man of the Mountain. This prince was named Alaodin. He had a lovely garden full of all manner of trees and fruits, in a beautiful valley, surrounded by high hills; and all round these plantations were various palaces and pavilions, decorated with works of art in gold, with paintings, and with furniture of silk. Therein were to be seen rivulets of wine, as well as milk, honey, and gentle streams of limpid water. He had placed therein damsels of transcendent beauty and endowed with great charms, who were taught to sing and to play all manner of instruments; they were dressed in silk and gold, and continually walked in these gardens and palaces. The reasons for which the Old Man had these palaces built were the following. Mahomet having said that those who should obey his will should go to paradise, and there find all kinds of luxuries, this prince wished it to be believed that he was the prophet and companion of Mahomet, and that he had the power of sending whom he chose to paradise. No one could succeed in entering the garden, because an impregnable castle had been built at the entrance of the valley, and it could only be approached by a covered and secret way. The Old Man had in his court some young men from ten to twenty years of age, chosen from those inhabitants of the hills who seemed to him capable of bearing arms, and who were bold and courageous.

From time to time he administered a certain drink to ten or twelve of these young men, which sent them to sleep, and when they were in deep stupor, he had them carried into the garden. When they awoke, they saw all we have described: they were surrounded by the young damsels, who sang, played instruments together, caressed them, played all sorts of games, and presented them with the most exquisite wines and meats (Fig. 317). So that these young men, satiated with such pleasures, did not doubt that they were in paradise, and would willingly have never gone out of it again.

"At the end of four or five days, the Old Man sent them to sleep again, and had them removed from the garden in the same way in which they had been brought in. He then called them before him, and asked them where they had been. 'By your grace, lord,' they answered, 'we have been in paradise.' And then they related, in the presence of everybody, what they had seen there. This tale excited the astonishment of all those who heard it, and the desire that they might be equally fortunate. The Old Man would then formally announce to those who were present, as follows: 'Thus saith the law of our prophet, He causes all who fight for their Lord to enter into paradise; if you obey me you shall enjoy that happiness.' By such words and plans this prince had so accustomed them to believe in him, that he whom he ordered to die for his service considered himself lucky. All the nobles or other enemies of the Old Man of the Mountain were put to death by the assassins in his service; for none of them feared death, provided he complied with the orders and wishes of his lord. However powerful a man might be, therefore, if he was an enemy of the Old Man's, he was sure to meet with an untimely end."

[Illustration: Fig. 317.—The Castle of Alamond and its Enchantments.—Fac–simile of a Miniature in "Marco Polo's Travels," Manuscript of the Fifteenth. Century, in the Library of the Arsenal of Paris.]

In his story, which we translate literally from the original, written in ancient French, the venerable traveller attributes the origin of this singular system of exercising power over the minds of persons to a prince who in reality did but keep up a tradition of his family; for the Alaodin herein mentioned is no other than a successor of the famous Hassan, son of Ali, who, in the middle of the eleventh century, took advantage of the wars which devastated Asia to create himself a kingdom, comprising the three provinces of Turkistan, Djebel, and Syria. Hassan had embraced the doctrine of the Ishmaelian sect, who pretended to explain allegorically all the precepts of the Mahometan religion, and who did away with public worship, and originated a creed which was altogether philosophical.

He made himself the chief exponent of this doctrine, which, by its very simplicity, was sure to attract to him many people of simple and sincere minds. Attacked by the troops of the Sultan Sindgar, he defended himself vigorously and not unsuccessfully; but, fearing lest he should fall in an unequal and protracted struggle against an adversary more powerful than himself, he had recourse to cunning so as to obtain peace. He entranced, or fascinated probably, by means analogous to those related by Marco Polo, a slave, who had the daring, during Sindgar's sleep, to stick a sharp dagger in the ground by the side of the Sultan's head. On waking, Sindgar was much alarmed. A few days after, Hassan wrote to him, "If one had not good intentions towards the Sultan, one might have driven the dagger, which was stuck in the earth by his head, into his bosom." The Sultan Sindgar then made peace with the chief of the Ishmaelians, whose dynasty lasted for one hundred and seventy years.

The Castle of Alamond, built on the confines of Persia, on the top of a high mountain surrounded with trees, after having been the usual residence of Hassan, became that of his successors. As in the native language the same word means both *prince* and *old man*, the Crusaders who had heard the word pronounced confounded the two, and gave the name of *Old Man of the Mountain* to the Ishmaelian prince at that time inhabiting the Castle of Alamond, a name which has remained famous in history since the period when the Sire de Joinville published his "Memoires."

Ancient authors call the subjects of Hassan, *Haschichini, Heississini, Assissini, Assassini,* various forms of the same expression, which, in fact, has passed into French with a signification which recalls the sanguinary exploits of the Ishmaelians. In seeking for the etymology of this name, one must suppose that Haschichini is the Latin transformation of the Arabic word Hachychy, the name of the sect of which we are speaking, because the ecstacies during which they believed themselves removed to paradise were produced by means of *haschisch* or *haschischa*. We know that this inebriating preparation, extracted from hemp, really produces the most strange and delicious hallucinations on those who use it. All travellers who have visited the East agree in saying that its effects are very superior to those of opium. We evidently must attribute to some ecstatic vision the supposed existence of the enchanted gardens, which Marco Polo described from popular tales, and which, of course, never existed but in the imagination of the young men, who were either mentally excited after fasting and prayer, or intoxicated by the haschischa, and consequently for a time lulled in dreams of celestial bliss which they imagined awaited them under the guidance of Hassan and his descendants.

[Illustration: Fig. 318.—The Old Man of the Mountain giving Orders to his Followers.—Fac–simile of a Miniature in the "Travels of Marco Polo," Manuscript of the Fifteenth Century (Library of the Arsenal of Paris).]

The Haschischini, whom certain contemporary historians describe to us as infatuated by the hope of some future boundless felicity, owe their melancholy celebrity solely to the blind obedience with which they executed the orders of their chiefs, and to the coolness with which they sought the favourable moment for fulfilling their sanguinary missions (Fig. 318). The Old Man of the Mountain (the master of daggers, *magister cultellorum*, as he is also called by the chronicler Jacques de Vintry), was almost continually at war with the Mussulman princes who reigned from the banks of the Nile to the borders of the Caspian Sea. He continually opposed them with the steel of his fanatical emissaries; at times, also, making a traffic and merchandise of murder, he treated for a money payment with the sultans or emirs, who were desirous of ridding themselves of an enemy. The Ishmaelians thus put to death a number of princes and Mahometan nobles; but, at the time of the Crusades, religious zeal having incited them against the Christians, they found more than one notable victim in the ranks of the Crusaders. Conrad, Marquis of Montferrat, was assassinated by them; the great Salah–Eddin (Saladin) himself narrowly escaped them; Richard Coeur de Lion and Philip Augustus were pointed out to the assassins by the Old Man, who subsequently, on hearing of the immense preparations which Louis IX. was making for the Holy War, had the daring to send two of his followers to France, and even into Paris, with orders to kill that monarch in the midst of his court. This king, after having again escaped, during his sojourn in Palestine, from the murderous attempts of the savage messengers of the Prince of Alamond, succeeded, by his courage, his firmness, and his virtues, in inspiring these fanatics with so much respect, that their chief, looking upon him as protected by heaven, asked for his friendship, and offered him presents, amongst which was a magnificent set of chessmen, in crystal, ornamented with gold and amber.

The successors of Hassan, simultaneously attacked by the Moguls under Houlayon, and by the Egyptians commanded by the Sultan Bibars, were conquered and dispossessed of their States towards the middle of the thirteenth century; but, long after, the Ishmaelians, either because their chiefs sought to recover their power, or because they had placed their daggers at the disposal of some foreign foe, continued notorious in history. At last the sect became extinct, or, at least, retired into obscurity, and renounced its murderous profession, which had for so long made its members such objects of terror.

We have thus seen how a legion of fanatics in the East made themselves the blind and formidable tools of a religious and political chieftain, who was no less ambitious than revengeful. If we now turn our attention to Germany, we shall here find, almost at the same period, a local institution which, although very different from the sanguinary court of the Old Man of the Mountain, was of an equally terrible and mysterious character. We must not, however, look at it from the same point of view, for, having been founded with the object of furthering and defending the establishment of a regular social state, which had been approved and sanctioned by the sovereigns, and recognised by the Church, it at times rendered great service to the cause of justice and humanity at a period when might usurped right, and when the excesses and the crimes of shameless evil–doers, and of petty tyrants, entrenched in their impregnable strongholds, were but too often made lawful from the simple fact that there was no power to oppose them.

The secret tribunal of Westphalia, which held its sittings and passed sentence in private, and which carried out its decrees on the spot, and whose rules, laws, and actions were enveloped in deep mystery, must unquestionably be looked upon as one of the most remarkable institutions of the Middle Ages.

[Illustration: Figs. 319 and 320.—Hermensul or Irmensul and Crodon, Idols of the Ancient Saxons.—Fac–simile of a Woodcut in the "Annales Circuli Westphaliae," by Herman Stangefol: in 4to, 1656.—The Idol Hermensul appears to have presided over Executive Justice, the attributes of which it holds in its hands.]

It would be difficult to state exactly at what period this formidable institution was established. A few writers, and amongst these Sebastian Munster, wish us to believe that it was founded by Charlemagne himself. They affirm that this monarch, having subjugated the Saxons to his sway, and having forced them to be baptized, created a secret tribunal, the duties of which were to watch over them, in order that they might not return to the errors of Paganism. However, the Saxons were incorrigible, and, although Christians, they still carried on the worship of their idols (Figs. 319 and 320); and, for this reason, it is said by these authorities that the laws of the tribunal of Westphalia were founded by Charlemagne. It is well known that from the ninth to the thirteenth century, all that part of Germany between the Rhine and the Weser suffered under the most complete anarchy. In consequence of this, and of the increase of crime which remained unpunished, energetic men established a rigorous jurisdiction, which, to a certain extent, suppressed these barbarous disorders, and gave some assurance to social intercourse; but the very mystery which gave weight to the institution was the cause of its origin being unknown. It is only mentioned, and then cursorily, in historical documents towards the early part of the fifteenth century. This court of judicature received the name of *Femgericht*, or *Vehmgericht*, which means Vehmic tribunal. The origin of the word *Fem*, *Vehm*, or *Fam*, which has given rise to many scientific discussions, still remains in doubt. The most generally accepted opinion is, that it is derived from a Latin expression—*vemi* (*vae mihi*), "woe is me!"

The special dominion over which the Vehmic tribunal reigned supreme was Westphalia, and the country which was subjected to its laws was designated as the *Terre Rouge*. There was no assembly of this tribunal beyond the limits of this Terre Rouge, but it would be quite impossible to define these limits with any accuracy. However, the free judges, assuming the right of suppressing certain crimes committed beyond their territory, on more than one occasion summoned persons living in various parts of Germany, and even in provinces far from Westphalia, to appear before them. We do not know all the localities wherein the Vehmic tribunal sat; but the most celebrated of them, and the one which served as a model for all the rest, held its sittings under a lime–tree, in front of the castle–gate of Dortmund (Fig. 321). There the chapters–general of the association usually assembled; and, on certain occasions, several thousands of the free judges were to be seen there.

Each tribunal was composed of an unlimited number of free judges, under the presidency of a free count, who was charged with the higher administration of Vehmic justice. A *free county* generally comprised several free tribunals, or *friestuhle*. The free count, who was chosen by the prince of the territory in which the tribunal sat, had two courts, one secret, the other public. The public assizes, which took place at least three times a year, were announced fourteen days beforehand, and any person living within the *county*, and who was summoned before the free count, was bound to appear, and to answer all questions which might be put to him. It was required that the free judges (who are generally mentioned as *femnoten*—that is to say, *sages*—and who are, besides, denoted by writers of the time by the most honourable epithets: such as, "serious men," "very pious," "of very pure morals," "lovers of justice," &c.) should be persons who had been born in lawful wedlock, and on German soil; they were not allowed to belong to any religions order, or to have ever themselves been summoned before the Vehmic tribunal. They were nominated by the free counts, but subject to the approval of their sovereigns. They were not allowed to sit as judges before having been initiated into the mysteries of the tribunals.

[Illustration: Fig. 321.—View of the Town of Dortmund in the Sixteenth Century.—From an Engraving on Copper in P. Bertius's "Theatrum Geographicum."]

The initiation of a free judge was accompanied by extraordinary formalities. The candidate appeared bareheaded; he knelt down, and, placing two fingers of his right hand on his naked sword and on a rope, he took oath to adhere to the laws and customs of the holy tribunal, to devote his five senses to it, and not to allow himself to be allured therefrom either by silver, gold, or even precious stones; to forward the interests of the tribunal "above everything illumined by the sun, and all that the rain reaches;" and to defend them "against everything which is between heaven and earth." The candidate was then given the sign by which members of the association recognised each other. This sign has remained unknown; and nothing, even in the deeds of the Vehmic archives, leads one even to guess what it was, and every hypothesis on this subject must be looked upon as uncertain or erroneous. By one of the fundamental statutes of the Terre Rouge, a member convicted of betraying the secrets of the order was condemned to the most cruel punishment; but we have every reason for asserting that this sentence was never carried out, or even issued against a free judge.

[Illustration: Fig. 322.—The Landgrave of Thuringia and his Wife.—Fac-simile of a Miniature in the Collection of the Minnesinger, Manuscript of the Fourteenth Century.]

In one case alone during the fourteenth century, was an accusation of this sort made, and that proved to be groundless.

It would have been considered the height of treason to have given a relation, or a friend, the slightest hint that he was being pursued, or that he had been condemned by the Holy Vehme, in order that he might seek refuge by flight. And in consequence of this, there was a general mistrust of any one belonging to the tribunal, so much so that "a brother," says a German writer, "often feared his brother, and hospitality was no longer possible."

The functions of free judges consisted in going about the country seeking out crimes, denouncing them, and inflicting immediate punishment on any evil-doer caught in the act (Figs. 323 and 324). The free judges might assemble provided there were at least seven in number to constitute a tribunal; but we hear of as many as three hundred assisting at a meeting.

[Illustration: Figs. 323 and 324.—Free Judges.—Fac–simile of two Woodcuts in the "Cosmographie Universelle" of Munster: in folio, 1552.]

It has been erroneously stated that the sittings of the Vehmic tribunals were held at night in the depths of forests, or in subterranean places; but it appears that all criminal business was first heard in public, and could only be subjected to a secret judgment when the accused had failed either publicly to justify himself or to appear in person.

When three free judges caught a malefactor in the very act, they could seize him, judge him, and inflict the penalty on the spot. In other cases, when a tribunal considered that it should pursue an individual, it summoned him to appear before it. The summons had to be written, without erasures, on a large sheet of vellum, and to bear at least seven seals—that of the free count, and those of six free judges; and these seals generally represented either a man in full armour holding a sword, or a simple sword blade, or other analagous emblems (Figs. 325 to 327). Two free judges delivered the summons personally where a member of the association was concerned; but if the summons affected an individual who was not of the Vehmic order, a sworn messenger bore it, and placed it in the very hands of the person, or slipped it into his house. The time given for putting in an appearance was originally six weeks and three days at least, but at a later period this time was shortened. The writ of summons was repeated three times, and each time bore a greater number of seals of free judges, so as to verify the legality of the instrument. The accused, whether guilty or not, was liable to a fine for not answering the first summons, unless he could prove that it was impossible for him to have done so. If he failed to appear on the third summons, he was finally condemned *en corps et en honneur*.

[Illustration: Fig. 325.—Seal of Herman Loseckin, Free Count of Medebach, in 1410.]

[Illustration: Fig. 326.—Seal of the Free Count, Hans Vollmar von Twern, at Freyenhagen, in 1476–1499.]

[Illustration: Fig. 327.—Seal of Johann Croppe, Free Count of Kogelnberg, in 1413.]

We have but imperfect information as to the formalities in use in the Vehmic tribunals. But we know that the sittings were invested with a certain solemnity and pomp. A naked sword—emblematical of justice, and recalling our Saviour's cross in the shape of its handle—and a rope—emblematical of the punishment deserved by the guilty—were placed on the table before the president. The judges were bareheaded, with bare hands, and each wore a cloak over his shoulder, and carried no arms of any sort.

[Illustration: Fig. 328.—The Duke of Saxony and the Marquis of Brandenburg.—From the "Theatrum Orbis Terrarum sive Tabula veteris Geographiae," in folio. Engraved by Wieriex, after Gerard de Jode.]

The plaintiff and the defendant were each allowed to produce thirty witnesses. The defendant could either defend himself, or entrust his case to an advocate whom he brought with him. At first, any free judge being defendant in a suit, enjoyed the privilege of justifying himself on oath; but it having been discovered that this privilege was abused, all persons, of whatever station, were compelled to be confronted with the other side. The witnesses, who were subpoened by either accuser or accused, had to give their evidence according to the truth, dispassionately and voluntarily. In the event of the accused not succeeding in bringing sufficient testimony to clear himself, the prosecutor claimed a verdict in his favour from the free count presiding at the tribunal, who appointed one of the free judges to declare it. In case the free judge did not feel satisfied as to the guilt, he could, by making oath, temporarily divest himself of his office, which devolved upon a second, a third, or even a fourth free judge. If four free judges were unable to decide, the matter was referred to another sitting; for judgment had to be pronounced by the appointed free judge at the sitting.

The various penalties for different crimes were left to the decision of the tribunal. The rules are silent on the subject, and simply state that the culprits will be punished "according to the authority of the secret bench." The *royale, i.e.* capital punishment, was strictly applied in all serious cases, and the manner of execution most in use was hanging (Figs. 329, 330).

A person accused who did not appear after the third summons, was out–lawed by a terrible sentence, which deprived him of all rights, of common peace, and forbad him the company of all Christians; by the wording of this sentence, his wife was looked upon as a widow, his children as orphans; his neck was abandoned to the birds of the air, and his body to the beasts of the field, "but his soul was recommended to God." At the expiration of one year and a day, if the culprit had not appeared, or had not established his common rights, all his goods were confiscated, and appropriated by the King or Emperor. When the condemnation referred to a prince, a town, or a corporation (for the accusations of the tribunal frequently were issued against groups of individuals), it caused the loss of all honour, authority, and privileges. The free count, in pronouncing the sentence, threw the rope, which was before him, on to the ground; the free judges spat upon it, and the name of the culprit was inscribed on the book of blood. The sentence was kept secret; the prosecutor alone was informed of it by a written notice, which was sealed with seven seals. When the condemned was present, the execution took place immediately, and, according to the custom of the Middle Ages, its carrying out was deputed to the youngest of the free judges. The members of the Vehmic association enjoyed the privilege of being hung seven feet higher than those who were not associates.

The Vehmic judgments were, however, liable to be appealed against: the accused might, at the sitting, appeal either to what was termed the imperial chamber, a general chapter of the association, which assembled at Dortmund, or (and this was the more frequent custom) to the emperor, or ruler of the country, whether he were king, prince, duke, or bishop, provided that these authorities belonged to the association. The revision of the judgment could only be entrusted to members of the tribunal, who, in their turn, could only act in Westphalia. The condemned might also appeal to the lieutenant–general of the emperor, or to the grand master of the Holy Vehme, a title which, from the remotest times, was given to the Archbishop of Cologne. There are even instances of appeals having been made to the councils and to the Popes, although the Vehmic association never had any communication or intercourse with the court of Rome. We must not forget a very curious privilege which, in certain cases, was left to the culprit as a last resource; he might appeal to the emperor, and solicit an order which required the execution of the sentence to be applied after a delay *of one hundred years, six weeks, and one day.*

[Illustration: Figs. 329 and 330.—Execution of the Sentences of the Secret Tribunal.—Fac–simile of Woodcuts in the "Cosmographie Universelle" of Munster: in folio, Basle, 1552.]

The chapter–general of the association was generally summoned once a year by the emperor or his lieutenant, and assembled either at Dortmund or Arensberg, in order to receive the returns of causes judged by the various Vehmic tribunals; to hear the changes which had taken place among the members of the order; to receive the free judges; to hear appeals; and, lastly, to decide upon reforms to be introduced into the rules. These reforms usually had reference to the connection of imperial authority with the members of the secret jurisdiction, and were generally suggested by the emperors, who were jealous of the increasing power of the association.

From what we have shown, on the authority of authentic documents, we understand how untrue is the tradition, or rather the popular idea, that the *Secret Tribunal* was an assembly of bloodthirsty judges, secretly perpetrating acts of mere cruelty, without any but arbitrary laws. It is clear, on the contrary, that it was a regular institution, having, it is true, a most mysterious and complex organization, but simply acting in virtue of legal prescriptions, which were rigorously laid down, and arranged in a sort of code which did honour to the wisdom of those who had created it.

It was towards the end of the fourteenth and the beginning of the fifteenth centuries that the Vehmic jurisdiction reached its highest degree of power; its name was only pronounced in a whisper and with trembling; its orders were received with immediate submission, and its chastisements always fell upon the guilty and those who resisted its authority. There cannot be a doubt but that the Westphalian tribunal prevented many great crimes and public misfortunes by putting a wholesome check on the nobles, who were ever ready to place themselves above all human authority; and by punishing, with pitiless severity, the audacity of bandits, who would otherwise have been encouraged to commit the most daring acts with almost the certainty of escaping with impunity. But the Holy Vehme, blinded by the terror it inspired, was not long without displaying the most extravagant assumption of power, and digressing from the strict path to which its action should have been confined. It summoned before its tribunals princes, who openly denied its authority, and cities, which did not condescend to answer to its behests. In the fifteenth century, the free judges were composed of men who could not be called of unimpeachable integrity; many persons of doubtful morals having been raised to the dignity by party influence and by money. The partiality and the spirit of revenge which at times prompted their judgments, were complained of; they were accused of being open to corruption; and this accusation appears to have been but too well founded. It is known that, according to a feudal practice established in the Vehmic system, every new free judge was obliged to make a present to the free count who had admitted him into the order; and the free counts did not hesitate to make this an important source of revenue to themselves by admitting, according to an historian, "many people as *judges* who, in reality, deserved to be *judged*."

[Illustration: Fig. 331.—View of Cologne in the Sixteenth Century.—From a Copper–plate in the "Theatrum Geographicum" of P. Bertius. The three large stars represent, it is supposed, the Three Persons of the Trinity, and the seven small ones the Electors of the Empire.]

[Illustration: Fig. 332.—German Knights (Fifteenth Century).—From a Plate in the "Life of the Emperor Maximilian," engraved by Burgmayer, from Drawings by Albert Durer.]

Owing to the most flagrant and most insolent abuses of power, the ancient authority of the institution became gradually more and more shaken. On one occasion, for instance, in answer to a summons issued by the Imperial Tribunal against some free judges, the tribunal of the Terre–Rouge had the daring to summon the Emperor Frederick III. before it to answer for this want of respect. On another occasion, a certain free count, jealous of one of his associates, hung him with his own hands while out on a hunting excursion, alleging that his rank of free judge authorised him to execute summary justice. From that time there was a perpetual cry of horror and indignation against a judicial institution which thus interpreted its duties, and before long the State undertook the suppression of these secret tribunals. The first idea of this was formed by the electors of the empire at the diet of Treves in 1512. The Archbishop of Cologne succeeded, however, in parrying the blow, by convoking the chapter–general of the order, on the plea of the necessity of reform. But, besides being essentially corrupt, the Holy Vehme had really run its course, and it gradually became effete as, by degrees, a better organized and more defined social and political state succeeded to the confused anarchy of the Middle Ages, and as the princes and free towns adopted the custom of dispensing justice either in person or through regular tribunals. Its proceedings, becoming more and more summary and rigorous, daily gave rise to feelings of greater and greater abhorrence. The common saying over all Germany was, "They first hang you, and afterwards inquire into your innocence." On all sides opposition arose against the jurisdiction of the free judges. Princes, bishops, cities, and citizens, agreed instinctively to counteract this worn–out and degenerate institution. The struggle was long and tedious. During the last convulsions of the expiring Holy Vehme, there was more than one sanguinary episode, both on the side of the free judges themselves, as well as on that of their adversaries. Occasionally the secret tribunal broke out into fresh signs of life, and proclaimed its existence by some terrible execution; and at times, also, its members paid dearly for their acts. On one occasion, in 1570, fourteen free judges, whom Kaspar Schwitz, Count of Oettingen, caused to be seized, were already tied up in bags, and about to be drowned, when the mob, pitying their fate, asked for and obtained their reprieve.

The death-blow to the Vehmic tribunal was struck by its own hand. It condenmed summarily, and executed without regular procedure, an inhabitant of Munster, who used to scandalize the town by his profligacy. He was arrested at night, led to a small wood, where the free judges awaited him, and condemned to death without being allowed an advocate; and, after being refused a respite even of a few hours, that he might make his peace with heaven, he was confessed by a monk, and his head was severed from his body by the executioner on the spot.

[Illustration: Fig. 333.—Interior Court of the Palace of the Doges of Venice: Buildings in which are the Cells and *the Leads*.—From Cesare Vecellio.]

Dating from this tragical event, which excited universal indignation, the authority of the free judges gradually declined, and, at last, the institution became almost defunct, and merely confined itself to occasionally adjudicating in simple civil matters.

We must not omit to mention the Council of Ten of Venice when speaking on the subject of arbitrary executions and of tyrannical and implacable justice. In some respects it was more notorious than the Vehmic tribunal, exercising as it did a no less mysterious power, and inspiring equal terror, though in other countries.

This secret tribunal was created after a revolt which burst on the republic of Venice on the 15th of June, 1310. At first it was only instituted for two months, but, after various successive prorogations, it was confirmed for five years, on the 31st of January, 1311. In 1316 it was again appointed for five years; on the 2nd of May, 1327, for ten years more; and at last was established permanently. In the fifteenth century the authority of the Council of Ten was consolidated and rendered more energetic by the creation of the Inquisitors of State. These were three in number, elected by the Council of Ten; and the citizens on whom the votes fell could not refuse the functions which were thus spontaneously, and often unexpectedly, assigned to them. The authority of Inquisitors of State was declared to be "unlimited."

In order to show the power and mode of action of this terrible tribunal, it is perhaps better to make a few extracts from the code of rules which it established for itself in June, 1454.

This document—several manuscript copies of which are to be found in the public libraries of Paris—says, "The inquisitors may proceed against any person whomsoever, no rank giving the right of exemption from their jurisdiction. They may pronounce any sentence, even that of death; only their final sentences must be passed unanimously. They shall have complete charge of the prisons and *the leads* (Fig. 333). They may draw at sight from the treasury of the Council of Ten, without having to give any account of the use made of the funds placed in their hands.

"The proceedings of the tribunal shall always be secret; its members shall wear no distinctive badge. No open arrests shall be made. The chief of the bailiffs (*sbirri*) shall avoid making domiciliary arrests, but he shall try to seize the culprit unawares, away from his home, and so securely get him under *the leads* of the Palace of the Doges. When the tribunal shall deem the death of any person necessary, the execution shall never be public; the condemned shall be drowned at night in the Orfano Canal.

"The tribunal shall authorise the generals commanding in Cyprus or in Candia, in the event of its being for the welfare of the Republic, to cause any patrician or other influential person in either of those Venetian provinces to disappear, or to be assassinated secretly, if such a measure should conscientiously appear to them indispensable; but they shall be answerable before God for it.

[Illustration: Fig. 334.—Member of the Brotherhood of Death, whose duty it was to accompany those sentenced to death.—From Cesare Vecellio.]

"If any workman shall practise in a foreign land any art or craft to the detriment of the Republic, he shall be ordered to return to his country; and should he not obey, all his nearest relatives shall be imprisoned, in order that his affection for them may bring him to obedience. Should he still persist in his disobedience, secret measures shall be taken to put him to death, wherever he may be.

"If a Venetian noble reveal to the tribunal propositions which have been made to him by some foreign ambassador, the agent, excepting it should be the ambassador himself, shall be immediately carried off and drowned.

"If a patrician having committed any misdeed shall take refuge under the protection of a foreign ambassador, he shall be put to death forthwith.

"If any noble in full senate take upon himself to question the authority of the Council of Ten, and persist in attacking it, he shall be allowed to speak without interruption; immediately afterwards he shall be arrested, and instructions as to his trial shall be given, so that he may be judged by the ordinary tribunals; and, if this does not succeed in preventing his proceedings, he shall be put to death secretly.

"In case of a complaint against one of the heads of the Council of Ten, the instructions shall be made secretly, and, in case of sentence of death, poison shall be the agent selected.

"Should any dissatisfied noble speak ill of the Government, he shall first be forbidden to appear in the councils and public places for two years. Should he not obey, or should he repeat the offence after the two years, he shall be drowned as incorrigible...." &c.

One can easily understand that in order to carry out these laws the most careful measures were taken to organize a system of espionage. The nobles were subjected to a rigorous supervision; the privacy of letters was not respected; an ambassador was never lost sight of, and his smallest acts were narrowly watched. Any one who dared to throw obstacles in the way of the spies employed by the Council of Ten, was put on the rack, and "made afterwards to receive the punishment which the State inquisitors might consider befitting." Whole pages of the secret statutes bear witness that lying and fraud formed the basis of all the diplomatic relations of the Venetian Government. Nevertheless the Council of Ten, which was solely instituted with the view of watching over the safety of the Republic, could not inter-meddle in civil cases, and its members were forbidden to hold any sort of communication with foreigners.

[Illustration: Figs. 335 and 336.—Chiefs of Sbirri, in the Secret Service of the Council of Ten.—From Cesare Vecellio.]

The list of names of Venetian nobles and distinguished persons who became victims to the suspicions tyranny of the Council of Ten, and of the State inquisitors, would be very long and of little interest. We may mention a few, however. We find that in 1385, Peter Justiniani, and, in 1388, Stephen Monalesco, were punished for holding secret transactions with the Lord of Padua; in 1413, John Nogarola, for having tried to set fire to Verona; in 1471, Borromeo Memo, for having uttered defamatory speeches against the Podestat of Padua. Not only was this Borromeo Memo punished, but three witnesses of the crime which was imputed to him were condemned to a year's imprisonment and three years' banishment, for not having denounced the deed "between evening and morning." In 1457 we find the Council of Ten attacking the Doge himself, by requiring the abdication of Francis Foscari. A century earlier it had caused the Doge, Marino Faliero, who was convicted of having taken part in a plot to destroy the influence of the nobility, to be executed on the very staircase of the ducal palace, where allegiance to the Republic was usually sworn.

[Illustration: Fig. 337.—Doge of Venice. Costume before the Sixteenth Century. From Cesare Vecellio.]

[Illustration: Fig. 338.—Doge of Venice in Ceremonial Costume of the Sixteenth Century. From Cesare Vecellio.]

Like the Holy Vehme, the Council of Ten compromised its authority by the abuse of power. In 1540, unknown to the Senate, and in spite of the well-prescribed limit of its authority, it concluded a treaty with the Turkish Sultan, Soliman II. The Senate at first concealed its indignation at this abuse of power, but, in 1582, it took measures so as considerably to restrain the powers of the Council of Ten, which, from that date, only existed in name.

[Illustration: Fig. 339.—Seal of the Free Count Heinrich Beckmann, of Medebach. (1520—1533).]

Punishments.

Refinements of Penal Cruelty.—Tortures for different Purposes.—Water, Screw-boards, and the Rack.—The Executioner.—Female Executioners.—Tortures.—Amende Honorable.—Torture of Fire, Real and Feigned.—Auto-da-fe.—Red-hot Brazier or Basin.—Beheading.—Quartering.—Wheel.—Garotte.—Hanging.—The Whip.—The Pillory.—The Arquebuse.—Tickling.—Flaying.—Drowning.—Imprisonment.—Regulations of Prisons.—The Iron Cage.—The Leads of Venice.

"It is very sad," says the learned M. de Villegille, "to observe the infinite variety of tortures which have existed since the beginning of the world. It is, in fact, difficult to realise the amount of ingenuity exercised by men in inventing new tortures, in order to give themselves the satisfaction of seeing their fellow-creatures agonizing in the most awful sufferings."

In entering upon the subject of ancient modes of punishment, we must first speak of the torture, which, according to the received phrase, might be either *previous* or *preparatory*: *previous*, when it consisted of a torture which the condemned had to endure previous to capital punishment; and *preparatory*, when it was applied in order to elicit from the culprit an avowal of his crime, or of that of his accomplices. It was also called *ordinary*, or *extraordinary*, according to the duration or violence with which it was inflicted. In some cases the torture lasted five or six consecutive hours; in others, it rarely exceeded an hour. Hippolyte de Marsillis, the learned and venerable jurisconsult of Bologna, who lived at the beginning of the fifteenth century, mentions fourteen ways of inflicting torture. The compression of the limbs by special instruments, or by ropes only; injection of water, vinegar, or oil, into the body of the accused; application of hot pitch, and starvation, were the processes most in use. Other means, which were more or less applied according to the fancy of the magistrate and the tormentor or executioner, were remarkable for their singular atrocities. For instance, placing hot eggs under the arm-pits; introducing dice between the skin and flesh; tying lighted candles to the fingers, so that they might be consumed simultaneously with the wax; letting water trickle drop by drop from a great height on the stomach; and also the custom, which was, according to writers on criminal matters, an indescribable torture, of watering the feet with salt water and allowing goats to lick them. However, every country had special customs as to the manner of applying torture.

In France, too, the torture varied according to the provinces, or rather according to the parliaments. For instance, in Brittany the culprit, tied in an iron chair, was gradually brought near a blazing furnace. In Normandy, one thumb was squeezed in a screw in the ordinary, and both thumbs in the extraordinary torture. At Autun, after high boots made of spongy leather had been placed on the culprit's feet, he was tied on to a table near a large fire, and a quantity of boiling water was poured on the boots, which penetrated the leather, ate away the flesh, and even dissolved the bones of the victim.

At Orleans, for the ordinary torture the accused was stripped half naked, and his hands were tightly tied behind his back, with a ring fixed between them. Then by means of a rope fastened to this ring, they raised the poor man, who had a weight of one hundred and eighty pounds attached to his feet, a certain height from the ground. For the extraordinary torture, which then took the name of *estrapade*, they raised the victim, with two hundred and fifty pounds attached to his feet, to the ceiling by means of a capstan; he was then allowed to fall several times successively by jerks to the level of the ground, by which means his arms and legs were completely dislocated (Fig. 340).

At Avignon, the ordinary torture consisted in hanging the accused by the wrists, with a heavy iron ball at each foot; for the extraordinary torture, which was then much in use in Italy under the name of *veglia*, the body was stretched horizontally by means of ropes passing through rings riveted into the wall, and attached to the four limbs, the only support given to the culprit being the point of a stake cut in a diamond shape, which just touched the end of the back–bone. A doctor and a surgeon were always present, feeling the pulse at the temples of the patient, so as to be able to judge of the moment when he could not any longer bear the pain.

[Illustration: Fig. 340.—The Estrapade, or Question Extraordinary.—Fac–simile of a Woodcut in the Work of J. Millaeus, "Praxis Criminis Persequendi." folio, Paris, 1541.]

[Illustration: Fig. 341.—The Water Torture.—Fac–simile of a Woodcut in J. Damhoudere's "Praxis Rerum Criminalium:" in 4to, Antwerp, 1556.]

At that moment he was untied, hot fomentations were used to revive him, restoratives were administered, and, as soon as he had recovered a little strength, he was again put to the torture, which went on thus for six consecutive hours.

In Paris, for a long time, the *water torture* was in use; this was the most easily borne, and the least dangerous. A person undergoing it was tied to a board which was supported horizontally on two trestles. By means of a horn, acting as a funnel, and whilst his nose was being pinched, so as to force him to swallow, they slowly poured four *coquemars* (about nine pints) of water into his mouth; this was for the ordinary torture. For the extraordinary, double that quantity was poured in (Fig. 341). When the torture was ended, the victim was untied, "and taken to be warmed in the kitchen," says the old text.

At a later period, the *brodequins* were preferred. For this torture, the victim was placed in a sitting posture on a massive bench, with strong narrow boards fixed inside and outside of each leg, which were tightly bound together with strong rope; wedges were then driven in between the centre boards with a mallet; four wedges in the ordinary and eight in the extraordinary torture. Not unfrequently during the latter operation the bones of the legs were literally burst.

The *brodequins* which were often used for ordinary torture were stockings of parchment, into which it was easy enough to get the feet when it was wet, but which, on being held near the fire, shrunk so considerably that it caused insufferable agony to the wearer.

Whatever manner of torture was applied, the accused, before undergoing it, was forced to remain eight or ten hours without eating. Damhoudere, in his famous technical work, called "Practique et Enchiridion des Causes Criminelles" (1544), also recommends that the hair should be carefully shaved from the bodies of persons about to undergo examination by torture, for fear of their concealing some countercharm which would render them insensible to bodily pain. The same author also recommends, as a rule, when there are several persons "to be placed on the rack" for the same deed, to begin with those from whom it would be most probable that confession would be first extorted. Thus, for instance, when a man and a woman were to suffer one after the other, he recommended that the woman be first tortured, as being the weaker of the two; when a father and son were concerned, the son should be tortured in presence of the father, "who naturally fears more for his son than for himself." We thereby see that the judges were adepts in the art of adding moral to physical tortures. The barbarous custom of punishment by torture was on several occasions condemned by the Church. As early as 866, we find, from Pope Nicholas V.'s letter to the Bulgarians, that their custom of torturing the accused was considered contrary to divine as well as to human law: "For," says he, "a confession should be voluntary, and not forced. By means of the torture, an innocent man may suffer to the utmost without making any avowal; and, in such a case, what a crime for the judge! Or the person may be subdued by pain, and may acknowledge himself guilty, although he be not so, which throws an equally great sin upon the judge."

[Illustration: Fig. 342.—Type of Executioner in the Decapitation of John the Baptist (Thirteenth Century).—Fac-simile of a Miniature in the Psalm-book of St. Louis. Manuscript preserved in the Musee des Souverains.]

After having endured the *previous* torture, the different phases of which were carried out by special tormentors or executioners, the condemned was at last handed over to the *maistre des haultes oeuvres*—that is to say, the *executioner*—whose special mission was that of sending culprits to another world (Fig. 342).

[Illustration: Fig. 343.—Swiss Grand Provost (Fifteenth Century).—From a Painting in the "Danse des Morts" of Basle, engraved by Merian.]

The executioner did not hold the same position in all countries. For whereas in France, Italy, and Spain, a certain amount of odium was attached to this terrible craft, in Germany, on the contrary, successfully carrying out a certain number of capital sentences was rewarded by titles and the privileges of nobility (Fig. 343). At Reutlingen, in Suabia, the last of the councillors admitted into the tribunal had to carry out the sentence with his own hand. In Franconia, this painful duty fell upon the councillor who had last taken a wife.

In France, the executioner, otherwise called the *King's Sworn Tormentor,* was the lowest of the officers of justice. His letters of appointment, which he received from the King, had, nevertheless, to be registered in Parliament; but, after having put the seal on them, it is said that the chancellor threw them under the table, in token of contempt. The executioner was generally forbidden to live within the precincts of the city, unless it was on the grounds where the pillory was situated; and, in some cases, so that he might not be mistaken amongst the people, he was forced to wear a particular coat, either of red or yellow. On the other hand, his duties ensured him certain privileges. In Paris, he possessed the right of *havage*, which consisted in taking all that he could hold in his hand from every load of grain which was brought into market; however, in order that the grain might be preserved from ignominious contact, he levied his tax with a wooden spoon. He enjoyed many similar rights over most articles of consumption, independently of benefiting by several taxes or fines, such as the toll on the Petit–Pont, the tax on foreign traders, on boats arriving with fish, on dealers in herrings, watercress, &c.; and the fine of five sous which was levied on stray pigs (see previous chapter), &c. And, lastly, besides the personal property of the condemned, he received the rents from the shops and stalls surrounding the pillory, in which the retail fish trade was carried on.

It appears that, in consequence of the receipts from these various duties forming a considerable source of revenue, the prestige of wealth by degrees dissipated the unfavourable impressions traditionally attached to the duties of executioner. At least, we have authority for supposing this, when, for instance, in 1418, we see the Paris executioner, who was then captain of the bourgeois militia, coming in that capacity to touch the hand of the Duke of Burgundy, on the occasion of his solemn entry into Paris with Queen Isabel of Bavaria. We may add that popular belief generally ascribed to the executioner a certain practical knowledge of medicine, which was supposed inherent in the profession itself; and the acquaintance with certain methods of cure unknown to doctors, was attributed to him; people went to buy from him the fat of culprits who had been hung, which was supposed to be a marvellous panacea. We may also remark that, in our day, the proficiency of the executioner in setting dislocated limbs is still proverbial in many countries.

[Illustration: Fig. 344.—Amende Honorable before the Tribunal.—Fac-simile of a Woodcut in J. Damhoudere's "Praxis Rerum Criminalium:" in 4to, Antwerp, 1556.]

More than once during the thirteenth century the duties of the executioner were performed by women, but only in those cases in which their own sex was concerned; for it is expressly stated in an order of St. Louis, that persons convicted of blasphemy shall be beaten with birch rods, "the men by men, and the women by women only, without the presence of men." This, however, was not long tolerated, for we know that a period soon arrived when women were exempted from a duty so little adapted to their physical weakness and moral sensitiveness.

The learned writer on criminal cases, Josse Damhoudere, whom we have already mentioned, and whom we shall take as our special guide in the enumeration of the various tortures, specifies thirteen ways in which the executioner "carries out his executions," and places them in the following order:—"Fire"—"the sword"—"mechanical force"—"quartering"—"the wheel"—"the fork"—"the gibbet"—"drawing"—"spiking"—"cutting off the ears"—"dismembering"—"flogging or beating"—and the "pillory."

[Illustration: Fig. 345.—The Punishment by Fire.—Fac-simile of a Woodcut of the "Cosmographie Universelle" of Munster: in folio, Basle, 1552.]

But before entering upon the details of this revolting subject, we must state that, whatever punishment was inflicted upon a culprit, it was very rare that its execution had not been preceded by the *amende honorable*, which, in certain cases, constituted a distinct punishment, but which generally was but the prelude to the torture itself. The *amende honorable* which was called *simple* or *short*, took place without the assistance of the executioner in the council chamber, where the condemned, bareheaded and kneeling, had to state that "he had falsely said or done something against the authority of the King or the honour of some person" (Fig. 344). For the *amende honorable in figuris*—that is to say, in public—the condemned, in his shirt, barefooted, the rope round his neck, followed by the executioner, and holding in his hand a wax taper, with a weight, which was definitely specified in the sentence which had been passed upon him, but which was generally of two or four pounds, prostrated himself at the door of a church, where in a loud voice he had to confess his sin, and to beg the pardon of God and man.

When a criminal had been condemned to be burnt, a stake was erected on the spot specially designed for the execution, and round it a pile was prepared, composed of alternate layers of straw and wood, and rising to about the height of a man. Care was taken to leave a free space round the stake for the victim, and also a passage by which to lead him to it. Having been stripped of his clothes, and dressed in a shirt smeared with sulphur, he had to walk to the centre of the pile through a narrow opening, and was then tightly bound to the stake with ropes and chains. After this, faggots and straw were thrown into the empty space through which he had passed to the stake, until he was entirely covered by them; the pile was then fired on all sides at once (Fig. 345).

Sometimes, the sentence was that the culprit should only be delivered to the flames after having been previously strangled. In this case, the dead corpse was then immediately placed where the victim would otherwise have been placed alive, and the punishment lost much of its horror. It often happened that the executioner, in order to shorten the sufferings of the condemned, whilst he prepared the pile, placed a large and pointed iron bar amongst the faggots and opposite the stake breast high, so that, directly the fire was lighted, the bar was quickly pushed against the victim, giving a mortal blow to the unfortunate wretch, who would otherwise have been slowly devoured by the flames. If, according to the wording of the sentence, the ashes of the criminal were to be scattered to the winds, as soon as it was possible to approach the centre of the burning pile, a few ashes were taken in a shovel and sprinkled in the air.

They were not satisfied with burning the living, they also delivered to the flames the bodies of those who had died a natural death before their execution could be carried out,

274

as if an anticipated death should not be allowed to save them from the punishment which they had deserved. It also happened in certain cases, where a person's guilt was only proved after his decease, that his body was disinterred, and carried to the stake to be burnt.

The punishment by fire was always inflicted in cases of heresy, or blasphemy. The Spanish Inquisition made such a constant and cruel use of it, that the expression *auto−da−fe* (act of faith), strangely perverted from its original meaning, was the only one employed to denote the punishment itself. In France, in the beginning of the fourteenth century, fifty−nine Templars were burned at the same time for the crimes of heresy and witchcraft. And three years later, on the 18th March, 1314, Jacques Molay, and a few other dignitaries of the Order of the Templars, also perished in the flames at the extremity of the island of Notre Dame, on the very spot where the equestrian statue of Henry IV. now stands.

Every one is acquainted with the fact that judges were found iniquitous enough to condemn Joan of Arc to death by fire as a witch and a heretic. Her execution, which took place in the market−place of Rouen, is remarkable from a circumstance which is little known, and which had never taken place on any other occasion. When it was supposed that the fire which surrounded the young heroine on all sides had reached her and no doubt suffocated her, although sufficient time had not elapsed for it to consume her body, a part of the blazing wood was withdrawn, "in order to remove any doubts from the people," and when the crowd had satisfied themselves by seeing her in the middle of the pile, "chained to the post and quite dead, the executioner replaced the fire...." It should be stated in reference to this point, that Joan having been accused of witchcraft, there was a general belief among the people that the flames would be harmless to her, and that she would be seen emerging from her pile unscathed.

The sentence of punishment by fire did not absolutely imply death at the stake, for there was a punishment of this description which was specially reserved for base coiners, and which consisted in hurling the criminals into a cauldron of scalding water or oil.

We must include in the category of punishment by fire certain penalties, which were, so to speak, but the preliminaries of a more severe punishment, such as the sulphur−fire, in which the hands of parricides, or of criminals accused of high treason, were burned. We must also add various punishments which, if they did not involve death, were none the less cruel, such as the red–hot brazier, *bassin ardent*, which was passed backwards and forwards before the eyes of the culprit, until they were destroyed by the scorching heat; and the process of branding various marks on the flesh, as an ineffaceable stigma, the use of which has been continued to the present day.

In certain countries decapitation was performed with an axe; but in France, it was carried out usually by means of a two–handed sword or glave of justice, which was furnished to the executioner for that purpose (Fig. 346). We find it recorded that in 1476, sixty sous parisis were paid to the executioner of Paris "for having bought a large *espee a feuille*," used for beheading the condemned, and "for having the old sword done up, which was damaged, and had become notched whilst carrying out the sentence of justice upon Messire Louis de Luxembourg."

[Illustration: Fig. 346.—Beheading.—Fac–simile of a Miniature on Wood in the "Cosmographie Universelle" of Munster: in folio, Basle, 1552.]

Originally, decapitation was indiscriminately inflicted on all criminals condemned to death; at a later period, however, it became the particular privilege of the nobility, who submitted to it without any feeling of degradation. The victim—unless the sentence prescribed that he should be blindfolded as an ignominious aggravation of the penalty—was allowed to choose whether he would have his eyes covered or not. He knelt down on the scaffold, placed his head on the block, and gave himself up to the executioner (Fig. 347). The skill of the executioner was generally such that the head was almost invariably severed from the body at the first blow. Nevertheless, skill and practice at times failed, for cases are on record where as many as eleven blows were dealt, and at times it happened that the sword broke. It was no doubt the desire to avoid this mischance that led to the invention of the mechanical instrument, now known under the name of the *guillotine*, which is merely an improvement on a complicated machine which was much more ancient than is generally supposed. As early as the sixteenth century the modern guillotine already existed in Scotland under the name of the *Maiden*, and English historians relate that Lord Morton, regent of Scotland during the minority of James VI., had it constructed after a model of a similar machine, which had long been in use at Halifax, in Yorkshire. They add, and popular tradition also has invented an analogous tale in France, that this Lord Morton, who was the inventor or the first to introduce this kind of punishment, was himself the first to experience it. The guillotine is, besides, very accurately described in the "Chronicles of Jean d'Auton," in an account of an execution which took place at Genoa at the beginning of the sixteenth century. Two German engravings, executed about 1550 by Pencz and Aldegrever, also represent an instrument of death almost identical with the guillotine; and the same instrument is to be found on a bas–relief of that period, which is still existing in one of the halls of the Tribunal of Luneburg, in Hanover.

[Illustration: Decapitation of Guillaume de Pommiers.

[Illustration: Fig. 347.—Public Executions.—Fac–simile of a Woodcut in the Latin Work of J. Millaeus, "Praxis Criminis Persequendi:" small folio, Parisis, Simon de Colines, 1541.]

And his Confessor, at Bordeaux in 1377, by order of the King of England's Lieutenant. *Froissart's Chronicles.* No. 2644, Bibl. nat'le de Paris.]

Possibly the invention of such a machine was prompted by the desire to curtail the physical sufferings of the victim, instead of prolonging them, as under the ancient system. It is, however, difficult to believe that the mediaeval judges were actuated by any humane feelings, when we find that, in order to reconcile a respect for *propriety* with a due compliance with the ends of justice, the punishment of burying alive was resorted to for women, who could not with decency be hung up to the gibbets. In 1460, a woman named Perette, accused of theft and of receiving stolen goods, was condemned by the Provost of Paris to be "buried alive before the gallows," and the sentence was literally carried out.

Quartering may in truth be considered the most horrible penalty invented by judicial cruelty. This punishment really dates from the remotest ages, but it was scarcely ever inflicted in more modern times, except on regicides, who were looked upon as having committed the worst of crimes. In almost all cases, the victim had previously to undergo various accessory tortures: sometimes his right hand was cut off, and the mutilated stump was burnt in a cauldron of sulphur; sometimes his arms, thighs, or breasts were lacerated with red–hot pincers, and hot oil, pitch, or molten lead was poured into the wounds.

[Illustration: Fig. 348.—Demons applying the Torture of the Wheel.—Fac–simile of a Woodcut in the "Grand Kalendrier ou Compost des Bergers:" small folio, Troyes, Nicholas le Rouge, 1529.]

After these horrible preliminaries, a rope was attached to each of the limbs of the criminal, one being bound round each leg from the foot to the knee, and round each arm from the wrist to the elbow. These ropes were then fastened to four bars, to each of which a strong horse was harnessed, as if for towing a barge. These horses were first made to give short jerks; and when the agony had elicited heart–rending cries from the unfortunate man, who felt his limbs being dislocated without being broken, the four horses were all suddenly urged on with the whip in different directions, and thus all the limbs were strained at one moment. If the tendons and ligaments still resisted the combined efforts of the four horses, the executioner assisted, and made several cuts with a hatchet on each joint. When at last—for this horrible torture often lasted several hours—each horse had drawn out a limb, they were collected and placed near the hideous trunk, which often still showed signs of life, and the whole were burned together. Sometimes the sentence was, that the body should be hung to the gibbet, and that the limbs should be displayed on the gates of the town, or sent to four principal towns in the extremities of the kingdom. When this was done, "an inscription was placed on each of the limbs, which stated the reason of its being thus exposed."

The *wheel* is the name applied to a torture of very ancient origin, but which was applied during the Middle Ages to quite a different torture from that used in olden times. The modern instrument might indeed have been called the cross, for it only served for the public exhibition of the body of the criminal whose limbs had been previously broken alive. This torture, which does not date earlier than the days of Francis I., is thus described: —The victim was first tied on his back to two joists forming a St. Andrew's cross, each of his limbs being stretched out on its arms. Two places were hollowed out under each limb, about a foot apart, in order that the joints alone might touch the wood. The executioner then dealt a heavy blow over each hollow with a square iron bar, about two inches broad and rounded at the handle, thus breaking each limb in two places. To the eight blows required for this, the executioner generally added two or three on the chest, which were called *coups de grace*, and which ended this horrible execution. It was only after death that the broken body was placed on a wheel, which was turned round on a pivot. Sometimes, however, the sentence ordered that the condemned should be strangled before being broken, which was done in such cases by the instantaneous twist of a rope round the neck.

Strangling, thus carried out, was called *garotting*. This method is still in use in Spain, and is specially reserved for the nobility. The victim is seated on a scaffold, his head leaning

278

against a beam and his neck grasped by an iron collar, which the executioner suddenly tightens from behind by means of a screw.

For several centuries, and down to the Revolution, hanging was the most common mode of execution in France; consequently, in every town, and almost in every village, there was a permanent gibbet, which, owing to the custom of leaving the bodies to hang till they crumbled into dust, was very rarely without having some corpses or skeletons attached to it. These gibbets, which were called *fourches patibulaires* or *justices*, because they represented the authority of the law, were generally composed of pillars of stone, joined at their summit by wooden traverses, to which the bodies of criminals were tied by ropes or chains. The gallows, the pillars of which varied in number according to the will of the authorities, were always placed by the side of frequented roads, and on an eminence.

[Illustration: Fig. 349.—The Gibbet of Montfaucon.—From an Engraving of the Topography of Paris, in the Collection of Engravings of the National Library.]

According to prescribed rule, the gallows of Paris, which played such an important part in the political as well as the criminal history of that city, were erected on a height north of the town, near the high road leading into Germany. Montfaucon, originally the name of the hill, soon became that of the gallows itself. This celebrated place of execution consisted of a heavy mass of masonry, composed of ten or twelve layers of rough stones, and formed an enclosure of forty feet by twenty–five or thirty. At the upper part there was a platform, which was reached by a stone staircase, the entrance to which was closed by a massive door (Fig. 349). On three sides of this platform rested sixteen square pillars, about thirty feet high, made of blocks of stone a foot thick. These pillars were joined to one another by double bars of wood, which were fastened into them, and bore iron chains three feet and a half long, to which the criminals were suspended. Underneath, half–way between these and the platform, other bars were placed for the same purpose. Long and solid ladders riveted to the pillars enabled the executioner and his assistants to lead up criminals, or to carry up corpses destined to be hung there. Lastly, the centre of the structure was occupied by a deep pit, the hideous receptacle of the decaying remains of the criminals.

One can easily imagine the strange and melancholy aspect of this monumental gibbet if one thinks of the number of corpses continually attached to it, and which were feasted upon by thousands of crows. On one occasion only it was necessary to replace *fifty—two* chains, which were useless; and the accounts of the city of Paris prove that the expense of executions was more heavy than that of the maintenance of the gibbet, a fact easy to be understood if one recalls to mind the frequency of capital sentences during the Middle Ages. Montfaucon was used not only for executions, but also for exposing corpses which were brought there from various places of execution in every part of the country. The mutilated remains of criminals who had been boiled, quartered, or beheaded, were also hung there, enclosed in sacks of leather or wickerwork. They often remained hanging for a considerable time, as in the case of Pierre des Essarts, who had been beheaded in 1413, and whose remains were handed over to his family for Christian burial after having hung on Montfaucon for three years.

The criminal condemned to be hanged was generally taken to the place of execution sitting or standing in a waggon, with his back to the horses, his confessor by his side, and the executioner behind him. He bore three ropes round his neck; two the size of the little finger, and called *tortouses*, each of which had a slip—knot; the third, called the *jet*, was only used to pull the victim off the ladder, and so to launch him into eternity (Fig. 350). When the cart arrived at the foot of the gallows, the executioner first ascended the ladder backwards, drawing the culprit after him by means of the ropes, and forcing him to keep pace with him; on arriving at the top, he quickly fastened the two *tortouses* to the arm of the gibbet, and by a jerk of his knee he turned the culprit off the ladder, still holding the *jet* in his own hand. He then placed his feet on the tied hands of the condemned, and suspending himself by his hands to the gibbet, he finished off his victim by repeated jerks, thus ensuring complete strangulation.

When the words "shall be hung until death doth ensue" are to be found in a sentence, it must not be supposed that they were used merely as a form, for in certain cases the judge ordered that the sentence should be only carried out as far as would prove to the culprit the awful sensation of hanging. In such cases, the victim was simply suspended by ropes passing under the arm—pits, a kind of exhibition which was not free from danger when it was too prolonged, for the weight of the body so tightened the rope round the chest that the circulation might be stopped. Many culprits, after hanging thus an hour, when brought down, were dead, or only survived this painful process a short time.

[Illustration: Fig. 350.—Hanging to Music. (A Minstrel condemned to the Gallows obtained permission that one of his companions should accompany him to his execution, and play his favourite instrument on the ladder of the Gallows.)—Fac—simile of a Woodcut in Michault's "Doctrinal du Temps Present:" small folio, goth., Bruges, about 1490.]

We have seen elsewhere (chapter on *Privileges and Rights, Feudal and Municipal*) that, when the criminal passed before the convent of the *Filles—Dieu*, the nuns of that establishment were bound to bring him out a glass of wine and three pieces of bread, and this was called *le dernier morceau des patients*. It was hardly ever refused, and an immense crowd assisted at this sad meal. After this the procession went forward, and on arriving near the gallows, another halt was made at the foot of a stone cross, in order that the culprit might receive the religions exhortations of his confessor. The moment the execution was over, the confessor and the officers of justice returned to the Chatelet, where a repast provided by the town awaited them.

[Illustration: Fig. 351.—View of the Pillory in the Market—place of Paris in the Sixteenth Century, after a Drawing by an unknown Artist of 1670.]

Sometimes the criminals, in consequence of a peculiar wording of the sentence, were taken to Montfaucon, whether dead or alive, on a ladder fastened behind a cart. This was an aggravation of the penalty, which was called *trainer sur la claie*.

The penalty of the lash was inflicted in two ways: first, under the *custode*, that is to say within the prison, and by the hand of the gaoler himself, in which case it was simply a correction; and secondly, in public, when its administration became ignominious as well as painful. In the latter case the criminal was paraded about the town, stripped to the waist, and at each crossway he received a certain number of blows on the shoulders, given by the public executioner with a cane or a knotted rope.

When it was only required to stamp a culprit with infamy he was put into the *pillory*, which was generally a kind of scaffold furnished with chains and iron collars, and bearing on its front the arms of the feudal lord. In Paris, this name was given to a round isolated tower built in the centre of the market. The tower was sixty feet high, and had large openings in its thick walls, and a horizontal wheel was provided, which was capable of turning on a pivot. This wheel was pierced with several holes, made so as to hold the hands and head of the culprit, who, on passing and repassing before the eyes of the crowd, came in full view, and was subjected to their hootings (Fig. 351). The pillories were always situated in the most frequented places, such as markets, crossways, &c.

Notwithstanding the long and dreadful enumeration we have just made of mediaeval punishments, we are far from having exhausted the subject; for we have not spoken of several more or less atrocious punishments, which were in use at various times and in various countries; such as the *Pain of the Cross*, specially employed against the Jews; the *Arquebusade*, which was well adapted for carrying out prompt justice on soldiers; the *Chatouillement*, which resulted in death after the most intense tortures; the *Pal* (Fig. 352), *flaying alive*, and, lastly, *drowning*, a kind of death frequently employed in France. Hence the common expression, *gens de sac et de corde*, which was derived from the sack into which persons were tied who were condemned to die by immersion.... But we will now turn away from these horrible scenes, and consider the several methods of penal sequestration and prison arrangements.

It is unnecessary to state that in barbarous times the cruel and pitiless feeling which induced legislators to increase the horrors of tortures, also contributed to the aggravation of the fate of prisoners. Each administrator of the law had his private gaol, which was entirely under his will and control (Fig. 353). Law or custom did not prescribe any fixed rules for the internal government of prisons. There can be little doubt, however, that these prisons were as small as they were unhealthy, if we may judge from that in the Rue de la Tannerie, which was the property of the provost, the merchants, and the aldermen of Paris in 1383. Although this dungeon was only eleven feet long by seven feet wide, from ten to twenty prisoners were often immured in it at the same time.

[Illustration: Fig. 352.—Empalement.—Fac–simile of a Woodcut in the "Cosmographie Universelle" of Munster: in folio, Basle, 1552.]

Paris alone contained twenty–five or thirty special prisons, without counting the *vade in pace* of the various religious communities. The most important were the Grand Chatelet, the Petit Chatelet, the Bastille, the Conciergerie, and the For–l'Eveque, the ancient seat of the ecclesiastical jurisdiction of the Bishop of Paris. Nearly all these places of confinement contained subterranean cells, which were almost entirely deprived of air and light. As examples of these may be mentioned the *Chartres basses* of the Petit Chatelet, where, under the reign of Charles VI., it was proved that no man could pass an entire day without being suffocated; and the fearful cells excavated thirty feet below the surface of the earth, in the gaol of the Abbey of Saint Germain des Pres, the roof of which was so low that a man of middle height could not stand up in them, and where the straw of the prisoners' beds floated upon the stagnant water which had oozed through the walls.

[Illustration: Fig. 353.—The Provost's Prison.—Fac–simile of a Woodcut in J. Damhoudere's "Praxis Rerum Civilium."]

The Grand Chatelet was one of the most ancient prisons of Paris, and probably the one which held the greatest number of prisoners. By a curious and arbitrary custom, prisoners were compelled to pay a gaol fee on entering and going out of this prison, which varied according to their rank, and which was established by a law of the year 1425. We learn from this enactment the names by which the various places of confinement composing this spacious municipal prison were known. A prisoner who was confined in the *Beauvoir, La Mate* or *La Salle*, had the right of "having a bed brought from his own house," and only had to pay the *droit de place* to the gaoler; any one who was placed in the *Boucherie*, in the *Beaumont*, or in the *Griseche*, "which are closed prisons," had to pay four deniers "*pour place;*" any one who was confined in the *Beauvais*, "lies on mats or on layers of rushes or straw" (*gist sur nates ou sur couche de feurre ou de paille*); if he preferred, he might be placed *au Puis*, in the *Gourdaine*, in the *Bercueil*, or in the *Oubliette*, where he did not pay more than in the *Fosse*. For this, no doubt, the smallest charge was made. Sometimes, however, the prisoner was left between two doors (" *entre deux huis*"), and he then paid much less than he would in the *Barbarie* or in the *Gloriette*. The exact meaning of these curious names is no longer intelligible to us, notwithstanding the terror which they formerly created, but their very strangeness gives us reason to suppose that the prison system was at that time subjected to the most odious refinement of the basest cruelty.

From various reliable sources we learn that there was a place in the Grand Chatelet, called the *Chausse d'Hypocras*, in which the prisoners had their feet continually in water, and where they could neither stand up nor lie down; and a cell, called *Fin d'aise*, which was a horrible receptacle of filth, vermin, and reptiles; as to the *Fosse*, no staircase being attached to it, the prisoners were lowered down into it by means of a rope and pulley.

By the law of 1425, the gaoler was not permitted to put more than *two or three* persons in the same bed. He was bound to give "bread and water" to the poor prisoners who had no means of subsistence; and, lastly, he was enjoined "to keep the large stone basin, which was on the pavement, full of water, so that prisoners might get it whenever they wished."

In order to defray his expenses, he levied on the prisoners various charges for attendance and for bedding, and he was authorised to detain in prison any person who failed to pay him. The power of compelling payment of these charges continued even after a judge's order for the release of a prisoner had been issued.

[Illustration: Fig. 354.—The Bastille.—From an ancient Engraving of the Topography of Paris, in the Collection of Engravings of the National Library.]

The subterranean cells of the Bastille (Fig. 354) did not differ much from those of the Chatelet. There were several, the bottoms of which were formed like a sugar–loaf upside down, thus neither allowing the prisoner to stand up, nor even to adopt a tolerable position sitting or lying down. It was in these that King Louis XI., who seemed to have a partiality for filthy dungeons, placed the two young sons of the Duke de Nemours (beheaded in 1477), ordering, besides, that they should be taken out twice a week and beaten with birch rods, and, as a supreme measure of atrocity, he had one of their teeth extracted every three months. It was Louis XI., too, who, in 1476, ordered the famous *iron cage*, to be erected in one of the towers of the Bastille, in which Guillaume, Bishop of Verdun, was incarcerated for fourteen years.

The Chateau de Loches also possessed one of these cages, which received the name of *Cage de Balue*, because the Cardinal Jean de la Balue was imprisoned in it. Philippe de Commines, in his "Memoires," declares that he himself had a taste of it for eight months. Before the invention of cages, Louis XI. ordered very heavy chains to be made, which were fastened to the feet of the prisoners, and attached to large iron balls, called, according to Commines, the King's little daughters (*les fillettes du roy*).

[Illustration: Fig. 355.—Movable Iron Cage.—Fac–simile of a Woodcut in the "Cosmographie Universelle" of Munster, in folio, Basle, 1552.]

The prison known by the name of The Leads of Venice is of so notorious a character that its mere mention is sufficient, without its being necessary for us to describe it. To the subject of voluntary seclusions, to which certain pious persons submitted themselves as acts of extreme religious devotion, it will only be necessary to allude here, and to remark that there are examples of this confinement having been ordered by legal authority. In 1485, Renee de Vermandois, the widow of a squire, had been condemned to be burnt for adultery and for murdering her husband; but, on letters of remission from the King,

284

Parliament commuted the sentence pronounced by the Provost of Paris, and ordered that Renee de Vermandois should be "shut up within the walls of the cemetery of the Saints–Innocents, in a small house, built at her expense, that she might therein do penance and end her days." In conformity with this sentence, the culprit having been conducted with much pomp to the cell which had been prepared for her, the door was locked by means of two keys, one of which remained in the hands of the churchwarden (*marguillier*) of the Church of the Innocents, and the other was deposited at the office of the Parliament. The prisoner received her food from public charity, and it is said that she became an object of veneration and respect by the whole town.

[Illustration: Fig. 356.—Cat–o'–nine–tails.—Fac–simile of a Woodcut in the "Cosmographie Universelle" of Munster.]

Jews.

Dispersion of the Jews.—Jewish Quarters in the Mediaeval Towns.—The *Ghetto* of Rome.—Ancient Prague.—The *Giudecca* of Venice.—Condition of the Jews.—Animosity of the People against them—Severity and vexatious Treatment of the Sovereigns.—The Jews of Lincoln.—The Jews of Blois.—Mission of the *Pastoureaux*.—Extermination of the Jews.—The Price at which the Jews purchased Indulgences.—Marks set upon them.—Wealth, Knowledge, Industry, and Financial Aptitude of the Jews.—Regulations respecting Usury as practised by the Jews.—Attachment of the Jews to their Religion.

A painful and gloomy history commences for the Jewish race from the day when the Romans seized upon Jerusalem and expelled its unfortunate inhabitants, a race so essentially homogeneous, strong, patient, and religious, and dating its origin from the remotest period of the patriarchal ages. The Jews, proud of the title of "the People of God," were scattered, proscribed, and received universal reprobation (Fig. 357), notwithstanding that their annals, collected under divine inspiration by Moses and the sacred writers, had furnished a glorious prologue to the annals of all modern nations, and had given to the world the holy and divine history of Christ, who, by establishing the Gospel, was to become the regenerator of the whole human family.

Their Temple is destroyed, and the crowd which had once pressed beneath its portico as the flock of the living God has become a miserable tribe, restless and unquiet in the present, but full of hope as regards the future. The Jewish *nation* exists nowhere, nevertheless, the Jewish *people* are to be found everywhere. They are wanderers upon the face of the earth, continually pursued, threatened, and persecuted. It would seem as if the existence of the offspring of Israel is perpetuated simply to present to Christian eyes a clear and awful warning of the Divine vengeance, a special, and at the same time an overwhelming example of the vicissitudes which God alone can determine in the life of a people.

[Illustration: Fig. 357.—Expulsion of the Jews in the Reign of the Emperor Hadrian (A.D. 135): "How Heraclius turned the Jews out of Jerusalem."—Fac-simile of a Miniature in the "Histoire des Empereurs," Manuscript of the Fifteenth Century, in the Library of the Arsenal, Paris.]

M. Depping, an historian of this race so long accursed, after having been for centuries blessed and favoured by God, says, "A Jewish community in an European town during the Middle Ages resembled a colony on an island or on a distant coast. Isolated from the rest of the population, it generally occupied a district or street which was separated from the town or borough. The Jews, like a troop of lepers, were thrust away and huddled together into the most uncomfortable and most unhealthy quarter of the city, as miserable as it vas disgusting. There, in ill-constructed houses, this poor and numerous population was amassed; in some cases high walls enclosed the small and dark narrow streets of the quarter occupied by this branded race, which prevented its extension, though, at the same time, it often protected the inhabitants from the fury of the populace."

In order to form a just appreciation of what the Jewish quarters were like in the mediaeval towns, one must visit the *Ghetto* of Rome or ancient Prague. The latter place especially has, in all respects, preserved its antique appearance. We must picture to ourselves a large enclosure of wretched houses, irregularly built, divided by small streets with no attempt at uniformity. The principal thoroughfare is lined with stalls, in which are sold not only old clothes, furniture, and utensils, but also new and glittering articles. The inhabitants of this enclosure can, without crossing its limits, procure everything necessary to material life. This quarter contains the old synagogue, a square building begrimed with the dirt of ages, and so covered with dirt and moss that the stone of which it is built is scarcely visible. The building, which is as mournful as a prison, has only narrow loopholes by way of windows, and a door so low that one must stoop to enter it. A dark passage leads to the interior, into which air and light can scarcely penetrate. A few lamps contend with the darkness, and lighted fires serve to modify a little the icy temperature of this cellar. Here and there pillars seem to support a roof which is too high and too darkened for the eye of the visitor to distinguish. On the sides are dark and damp recesses, where women assist at the celebration of worship, which is always carried on, according to ancient custom, with much wailing and strange gestures of the body. The book of the law which is in use is no less venerable than the edifice in which it is contained. It appears that this synagogue has never undergone the slightest repairs or changes for many centuries. The successive generations who have prayed in this ancient temple rest under thousands of sepulchral stones, in a cemetery which is of the same date as the synagogue, and is about a league in circumference.

Paris has never possessed, properly speaking, a regular *Jewish quarter*; it is true that the Israelites settled down in the neighbourhood of the markets, and in certain narrow streets, which at some period or other took the name of *Juiverie* or *Vieille Juiverie (Old Jewry)*; but they were never distinct from the rest of the population; they only had a separate cemetery, at the bottom or rather on the slope of the hill of Sainte–Genevieve. On the other hand, most of the towns of France and of Europe had their *Jewry*. In certain countries, the colonies of Jews enjoyed a share of immunities and protections, thus rendering their life a little less precarious, and their occupations of a rather more settled character.

In Spain and in Portugal, the Jews, in consequence of their having been on several occasions useful to the kings of those two countries, were allowed to carry on their trade, and to engage in money speculations, outside their own quarters; a few were elevated to positions of responsibility, and some were even tolerated at court.

In the southern towns of France, which they enriched by commerce and taxes, and where they formed considerable communities, the Jews enjoyed the protection of the nobles. We find them in Languedoc and Provence buying and selling property like Christians, a privilege which was not permitted to them elsewhere: this is proved by charters of contracts made during the twelfth and thirteenth centuries, which bear the signature of certain Jews in Hebrew characters. On Papal lands, at Avignon, at Carpentras, and at Cavaillon, they had *bailes*, or consuls of their nation. The Jews of Rousillon during the Spanish rule (fifteenth century) were governed by two syndics and a scribe, elected by the community. The latter levied the taxes due to the King of Aragon. In Burgundy they cultivated the vines, which was rather singular, for the Jews generally preferred towns where they could form groups more compact, and more capable of mutual assistance. The name of *Sabath*, given to a vineyard in the neighbourhood of Macon, still points out the position of their synagogue. The hamlet of *Mouys*, a dependency of the communes of Prissey, owes its name to a rich Israelite, Moses, who had received that land as an indemnity for money lent to the Count Gerfroy de Macon, which the latter had been unable to repay. In Vienna, where the Israelites had a special quarter, still called *the Jews'*

[Illustration: Fig. 358.—Jews taking the Blood from Christian Children, for their Mystic Rites.—From a Pen–and–ink Drawing, illuminated, in the Book of the Cabala of Abraham the Jew (Library of the Arsenal, Paris).]

Square, a special judge named by the duke was set over them. Exempted from the city rates, they paid a special poil tax, and they contributed, but on the same footing as Christian vassals, to extraordinary rates, war taxes, and travelling expenses of the nobles, &c. This community even became so rich that it eventually held mortgages on the greater part of the houses of the town.

In Venice also, the Jews had their quarter—the *Giudecca* —which is still one of the darkest in the town; but they did not much care about such trifling inconveniences, as the republic allowed them to bank, that is, to lend money at interest; and although they were driven out on several occasions, they always found means to return and recommence their operations. When they were authorised to establish themselves in the towns of the Adriatic, their presence did not fail to annoy the Christian merchants, whose rivals they were; but neither in Venice nor in the Italian republics had they to fear court intrigues, nor the hatred of corporations of trades, which were so powerful in France and in Germany.

It was in the north of Europe that the animosity against the Jews was greatest. The Christian population continually threatened the Jewish quarters, which public opinion pointed to as haunts and sinks of iniquity. The Jews were believed to be much more amenable to the doctrines of the Talmud than to the laws of Moses. However secret they may have kept their learning, a portion of its tenets transpired, which was supposed to inculcate the right to pillage and murder Christians; and it is to the vague knowledge of these odious prescriptions of the Talmud that we must attribute the readiness with which the most atrocious accusations against the Jews were always welcomed.

Besides this, the public mind in those days of bigotry was naturally filled with a deep antipathy against the Jewish deicides. When monks and priests came annually in Holy week to relate from the pulpit to their hearers the revolting details of the Passion, resentment was kindled in the hearts of the Christians against the descendants of the judges and executioners of the Saviour. And when, on going out of the churches, excited by the sermons they had just heard, the faithful saw in pictures, in the cemeteries, and elsewhere, representations of the mystery of the death of our Saviour, in which the Jews played so odious a part, there was scarcely a spectator who did not feel an increased hatred against the condemned race. Hence it was that in many towns, even when the authorities did not compel them to do so, the Israelites found it prudent to shut themselves up in their own quarter, and even in their own houses, during the whole of Passion week; for, in consequence of the public feeling roused during those days of mourning and penance, a false rumour was quite sufficient to give the people a pretext for offering violence to the Jews.

In fact, from the earliest days of Christianity, a certain number of accusations were always being made, sometimes in one country, sometimes in another, against the Israelites, which always ended in bringing down the same misfortunes on their heads. The most common, and most easily credited report, was that which attributed to them the murder of some Christian child, said to be sacrificed in Passion week in token of their hatred of Christ; and in the event of this terrible accusation being once uttered, and maintained by popular opinion, it never failed to spread with remarkable swiftness. In such cases, popular fury, not being on all occasions satisfied with the tardiness of judicial forms, vented itself upon the first Jews who had the misfortune to fall into the hands of their enemies. As soon as the disturbance was heard the Jewish quarter was closed; fathers and mothers barricaded themselves in with their children, concealed whatever riches they possessed, and listened tremblingly to the clamour of the multitude which was about to besiege them.

[Illustration: Fig. 359.—Secret Meeting of the Jews at the Rabbi's House.—Fac-simile of a Miniature of the "Pelerinage de la Vie Humaine," Manuscript of the Fourteenth Century, in the National Library of Paris.]

In 1255, in Lincoln, the report was suddenly spread that a child of the name of Hughes had been enticed into the Jewish quarter, and there scourged, crucified, and pierced with lances, in the presence of all the Israelites of the district, who were convoked and assembled to take part in this horrible barbarity. The King and Queen of England, on their return from a journey to Scotland, arrived in Lincoln at the very time when the inhabitants were so much agitated by this mysterious announcement. The people called for vengeance. An order was issued to the bailiffs and officers of the King to deliver the murderer into the hands of justice, and the quarter in which the Jews had shut themselves up, so as to avoid the public animosity, was immediately invaded by armed men. The rabbi, in whose house the child was supposed to have been tortured, was seized, and at once condemned to be tied to the tail of a horse, and dragged through the streets of the town. After this, his mangled body, which was only half dead, was hung (Fig. 359). Many of the Jews ran away and hid themselves in all parts of the kingdom, and those who had the misfortune to be caught were thrown into chains and led to London. Orders were given in the provinces to imprison all the Israelites who were accused or even suspected of having taken any part, whether actively or indirectly, in the murder of the Lincoln child; and suspicion made rapid strides in those days. In a short space of time, eighteen Israelites in London shared the fate of the rabbi of their community in Lincoln. Some Dominican monks, who were charitable and courageous enough to interfere in favour of the wretched prisoners, brought down odium on their own heads, and were accused of having allowed themselves to be corrupted by the money of the Jews. Seventy–one prisoners were retained in the dungeons of London, and seemed inevitably fated to die, when the king's brother, Richard, came to their aid, by asserting his right over all the Jews of the kingdom—a right which the King had pledged to him for a loan of 5,000 silver marks. The unfortunate prisoners were therefore saved, thanks to Richard's desire to protect his securities. History does not tell what their liberty cost them; but we must hope that a sense of justice alone guided the English prince, and that the Jews found other means besides money by which to show their gratitude.

There is scarcely a country in Europe which cannot recount similar tales. In 1171, we find the murder of a child at Orleans, or Blois, causing capital punishment to be inflicted on several Jews. Imputations of this horrible character were continually renewed during the Middle Ages, and were of very ancient origin; for we hear of them in the times of Honorius and Theodosius the younger; we find them reproduced with equal vehemence in 1475 at Trent, where a furious mob was excited against the Jews, who were accused of having destroyed a child twenty–nine months old named Simon. The tale of the martyrdom of this child was circulated widely, and woodcut representations of it were freely distributed, which necessarily increased, especially in Germany, the horror which was aroused in the minds of Christians against the accursed nation (Fig. 361).

[Illustration: Fig. 360.—The Infant Richard crucified by the Jews, at Pontoise.—Fac-simile of a Woodcut, with Figures by Wohlgemuth, in the "Liber Chronicarum Mundi:" large folio, Nuremberg, 1493.]

[Illustration: Fig. 361.—Martyrdom of Simon at Trent.—Fac-simile, reduced, of a Woodcut of Wohlgemuth, in the "Liber Chronicarum Mundi:" large folio, Nuremberg, 1493.]

The Jews gave cause for other accusations calculated to keep up this hatred; such as the desecration of the consecrated host, the mutilation of the crucifix. Tradition informs us of a miracle which took place in Paris in 1290, in the Rue des Jardins, when a Jew dared to mutilate and boil a consecrated host. This miracle was commemorated by the erection of a chapel on the spot, which was afterwards replaced by the church and convent of the Billettes. In 1370, the people of Brussels were startled in consequence of the statements of a Jewess, who accused her co-religionists of having made her carry a pyx full of stolen hosts to the Jews of Cologne, for the purpose of submitting them to the most horrible profanations. The woman added, that the Jews having pierced these hosts with sticks and knives, such a quantity of blood poured from them that the culprits were struck with terror, and concealed themselves in their quarter. The Jews were all imprisoned, tortured, and burnt alive (Fig. 362). In order to perpetuate the memory of the miracle of the bleeding hosts, an annual procession took place, which was the origin of the great kermesse, or annual fair.

In the event of any unforeseen misfortune, or any great catastrophe occurring amongst Christians, the odium was frequently cast on the Jews. If the Crusaders met with reverses in Asia, fanatics formed themselves into bands, who, under the name of *Pastoureaux*, spread over the country, killing and robbing not only the Jews, but many Christians also. In the event of any general sickness, and especially during the prevalence of epidemics, the Jews were accused of having poisoned the water of fountains and pits, and the people massacred them in consequence. Thousands perished in this way when the black plague made ravages in Europe in the fourteenth century. The sovereigns, who were tardy in suppressing these sanguinary proceedings, never thought of indemnifying the Jewish families which so unjustly suffered.

[Illustration: Fig. 362.—The Jews of Cologne burnt alive.—From a Woodcut in the "Liber Chronicarum Mundi:" large folio, Nuremberg, 1493.]

In fact, it was then most religiously believed that, by despising and holding the Jewish nation under the yoke, banished as it was from Judaea for the murder of Jesus Christ, the will of the Almighty was being carried out, so much so that the greater number of kings and princes looked upon themselves as absolute masters over the Jews who lived under their protection. All feudal lords spoke with scorn of *their Jews*; they allowed them to establish themselves on their lands, but on the condition that as they became the subjects and property of their lord, the latter should draw his best income from them.

We have shown by an instance borrowed from the history of England that the Jews were often mortgaged by the kings like land. This was not all, for the Jews who inhabited Great Britain during the reign of Henry III., in the middle of the thirteenth century, were not only obliged to acknowledge, by voluntarily contributing large sums of money, the service the King's brother had rendered them in clearing them from the imputation of having had any participation in the murder of the child Richard, but the loan on mortgage, for which they were the material and passive security, became the cause of odious extortions from them. The King had pledged them to the Earl of Cornwall for 5,000 marks, but they themselves had to repay the royal loan by means of enormous taxes. When they had succeeded in cancelling the King's debt to his brother, that necessitous monarch again mortgaged them, but on this occasion to his son Edward. Soon after, the son having rebelled against his father, the latter took back his Jews, and having assembled six elders from each of their communities, he told them that he required 20,000 silver marks, and ordered them to pay him that sum at two stated periods. The payments were rigorously exacted; those who were behind-hand were imprisoned, and the debtor who was in arrear for the second payment was sued for the whole sum. On the King's death his successor continued the same system of tyranny against the Jews. In 1279 they were charged with having issued counterfeit coin, and on this vague or imaginary accusation two hundred and eighty men and women were put to death in London alone. In the counties there were also numerous executions, and many innocent persons were thrown into dungeons; and, at last, in 1290 King Edward, who wished to enrich himself by taking possession of their properties, banished the Jews from his kingdom. A short time before this, the English people had offered to pay an annual fine to the King on condition of his expelling the Jews from the country; but the Jews outbid them, and thus obtained the repeal of the edict of banishment. However, on this last occasion there was no mercy shown, and the Jews, sixteen thousand in number, were expelled from England, and the King seized upon their goods.

At the same period Philippe le Bel of France gave the example of this system of persecuting the Jews, but, instead of confiscating all their goods, he was satisfied with taking one–fifth; his subjects, therefore, almost accused him of generosity.

[Illustration: Fig. 363.—Jewish Conspiracy in France.—From a Miniature in the "Pelerinage de la Vie Humaine" (Imperial Library, Paris).]

The Jews often took the precaution of purchasing certain rights and franchises from their sovereign or from the feudal lord under whose sway they lived; but generally these were one–sided bargains, for not being protected by common rights, and only forming a very small part of the population, they could nowhere depend upon promises or privileges which had been made to them, even though they had purchased them with their own money.

To the uncertainty and annoyance of a life which was continually being threatened, was added a number of vexatious and personal insults, even in ordinary times, and when they enjoyed a kind of normal tolerance. They were almost everywhere obliged to wear a visible mark on their dress, such as a patch of gaudy colour attached to the shoulder or chest, in order to prevent their being mistaken for Christians. By this or some other means they were continually subject to insults from the people, and only succeeded in ridding themselves of it by paying the most enormous fines. Nothing was spared to humiliate and insult them. At Toulouse they were forced to send a representative to the cathedral on every Good Friday, that he might there publicly receive a box on the ears. At Beziers, during Passion week, the mob assumed the right of attacking the Jews' houses with stones. The Jews bought off this right in 1160 by paying a certain sum to the Vicomte de Beziers, and by promising an annual poll–tax to him and to his successors. A Jew, passing on the road of Etampes, beneath the tower of Montlhery, had to pay an obole; if he had in his possession a Hebrew book, he paid four deniers; and, if he carried his lamp with him, two oboles. At Chateauneuf–sur–Loire a Jew on passing had to pay twelve deniers and a Jewess six. It has been said that there were various ancient rates levied upon Jews, in which they were treated like cattle, but this requires authentication.

During the Carnival in Rome they were forced to run in the lists, amidst the jeers of the populace. This public outrage was stopped at a subsequent period by a tax of 300 ecus, which a deputation from the Ghetto presented on their knees to the magistrates of the city, at the same time thanking them for their protection.

When Pope Martin IV. arrived at the Council of Constance, in 1417, the Jewish community, which was as numerous as it was powerful in that old city, came in great state to present him with the book of the law (Fig. 364). The holy father received the Jews kindly, and prayed God to open their eyes and bring them back into the bosom of his church. We know, too, how charitable the popes were to the Jews.

In the face of the distressing position they occupied, it may be asked what powerful motive induced the Jews to live amongst nations who almost invariably treated them as enemies, and to remain at the mercy of sovereigns whose sole object was to oppress, plunder, and subject them to all kinds of vexations? To understand this it is sufficient to remember that, in their peculiar aptness for earning and hoarding money, they found, or at least hoped to find, a means of compensation whereby they might be led to forget the servitude to which they were subjected.

There existed amongst them, and especially in the southern countries, some very learned men, who devoted themselves principally to medicine; and in order to avoid having to struggle against insuperable prejudice, they were careful to disguise their nationality and religion in the exercise of that art.

[Illustration: Fig. 364.—The Jewish Procession going to meet the Pope at the Council of Constance, in 1417.—After a Miniature in the Manuscript Chronicle of Ulrie de Reichental, in the Library of the Mansion–house of Basle, in Switzerland.]

They pretended, in order not to arouse the suspicion of their patients, to be practitioners from Lombardy or Spain, or even from Arabia; whether they were really clever, or only made a pretence of being so, in an art which was then very much a compound of quackery and imposture, it is difficult to say, but they acquired wealth as well as renown in its practice. But there was another science, to the study of which they applied themselves with the utmost ardour and perseverance, and for which they possessed in a marvellous degree the necessary qualities to insure success, and that science was the science of finance. In matters having reference to the recovering of arrears of taxes, to contracts for the sale of goods and produce of industry, to turning a royalty to account, to making hazardous commercial enterprises lucrative, or to the accumulating of large sums of money for the use of sovereigns or poor nobles, the Jews were always at hand, and might invariably be reckoned upon. They created capital, for they always had funds to dispose of, even in the midst of the most terrible public calamities, and, when all other means were exhausted, when all expedients for filling empty purses had been resorted to without success, the Jews were called in. Often, in consequence of the envy which they excited from being known to possess hoards of gold, they were exposed to many dangers, which they nevertheless faced, buoying themselves up with the insatiable love of gain.

Few Christians in the Middle Ages were given to speculation, and they were especially ignorant of financial matters, as demanding interest on loans was almost always looked upon as usury, and, consequently, such dealings were stigmatized as disgraceful. The Jews were far from sharing these high-minded scruples, and they took advantage of the ignorance of Christians by devoting themselves as much as possible to enterprises and speculations, which were at all times the distinguishing occupation of their race. For this reason we find the Jews, who were engaged in the export trade from the twelfth to the fifteenth centuries, doing a most excellent business, even in the commercial towns of the Mediterranean. We can, to a certain extent, in speaking of the intercourse of the Jews with the Christians of the Middle Ages, apply what Lady Montague remarked as late as 1717, when comparing the Jews of Turkey with the Mussulmans: "The former," she says, "have monopolized all the commerce of the empire, thanks to the close ties which exist amongst them, and to the laziness and want of industry of the Turks. No bargain is made without their connivance. They are the physicians and stewards of all the nobility. It is easy to conceive the unity which this gives to a nation which never despises the smallest profits. They have found means of rendering themselves so useful, that they are certain of protection at court, whoever the ruling minister may be. Many of them are enormously rich, but they are careful to make but little outward display, although living in the greatest possible luxury."

[Illustration: Fig. 365.—Costume of an Italian Jew of the Fourteenth Century.—From a Painting by Sano di Pietro, preserved in the Academy of the Fine Arts, at Sienna.]

[Illustration: The Jews' Passover.

Fac—simile of a miniature from a missel of fifteenth century ornamented with paintings of the School of Van Eyck. Bibl. de l'Arsenal, Th. lat., no 199.]

The condition of the Jews in the East was never so precarious nor so difficult as it was in the West. From the Councils of Paris, in 615, down to the end of the fifteenth century, the nobles and the civil and ecclesiastical authorities excluded the Jews from administrative positions; but it continually happened that a positive want of money, against which the Jews were ever ready to provide, caused a repeal or modification of these arbitrary measures. Moreover, Christians did not feel any scruple in parting with their most valued treasures, and giving them as pledges to the Jews for a loan of money when they were in need of it. This plan of lending on pledge, or usury, belonged specially to the Jews in Europe during the Middle Ages, and was both the cause of their prosperity and of their misfortune. Of their prosperity, because they cleverly contrived to become possessors of all the coin; and of their misfortune, because their usurious demands became so detrimental to the public welfare, and were often exacted with such unscrupulous severity, that people not unfrequently became exasperated, and acts of violence were committed, which as often fell upon the innocent as upon the guilty. The greater number of the acts of banishment were those for which no other motive was assigned, or, at all events, no other pretext was made, than the usury practised by these strangers in the provinces and in the towns in which they were permitted to reside. When the Christians heard that these rapacious guests had harshly pressed and entirely stripped certain poor debtors, when they learned that the debtors, ruined by usury, were still kept prisoners in the house of their pitiless creditors, general indignation often manifested itself by personal attacks. This feeling was frequently shared by the authorities themselves, who, instead of dispensing equal justice to the strangers and to the citizens, according to the spirit of the law, often decided with partiality, and even with resentment, and in some cases abandoned the Jews to the fury of the people.

The people's feelings of hatred against the sordid avarice of the Jews was continually kept up by ballads which were sung, and legends which were related, in the public streets of the cities and in the cottages of the villages—ballads and legends in which usurers were depicted in hideous colours (Fig. 366). The most celebrated of these popular compositions was evidently that which must have furnished the idea to Shakespeare of the *Merchant of Venice*, for in this old English drama mention is made of a bargain struck between a Jew and a Christian, who borrows money of him, on condition that, if he cannot refund it on a certain day, the lender shall have the right of cutting a pound of flesh from his body. All the evil which the people said and thought of the Jews during the Middle Ages seems concentrated in the Shylock of the English poet.

The rate of interest for loans was, nevertheless, everywhere settled by law, and at all times. This rate varied according to the scarcity of gold, and was always high enough to give a very ample profit to the lenders, although they too often required a very much higher rate. In truth, the small security offered by those borrowing, and the arbitrary manner in which debts were at times cancelled, increased the risks of the lender and the normal difficulties of obtaining a loan. We find everywhere, in all ancient legislations, a mass of rules on the rate of pecuniary interest to be allowed to the Jews.

[Illustration: Fig. 366.—Legend of the Jew calling the Devil from a Vessel of Blood.—Fac-simile of a Woodcut in Boaistuau's "Histoires Prodigieuses:" in 4to, Paris, Annet Briere, 1560.]

In some countries, especially in England, precautionary measures were taken for regulating the compacts entered into between Christians and Jews. One of the departments of the Exchequer received the register of these compacts, which thus acquired a legal value. However, it was not unfrequent for the kings of England to grant, of their own free will, letters of release to persons owing money to Jews; and these letters, which were often equivalent to the cancelling of the entire debt, were even at times actually purchased from the sovereign. Mention of sums received by the royal treasury for the liberation of debtors, or for enabling them to recover their mortgaged lands without payment, may still be found in the registers of the Exchequer of London; at the same time, Jews, on the other hand, also paid the King large sums, in order that he might allow justice to take its course against powerful debtors who were in arrear, and who could not be induced to pay. We thus see that if the Jews practised usury, the Christians, and especially kings and powerful nobles, defrauded the Jews in every way, and were too often disposed to sell to them the smallest concessions at a great price. Indeed, Christians often went so far as to persecute them, in order to obtain the greatest possible amount from them; and the Jews of the Middle Ages put up with anything provided they could enrich themselves.

[Illustration: Fig. 367.—View and Plan of Jerusalem.—Fac-simile of a Woodout in the "Liber Chronicarum Mundi" large folio, Nuremberg, 1493.]

It must not be supposed, however, that, great as were their capabilities, the Jews exclusively devoted themselves to financial matters. When they were permitted to trade they were well satisfied to become artisans or agriculturists. In Spain they proved themselves most industrious, and that kingdom suffered a great loss in consequence of their being expelled from it. In whatever country they established themselves, the Jews carried on most of the mechanical and manual industries with cleverness and success; but they could not hope to become landed proprietors in countries where they were in such bad odour, and where the possession of land, far from offering them any security, could not fail to excite the envy of their enemies.

If, as is the case, Oriental people are of a serious turn of mind, it is easy to understand that the Jews should have been still more so, since they were always objects of hatred and abhorrence. We find a touching allegory in the Talmud. Each time that a human being is created God orders his angels to bring a soul before his throne, and orders this soul to go and inhabit the body which is about to be born on earth. The soul is grieved, and supplicates the Supreme Being to spare it that painful trial, in which it only sees sorrow and affliction. This allegory may be suitably applied to a people who have only to expect contempt, mistrust, and hatred, everywhere. The Israelites, therefore, clung enthusiastically to the hope of the advent of a Messiah who should bring back to them the happy days of the land of promise, and they looked upon their absence from Palestine as only a passing exile. "But," the Christians said to them, "this Messiah has long since come." "Alas!" they answered, "if He had appeared on earth should we still be miserable?" Fulbert, Bishop of Chartres, preached three sermons to undeceive the Jews, by endeavouring to prove to them that their Messiah was no other than Jesus Christ; but he preached to the winds, for the Jews remained obstinately attached to their illusion that the Messiah was yet to come.

In any case, the Jews, who mixed up the mysteries and absurdities of the Talmud with the ancient laws and numerous rules of the religion of their ancestors, found in the practice of their national customs, and in the celebration of their mysterious ceremonies, the sweetest emotions, especially when they could devote themselves to them in the peaceful retirement of the Ghetto; for, in all the countries in which they lived scattered and isolated amongst Christians, they were careful to conceal their worship and to conduct their ceremonial as secretly as possible.

The clergy, in striving to convert the Jews, repeatedly had conferences with the rabbis of a controversial character, which often led to quarrels, and aggravated the lot of the Jewish community. If Catholic proselystism succeeded in completely detaching a few individuals or a few families from the Israelitish creed, these ardent converts rekindled the horror of the people against their former co-religionists by revealing some of the precepts of the Talmud. Sometimes the conversion of whole masses of Jews was effected, but this happened much less through conviction on their part than through the fear of exile, plunder, or execution.

These pretended conversions, however, did not always protect them from danger. In Spain the Inquisition kept a close watch on converted Jews, and, if they were not true to their new faith, severe punishment was inflicted upon them. In 1506, the inhabitants of Abrantes, a town of Portugal, massacred all the baptized Jews. Manoel, a king of Portugal, forbad the converts from selling their goods and leaving his dominions. The Church excluded them from ecclesiastical dignities, and, when they succeeded in obtaining civil employments, they were received with distrust. In France the Parliaments tried, with a show of justice, to prevent converted Jews from being reproached for their former condition; but Louis XII., during his pressing wants, did not scruple to exact a special tax from them. And, in 1611, we again find that they were unjustly denounced, and under the form of a *Remonstrance to the King and the Parliament of Provence, on account of the great family alliances of the new converts*, an appeal was made for the most cruel reprisals against this unfortunate race, "which deserved only to be banished and their goods confiscated."

[Illustration: Fig. 368.—Jewish Ceremony before the Ark.—Fac-simile of a woodcut printed at Troyes.]

Gipsies, Tramps, Beggars, and Cours des Miracles.

First Appearance of Gipsies in the West.—Gipsies in Paris.—Manners and Customs of these Wandering Tribes.—Tricks of Captain Charles.—Gipsies expelled by Royal Edict.—Language of Gipsies.—The Kingdom of Slang.—The Great Coesre, Chief of the Vagrants; his Vassals and Subjects.—Divisions of the Slang People; its Decay and the Causes thereof.—Cours des Miracles.—The Camp of Rognes.—Cunning Language, or

Slang.—Foreign Rogues, Thieves, and Pickpockets.

In the year 1417 the inhabitants of the countries situated near the mouth of the Elbe were disturbed by the arrival of strangers, whose manners and appearance were far from pre—possessing. These strange travellers took a course thence towards the Teutonic Hanse, starting from Luneburg: they subsequently proceeded to Hamburg, and then, going from east to west along the Baltic, they visited the free towns of Lubeck, Wismar, Rostock, Stralsund, and Greifswald.

These new visitors, known in Europe under the names of *Zingari, Cigani, Gipsies, Gitanos, Egyptians*, or *Bohemians*, but who, in their own language, called themselves *Romi*, or *gens maries*, numbered about three hundred men and women, besides the children, who were very numerous. They divided themselves into seven bands, all of which followed the same track. Very dirty, excessively ugly, and remarkable for their dark complexions, these people had for their leaders a duke and a count, as they were called, who were superbly dressed, and to whom they acknowledged allegiance. Some of them rode on horseback, whilst others went on foot. The women and children travelled on beasts of burden and in waggons (Fig. 369). If we are to believe their own story, their wandering life was caused by their return to Paganism after having been previously converted to the Christian faith, and, as a punishment for their sin, they were to continue their adventurous course for a period of seven years. They showed letters of recommendation from various princes, among others from Sigismund, King of the Romans, and these letters, whether authentic or false, procured for them a welcome wherever they went. They encamped in the fields at night, because the habit they indulged in of stealing everything for which they had a fancy, caused them to fear being disturbed in the towns. It was not long, however, before many of them were arrested and put to death for theft, when the rest speedily decamped.

[Illustration: Fig. 369.—Gipsies on the March.—Fifteenth Century Piece of old Tapestry in the Chateau d'Effiat, contributed by M.A. Jubinal.]

In the course of the following year we find them at Meissen, in Saxony, whence they were driven out on account of the robberies and disturbances they committed; and then in Switzerland, where they passed through the countries of the Grisons, the cantons of Appenzell, and Zurich, stopping in Argovie. Chroniclers who mention them at that time speak of their chief, Michel, as Duke of Egypt, and relate that these strangers, calling themselves Egyptians, pretended that they were driven from their country by the Sultan of Turkey, and condemned to wander for seven years in want and misery. These chroniclers add that they were very honest people, who scrupulously followed all the practices of the Christian religion; that they were poorly clad, but that they had gold and silver in abundance; that they lived well, and paid for everything they had; and that, at the end of seven years, they went away to return home, as they said. However, whether because a considerable number remained on the road, or because they had been reinforced by others of the same tribe during the year, a troop of fifty men, accompanied by a number of hideous women and filthy children, made their appearance in the neighbourhood of Augsburg. These vagabonds gave out that they were exiles from Lower Egypt, and pretended to know the art of predicting coming events. It was soon found out that they were much less versed in divination and in the occult sciences than in the arts of plundering, roguery, and cheating.

In the following year a similar horde, calling themselves Saracens, appeared at Sisteron, in Provence; and on the 18th. of July, 1422, a chronicler of Bologna mentions the arrival in that town of a troop of foreigners, commanded by a certain Andre, Duke of Egypt, and composed of at least one hundred persons, including women and children. They encamped inside and outside the gate *di Galiera*, with the exception of the duke, who lodged at the inn *del Re*. During the fifteen days which they spent at Bologna a number of the people of the town went to see them, and especially to see "the wife of the duke," who, it was said, knew how to foretell future events, and to tell what was to happen to people, what their fortunes would be, the number of their children, if they were good or bad, and many other things (Fig. 370). Few men, however, left the house of the so–called Duke of Egypt without having their purses stolen, and but few women escaped without having the skirts of their dresses cut. The Egyptian women walked about the town in groups of six or seven, and whilst some were talking to the townspeople, telling them their fortunes, or bartering in shops, one of their number would lay her hands on anything which was within reach. So many robberies were committed in this way, that the magistrates of the town and the ecclesiastical authorities forbad the inhabitants from visiting the Egyptians' camp, or from having any intercourse with them, under penalty of excommunication and of a fine of fifty livres. Besides this, by a strange application of the laws of retaliation, those who had been robbed by these foreigners were permitted to rob them to the extent of the value of the things stolen. In consequence of this, the Bolognians entered a stable in which several of the Egyptians' horses were kept, and took out one of the finest of them. In order to recover him the Egyptians agreed to restore what

301

they had taken, and the restitution was made. But perceiving that they could no longer do any good for themselves in this province, they struck their tents and started for Rome, to which city they said they were bound to go, not only in order to accomplish a pilgrimage imposed upon them by the Sultan, who had expelled them from their own land, but especially to obtain letters of absolution from the Holy Father.

[Illustration: Fig. 370.—Gipsies Fortune–telling.—Fac–simile of a Woodcut in the "Cosmographie Universelle" of Munster: in folio, Basle, 1552.]

In 1422 the band left Italy, and we find them at Basle and in Suabia. Then, besides the imperial passports, of which they had up to that time alone boasted, they pretended to have in their possession bulls which they stated that they had obtained from the Pope. They also modified their original tale, and stated that they were descendants of the Egyptians who refused hospitality to the Holy Virgin and to St. Joseph during their flight into Egypt: they also declared that, in consequence of this crime, God had doomed their race to perpetual misery and exile.

Five years later we find them in the neighbourhood of Paris. "The Sunday after the middle of August," says "The Journal of a Bourgeois of Paris," "there came to Paris twelve so–called pilgrims, that is to say, a duke, a count, and ten men, all on horseback; they said that they were very good Christians, and that they came from Lower Egypt; ... and on the 29th of August, the anniversary of the beheading of St. John, the rest of the band made their appearance. These, however, were not allowed to enter Paris, but, by order of the provost, were lodged in the Chapel of St. Denis. They did not number more than one hundred and twenty, including women and children. They stated that, when they left their own country, they numbered from a thousand to twelve hundred, but that the rest had died on the road..... Whilst they were at the chapel never was such a concourse of people collected, even at the blessing of the fair of Landit, as went from Paris, St. Denis, and elsewhere, to see these strangers. Almost all of them had their ears pierced, and in each one or two silver rings, which in their country, they said, was a mark of nobility. The men were very swarthy, with curly hair; the women were very ugly, and extremely dark, with long black hair, like a horse's tail; their only garment being an old rug tied round the shoulder by a strip of cloth or a bit of rope (Fig. 371). Amongst them were several fortune–tellers, who, by looking into people's hands, told them what had happened or what was to happen to them, and by this means often did a good deal to sow discord in families. What was worse, either by magic, by Satanic agency, or by sleight of hand, they managed to empty people's purses whilst talking to them.... So, at least, every one said. At last accounts respecting them reached the ears of the Bishop of Paris. He went to them with a Franciscan friar, called Le Petit Jacobin, who, by the bishop's order, delivered an earnest address to them, and excommunicated all those who had anything to do with them, or who had their fortunes told. He further advised the gipsies to go away, and, on the festival of Notre–Dame, they departed for Pontoise."

[Illustration: Fig. 371.—A Gipsy Family.—Fac–simile of a Woodcut in the "Cosmographie Universelle" of Munster: in folio, Basle, 1552.]

Here, again, the gipsies somewhat varied their story. They said that they were originally Christians; but that, in consequence of an invasion by the Saracens, they had been forced to renounce their religion; that, at a subsequent period, powerful monarchs had come to free them from the yoke of the infidels, and had decreed that, as a punishment to them for having renounced the Christian faith, they should not be allowed to return to their country before they had obtained permission from the Pope. They stated that the Holy Father, to whom they had gone to confess their sins, had then ordered them to wander about the world for seven years, without sleeping in beds, at the same time giving direction to every bishop and every priest whom they met to offer them ten livres; a direction which the abbots and bishops were in no hurry to obey. These strange pilgrims stated that they had been only five years on the road when they arrived in Paris.

Enough has been said to show that, although the object of their long pilgrimage was ostensibly a pious one, the Egyptians or gipsies were not very slow in giving to the people whom they visited a true estimate of their questionable honesty, and we do not think it would be particularly interesting to follow step by step the track of this odious band, which from this period made its appearance sometimes in one country and sometimes in another, not only in the north but in the south, and especially in the centre of Europe. Suffice it to say that their quarrels with the authorities, or the inhabitants of the countries which had the misfortune to be periodically visited by them, have left numerous traces in history.

On the 7th of November, 1453, from sixty to eighty gipsies, coming from Courtisolles, arrived at the entrance of the town of Cheppe, near Chalons–sur–Marne. The strangers, many of whom carried "javelins, darts, and other implements of war," having asked for hospitality, the mayor of the town informed them "that it was not long since some of the same company, or others very like them, had been lodged in the town, and had been guilty of various acts of theft." The gipsies persisted in their demands, the indignation of the people was aroused, and they were soon obliged to resume their journey. During their unwilling retreat, they were pursued by many of the inhabitants of the town, one of whom killed a gipsy named Martin de la Barre: the murderer, however, obtained the King's pardon.

In 1532, at Pleinpalais, a suburb of Geneva, some rascals from among a band of gipsies, consisting of upwards of three hundred in number, fell upon several of the officers who were stationed to prevent their entering the town. The citizens hurried up to the scene of disturbance. The gipsies retired to the monastery of the Augustin friars, in which they fortified themselves: the bourgeois besieged them, and would have committed summary justice on them, but the authorities interfered, and some twenty of the vagrants were arrested, but they sued for mercy, and were discharged.

[Illustration: Fig. 372.—Gipsy Encampment.—Fac-simile of a Copper-plate by Callot.]

In 1632, the inhabitants of Viarme, in the Department of Lot-et-Garonne, made an onslaught upon a troop of gipsies who wanted to take up their quarters in that town. The whole of them were killed, with the exception of their chief, who was taken prisoner and brought before the Parliament of Bordeaux, and ordered to be hung. Twenty-one years before this, the mayor and magistrates of Bordeaux gave orders to the soldiers of the watch to arrest a gipsy chief, who, having shut himself up in the tower of Veyrines, at Merignac, ransacked the surrounding country. On the 21st of July, 1622, the same magistrates ordered the gipsies to leave the parish of Eysines within twenty-four hours, under penalty of the lash.

It was not often that the gipsies used violence or openly resisted authority; they more frequently had recourse to artifice and cunning in order to attain their end. A certain Captain Charles acquired a great reputation amongst them for the clever trickeries which he continually conceived, and which his troop undertook to carry out. A chronicler of the time says, that by means of certain herbs which he gave to a half-starved horse, he made him into a fat and sleek animal; the horse was then sold at one of the neighbouring fairs or markets, but the purchaser detected the fraud within a week, for the horse soon became thin again, and usually sickened and died.

Tallemant des Reaux relates that, on one occasion, Captain Charles and his attendants took up their quarters in a village, the cure of which being rich and parsimonious, was much disliked by his parishioners. The cure never left his house, and the gipsies could not, therefore, get an opportunity to rob him. In this difficulty, they pretended that one of them had committed a crime, and had been condemned to be hung a quarter of a league from the village, where they betook themselves with all their goods. The man, at the foot of the gibbet, asked for a confessor, and they went to fetch the cure. He, at first, refused to go, but his parishioners compelled him. During his absence some gipsies entered his house, took five hundred ecus from his strong box, and quickly rejoined the troop. As soon as the rascal saw them returning, he said that he appealed to the king of *la petite Egypte*, upon which the captain exclaimed, "Ah! the traitor! I expected he would appeal." Immediately they packed up, secured the prisoner, and were far enough away from the scene before the cure re-entered his house.

Tallemant relates another good trick. Near Roye, in Picardy, a gipsy who had stolen a sheep offered it to a butcher for one hundred sous (about sixty francs of our money), but the butcher declined to give more than four livres for it. The butcher then went away; whereupon the gipsy pulled the sheep from a sack into which he had put it, and substituted for it a child belonging to his tribe. He then ran after the butcher, and said, "Give me five livres, and you shall have the sack into the bargain." The butcher paid him the money, and went away. When he got home he opened the sack, and was much astonished when he saw a little boy jump out of it, who, in an instant, caught up the sack and ran off. "Never was a poor man so thoroughly hoaxed as this butcher," says Tallemant des Reaux.

The gipsies had thousands of other tricks in stock as good as the ones we have just related, in proof of which we have but to refer to the testimony of one of their own tribe, who, under the name of Pechon de Ruby, published, towards the close of the sixteenth century, "La Vie Genereuse des Mattois, Guex, Bohemiens, et Cagoux." "When they want to leave a place where they have been stopping, they set out in an opposite direction to that in which they are going, and after travelling about half a league they take their right course. They possess the best and most accurate maps, in which are laid down not only all the towns, villages, and rivers, but also the houses of the gentry and others; and they fix upon places of rendezvous every ten days, at twenty leagues from the point from whence they set out.... The captain hands over to each of the chiefs three or four families to take charge of, and these small bands take different cross-roads towards the place of

305

rendezvous. Those who are well armed and mounted he sends off with a good almanac, on which are marked all the fairs, and they continually change their dress and their horses. When they take up their quarters in any village they steal very little in its immediate vicinity, but in the neighbouring parishes they rob and plunder in the most daring manner. If they find a sum of money they give notice to the captain, and make a rapid flight from the place. They coin counterfeit money, and put it into circulation. They play at all sorts of games; they buy all sorts of horses; whether sound or unsound, provided they can manage to pay for them in their own base coin. When they buy food they pay for it in good money the first time, as they are held in such distrust; but, when they are about to leave a neighbourhood, they again buy something, for which they tender false coin, receiving the change in good money. In harvest time all doors are shut against them; nevertheless they contrive, by means of picklocks and other instruments, to effect an entrance into houses, when they steal linen, cloaks, silver, and any other movable article which they can lay their hands on. They give a strict account of everything to their captain, who takes his share of all they get, except of what they earn by fortune–telling. They are very clever at making a good bargain; when they know of a rich merchant being in the place, they disguise themselves, enter into communications with him, and swindle him, ... after which they change their clothes, have their horses shod the reverse way, and the shoes covered with some soft material lest they should be heard, and gallop away."

[Illustration: Fig. 373.—The Gipsy who used to wash his Hands in Molten Lead.—Fac–simile of a Woodcut in the "Histoires Merveilleuses" of Pierre Boaistuau: in 4to, 1560.]

In the "Histoire Generale des Larrons" we read that the vagabonds called gipsies sometimes played tricks with goblets, sometimes danced on the tight–rope, turned double–somersaults, and performed other feats (Fig. 373), which proves that these adventurers adopted all kinds of methods of gaining a livelihood, highway robbery not excepted. We must not, therefore, be surprised if in almost all countries very severe police measures were taken against this dangerous race, though we must admit that these measures sometimes partook of a barbarous character.

After having forbidden them, with a threat of six years at the galleys, to sojourn in Spain, Charles V. ordered them to leave Flanders under penalty of death. In 1545, a gipsy who had infringed the sentence of banishment was condemned by the Court of Utrecht to be flogged till the blood appeared, to have his nostrils slit, his hair removed, his beard shaved off, and to be banished for life. "We can form some idea," says the German historian Grellman, "of the miserable condition of the gipsies from the following facts: many of them, and especially the women, have been burned by their own request, in order to end their miserable state of existence; and we can give the case of a gipsy who, having been arrested, flogged, and conducted to the frontier, with the threat that if he reappeared in the country he would be hanged, resolutely returned after three successive and similar threats, at three different places, and implored that the capital sentence might be carried out, in order that he might be released from a life of such misery. These unfortunate people," continues the historian, "were not even looked upon as human beings, for, during a hunting party, consisting of members of a small German court, the huntsmen had no scruple whatever in killing a gipsy woman who was suckling her child, just as they would have done any wild beast which came in their way."

M. Francisque Michel says, "Amongst the questions which arise from a consideration of the existence of this remarkable people, is one which, although neglected, is nevertheless of considerable interest, namely, how, with a strange language, unlike any used in Europe, the gipsies could make themselves understood by the people amongst whom they made their appearance for the first time: newly arrived in the west, they could have none of those interpreters who are only to be found amongst a long–established people, and who have political and commercial intercourse with other nations. Where, then, did the gipsies obtain interpreters? The answer seems to us to be clear. Receiving into their ranks all those whom crime, the fear of punishment, an uneasy conscience, or the charm of a roaming life, continually threw in their path, they made use of them either to find their way into countries of which they were ignorant, or to commit robberies which would otherwise have been impracticable. Themselves adepts in all sorts of bad practices, they were not slow to form an alliance with profligate characters who sometimes worked in concert with them, and sometimes alone, and who always framed the model for their own organization from that of the gipsies."

[Illustration: Fig. 374.—Orphans, *Callots*, and the Family of the Grand Coesre.—From painted Hangings and Tapestry from the Town of Rheims, executed during the Fifteenth Century.]

This alliance—governed by statutes, the honour of compiling which has been given to a certain Ragot, who styled himself captain—was composed of *matois*, or sharpers; of *mercelots*, or hawkers, who were very little better than the former; of *gueux*, or dishonest beggars, and of a host of other swindlers, constituting the order or hierarchy of the *Argot*, or Slang people. Their chief was called the *Grand Coesre*, "a vagabond broken to all the tricks of his trade," says M. Francisque Michel, and who frequently ended his days on the rack or the gibbet. History has furnished us with the story of a "miserable cripple" who used to sit in a wooden bowl, and who, after having been Grand Coesre for three years, was broken alive on the wheel at Bordeaux for his crimes. He was called *Roi de Tunes* (Tunis), and was drawn about by two large dogs. One of his successors, the Grand Coesre surnamed Anacreon, who suffered from the same infirmity, namely, that of a cripple, rode about Paris on a donkey begging. He generally held his court on the Port–au–Foin, where he sat on his throne dressed in a mantle made of a thousand pieces. The Grand Coesre had a lieutenant in each province called *cagou*, whose business it was to initiate apprentices in the secrets of the craft, and who looked after, in different localities, those whom the chief had entrusted to his care. He gave an account of the property he received in thus exercising his stewardship, and of the money as well as of the clothing which he took from the *Argotiers* who refused to recognise his authority. As a remuneration for their duties, the cagoux were exempt from all tribute to their chief; they received their share of the property taken from persons whom they had ordered to be robbed, and they were free to beg in any way they pleased. After the cagoux came the *archisuppots*, who, being recruited from the lowest dregs of the clergy and others who had been in a better position, were, so to speak, the teachers of the law. To them was intrusted the duty of instructing the less experienced rogues, and of determining the language of Slang; and, as a reward for their good and loyal services, they had the right of begging without paying any fees to their chiefs.

[Illustration: Fig. 375.—The Blind and the Poor Sick of St. John.—From painted Hangings and Tapestry in the Town of Rheims, executed during the Fifteenth Century.]

The Grand Coesre levied a tax of twenty–four sous per annum upon the young rogues, who went about the streets pretending to shed tears (Fig. 374), as "helpless orphans," in order to excite public sympathy. The *marcandiers* had to pay an ecu; they were tramps clothed in a tolerably good doublet, who passed themselves off as merchants ruined by war, by fire, or by having been robbed on the highway. The *malingreux* had to pay forty sous; they were covered with sores, most of which were self–inflicted, or they pretended to have swellings of some kind, and stated that they were about to undertake a pilgrimage to St. Meen, in Brittany, in order to be cured. The *pietres*, or lame rogues, paid half an ecu, and walked with crutches. The *sabouleux*, who were commonly called the *poor sick of St. John*, were in the habit of frequenting fairs and markets, or the vicinity of churches; there, smeared with blood and appearing as if foaming at the mouth by means of a piece of soap they had placed in it, they struggled on the ground as if in a fit, and in this way realised a considerable amount of alms. These consequently paid the largest fees to the Coesre (Fig. 375).

[Illustration: Fig. 376.—The *Ruffes* and the *Millards*.—From painted Hangings and Tapestry of Rheims, executed about the Fifteenth Century.]

Besides these, there were the *callots*, who were either affected with a scurfy disease or pretended to be so, and who were contributors to the civil list of their chief to the amount of sevens sous; as also the *coquillards*, or pretended pilgrims of St. James or St. Michael; and the *hubins*, who, according to the forged certificate which they carried with them, were going to, or returning from, St. Hubert, after having been bitten by a mad dog. The *polissons* paid two ecus to the Coesre, but they earned a considerable amount, especially in winter; for benevolent people, touched with their destitution and half–nakedness, gave them sometimes a doublet, sometimes a shirt, or some other article of clothing, which of course they immediately sold. The *francs mitoux*, who were never taxed above five sous, were sickly members of the fraternity, or at all events pretended to be such; they tied their arms above the elbow so as to stop the pulse, and fell down apparently fainting on the public footpaths. We must also mention the *ruffes* and the *millards*, who went into the country in groups begging (Fig. 376). The *capons* were cut–purses, who hardly ever left the towns, and who laid hands on everything within their reach. The *courtauds de boutanche* pretended to be workmen, and were to be met with everywhere with the tools of their craft on their back, though they never used them. The *convertis* pretended to have been impressed by the exhortations of some excellent preacher, and made a public profession of faith; they afterwards stationed themselves at church doors, as recently converted Catholics, and in this way received liberal contributions.

Lastly, we must mention the *drilles*, the *narquois*, or the people of the *petite flambe*, who for the most part were old pensioners, and who begged in the streets from house to house, with their swords at their sides (Fig. 377). These, who at times lived a racketing and luxurious life, at last rebelled against the Grand Coesre, and would no longer be reckoned among his subjects—a step which gave a considerable shock to the Argotic monarchy.

[Illustration: Fig. 377.—The *Drille* or *Narquois*.—From painted Hangings from the Town of Rheims (Fifteenth Century).]

[Illustration: Fig. 378.—Perspective View of Paris in 1607.—Fac–simile of a Copper–plate by Leonard Gaultier. (Collection of M. Guenebault, Paris.)]

There was another cause which greatly contributed to diminish the power as well as the prestige of this eccentric sovereign, and this was, that the cut–purses, the night–prowlers and wood–thieves, not finding sufficient means of livelihood in their own department, and seeing that the Argotiers, on the contrary, were always in a more luxurious position, tried to amalgamate robbery with mendicity, which raised an outcry amongst these sections of their community. The archisuppots and the cagoux at first declined such an alliance, but eventually they were obliged to admit all, with the exception of the wood–thieves, who were altogether excluded. In the seventeenth century, therefore, in order to become a thorough Argotier, it was necessary not only to solicit alms like any mere beggar, but also to possess the dexterity of the cut–purse and the thief. These arts were to be learned in the places which served as the habitual rendezvous of the very dregs of society, and which were generally known as the *Cours des Miracles*. These houses, or rather resorts, had been so called, if we are to believe a writer of the early part of the seventeenth century, "Because rogues ... and others, who have all day been cripples, maimed, dropsical, and beset with every sort of bodily ailment, come home at night, carrying under their arms a sirloin of beef, a joint of veal, or a leg of mutton, not forgetting to hang a bottle of wine to their belt, and, on entering the court, they throw aside their crutches, resume their healthy and lusty appearance, and, in imitation of the ancient Bacchanalian revelries, dance all kinds of dances with their trophies in their hands, whilst the host is preparing their suppers. Can there be a greater *miracle* than is to be seen in this court, where the maimed walk upright?"

[Illustration: Fig. 379.—*Cour des Miracles* of Paris. Talebot the Hunchback, a celebrated Scamp during the Seventeenth Century.—From an old Engraving in the Collection of Engravings in the National Library of Paris.]

In Paris there were several *Cours des Miracles*, but the most celebrated was that which, from the time of Sauval, the singular historian of the "Antiquities of Paris," to the middle of the seventeenth century, preserved this generic name *par excellence*, and which exists to this day (Fig. 379). He says, "It is a place of considerable size, and is in an unhealthy, muddy, and irregular blind alley. Formerly it was situated on the outskirts of Paris, now it is in one of the worst built, dirtiest, and most out-of-the-way quarters of the town, between the Rue Montorgueil, the convent of the Filles-Dieu, and the Rue Neuve-Saint-Sauveur. To get there one must wander through narrow, close, and by-streets; and in order to enter it, one must descend a somewhat winding and rugged declivity. In this place I found a mud house, half buried, very shaky from old age and rottenness, and only eight metres square; but in which, nevertheless, some fifty families are living, who have the charge of a large number of children, many of whom are stolen or illegitimate.... I was assured that upwards of five hundred large families occupy that and other houses adjoining.... Large as this court is, it was formerly even bigger.... Here, without any care for the future, every one enjoys the present; and eats in the evening what he has earned during the day with so much trouble, and often with so many blows; for it is one of the fundamental rules of the Cour des Miracles never to lay by anything for the morrow. Every one who lives there indulges in the utmost licentiousness; both religion and law are utterly ignored.... It is true that outwardly they appear to acknowledge a God; for they have set up in a niche an image of God the Father, which they have stolen from some church, and before which they come daily to offer up certain prayers; but this is only because they superstitiously imagine that by this means they are released from the necessity of performing the duties of Christians to their pastor and their parish, and are even absolved from the sin of entering a church for the purpose of robbery and purse-cutting."

Paris, the capital of the kingdom of rogues, was not the only town which possessed a Cour des Miracles, for we find here and there, especially at Lyons and Bordeaux, some traces of these privileged resorts of rogues and thieves, which then flourished under the sceptre of the Grand Coesre. Sauval states, on the testimony of people worthy of credit, that at Sainte-Anne d'Auray, the most holy place of pilgrimage in Brittany, under the superintendence of the order of reformed Carmelite friars, there was a large field called the *Rogue's Field*. This was covered with mud huts; and here the Grand Coesre resorted annually on the principal solemn festivals, with his officers and subjects, in order "to hold his council of state," that is to say, in order to settle and arrange respecting robbery. At these *state* meetings, which were not always held at Sainte-Anne d'Auray, all the subjects of the Grand Coesre were present, and paid homage to their lord and master. Some came and paid him the tribute which was required of them by the statutes of the craft; others rendered him an account of what they had done, and what they had earned during the year. When they had executed their work badly, he ordered them to be punished, either corporally or pecuniarily, according to the gravity of their offences. When he had not himself properly governed his people, he was dethroned, and a successor was appointed by acclamation.

[Illustration: Fig. 380.—Beggar playing the Fiddle, and his Wife accompanying him with the Bones.—From an old Engraving of the Seventeenth Century.]

At these assemblies, as well as in the Cours des Miracles, French was not spoken, but a strange and artificial language was used called *jargon, langue matoise, narquois,* &c. This language, which is still in use under the name of *argot*, or slang, had for the most part been borrowed from the jargon or slang of the lower orders. To a considerable extent, according to the learned philologist of this mysterious language, M. Francisque Michel, it was composed of French words lengthened or abbreviated; of proverbial expressions; of words expressing the symbols of things instead of the things themselves; of terms either intentionally or unintentionally altered from their true meaning; and of words which resembled other words in sound, but which had not the same signification. Thus, for mouth, they said *pantiere*, from *pain* (bread), which they put into it; the arms were *lyans* (binders); an ox was a *cornant* (horned); a purse, a *fouille*, or *fouillouse*; a cock, a *horloge*, or timepiece; the legs, *des quilles* (nine–pins); a sou, a *rond*, or round thing; the eyes, *des luisants* (sparklers), &c. In jargon several words were also taken from the ancient language of the gipsies, which testifies to the part which these vagabonds played in the formation of the Argotic community. For example, a shirt was called *lime*; a chambermaid, *limogere; sheets, limans—words all derived from the gipsy word lima, a shirt: they called an ecu, a rusquin or rougesme, from rujia, the common word for money; a rich man, rupin; a house, turne; a knife, chourin, from rup, turna, and chori, which, in the gipsy tongue, mean respectively silver, castle, and knife.*

From what we have related about rogues and the Cours des Miracles, one might perhaps be tempted to suppose that France was specially privileged; but it was not so, for Italy was far worse in this respect. The rogues were called by the Italians *bianti*, or *ceretani*, and were subdivided into more than forty classes, the various characteristics of which have been described by a certain Rafael Frianoro. It is not necessary to state that the analogue of more than one of these classes is to be found in the short description we have given of the Argotic kingdom in France. We will therefore only mention those which were more especially Italian. It must not be forgotten that in the southern countries, where religions superstition was more marked than elsewhere, the numerous family of rogues had no difficulty in practising every description of imposture, inasmuch as they trusted to the various manifestations of religions feeling to effect their purposes. Thus the *affrati*, in order to obtain more alms and offerings, went about in the garb of monks and priests, even saying mass, and pretending that it was the first time they had exercised their sacred office. So the *morghigeri* walked behind a donkey, carrying a bell and a lamp, with their string of beads in their hands, and asking how they were to pay for the bell, which they were always "just going to buy." The *felsi* pretended that they were divinely inspired and endowed with the gift of second sight, and announced that there were hidden treasures in certain houses under the guardianship of evil spirits. They asserted that these treasures could not be discovered without danger, except by means of fastings and offerings, which they and their brethren could alone make, in consideration of which they entered into a bargain, and received a certain sum of money from the owners. The *accatosi* deserve mention on account of the cleverness with which they contrived to assume the appearance of captives recently escaped from slavery. Shaking the chains with which they said they had been bound, jabbering unintelligible words, telling heart–rending tales of their sufferings and privations, and showing the marks of blows which they had received, they went on their knees, begging for money that they might buy off their brethren or their friends, whom they said they had left in the hands of the Saracens or the Turks, We must mention, also, the *allacrimanti*, or weepers, who owed their name to the facility which they possessed of shedding tears at will; and the *testatori*, who, pretending to be seriously ill and about to die, extorted money from all those to whom they promised to leave their fortunes, though, of course, they had not a son to leave behind them. We must not forget the *protobianti* (master rogues), who made no scruple of exciting compassion from their own comrades (Fig. 381), nor the *vergognosi*, who, notwithstanding their poverty, wished to be thought rich, and considered that assistance was due to them from the mere fact of their being noble. We must here conclude, for it would occupy too much time to go through the list of these Italian vagabonds. As for the German (Figs. 382 and 383), Spanish, and English rogues, we may simply remark that no type exists among them which is not to be met with amongst the Argotiers of France or the Bianti of Italy. In giving a description, therefore, of the mendicity practised in these two countries during the Middle Ages, we are sure to be representing what it was in other parts of Europe.

[Illustration: Fig. 381.—Italian Beggar.—From an Engraving by Callot.]

[Illustration: Figs. 382 and 383.—German Beggars.—Fac–simile of a Woodcut in the "Cosmographie Universelle" of Munster: in folio, Basle, 1552.]

The history of regular robbers and highwaymen during this long period is more difficult to describe; it contains only disconnected anecdotes of a more or less interesting character. It is probable, moreover, that robbers did not always commit their depredations singly, and that they early understood the advantages of associating together. The *Tafurs*, or *Halegrins*, whom we notice as followers of Godefroy de Bouillon at the time of the Crusades, towards the end of the eleventh century, were terribly bad characters, and are actually accused by contemporary writers of violating tombs, and of living on human flesh. On this account they were looked upon with the utmost horror by the infidels, who dreaded more their savage ferocity than the valour of the Crusaders. The latter even, who had these hordes of Tafurs under their command, were not without considerable mistrust of them, and when, during their march through Hungary, under the protection of the cross, these miscreants committed depredations, Godefroy de Bouillion was obliged to ask pardon for them from the king of that country.

An ancient poet has handed down to us a story in verse setting forth the exploits of Eustace the monk, who, after having thrown aside his frock, embraced the life of a robber, and only abandoned it to become Admiral of France under Philip Augustus. He was killed before Sandwich, in 1217. We have satisfactory proof that as early as the thirteenth century sharpers were very expert masters of their trade, for the ingenious and amusing tricks of which they were guilty are quite equal to the most skilled of those now recorded in our police reports. In the two following centuries the science of the *pince* and of the *croc* (pincers and hook), as it was then called, alone made progress, and Pathelin (a character in comedy, and an incomparable type of craft and dishonesty) never lacked disciples any more than Villon did imitators. We know that this charming poet, who was at the same time a most expert thief, narrowly escaped hanging on two occasions. His contemporaries attributed to him a poem of twelve hundred verses, entitled "Les Repues Franches," in which are described the methods in use among his companions for procuring wine, bread, meat, and fish, without having to pay for them. They form a series of interesting stories, the moral of which is to be gathered from the following lines:—

"C'est bien, disne, quand on eschappe
Sans desbourcer pas ung denier,
Et dire adieu an tavernier,

314

En torchant son nez a la nappe."

The meaning of this doggrel, which is somewhat broad, may be rendered—"He dines well who escapes without paying a penny, and who bids farewell to the innkeeper by wiping his nose on the tablecloth."

Side by side with this poem of Villon we ought to cite one of a later period—"La Legende de Maitre Faifeu," versified by Charles Boudigne. This Faifeu was a kind of Villon of Anjou, who excelled in all kinds of rascality, and who might possibly have taught it even to the gipsies themselves. The character of Panurge, in the "Pantagruel," is no other than the type of Faifeu, immortalised by the genius of Rabelais. We must also mention one of the pamphlets of Guillaume Bouchet, written towards the end of the sixteenth century, which gives a very amusing account of thieves of every description, and also "L'Histoire Generale des Larrons," in which are related numerous wonderful tales of murders, robberies, and other atrocities, which made our admiring ancestors well acquainted with the heroes of the Greve and of Montfaucon. It must not be supposed that in those days the life of a robber who pursued his occupation with any degree of industry and skill was unattended with danger, for the most harmless cut–purses were hung without mercy whenever they were caught; the fear, however, of this fate did not prevent the *Enfants de la Matte* from performing wonders.

Brantome relates that King Charles IX. had the curiosity to wish to "know how the cut–purses performed their arts with so much skill and dexterity," and begged Captain La Chambre to introduce to him, on the occasion of a banquet and a ball, the cleverest cut–purses, giving them full liberty to exhibit their skill. The captain went to the Cours des Miracles and fetched ten of the most expert of these thieves, whom he presented to the King. Charles, "after the dinner and the ball had taken place, wished to see all the plunder, and found that they had absolutely earned three thousand ecus, either in money from purses, or in precious stones, pearls, or other jewels; some of the guests even lost their cloaks, at which the King thought he should die of laughter." The King allowed them to keep what they had thus earned at the expense of his guests; but he forbad them "to continue this sort of life," under penalty of being hung, and he had them enrolled in the army, in order to recompense them for their clever feats. We may safely assert that they made but indifferent soldiers.

[Illustration: Fig. 384.—The Exhibitor of strange Animals (Twelfth Century Manuscript, Royal Library of Brussels).]

Ceremonials.

Origin of Modern Ceremonial.—Uncertainty of French Ceremonial up to the End of the Sixteenth Century.—Consecration of the Kings of France.—Coronation of the Emperors of Germany.—Consecration of the Doges of Venice.—Marriage of the Doge with the Sea.—State Entries of Sovereigns.—An Account of the Entry of Isabel of Bavaria into Paris.—Seats of Justice.—Visits of Ceremony between Persons of rank.—Mourning.—Social Courtesies.—Popular Demonstrations and National Commemorations.—New Year's Day.—Local Festivals.— *Vins d'Honneur.*—Processions of Trades.

Although society during the Middle Ages was, as a whole, closely cemented together, being animated by the same sentiments and imbued with the same spirit, it was divided, as we have already stated, into three great classes, namely, the clergy, the nobility, and the *liers–etat.* These classes, each of which formed a distinct body within the State, carried on an existence peculiar to itself, and presented in its collective capacity a separate individuality. Hence there was a distinct ceremonial for each class. We will not attempt to give in detail the innumerable laws of these three kinds of ceremonial; our attention will be directed solely to their most characteristic customs, and to their most remarkable and interesting aspects taken as a whole. We must altogether lay aside matters relating specially to ceremonies of a purely religions character, as they are connected more or less with the traditions and customs of the Church, and belong to quite a distinct order of things.

"When the Germans, and especially the Franks," says the learned paleographer Vallet de Viriville, "had succeeded in establishing their own rule in place of that of the Romans, these almost savage nations, and the barbarian chiefs who were at their head under the title of kings, necessarily borrowed more or less the refined practices relating to ceremonial possessed by the people whom they had conquered. The elevation of the elected chief or king on the shield and the solemn taking of arms in the midst of the tribe seem to be the only traces of public ceremonies which we can discover among the

316

Grermans. The marvellous display and the imposing splendour of the political hierarchy of the Roman Empire, especially in its outward arrangements, must have astonished the minds of these uncultivated people. Thus we find the Frank kings becoming immediately after a victory the simple and clumsy imitators of the civilisation which they had broken up." Clovis on returning to Tours in 507, after having defeated Alaric, received the titles of *Patrician* and *Consul* from the Emperor Anastasius, and bedecked himself with the purple, the chlamys, and the diadem. The same principle of imitation was afterwards exhibited in the internal and external court ceremonial, in proportion as it became developed in the royal person. Charlemagne, who aimed at everything which could adorn and add strength to a new monarchy, established a regular method for the general and special administration of his empire, as also for the internal arrangement and discipline of his palace. We have already referred to this twofold organization (*vide* chapters on Private Life and on Food), but we may here remark that, notwithstanding these ancient tendencies to the creation of a fixed ceremonial, the trifling rules which made etiquette a science and a law, were introduced by degrees, and have only very recently been established amongst us.

In 1385, when King Charles VI. married the notorious Isabel of Bavaria, then scarcely fourteen years of age, he desired to arrange for her a magnificent entry into Paris, the pomp and brilliancy of which should be consistent with the rank and illustrious descent of his young bride. He therefore begged the old Queen Blanche, widow of Philippe de Valois, to preside over the ceremony, and to have it conducted according to the custom of olden times. She was consequently obliged, in the absence of any fixed rules on the subject, to consult the official records,—that is to say, the "Chronique du Monastere de Saint–Denis." The first embodiment of rules relating to these matters in use among the nobility, which had appeared in France under the title of "Honneurs de la Cour," only goes back to the end of the fifteenth century. It appears, however, that even then this was not generally admitted among the nobility as the basis of ceremonial, for in 1548 we find that nothing had been definitely settled. This is evident from the fact that when King Henri III. desired to know the rank and order of precedence of the princes of the royal blood, both dukes and counts—as also that of the other princes, the barons, the nobles of the kingdom, the constables, the marshals of France and the admirals, and what position they had held on great public occasions during the reigns of his predecessors—he commissioned Jean du Tillet, the civil registrar of the Parliament of Paris, to search among the royal archives for the various authentic documents which might throw light on this question, and serve as a precedent for the future. In fact, it was Henri III. who, in

1585, created the office of Grand Master of the Ceremonies of France, entrusting it to Guillaume Pot, a noble of Rhodes, which office for many generations remained hereditary in his family.

[Illustration: Fig. 385.—Herald (Fourteenth Century).—From a Miniature in the "Chroniques de Saint–Denis" (Imperial Library of Paris).]

Nevertheless the question of ceremonial, and especially that of precedence, had already more than once occupied the attention of sovereigns, not only within their own states, but also in relation to diplomatic matters. The meetings of councils, at which the ambassadors of all the Christian Powers, with the delegates of the Catholic Church, were assembled, did not fail to bring this subject up for decision. Pope Julius II. in 1504 instructed Pierre de Crassis, his Master of the Ceremonies, to publish a decree, determining the rank to be taken by the various sovereigns of Europe or by their representatives; but we should add that this Papal decree never received the sanction of the parties interested, and that the question of precedence, even at the most unimportant public ceremonies, was during the whole of the Middle Ages a perpetual source of litigation in courts of law, and of quarrels which too often ended in bloodshed.

It is right that we should place at the head of political ceremonies those having reference to the coronation of sovereigns, which were not only political, but owed their supreme importance and dignity to the necessary intervention of ecclesiastical authority. We will therefore first speak of the consecration and coronation of the kings of France.

Pepin le Bref, son of Charles Martel and founder of the second dynasty, was the first of the French kings who was consecrated by the religions rite of anointing. But its mode of administration for a long period underwent numerous changes, before becoming established by a definite law. Thus Pepin, after having been first consecrated in 752 in the Cathedral of Boissons, by the Archbishop of Mayence, was again consecrated with his two sons Charlemagne and Carloman, in 753, in the Abbey of St. Denis, by Pope Stephen III. Charlemagne was twice anointed by the Sovereign Pontiff, first as King of Lombardy, and then as Emperor. Louis le Debonnaire, his immediate successor, was consecrated at Rheims by Pope Stephen IV. in 816. In 877 Louis le Begue received unction and the sceptre, at Compiegne, at the hands of the Archbishop of Rheims. Charles le Simple in 893, and Robert I. in 922, were consecrated and crowned at Rheims; but the coronation of Raoul, in 923, was celebrated in the Abbey of St. Medard de Soissons, and that of Louis d'Outremer, in 936, at Laon. From the accession of King Lothaire to that of Louis VI. (called Le Gros), the consecration of the kings of France sometimes took place in the metropolitan church of Rheims, and sometimes in other churches, but more frequently in the former. Louis VI. having been consecrated in the Cathedral of Orleans, the clergy of Rheims appealed against this supposed infraction of custom and their own special privileges. A long discussion took place, in which were brought forward the titles which the Church of Rheims possessed subsequently to the reign of Clovis to the exclusive honour of having kings consecrated in it; and King Louis le Jeune, son of Louis le Gros, who was himself consecrated at Rheims, promulgated a special decree on this question, in anticipation of the consecration of his son, Philippe Auguste. This decree finally settled the rights of this ancient church, and at the same time defined the order which was to be observed in future at the ceremony of consecration. From that date, down to the end of the reign of the Bourbons of the elder line, kings were invariably consecrated, according to legal rite, in the metropolitan church of Rheims, with the exception of Henry IV., who was crowned at Chartres by the bishop of that town, on account of the civil wars which then divided his kingdom, and caused the gates of Rheims to be closed against him.

[Illustration: Fig. 386.—Coronation of Charlemagne.—Fac–simile of a Miniature in the "Chroniques de Saint–Denis," Manuscript of the Fourteenth Century (Imperial Library of Paris).]

The consecration of the kings of France always took place on a Sunday. On the previous day, at the conclusion of evening prayers, the custody of the cathedral devolved upon certain royal officers, assisted by the ordinary officials. During the evening the monarch came to the church for devotion, and "according to his religions feelings, to pass part of the night in prayer," an act which was called *la veillee des armes*. A large platform, surmounted by a throne, was erected between the chancel and the great nave. Upon this assembled, besides the King and his officers of State, twelve ecclesiastical peers, together with those prelates whom the King might be pleased to invite, and six lay peers, with other officers or nobles. At daybreak, the King sent a deputation of barons to the Abbey of St. Remi for the holy vial, which was a small glass vessel called *ampoule*, from the Latin word *ampulla*, containing the holy oil to be used at the royal anointing. According to tradition, this vial was brought from heaven by a dove at the time of the consecration of Clovis. Four of the nobles remained as hostages at the abbey during the time that the Abbot of St. Remi, followed by his monks and escorted by the barons, went in procession to the cathedral to place the sacred vessel upon the altar. The abbot of St. Denis in France had in a similar manner to bring from Rheims with great pomp, and deposit by the side of the holy vial, the royal insignia, which were kept in the treasury of his monastery, and had been there since the reign of Charlemagne. They consisted of the crown, the sword sheathed, the golden spurs, the gilt sceptre, the rod adorned with an ivory handle in the form of a hand, the sandals of blue silk, embroidered with fleur de lis, the chasuble or *dalmatique*, and the *surcot*, or royal mantle, in the shape of a cape without a hood. The King, immediately on rising from his bed, entered the cathedral, and forthwith took oath to maintain the Catholio faith and the privileges of the Church, and to dispense good and impartial justice to his subjects. He then walked to the foot of the altar, and divested himself of part of his dress, having his head bare, and wearing a tunic with openings on the chest, on the shoulders, at the elbows, and in the middle of the back; these openings were closed by means of silver aigulets. The Archbishop of Rheims then drew the sword from the scabbard and handed it to the King, who passed it to the principal officer in attendance. The prelate then proceeded with the religious part of the ceremony of consecration, and taking a drop of the miraculous oil out of the holy vial by means of a gold needle, he mixed it with the holy oil from his own church. This being done, and sitting in the posture of consecration, he anointed the King, who was kneeling before him, in five different parts of the body, namely, on the forehead, on the breast, on the back, on the shoulders, and on the joints of the arms. After this the King rose up, and with the assistance of his officers, put on his royal robes. The Archbishop handed to him successively the ring, the sceptre, and the rod of justice, and lastly placed the crown on his head. At this moment the twelve peers formed themselves into a group, the lay peers being in the first rank, immediately around the sovereign, and raising their hands to the crown, they held it for a moment, and then they conducted the King to the throne. The consecrating prelate, putting down his mitre, then knelt at the feet of the monarch and took the oath of allegiance, his example being followed by the other peers and their vassals who were in attendance. At the same time, the cry of "*Vive le Roi!*" uttered by the archbishop, was repeated three times outside the cathedral by the heralds—at—arms, who shouted it to the assembled multitude. The latter replied, "*Noel! Noel! Noel!*" and scrambled for the small pieces of money thrown to them by the officers, who at the same time cried out, "*Largesse, largesse aux manants*!" Every part of this ceremony was accompanied by benedictions and prayers, the form of which was read out of the consecration service as ordered by the bishop, and the proceedings terminated by the return of the civil and religious procession which had composed the *cortege*. When the sovereign was married, his wife participated with him in the honours of the consecration, the symbolical investiture, and the coronation; but she only partook of the homage rendered to the King to a limited degree, which was meant to imply that the Queen had a less extended authority and a less exalted rank.

[Illustration: Fig. 387.—Dalmatica and Sandals of Charlemagne, Insignia of the Kings of France at their Coronation, preserved in the Treasury of the Abbey of St. Denis.]

The ceremonies which accompanied the accessions of the emperors of Germany (Fig. 388) are equally interesting, and were settled by a decree which the Emperor Charles IX. promulgated in 1356, at the Diet of Nuremberg. According to the terms of this decree—which is still preserved among the archives of Frankfort–on–the–Main, and which is known as the *bulle d'or*, or golden bull, from the fact of its bearing a seal of pure gold—on the death of an emperor, the Archbishop of Mayence summoned, for an appointed day, the Prince Electors of the Empire, who, during the whole course of the Middle Ages, remained seven in number, "in honour," says the bull, "of the seven candlesticks mentioned in the Apocalypse." These Electors—who occupied the same position near the Emperor that the twelve peers did in relation to the King of France—were the Archbishops of Mayence, of Treves, and of Cologne, the King of Bohemia, the Count Palatine of the Rhine, the Duke of Saxony, and the Margrave of Brandenburg. On the appointed day, the mass of the Holy Spirit was duly solemnized in the Church of St. Bartholomew of Frankfort, a town in which not only the election of the Emperor, but also his coronation, almost always took place, though one might have supposed that Aix–la–Chapelle would have been selected for such ceremonies. The Electors attended, and after the service was concluded, they retired to the sacristy of the church, accompanied by their officers and secretaries, They had thirty days for deliberation, but beyond that period they were not allowed "to eat bread or drink water" until they had agreed, at least by a majority, to give *a temporal chief to the Christian people, that is to say, a King of the Romans, who should in due time be promoted to be Emperor,* The newly–elected prince was, in fact, at first simply *King of the Romans*, and this title was often borne by persons who were merely nominated for the office by the voice of the Electors, or by political combinations. In order to be promoted to the full measure of power and authority, the King of the Romans had to receive both religions consecration and the crown. The ceremonies adopted at this solemnity were very analogous to those used at the consecrations of the kings of France, as well as to those of installation of all Christian princes. The service was celebrated by the Archbishop of Cologne, who placed the crown on the head of the sovereign–elect, whom he consecrated

321

Emperor. The symbols of his authority were handed to him by the Electors, and then he was proclaimed, *"Caesar, most sacred, ever august Majesty, Emperor, of the Holy Roman Empire of the nation of Germany."*

[Illustration: Fig. 388.—Costume of Emperors at their Coronation since the Time of Charlemagne.—From an Engraving in a Work entitled "Insignia Sacre Majistatis Caesarum Principum." Frankfort, 1579, in folio.]

The imperial *cortege* then came out from the Church of St. Bartholomew, and went through the town, halting at the town–hall (called the *Roemer*, in commemoration of the noble name of Rome), where a splendid banquet, prepared in the *Kaysersaal* (hall of the Caesars), awaited the principal performers in this august ceremony.

At the moment that the Emperor set foot on the threshold of the Roemer, the Elector of Saxony, Chief Marshal of the Empire, on horseback, galloped at full speed towards a heap of oats which was piled up in the middle of the square. Holding in one hand a silver measure, and in the other a scraper of the same metal, each of which weighed six marks, he filled the measure with oats, levelled it with the scraper, and handed it over to the hereditary marshal. The rest of the heap was noisily scrambled for by the people who had been witnesses of this allegorical performance. Then the Count Palatine, as chief seneschal, proceeded to perform his part in the ceremony, which consisted of placing before the Emperor, who was sitting at table, four silver dishes, each weighing three marks. The King of Bohemia, as chief butler, handed to the monarch wine and water in a silver cup weighing twelve marks; and then the Margrave of Magdeburg presented to him a silver basin of the same weight for washing his hands. The other three Electors, or arch–chancellors, provided at their own expense the silver baton, weighing twelve marks, suspended to which one of them carried the seals of the empire. Lastly, the Emperor, and with him the Empress if he was married, the princes, and the Electors, sat down to a banquet at separate tables, and were waited upon by their respective officers. On another table or stage were placed the Imperial insignia. The ceremony was concluded outside by public rejoicings: fountains were set to play; wine, beer, and other beverages were distributed; gigantic bonfires were made, at which whole oxen were roasted; refreshment tables were set out in the open air, at which any one might sit down and partake, and, in a word, every bounty as well as every amusement was provided. In this way for centuries public fetes were celebrated on these occasions.

[Illustration: Fig. 389.—Imperial Procession.—From an Engraving of the "Solemn Entry of Charles V. and Clement VII. into Bologna," by L. de Cranach, from a Fresco by Brusasorci, of Verona.]

The doges of Venice, as well as the emperors of Germany, and some other heads of states, differed from other Christian sovereigns in this respect, that, instead of holding their high office by hereditary or divine right, they were installed therein by election. At Venice, a conclave, consisting of forty electors, appointed by a much more numerous body of men of high position, elected the Doge, or president of *the most serene Republic*.

From the day when Laurent Tiepolo, immediately after his election in 1268, was spontaneously carried in triumph by the Venetian sailors, it became the custom for a similar ovation to take place in honour of any newly–elected doge. In order to do this, the workmen of the harbour had the new Doge seated in a splendid palanquin, and carried him on their shoulders in great pomp round the Piazza San Marco. But another still more characteristic ceremony distinguished this magisterial election. On Ascension Day, the Doge, entering a magnificent galley, called the *Bucentaur*, which was elegantly equipped, and resplendent with gold and precious stuffs, crossed the Grand Canal, went outside the town, and proceeded in the midst of a nautical *cortege*, escorted by bands of music, to the distance of about a league from the town on the Adriatic Gulf. Then the Patriarch of Venice gave his blessing to the sea, and the Doge, taking the helm, threw a gold ring into the water, saying, "O sea! I espouse thee in the name, and in token, of our true and perpetual sovereignty." Immediately the waters were strewed with flowers, and the shouts of joy, and the clapping of hands of the crowd, were intermingled with the strains of instruments of music of all sorts, whilst the glorious sky of Venice smiled on the poetic scene.

The greater part of the principal ceremonies of the Middle Ages acquired, from various accessory and local circumstances, a character of grandeur well fitted to impress the minds of the populace. On these memorable occasions the exhibition of some historical memorial, of certain traditional symbols, of certain relics, &c., brought to the recollection the most celebrated events in national history—events already possessing the prestige of antiquity as well as the veneration of the people. Thus, as a memorial of the consecration of the kings of Hungary, the actual crown of holy King Stephen was used; at the consecration of the kings of England, the actual chair of Edward the Confessor was used; at the consecration of the emperors of Germany, the imperial insignia actually used by

Charlemagne formed part of the display; at the consecration of the kings of France at a certain period, the hand of justice of St. Louis, which has been before alluded to, was produced.

[Illustration: Fig. 390.—Standards of the Church and the Empire.—Reduced from an Engraving of the "Entry of Charles V. and Clement VII. into Bologna," by Lucas de Cranach, from a Fresco by Brusasorci, of Verona.]

After their consecration by the Church and by the spiritual power, the sovereigns had simply to take actual possession of their dominions, and, so to speak, of their subjects. This positive act of sovereignty was often accompanied by another class of ceremonies, called *joyous entry*, or *public entry*. These entries, of which numerous accounts have been handed down to us by historians, and which for the most part were very varied in character, naturally took place in the capital city. We will limit ourselves to transcribing the account given by the ancient chronicler, Juvenal des Ursins, of the entry into Paris of Queen Isabel of Bavaria, wife of Charles VI., which was a curious specimen of the public fetes of this kind.

[Illustration: Fig. 391.—Grand Procession of the Doge, Venice (Sixteenth Century).—Reduced from one of fourteen Engravings representing this Ceremony, designed and engraved by J. Amman.]

"In the year 1389, the King was desirous that the Queen should make a public entry into Paris, and this he made known to the inhabitants, in order that they should make preparations for it. And there were at each cross roads divers *histoires* (historical representations, pictures, or tableaux vivants), and fountains sending forth water, wine, and milk. The people of Paris in great numbers went out to meet the Queen, with the Provost of the Merchants, crying 'Noel!' The bridge by which she passed was covered with blue taffeta, embroidered with golden fleurs–de–lys. A man of light weight, dressed in the guise of an angel, came down, by means of some well–constructed machinery, from one of the towers of Notre–Dame, to the said bridge through an opening in the said blue taffeta, at the moment when the Queen was passing, and placed a beautiful crown on her head. After he had done this, he withdrew through the said opening by the same means, and thus appeared as if he were returning to the skies of his own accord. Before the Grand Chastelet there was a splendid court adorned with azure tapestry, which was intended to be a representation of the *lit–de–justice*, and it was very large and richly

324

decorated. In the middle of it was a very large pure white artificial stag, its horns gilt, and its neck encircled with a crown of gold. It was so ingeniously constructed that its eyes, horns, mouth, and all its limbs, were put in motion by a man who was secreted within its body. Hanging to its neck were the King's arms—that is to say, three gold fleur–de–lys on an azure shield.... Near the stag there was a large sword, beautiful and bright, unsheathed; and when the Queen passed, the stag was made to take the sword in the right fore–foot, to hold it out straight, and to brandish it. It was reported to the King that the said preparations were made, and he said to Savoisy, who was one of those nearest to him, 'Savoisy, I earnestly entreat thee to mount a good horse, and I will ride behind thee, and we will so dress ourselves that no one will know us, and let us go and see the entry of my wife.' And, although Savoisy did all he could to dissuade him, the King insisted, and ordered that it should be done. So Savoisy did what the King had ordered, and disguised himself as well as he could, and mounted on a powerful horse with the King behind him. They went through the town, and managed so as to reach the Chastelet at the time the Queen was passing. There was a great crowd, and Savoisy placed himself as near as he could, and there were sergeants on all sides with thick birch wands, who, in order to prevent the crowd from pressing upon and injuring the court where the stag was, hit away with their wands as hard as they could. Savoisy struggled continually to get nearer and nearer, and the sergeants, who neither knew the King nor Savoisy, struck away at them, and the King received several very hard and well–directed blows on the shoulders. In the evening, in the presence of the ladies, the matter was talked over, and they began to joke about it, and even the King himself laughed at the blows he had received. The Queen on her entry was seated on a litter, and very magnificently dressed, as were also the ladies and maids of honour. It was indeed a splendid sight; and if any one wished to describe the dresses of the ladies, of the knights and squires, and of those who escorted the Queen, it would take a long time to do so. After supper, singing and dancing commenced, which continued until daylight. The next day there were tournaments and other sports" (Fig. 392).

[Illustration: Entry of Charles the Seventh into Paris

A miniature from *Monstrelet the Chronicles* in the Bibl. nat. de Paris, no 20,861 Costumes of the Sixteenth century.]

[Illustration: Fig. 392.—Tournaments in honour of the Entry of Queen Isabel into Paris—From a Miniature in the "Chroniques" of Froissart, Manuscript of the Fifteenth

[Illustration: Fig. 393.—Seat of Justice, held by King Philippe de Valois, on the 8th April, 1332, for the Trial of Robert, Comte d'Artois.—From a Pen–and–ink Sketch in an Original Manuscript (Arch. of the Empire)]

In the course of this simple and graphic description mention has been made of the *lit de justice* (seat of justice). All judicial or legislative assemblies at which the King considered it his duty to be present were thus designated; when the King came there simply as a looker–on, they were more commonly called *plaidoyers*, and, in this case, no change was made in the ordinary arrangements; but when the King presided they were called *conseils*, and then a special ceremonial was required. In fact, by *lit de justice* (Fig. 393), or *cour des pairs*, we understand a court consisting of the high officers of the crown, and of the great executive of the State, whose duty it was to determine whether any peer of France should be tried on a criminal charge; gravely to deliberate on any political matter of special interest; or to register, in the name of the absolute sovereignty of the King, any edict of importance. We know the prominent, and, we may say, even the fatal, part played by these solemnities, which were being continually re–enacted, and on every sort of pretext, during the latter days of monarchy. These courts were always held with impressive pomp. The sovereign usually summoned to them the princes of the blood royal and the officers of his household; the members of the Parliament took their seats in scarlet robes, the presidents being habited in their caps and their mantles, and the registrars of the court also wearing their official dress. The High Chancellor, the First Chamberlain, and the Provost of Paris, sat at the King's feet. The Chancellor of France, the presidents and councillors of the Parliament, occupied the bar, and the ushers of the court were in a kneeling posture.

Having thus mentioned the assemblies of persons of distinction, the interviews of sovereigns (Fig. 394), and the reception of ambassadors—without describing them in detail, which would involve more space than we have at our command—we will enter upon the subject of the special ceremonial adopted by the nobility, taking as our guide the standard book called "Honneurs de la Cour," compiled at the end of the fifteenth century by the celebrated Alienor de Poitiers. In addition to her own observations, she gives those of her mother, Isabelle de Souza, who herself had but continued the work of another noble lady, Jeanne d'Harcourt—married in 1391 to the Count William de Namur—who was considered the best authority to be found in the kingdom of France. This collection of the customs of the court forms a kind of family diary embracing three generations, and extending back over more than a century.

Notwithstanding the curious and interesting character of this book, and the authority which it possesses on this subject, we cannot, much to our regret, do more than borrow a few passages from it; but these, carefully selected, will no doubt suffice to give some idea of the manners and customs of the nobility during the fifteenth century, and to illustrate the laws of etiquette of which it was the recognised code.

One of the early chapters of the work sets forth this fundamental law of French ceremonial, namely, that, "according to the traditions or customs of France, women, however exalted their position, be they even king's daughters, rank with their husbands." We find on the occasion of the marriage of King Charles VII. with Mary of Anjou, in 1413, although probably there had never been assembled together so many princes and ladies of rank, that at the banquet the ladies alone dined with the Queen, "and no gentlemen sat with them." We may remark, whilst on this subject, that before the reign of Francis I. it was not customary for the two sexes to be associated together in the ordinary intercourse of court life; and we have elsewhere remarked (see chapter on Private Life) that this departure from ancient custom exerted a considerable influence, not only on manners, but also on public affairs.

[Illustration: Fig. 394.—Interview of King Charles V. with the Emperor Charles IV. in Paris in 1378.—Fac-simile of a Miniature in the Description of this Interview, Manuscript of the Fifteenth Century, in the Library of the Arsenal of Paris.]

The authoress of the "Honneurs de la Cour" specially mentions the respect which Queen Mary of Anjou paid to the Duchess of Burgundy when she was at Chalons in Champagne in 1445: "The Duchess came with all her retinue, on horseback and in carriages, into the courtyard of the mansion where the King and Queen were, and there alighted, her first maid of honour acting as her train-bearer. M. de Bourbon gave her his right hand, and the gentlemen went on in front. In this manner she was conducted to the hall which served as the ante-chamber to the Queen's apartment. There she stopped, and sent in M. de Crequi to ask the Queen if it was her pleasure that she should enter.... When the Duchess came to the door she took the train of her dress from the lady who bore it and let it trail on the ground, and as she entered she knelt and then advanced to the middle of the room. There she made the same obeisance, and moved straight towards the Queen, who was standing close to the foot of her throne. When the Duchess had performed a further act of homage, the Queen advanced two or three steps, and the Duchess fell on her knees; the Queen then put her hand on her shoulder, embraced her, kissed her, and commanded her to rise."

The Duchess then went up to Margaret of Scotland, wife of the Dauphin, afterwards Louis XI., "who was four or five feet from the Queen," and paid her the same honours as she had done to the Queen, although the Dauphine appeared to wish to prevent her from absolutely kneeling to her. After this she turned towards the Queen of Sicily (Isabelle de Lorraine, wife of Rene of Anjou, brother–in–law of the King), "who was two or three feet from the Dauphine," and merely bowed to her, and the same to another Princess, Madame de Calabre, who was still more distantly connected with the blood royal. Then the Queen, and after her the Dauphine, kissed the three maids of honour of the Duchess and the wives of the gentlemen. The Duchess did the same to the ladies who accompanied the Queen and the Dauphine, "but of those of the Queen of Sicily the Duchess kissed none, inasmuch as the Queen had not kissed hers. And the Duchess would not walk behind the Queen, for she said that the Duke of Burgundy was nearer the crown of France than was the King of Sicily, and also that she was daughter of the King of Portugal, who was greater than the King of Sicily."

Further on, from the details given of a similar reception, we learn that etiquette was not at that time regulated by the laws of politeness as now understood, inasmuch as the voluntary respect paid by men to the gentle sex was influenced much by social rank. Thus, at the time of a visit of Louis XI., then Dauphin, to the court of Brussels, to which place he went to seek refuge against the anger of his father, the Duchesses of Burgundy, of Charolais, and of Cleves, his near relatives, exhibited towards him all the tokens of submission and inferiority which he might have received from a vassal. The Dauphin, it is true, wished to avoid this homage, and a disussion on the subject of "more than a quarter of an hour ensued;" at last he took the Duchess of Burgundy by the arm and led her away, in order to cut short the ceremonies "about which Madame made so much to do." This, however, did not prevent the princesses, on their withdrawing, from kneeling to the ground in order to show their respect for the son of the King of France.

[Illustration: Fig. 395.—The Entry of Louis XI. into Paris.—Fac–simile of a Miniature in the "Chroniques" of Monstrelet, Manuscript of the Fifteenth Century (Imperial Library of Paris).]

We have already seen that the Duchess of Burgundy, when about to appear before the Queen, took her train from her train-bearer in order that she might carry it herself. In this she was only conforming to a general principle, which was, that in the presence of a superior, a person, however high his rank, should not himself receive honours whilst at the same time paying them to another. Thus a duke and a duchess amidst their court had all the things which were used at their table covered—hence the modern expression, *mettre le couvert* (to lay the cloth)—even the wash-hand basin and the *cadenas*, a kind of case in which the cups, knives, and other table articles were kept; but when they were entertaining a king all these marks of superiority were removed, as a matter of etiquette, from the table at which they sat, and were passed on as an act of respect to the sovereign present.

The book of Dame Alienor, in a series of articles to which we shall merely allude, speaks at great length and enters into detail respecting the interior arrangements of the rooms in which princes and other noble children were born. The formalities gone through on these occasions were as curious as they were complicated; and Dame Alienor regretted to see them falling into disuse, "owing to which," she says, "we fear that the possessions of the great houses of the nobility are getting too large, as every one admits, and chicanery or concealment of birth, so as to make away with too many children, is on the increase."

Mourning is the next subject which we shall notice. The King never wore black for mourning, not even for his father, but scarlet or violet. The Queen wore white, and did not leave her apartments for a whole year. Hence the name of *chateau, hotel,* or *tour de la Reine Blanche,* which many of the buildings of the Middle Ages still bear, from the fact that widowed queens inhabited them during the first year of their widowhood. On occasions of mourning, the various reception rooms of a house were hung with black. In deep mourning, such as that for a husband or a father, a lady wore neither gloves, jewels, nor silk. The head was covered with a low black head-dress, with trailing lappets, called *chaperons, barbettes, couvre-chefs*, and *tourets*. A duchess and the wife of a knight or a banneret, on going into mourning, stayed in their apartments for six weeks; the former, during the whole of this time, when in deep mourning, remained lying down all day on a bed covered with a white sheet; whereas the latter, at the end of nine days, got up, and until the six weeks were over, remained sitting in front of the bed on a black sheet. Ladies did not attend the funerals of their husbands, though it was usual for them to be present at those of their fathers and mothers. For an elder brother, they wore the same mourning as for a father, but they did not lie down as above described.

[Illustration: Fig. 396.—"How the King–at–Arms presents the Sword to the Duke of Bourbon."—From a Miniature in "Tournois du Roi Rene," Manuscript of the Fifteenth Century (Imperial Library of Paris).]

In their everyday intercourse with one another, kings, princes, dukes, and duchesses called one another *monsieur* and *madame*, adding the Christian name or that of the estate. A superior speaking or writing to an inferior, might prefix to his or her title of relationship *beau* or *belle*; for instance, *mon bel oncle, ma belle cousine*. People in a lower sphere of life, on being introduced to one another, did not say, "Monsieur Jean, ma belle tante"—"Mr. John, allow me to introduce you to my aunt"—but simply, "Jean, ma tante." The head of a house had his seat under a canopy or *dosseret* (Fig. 396), which he only relinquished to his sovereign, when he had the honour of entertaining him. "Such," says Alienor, in conclusion, "are the points of etiquette which are observed in Germany, in France, in Naples, in Italy, and in all other civilised countries and kingdoms." We may here remark, that etiquette, after having originated in France, spread throughout all Christian nations, and when it had become naturalised, as it were, amongst the latter, it acquired a settled position, which it retained more firmly than it did in France. In this latter country, it was only from the seventeenth century, and particularly under Louis XIV., that court etiquette really became a science, and almost a species of religions observance, whose minutiae were attended to as much as if they were sacramental rites, though they were not unfrequently of the most childish character, and whose pomp and precision often caused the most insufferable annoyance. But notwithstanding the perpetual changes of times and customs, the French nation has always been distinguished for nobility and dignity, tempered with good sense and elegance.

If we now direct our attention to the *tiers etat*, that class which, to quote a celebrated expression, "was destined to become everything, after having for a long time been looked upon as nothing," we shall notice that there, too, custom and tradition had much to do with ceremonies of all kinds. The presence of the middle classes not only gave, as it were, a stamp of grandeur to fetes of an aristocratic and religions character, but, in addition, the people themselves had a number of ceremonies of every description, in which etiquette was not one whit less strict than in those of the court. The variety of civic and popular ceremonies is so great, that it would require a large volume, illustrated with numerous engravings, to explain fully their characteristic features. The simple enumeration of the various public fetes, each of which was necessarily accompanied by a distinct ceremonial, would take up much time were we to attempt to give it even in the shortest manner.

[Illustration: Fig. 397.—Entry of the Roi de l'Epinette at Lille, in the Sixteenth Century.—From a Miniature in a Manuscript of the Library of Rouen.]

Besides the numerous ceremonies which were purely religious, namely, the procession of the *Fete–Dieu*, in Rogation week, and the fetes which were both of a superstitions and burlesque character, such as *des Fous, de l'Ane, des Innocents*, and others of the same kind, so much in vogue during the Middle Ages, and which we shall describe more in detail hereafter, we should like to mention the military or gymnastic fetes. Amongst these were what were called the processions of the *Confreres de l'Arquebuse*, the *Archers*, the *Papegaut*, the *roi de l'Epinette*, at Lille (Fig. 397), and the *Forestier* at Bruges. There were also what may be termed the fetes peculiar to certain places, such as those of *Behors*, of the *Champs Galat* at Epinal, of the *Laboureurs* at Montelimar, of *Guy l'an neuf* at Anjou. Also of the fetes of *May*, of the *sheaf*, of the *spring*, of the *roses*, of the *fires of St. John*, &c. Then there were the historical or commemorative fetes, such as those of the *Geant Reuss* at Dunkerque, of the *Gayant* at Douai, &c.; also of *Guet de Saint–Maxime* at Riez in Provence, the processions of *Jeanne d'Arc* at Orleans, of *Jeanne Hachette* at Beauvais; and lastly, the numerous fetes of public corporations, such as the *Ecoliers*, the *Nations*, the *Universites*; also the *Lendit*, the *Saint–Charlemagne*, the *Baillee des roses au Parlement*; the literary fetes of the *Pays et Chambres de rhetorique* of Picardy and Flanders, of the *Clemence Isaure* at Toulouse, and of the *Capitole* at Rome, &c.; the fetes of the *Serments, Metiers*, and *Devoirs* of the working men's corporation; and lastly, the *Fetes Patronales*, called also *Assemblees, Ducasses, Folies, Foires, Kermesses, Pardons*, &c.

From this simple enumeration, it can easily be understood what a useless task we should impose upon ourselves were we merely to enter upon so wide and difficult a subject. Apart from the infinite variety of details resulting from the local circumstances under which these ceremonies had been instituted, which were everywhere celebrated at fixed periods, a kind of general principle regulated and directed their arrangement. Nearly all these fetes and public rejoicings, which to a certain extent constituted the common basis of popular ceremonial, bore much analogy to one another. There are, however, certain peculiarities less known and more striking than the rest, which deserve to be mentioned, and we shall then conclude this part of our subject.

Manners, Custom and Dress During the Middle

[Illustration: Fig. 398.—Representation of a Ballet before Henri III. and his Court, in the Gallery of the Louvre.—Fac–simile of an Engraving on Copper of the "Ballet de la Royne," by Balthazar de Beaujoyeulx (folio, Paris, Mamert Patisson, 1582.)]

Those rites, ceremonies, and customs, which are the most commonly observed, and which most persistently keep their place amongst us, are far from being of modern origin. Thus, the custom of jovially celebrating the commencement of the new year, or of devoting certain particular days to festivity, is still universally followed in every country in the world. The practice of sending presents on *New Year's Day* is to be found among civilised nations in the East as well as in our own country. In the Middle Ages the intimate friends of princes, and especially of the kings of France, received Christmas gifts, for which they considered themselves bound to make an ample return. In England these interchanges of generosity also take place on Christmas Day. In Russia, on Easter Day, the people, on meeting in the street, salute one another by saying "Christ is risen." These practices, as well as many others, have no doubt been handed down to us from the early ages of Christianity. The same may be said of a vast number of customs of a more or less local character, which have been observed in various countries for centuries. In former times, at Ochsenbach, in Wurtemberg, during the carnival, women held a feast at which they were waited upon by men, and, after it was over, they formed themselves into a sort of court of plenary indulgence, from which the men were uniformly excluded, and sat in judgment on one another. At Ramerupt, a small town in Champagne, every year, on the 1st of May, twenty of the citizens repaired to the adjoining hamlet of St. Remy, hunting as they went along. They were called *the fools of Rameru*, and it was said that the greatest fool led the band. The inhabitants of St. Remy were bound to receive them gratuitously, and to supply them, as well as their horses and dogs, with what they required, to have a mass said for them, to put up with all the absurd vagaries of the captain and his troop, and to supply them with a *fine and handsome horned ram,* which was led back in triumph. On their return into Ramerupt they set up shouts at the door of the cure, the procurator fiscal, and the collector of taxes, and, after the invention of gunpowder, fireworks were let off. They then went to the market–place, where they danced round the ram, which was decorated with ribbons. No doubt this was a relic of the feasts of ancient heathenism.

A more curious ceremony still, whose origin, we think, may be traced to the Dionysian feasts of heathenism, has continued to be observed to this day at Beziers. It bears the names of the *Feast of Pepezuch*, the *Triumph of Beziers,* or the *Feast of Caritats* or

Charites. At the bottom of the Rue Francaise at Beziers, a statue is to be seen which, notwithstanding the mutilations to which it has been subjected, still distinctly bears traces of being an ancient work of the most refined period of art. This statue represents Pepezuch, a citizen of Beziers, who, according to somewhat questionable tradition, valiantly defended the town against the Goths, or, as some say, against the English; its origin, therefore, cannot be later than the thirteenth century. On Ascension Day, the day of the Feast of Pepezuch, an immense procession went about the town. Three remarkable machines were particularly noticeable; the first was an enormous wooden camel made to walk by mechanism, and to move its limbs and jaws; the second was a galley on wheels fully manned; the third consisted of a cart on which a travelling theatre was erected. The consuls and other civic authorities, the corporations of trades having the pastors walking in front of them, the farriers on horseback, all bearing their respective insignia and banners, formed the procession. A double column, composed of a division of young men and young women holding white hoops decorated with ribbons and many–coloured streamers, was preceded by a young girl crowned with flowers, half veiled, and carrying a basket. This brilliant procession marched to the sound of music, and, at certain distances, the youthful couples of the two sexes halted, in order to perform, with the assistance of their hoops, various figures, which were called the *Danse des Treilles.* The machines also stopped from time to time at various places. The camel was especially made to enter the Church of St. Aphrodise, because it was said that the apostle had first come on a camel to preach the Gospel in that country, and there to receive the palm of martyrdom. On arriving before the statue of Pepezuch the young people decorated it with garlands. When the square of the town was reached, the theatre was stopped like the ancient car of Thespis, and the actors treated the people to a few comical drolleries in imitation of Aristophanes. From the galley the youths flung sugar–plums and sweetmeats, which the spectators returned in equal profusion. The procession closed with a number of men, crowned with green leaves, carrying on their heads loaves of bread, which, with other provisions contained in the galley, were distributed amongst the poor of the town.

In Germany and in France it was the custom at the public entries of kings, princes, and persons of rank, to offer them the wines made in the district and commonly sold in the town. At Langres, for instance, these wines were put into four pewter vessels called *cimaises,* which are still to be seen. They were called the *lion, monkey, sheep,* and *pig* wines, symbolical names, which expressed the different degrees or phases of drunkenness which they were supposed to be capable of producing: the lion, courage; the monkey, cunning; the sheep, good temper; the pig, bestiality.

We will now conclude by borrowing, from the excellent work of M. Alfred Michiels on Dutch and Flemish painting, the abridged description of a procession of corporations of trades, which took place at Antwerp in 1520, on the Sunday after Ascension Day. "All the corporations of trades were present, every member being dressed in his best suit." In front of each guild a banner floated; and immediately behind an enormous lighted wax–taper was carried. March music was played on long silver trumpets, flutes, and drums. The goldsmiths, painters, masons, silk embroiderers, sculptors, carpenters, boatmen, fishermen, butchers, curriers, drapers, bakers, tailors, and men of every other trade marched two abreast. Then came crossbowmen, arquebusiers, archers, &c., some on foot and some on horseback. After them came the various monastic orders; and then followed a crowd of bourgeois magnificently dressed. A numerous company of widows, dressed in white from head to foot, particularly attracted attention; they constituted a sort of sisterhood, observing certain rules, and gaining their livelihood by various descriptions of manual work. The cathedral canons and the other priests walked in the procession in their gorgeous silk vestments sparkling with gold. Twenty persons carried on their shoulders a huge figure of the Virgin, with the infant Saviour in her arms, splendidly decorated. At the end of the procession were chariots and ships on wheels. There were various groups in the procession representing scenes from the Old and New Testament, such as the *Salutation of the Angels*, the *Visitation of the Magi*, who appeared riding on camels, the *Flight into Egypt*, and other well–known historical incidents. The last machine represented a dragon being led by St. Margaret with a magnificent bridle, and was followed by St. George and several brilliantly attired knights.

[Illustration: Fig. 399.—Sandal and Buskin of Charlemagne.—From the Abbey of St. Denis.]

Costumes.

Influence of Ancient Costume.—Costume in the Fifth
Century.—Hair.—Costumes in the Time of Charlemagne.—Origin of Modern
National Dress.—Head–dresses and Beards: Time of St. Louis.—Progress
of Dress: Trousers, Hose, Shoes, Coats, Surcoats, Capes.—Changes in the
Fashions of Shoes and Hoods.—*Livree*,—Cloaks and Capes.—Edicts

against Extravagant Fashions.—Female Dress: Gowns, Bonnets, Head–dresses, &c.—Disappearance of Ancient Dress.—Tight–fitting Gowns.—General Character of Dress under Francis I.—Uniformity of Dress.

Long garments alone were worn by the ancients, and up to the period when the barbarous tribes of the North made their appearance, or rather, until the invasion of the Roman Empire by these wandering nations, male and female dress differed but little. The Greeks made scarcely any change in their mode of dress for centuries; but the Romans, on becoming masters of the world, partially adopted the dress and arms of the people they had conquered, where they considered them an improvement on their own, although the original style of dress was but little altered (Figs. 400 and 401).

Roman attire consisted of two garments—the under garment, or *tunic*, and the outer garment, or *cloak*; the latter was known under the various names of *chlamys, toga*, and *pallium*, but, notwithstanding these several appellations, there was scarcely any appreciable distinction between them. The simple tunic with sleeves, which answered to our shirt, was like the modern blouse in shape, and was called by various names. The *chiridota* was a tunic with long and large sleeves, of Asiatic origin; the *manuleata* was a tunic with long and tight sleeves coming to the wrists; the *talaris* was a tunic reaching to the feet; the *palmata* was a state tunic, embroidered with palms, which ornamentation was often found in other parts of dress. The *lacerna, loena, cucullus, chlamys, sagum, paludamentum*, were upper garments, more or less coarse, either full or scant, and usually short, and were analogous to our cloaks, mantles, &c., and were made both with and without hoods. There were many varieties of the tunic and cloak invented by female ingenuity, as well as of other articles of dress, which formed elegant accessories to the toilet, but there was no essential alteration in the national costume, nor was there any change in the shape of the numerous descriptions of shoes. The barbarian invasions brought about a revolution in the dress as well as in the social state of the people, and it is from the time of these invasions that we may date, properly speaking, the history of modern dress; for the Roman costume, which was in use at the same time as that of the Franks, the Huns, the Vandals, the Goths, &c., was subjected to various changes down to the ninth century. These modifications increased afterwards to such an extent that, towards the fourteenth century, the original type had altogether disappeared.

Manners, Custom and Dress During the Middle

[Illustration: Figs. 400 and 401.—Gallo-Roman Costumes.—From Bas-reliefs discovered in Paris in 1711 underneath the Choir of Notre-Dame.]

It was quite natural that men living in a temperate climate, and bearing arms only when in the service of the State, should be satisfied with garments which they could wear without wrapping themselves up too closely. The northern nations, on the contrary, had early learned to protect themselves against the severity of the climate in which they lived. Thus the garments known by them as *braies*, and by the Parthians as *sarabara*, doubtless gave origin to those which have been respectively called by us *chausses, haut-de-chausses, trousses, gregues, culottes, pantalons*, &c. These wandering people had other reasons for preferring the short and close-fitting garments to those which were long and full, and these were their innate pugnacity, which forced them ever to be under arms, their habit of dwelling in forests and thickets, their love of the chase, and their custom of wearing armour.

The ancient Greeks and Romans always went bareheaded in the towns; but in the country, in order to protect themselves from the direct rays of the sun, they wore hats much resembling our round hats, made of felt, plaited rushes, or straw. Other European nations of the same period also went bareheaded, or wore caps made of skins of animals, having no regularity of style, and with the shape of which we are but little acquainted.

Shoes, and head-dresses of a definite style, belong to a much more modern period, as also do the many varieties of female dress, which have been known at all times and in all countries under the general name of *robes*. The girdle was only used occasionally, and its adoption depended on circumstances; the women used it in the same way as the men, for in those days it was never attached to the dress. The great difference in modern female costume consists in the fact of the girdle being part of the dress, thus giving a long or short waist, according to the requirements of fashion. In the same manner, a complete revolution took place in men's dress according as loose or tight, long or short sleeves were introduced.

We shall commence our historical sketch from the fifth century, at which period we can trace the blending of the Roman with the barbaric costume—namely, the combination of the long, shapeless garment with that which was worn by the Germans, and which was accompanied by tight-fitting braies. Thus, in the recumbent statue which adorned the tomb of Clovis, in the Church of the Abbey of St. Genevieve, the King is represented as wearing the *tunic* and the *toga*, but, in addition, Gallo–Roman civilization had actually given him tight–fitting braies, somewhat similar to what we now call pantaloons. Besides this, his tunic is fastened by a belt; which, however, was not a novelty in his time, for the women then wore long dresses, fastened at the waist by a girdle. There is nothing very remarkable about his shoes, since we find that the shoe, or closed sandal, was worn from the remotest periods by nearly all nations (Figs. 402 and 403).

[Illustration: Fig. 402.—Costume of King Clovis (Sixth Century).—From a Statue on his Tomb, formerly in the Abbey of St. Genevieve.]

[Illustration: Fig. 403.—Costume of King Childebert (Seventh Century).—From a Statue formerly placed in the Refectory of the Abbey of St. Germain–des–Pres.]

The cloak claims an equally ancient origin. The principal thing worthy of notice is the amount of ornament with which the Franks enriched their girdles and the borders of their tunics and cloaks. This fashion they borrowed from the Imperial court, which, having been transferred from Rome to Constantinople during the third century, was not slow to adopt the luxury of precious stones and other rich decorations commonly in use amongst Eastern nations. Following the example of Horace de Vielcastel, the learned author of a history of the costumes of France, we may here state that it is very difficult, if not impossible, to define the exact costume during the time of the early Merovingian periods. The first writers who have touched upon this subject have spoken of it very vaguely, or not being contemporaries of the times of which they wrote, could only describe from tradition or hearsay. Those monuments in which early costume is supposed to be represented are almost all of later date, when artists, whether sculptors or painters, were not very exact in their delineations of costume, and even seemed to imagine that no other style could have existed before their time than the one with which they were daily familiar. In order to be as accurate as possible, although, after all, we can only speak hypothetically, we cannot do better than call to mind, on the one hand, what Tacitus says of the Germans, that they "were almost naked, excepting for a short and tight garment round their waists, and a little square cloak which they threw over the right shoulder," and, on the other, to carry ourselves back in imagination to the ancient Roman costume. We may notice, moreover, the curious description given of the Franks by Sidoine Apollinaire, who says, "They tied up their flaxen or light–brown hair above their foreheads, into a kind of tuft, and then made it fall behind the head like a horse's tail. The face was clean shaved, with the exception of two long moustaches. They wore cloth garments, fitting tight to the body and limbs, and a broad belt, to which they hung their swords." But this is a sketch made at a time when the Frankish race was only known among the Gauls through its marauding tribes, whose raids, from time to time, spread terror and dismay throughout the countries which they visited. From the moment when the uncultivated tribes of ancient Germany formally took possession of the territory which they had withdrawn from Roman rule, they showed themselves desirous of adopting the more gentle manners of the conquered nation. "In imitation of their chief," says M. Jules Quicherat, the eminent antiquarian, "more than once the Franks doffed the war coat and the leather Belt, and assumed the toga of Roman dignity. More than once their flaxen hair was shown to advantage by flowing over the imperial mantle, and the gold of the knights, the purple of the senators and patricians, the triumphal crowns, the fasces, and, in short, everything which the Roman Empire invented in order to exhibit its grandeur, assisted in adding to that of our ancestors."

[Illustration: Figs. 404 and 405.—Saints in the Costume of the Sixth to the Eighth Centuries.—From Miniatures in old Manuscripts of the Royal Library of Brussels (Designs by Count H. de Vielcastel).]

One great and characteristic difference between the Romans and the Franks should, however, be specially mentioned; namely, in the fashion of wearing the hair long, a fashion never adopted by the Romans, and which, during the whole of the first dynasty, was a distinguishing mark of kings and nobles among the Franks. Agathias, the Greek historian, says, "The hair is never cut from the heads of the Frankish kings' sons. From early youth their hair falls gracefully over their shoulders, it is parted on the forehead, and falls equally on both sides; it is with them a matter to which they give special attention." We are told, besides, that they sprinkled it with gold–dust, and plaited it in small bands, which they ornamented with pearls and precious metals.

Whilst persons of rank were distinguished by their long and flowing hair, the people wore theirs more or less short, according to the degree of freedom which they possessed, and the serfs had their heads completely shaved. It was customary for the noble and free classes to swear by their hair, and it was considered the height of politeness to pull out a hair and present it to a person. Fredegaire, the chronicler, relates that Clovis thus pulled out a hair in order to do honour to St. Germer, Bishop of Toulouse, and presented it to him; upon this, the courtiers hastened to imitate their sovereign, and the venerable prelate returned home with his hand full of hair, delighted at the flattering reception he had met with at the court of the Frankish king. Durinig the Merovingian period, the greatest insult that could be offered to a freeman was to touch him with a razor or scissors. The degradation of kings and princes was carried out in a public manner by shaving their heads and sending them into a monastery; on their regaining their rights and their authority, their hair was always allowed to grow again. We may also conclude that great importance was attached to the preservation of the hair even under the kings of the second dynasty, for Charlemagne, in his Capitulaires, orders the hair to be removed as a punishment in certain crimes.

The Franks, faithful to their ancient custom of wearing the hair long, gradually gave up shaving the face. At first, they only left a small tuft on the chin, but by degrees they allowed this to increase, and in the sixth and seventh centuries freemen adopted the usual form of beard. Amongst the clergy, the custom prevailed of shaving the crown of the head, in the same way as that adopted by certain monastic orders in the present day. Priests for a long time wore beards, but ceased to do so on their becoming fashionable amongst the laity (Figs. 406, 407). Painters and sculptors therefore commit a serious error in representing the prelates and monks of those times with large beards.

As far as the monumental relics of those remote times allow us to judge, the dress as worn by Clovis underwent but trifing modifications during the first dvnasty; but during the reigns of Pepin and Charlemagne considerable changes were effected, which resulted from the intercourse, either of a friendly or hostile nature, between the Franks and the southern nations. About this time, silk stuffs were introduced into the kingdom, and the upper classes, in order to distinguish themselves from the lower, had their garments trimmed round with costly furs (see chapter on Commerce).

[Illustration: Fig. 406 and 407.—Costume of the Prelates from the Eighth to the Tenth Centuries—After Miniatures in the "Missal of St. Gregory," in the National Library of Paris.]

We have before stated (see chapter on Private Life) that Charlemagne, who always was very simple in his tastes, strenuously set his face against these novel introductions of luxury, which he looked upon as tending to do harm. "Of what use are these cloaks?" he said; "in bed they cannot cover us, on horseback they can neither protect us from the rain nor the wind, and when we are sitting they can neither preserve our legs from the cold nor the damp." He himself generally wore a large tunic made of otters' skins. On one occasion his courtiers went out hunting with him, clothed in splendid garments of southern fashion, which became much torn by the briars, and begrimed with the blood of the animals they had killed. "Oh, ye foolish men!" he said to them the next day as he showed them his own tunic, which a servant had just returned to him in perfect condition, after having simply dried it before the fire and rubbed it with his hands. "Whose garments are the more valuable and the more useful? mine, for which I have only paid a sou (about twenty–two francs of present money), or yours, which have cost so much?" From that time, whenever this great king entered on a campaign, the officers of his household, even the most rich and powerful, did not dare to show themselves in any clothes but those made of leather, wool, or cloth; for had they, on such occasions, made their appearance dressed in silk and ornaments, he would have sharply reproved them and have treated them as cowards, or as effeminate, and consequently unfit for the work in which he was about to engage.

Nevertheless, this monarch, who so severely proscribed luxury in daily life, made the most magnificent display on the occasions of political or religious festivals, when the imperial dignity with which he was invested required to be set forth by pompous ceremonial and richness of attire.

During the reign of the other Carlovingian kings, in the midst of political troubles, of internal wars, and of social disturbances, they had neither time nor inclination for inventing new fashions. Monuments of the latter part of the ninth century prove, indeed, that the national dress had hardly undergone any change since the time of Charlemagne, and that the influence of Roman tradition, especially on festive occasions, was still felt in the dress of the nobles (Figs. 408 to 411).

In a miniature of the large MS. Bible given by the canons of Saint–Martin of Tours in 869 to Charles the Bald (National Library of Paris), we find the King sitting on his throne surrounded by the dignitaries of his court, and by soldiers all dressed after the Roman fashion. The monarch wears a cloak which seems to be made of cloth of gold, and is attached to the shoulder by a strap or ribbon sliding through a clasp; this cloak is embroidered in red, on a gold ground; the tunic is of reddish brown, and the shoes are light red, worked with gold thread. In the same manuscript there is another painting, representing four women listening to the discourse of a prophet. From this we discover that the female costume of the time consisted of two tunics, the under one being longer but less capacious than the other, the sleeves of the former coming down tight to the wrists, and being plaited in many folds, whilst those of the latter open out, and only reach to the elbow. The lower part, the neck, and the borders of the sleeves are trimmed with ornamented bands, the waist is encircled by a girdle just above the hips, and a long veil, finely worked, and fastened on the head, covers the shoulders and hangs down to the feet, completely hiding the hair, so that long plaits falling in front were evidently not then in fashion. The under dress of these four women—who all wear black shoes, which were probably made of morocco leather—are of various colours, whereas the gowns or outer tunics are white.

[Illustration: Fig. 408.—Costume of a Scholar of the Carlovingian Period (St. Matthew writing his Gospel under the Inspiration of Christ).—From a Miniature in a Manuscript of the Ninth Century, in the Burgundian Library, Brussels (drawn by Count H. de Vielcastel).]

Notwithstanding that under the Carlovingian dynasty it was always considered a shame and a dishonour to have the head shaved, it must not be supposed that the upper classes continued to wear the long Merovingian style of hair. After the reign of Charlemagne, it was the fashion to shave the hair from above the forehead, the parting being thus widened, and the hair was so arranged that it should not fall lower than the middle of the neck. Under Charles the Bald, whose surname proves that he was not partial to long hair, this custom fell into disuse or was abandoned, and men had the greater part of their heads shaved, and only kept a sort of cap of hair growing on the top of the head. It is at this period that we first find the *cowl* worn. This kind of common head–dress, made from the furs of animals or from woollen stuffs, continued to be worn for many centuries, and indeed almost to the present day. It was originally only a kind of cap, light and very small; but it gradually became extended in size, and successively covered the ears, the neck, and lastly even the shoulders.

No great change was made in the dress of the two sexes during the tenth century. "Nothing was more simple than the head–dress of women," says M. Jules Quicherat; "nothing was less studied than their mode of wearing their hair; nothing was more simple, and yet finer, than their linen. The elegant appearance of their garments recalls that of the Greek and Roman, women. Their dresses were at times so tight as to display all the elegance of their form, whilst at others they were made so high as completely to cover the neck; the latter were called *cottes–hardies*. The *cotte–hardie*, which has at all times been part of the dress of French women, and which was frequently worn also by men, was a long tunic reaching to the heels, fastened in at the waist and closed at the wrists. Queens, princesses, and ladies of the nobility wore in addition a long cloak lined with ermine, or a tunic with or without sleeves; often, too, their dress consisted of two tunics, and of a veil or drapery, which was thrown over the head and fell down before and behind, thus entirely surrounding the neck."

[Illustration: Fig. 409.—Costume of a Scholar.

Fig. 410.—Costume of a Bishop or Abbot.

Fac–similes of Miniatures in a Manuscript of the Ninth Century ("Biblia Sacra"), in the Royal Library of Brussels.]

We cannot find that any very decided change was made in dress before the end of the eleventh century. The ordinary dress made of thick cloths and of coarse woollen stuffs was very strong and durable, and not easily spoiled; and it was usual, as we still find in some provinces which adhere to old customs, for clothes, especially those worn on festive occasions and at ceremonials, to be handed down as heirlooms from father to son, to the third or fourth generation. The Normans, who came from Scandinavia towards the end of the tenth century, A.D. 970, with their short clothes and coats of mail, at first adopted the dress of the French, and continued to do so in all its various changes. In the following century, having found the Saxons and Britons in England clad in the garb of their ancestors, slightly modified by the Roman style of apparel, they began to make great changes in their manner of dressing themselves. They more and more discarded Roman fashions, and assumed similar costumes to those made in France at the same period.

[Illustration: Fig. 411.—Costume of Charles the Simple (Tenth Century).—From a Miniature in the "Rois de France," by Du Tillet, Manuscript of the Sixteenth Century (Imperial Library of Paris).]

Before proceeding further in our history of mediaeval dress, we must forestall a remark which will not fail to be made by the reader, and this is, that we seem to occupy ourselves exclusively with the dress of kings, queens, and other people of note. But we must reply, that though we are able to form tolerably accurate notions relative to the dress of the upper classes during these remote periods, we do not possess any reliable information relative to that of the lower orders, and that the written documents, as well as the sculptures and paintings, are almost useless on this point. Nevertheless, we may suppose that the dress of the men in the lowest ranks of society has always been short and tight, consisting of *braies*, or tight drawers, mostly made of leather, of tight tunics, of *sayons* or doublets, and of capes or cloaks of coarse brown woollen. The tunic was confined at the waist by a belt, to which the knife, the purse, and sometimes the working tools were suspended. The head–dress of the people was generally a simple cap made of thick, coarse woollen cloth or felt, and often of sheep's skin. During the twelfth century, a person's rank or social position was determined by the head–dress. The cap was made of velvet for persons of rank, and of common cloth for the poor. The *cornette*, which was always an appendage to the cap, was made of cloth, with which the cap might be fastened or adjusted on the head. The *mortier*, or round cap, dates from the earliest centuries, and was altered both in shape and material according to the various changes of fashion; but lawyers of high position continued to wear it almost in its original shape, and it became like a professional badge for judges and advocates.

In the miniatures of that time we find Charles the Good, Count of Flanders, who died in 1127, represented with a cap with a point at the top, to which a long streamer is attached, and a peak turned up in front. A cap very similar, but without the streamer, and with the point turned towards the left, is to be seen in a portrait of Geoffroy le Bel, Comte de Maine, in 1150. About the same period, Agnes de Baudement is represented with a sort of cap made of linen or stuff, with lappets hanging down over the shoulders; she is dressed in a robe fastened round the waist, and having long bands attached to the sleeves near the wrists. Queen Ingeburge, second wife of Philip Augustus, also wore the tight gown, fastened at the collar by a round buckle, and two bands of stuff forming a kind of necklace; she also used the long cloak, and the closed shoes, which had then begun to be made pointed. Robert, Comte de Dreux, who lived at the same period, is also dressed almost precisely like the Queen, notwithstanding the difference of sex and rank; his robe, however, only descends to the instep, and his belt has no hangings in front. The Queen is represented with her hair long and flowing, but the count has his cut short.

[Illustration: Fig. 412.—Costume of King Louis le Jeune—Miniature of the "Rois de France," by Du Tillet (Sixteenth Century), in the National Library of Paris.]

[Illustration: Fig. 413.—Royal Costume.—From a Miniature in a Manuscript of the Twelfth Century, in the Burgundian Library, Brussels.]

Manners, Custom and Dress During the Middle

Women, in addition to their head–dress, often wore a broad band, which was tied under the chin, and gave the appearance of a kind of frame for the face. Both sexes wore coloured bands on their shoes, which were tied round the ankles like those of sandals, and showed the shape of the foot.

The beard, which was worn in full at the beginning of the twelfth century, was by degrees modified both as to shape and length. At first it was cut in a point, and only covered the end of the chin, but the next fashion was to wear it so as to join the moustaches. Generally, under Louis le Jeune (Fig. 412), moustaches went out of fashion. We next find beards worn only by country people, who, according to contemporary historians, desired to preserve a "remembrance of their participation in the Crusades." At the end of this century, all chins were shaved.

The Crusades also gave rise to the general use of the purse, which was suspended to the belt by a cord of silk or cotton, and sometimes by a metal chain. At the time of the Holy War, it had become an emblem characteristic of pilgrims, who, before starting for Palestine, received from the hands of the priest the cross, the pilgrim's staff, and the purse.

We now come to the time of Louis IX. (Figs. 414 to 418), of that good king who, according to the testimony of his historians, generally dressed with the greatest simplicity, but who, notwithstanding his usual modesty and economy, did not hesitate on great occasions to submit to the pomp required by the regal position which he held. "Sometimes," says the Sire de Joinville, "he went into his garden dressed in a camel's–hair coat, a surcoat of linsey-woolsey without sleeves, a black silk cloak without a hood, and a hat trimmed with peacocks' feathers. At other times he was dressed in a coat of blue silk, a surcoat and mantle of scarlet satin, and a cotton cap."

The surcoat (sur–cotte) was at first a garment worn only by females, but it was soon adopted by both sexes: it was originally a large wrapper with sleeves, and was thrown over the upper part of the robe (cotte), hence its name, sur–cotte. Very soon it was made without sleeves—doubtless, as M. Quicherat remarks, that the under garment, which was made of more costly material, might be seen; and then, with the same object, and in order that the due motion of the limbs might not be interfered with, the surcoat was raised higher above the hips, and the arm–holes were made very large.

344

[Illustration: Fig. 414.—Costume of a Princess dressed in a Cloak lined with Fur.—From a Miniature of the Thirteenth Century.]

[Illustration: Fig. 415.—Costume of William Malgeneste, the King's Huntsman, as represented on his Tomb, formerly in the Abbey of Long–Pont.]

At the consecration of Louis IX., in 1226, the nobles wore the cap (*mortier*) trimmed with fur; the bishops wore the cope and the mitre, and carried the crosier. Louis IX., at the age of thirteen, is represented, in a picture executed in 1262 (Sainte–Chapelle, Paris), with his hair short, and wearing a red velvet cap, a tunic, and over this a cloak open at the chest, having long sleeves, which are slit up for the arms to go through; this cloak, or surcoat, is trimmed with ermine in front, and has the appearance of what we should now call a fur shawl. The young King has long hose, and shoes similar in shape to high slippers. In the same painting Queen Margaret, his wife, wears a gown with tight bodice opened out on the hips, and having long and narrow sleeves; she also has a cloak embroidered with fleurs–de–lis, the long sleeves of which are slit up and bordered with ermine; a kind of hood, much larger than her head, and over this a veil, which passes under the chin without touching the face; the shoes are long, and seem to enclose the feet very tightly.

[Illustration: Fig. 416.—Costumes of the Thirteenth Century: Tristan and the beautiful Yseult.—From a Miniature in the Romance of "Tristan," Manuscript of the Fourteenth Century (Imperial Library of Paris).]

From this period gowns with tight bodices were generally adopted; the women wore over them a tight jacket, reaching to a little below the hips, often trimmed with fur when the gown was richly ornamented, and itself richly ornamented when the gown was plain. They also began to plait the hair, which fell down by the side of the face to the neck, and they profusely decorated it with pearls or gold or silver ornaments. Jeanne, Queen of Navarre, wife of Philippe le Bel, is represented with a pointed cap, on the turned–up borders of which the hair clusters in thick curls on each side of the face; on the chest is a frill turned down in two points; the gown, fastened in front by a row of buttons, has long and tight sleeves, with a small slit at the wrists closed by a button; lastly, the Queen wears, over all, a sort of second robe in the shape of a cloak, the sleeves of which are widely slit in the middle.

Manners, Custom and Dress During the Middle

At the end of the thirteenth century luxury was at its height at the court of France: gold and silver, pearls and precious stones were lavished on dress. At the marriage of Philip III., son of St. Louis, the gentlemen were dressed in scarlet; the ladies in cloth of gold, embroidered and trimmed with gold and silver lace. Massive belts of gold were also worn, and chaplets sparkling with the same costly metal. Moreover, this magnificence and display (see chapter on Private Life) was not confined to the court, for we find that it extended to the bourgeois class, since Philippe le Bel, by his edict of 1294, endeavoured to limit this extravagance, which in the eyes of the world had an especial tendency to obliterate, or at least to conceal, all distinctions of birth, rank, and condition. Wealth strove hard at that time to be the sole standard of dress.

As we approach the fourteenth century—an epoch of the Middle Ages at which, after many changes of fashion, and many struggles against the ancient Roman and German traditions, modern national costume seems at last to have assumed a settled and normal character—we think it right to recapitulate somewhat, with a view to set forth the nature of the various elements which were at work from time to time in forming the fashions in dress. In order to give more weight to our remarks, we will extract, almost word for word, a few pages from the learned and excellent work which M. Jules Quicherat has published on this subject.

"Towards the year 1280," he says, "the dress of a man—not of a man as the word was then used, which meant *serf*, but of one to whom the exercise of human prerogatives was permitted, that is to say, of an ecclesiastic, a bourgeois, or a noble—was composed of six indispensable portions: the *braies*, or breeches, the stockings, the shoes, the coat, the surcoat, or *cotte–hardie,* and the *chaperon*, or head–dress. To these articles those who wished to dress more elegantly added, on the body, a shirt; on the shoulders, a mantle; and on the head, a hat, or *fronteau*.

[Illustration: Fig. 417.—Costumes of the Common People in the Fourteenth Century: Italian Gardener and Woodman.—From two Engravings in the Bonnart Collection.]

"The *braies*, or *brayes*, were a kind of drawers, generally knitted, sometimes made of woollen stuff or silk, and sometimes even of undressed leather. .... Our ancestors derived this part of their dress from the ancient Gauls; only the Gallic braies came down to the ankle, whereas those of the thirteenth century only reached to the calf. They were fastened above the hips by means of a belt called the *braier*.

"By *chausses* was meant what we now call long stockings or hose. The stockings were of the same colour and material as the braies, and were kept up by the lower part of the braies being pulled over them, and tied with a string.

"The shoes were made of various kinds of leather, the quality of which depended on the way in which they were tanned, and were either of common leather, or of leather which was similar to that we know as morocco, and was called *cordouan* or *cordua* (hence the derivation of the word *cordouannier*, which has now become *cordonnier*). Shoes were generally made pointed; this fashion of the *poulaines*, or Polish points, was followed throughout the whole of Europe for nearly three hundred years, and, when first introduced, the Church was so scandalized by it that it was almost placed in the catalogue of heresies. Subsequently, the taste respecting the exaggerated length of the points was somewhat modified, but it had become so inveterate that the tendency for pointed shoes returning to their former absurd extremes was constantly showing itself. The pointed shoes became gradually longer during the struggles which were carried on in the reign of Philippe le Bel between Church and State.

"Besides the shoes, there were also the *estiviaux*, thus named from. *estiva* (summer thing), because, being generally made of velvet, brocade, or other costly material, they could only be worn in dry weather.

"The coat (*cotte*) corresponded with the tunic of the ancients, it was a blouse with tight sleeves. These sleeves were the only part of it which were exposed, the rest being completely covered by the surcoats, or *cotte–hardie,* a name the origin of which is obscure. In shape the surcoat somewhat resembled a sack, in which, at a later period, large slits were made in the arms, as well as over the hips and on the chest, through which appeared the rich furs and satins with which it was lined.... The ordinary material of the surcoat for the rich was cloth, either scarlet, blue, or reddish brown, or two or more of these colours mixed together; and for the poor, linsey–woolsey or fustian. The nobles, princes, or barons, when holding a court, wore surcoats of a colour to match their arms, which were embroidered upon them, but the lesser nobles who frequented the houses of the great spoke of themselves as in the robes of such and such a noble, because he whose patronage they courted was obliged to provide them with surcoats and mantles. These were of their patron's favourite colour, and were called the livery (*livree*), on account of their distribution (*livraison*), which took place twice a year. The word has remained in use ever since, but with a different signification; it is, however, so nearly akin to the original meaning that its affinity is evident."

[Illustration: Fig. 418.—Costume of English Servants in the Fourteenth Century.—From Manuscripts in the British Museum.]

[Illustration: Fig. 419.—Costume of Philip the Good, with Hood and "Cockade."—From a Miniature in a Manuscript of the Period.]

An interesting anecdote relative to this custom is to be found in the chronicles of Matthew Paris. When St. Louis, to the dismay of all his vassals, and of his inferior servants, had decided to take up the cross, he succeeded in associating the nobles of his court with him in his vow by a kind of pious fraud. Having had a certain number of mantles prepared for Christmas–day, he had a small white cross embroidered on each above the right shoulder, and ordered them to be distributed among the nobles on the morning of the feast when they were about to go to mass, which was celebrated some time before sunrise. Each courtier received the mantle given by the King at the door of his room, and put it on in the dark without noticing the white cross; but, when the day broke, to his great surprise, he saw the emblem worn by his neighbour, without knowing that he himself wore it also. "They were surprised and amused," says the English historian, "at finding that the King had thus piously entrapped them.... As it would have been unbecoming, shameful, and even unworthy of them to have removed these crosses, they laughed heartily, and said that the good King, on starting as a pilgrim–hunter, had found a new method of catching men."

"The chaperon," adds M. Quicherat, "was the national head–dress of the ancient French, as the *cucullus*, which was its model, was that of the Gauls. We can imagine its appearance by its resemblance to the domino now worn at masked balls. The shape was much varied during the reign of Philippe le Bel, either by the diminution of the cape or by the lengthening of the hood, which was always sufficiently long to fall on the shoulders. In the first of these changes, the chaperon no longer being tied round the neck, required to be held on the head by something more solid. For this reason it was set on a pad or roll, which changed it into a regular cap. The material was so stitched as to make it take certain folds, which were arranged as puffs, as ruffs, or in the shape of a cock's comb; this last fashion, called *cockade*, was especially in vogue (Fig. 419)—hence the origin of the French epithet *coquard*, which would be now expressed by the word *dandy*.

"Hats were of various shapes. They were made of different kinds of felt, or of otter or goat's skin, or of wool or cotton. The expression *chapeau de fleurs* (hat of flowers), which continually occurs in ancient works, did not mean any form of hat, but simply a coronet of forget–me–nots or roses, which was an indispensable part of dress for balls or festivities down to the reign of Philippe de Valois (1347). Frontlets (*fronteaux*), a species of fillet made of silk, covered with gold and precious stones, superseded the *chapeau de fleurs*, inasmuch as they had the advantage of not fading. They also possessed the merit of being much more costly, and were thus the means of establishing in a still more marked manner distinctions in the social positions of the wearers.

[Illustration: Fig. 420.—Costumes of a rich Bourgeoise, of a Peasant–woman, and of a Lady of the Nobility, of the Fourteenth Century.—From various painted Windows in the Churches of Moulins (Bourbonnais).]

[Illustration: Saint Catherine Surrounded by the Doctors of Alexandria.

A miniature from the *Breviary* of the cardinal Grimani, attributed to Memling.

Bibl. of Saint–Marc, Venice.

(From a copy belonging to M. Ambroise Firmin–Didot.)]

"There were two kinds of mantles; one was open in front, and fell over the back, and a strap which crossed the chest held it fixed on the shoulders; the other, enveloping the body like a bell, was slit up on the right side, and was thrown back over the left arm; it was made with a fur collar, cut in the shape of a tippet. This last has been handed down to us, and is worn by our judges under the name of *toge* and *epitoge*.

"It is a very common mistake to suppose that the shirt is an article of dress of modern invention; on the contrary, it is one of great antiquity, and its coming into general use is the only thing new about it.

"Lastly, we have to mention the *chape*, which was always regarded as a necessary article of dress. The *chape* was the only protection against bad weather at a period when umbrellas and covered carriages were unknown. It was sometimes called *chape de pluie*, on account of the use to which it was applied, and it consisted of a large cape with sleeves, and was completely waterproof. It was borne behind a master by his servant, who, on account of this service was called a *porte–chape*. It is needless to say that the common people carried it themselves, either slung over their backs, or folded under the arm."

If we now turn to female attire, we shall find represented in it all the component parts of male dress, and almost all of them under the same names. It must be remarked, however, that the women's coats and surcoats often trailed on the ground; that the hat—which was generally called a *couvre–chef,* and consisted of a frame of wirework covered over with stuff which was embroidered or trimmed with lace—was not of a conical shape; and, lastly, that the *chaperon*, which was always made with a tippet, or *chausse*, never turned over so as to form a cap. We may add that the use of the couvre–chef did not continue beyond the middle of the fourteenth century, at which time women adopted the custom of wearing any kind of head–dress they chose, the hair being kept back by a silken net, or *crepine*, attached either to a frontlet, or to a metal fillet, or confined by a veil of very light material, called a *mollequin* (Fig. 420).

With the aid of our learned guide we have now reached a period (end of the thirteenth century) well adapted for this general study of the dress of our ancestors, inasmuch as soon afterwards men's dress at least, and especially that of young courtiers, became most ridiculously and even indecently exaggerated. To such an extent was this the case, that serious calamities having befallen the French nation about this time, and its fashions having exercised a considerable influence over the whole continent of Europe, contemporary historians do not hesitate to regard these public misfortunes as a providential chastisement inflicted on France for its disgraceful extravagance in dress.

[Illustration: Fig. 421.—Costumes of a young Nobleman and of a Bourgeois in the Fourteenth Century.—From a painted Window in the Church of Saint–Ouen at Rouen, and from a Window at Moulins (Bourbonnais).]

"We must believe that God has permitted this as a just judgment on us for our sins," say the monks who edited the "Grande Chronique de St. Denis," in 1346, at the time of the unfortunate battle of Cressy, "although it does not belong to us to judge. But what we see we testify to; for pride was very great in France, and especially amongst the nobles and others, that is to say, pride of nobility, and covetousness. There was also much impropriety in dress, and this extended throughout the whole of France. Some had their clothes so short and so tight that it required the help of two persons to dress and undress them, and whilst they were being undressed they appeared as if they were being skinned. Others wore dresses plaited over their loins like women; some had chaperons cut out in points all round; some had tippets of one cloth, others of another; and some had their head–dresses and sleeves reaching to the ground, looking more like mountebanks than anything else. Considering all this, it is not surprising if God employed the King of England as a scourge to correct the excesses of the French people."

And this is not the only testimony to the ridiculous and extravagant tastes of this unfortunate period. One writer speaks with indignation of the *goats' beards* (with two points), which seemed to put the last finishing touch of ridicule on the already grotesque appearance of even the most serious people of that period. Another exclaims against the extravagant luxury of jewels, of gold and silver, and against the wearing of feathers, which latter then appeared for the first time as accessories to both male and female attire. Some censure, and not without reason, the absurd fashion of converting the ancient leather girdle, meant to support the waist, into a kind of heavy padded band, studded with gilded ornaments and precious stones, and apparently invented expressly to encumber the person wearing it. Other contemporary writers, and amongst these Pope Urban V. and King Charles V. (Fig. 422), inveigh against the *poulaines*, which had more than ever come into favour, and which were only considered correct in fashion when they were made as a kind of appendix to the foot, measuring at least double its length, and ornamented in the most fantastical manner. The Pope anathematized this deformity as "a mockery of God and the holy Church," and the King forbad craftsmen to make them, and his subjects to wear them. All this is as nothing in comparison with the profuse extravagance displayed in furs, which was most outrageous and ruinous, and of which we could not form an idea were it not for the items in certain royal documents, from which we gather that, in order to trim two complete suits for King John, no fewer than six hundred and seventy martens' skins were used. It is also stated that the Duke of Berry, the youngest son of that monarch, purchased nearly ten thousand of these same skins from a distant country in the north, in order to trim only five mantles and as many surcoats. We read also that a robe made for the Duke of Orleans, grandson of the same king, required two thousand seven hundred and ninety ermines' skins. It is unnecessary to state, that in consequence of this large consumption, skins could only be purchased at the most extravagant prices; for example, fifty skins cost about one hundred francs (or about six thousand of present currency), showing to what an enormous expense those persons were put who desired to keep pace with the luxury of the times (Fig. 424).

[Illustration: Fig. 422.—Costume of Charles V., King of France.—From a Statue formerly in the Church of the Celestins, Paris.]

[Illustration: Fig. 423.—Costume of Jeanne de Bourbon, Wife of Charles V.—From a Statue formerly in the Church of the Celestins, Paris.]

We have already seen that Charles V. used his influence, which was unfortunately very limited, in trying to restrain the extravagance of fashion. This monarch did more than decree laws against indelicate or unseemly and ridiculous dress; he himself never wore anything but the long and ample costume, which was most becoming, and which had been adopted in the preceding century. His example, it is true, was little followed, but it nevertheless had this happy result, that the advocates of short and tight dresses, as if suddenly seized with instinctive modesty, adopted an upper garment, the object of which seemed to be to conceal the absurd fashions which they had not the courage to rid themselves of. This heavy and ungraceful tunic, called a *housse*, consisted of two broad bands of a more or less costly material, which, starting from the neck, fell behind and before, thus almost entirely concealing the front and back of the person, and only allowing the under garments to be seen through the slits which naturally opened on each side of it.

A fact worthy of remark is, that whilst male attire, through a depravity of taste, had extended to the utmost limit of extravagance, women's dress, on the contrary, owing to a strenuous effort towards a dignified and elegant simplicity, became of such a character that it combined all the most approved fashions of female costume which had been in use in former periods.

The statue of Queen Jeanne de Bourbon, wife of Charles V., formerly placed with that of her husband in the Church of the Celestins at Paris, gives the most faithful representation of this charming costume, to which our artists continually have recourse when they wish to depict any poetical scenes of the French Middle Ages (Fig. 423).

[Illustration: Fig. 424.—Costumes of Bourgeois or Merchant, of a Nobleman, and of a Lady of the Court or rich Bourgeoise, with the Head–dress (*escoffion*) of the Fifteenth Century.—From a Painted Window of the Period, at Moulins (Bourbonnais), and from a Painting on Wood of the same Period, in the Musee de Cluny.]

This costume, without positively differing in style from that of the thirteenth century, inasmuch as it was composed of similar elements, was nevertheless to be distinguished by a degree of elegance which hitherto had been unknown. The coat, or under garment, which formerly only showed itself through awkwardly—contrived openings, now displayed the harmonious outlines of the figure to advantage, thanks to the large openings in the overcoat. The surcoat, kept back on the shoulders by two narrow bands, became a sort of wide and trailing skirt, which majestically draped the lower part of the body; and, lastly, the external corset was invented, which was a kind of short mantle, falling down before and behind without concealing any of the fine outlines of the bust. This new article of apparel, which was kept in its place in the middle of the chest by a steel busk encased in some rich lace—work, was generally made of fur in winter and of silk in summer. If we consult the numerous miniatures in manuscripts of this period, in which the gracefulness of the costume was heightened by the colours employed, we shall understand what variety and what richness of effect could be displayed without departing from the most rigid simplicity.

One word more in reference to female head—dress. The fashion of wearing false hair continued in great favour during the middle of the fourteenth century, and it gave rise to all sorts of ingenious combinations; which, however, always admitted of the hair being parted from the forehead to the back of the head in two equal masses, and of being plaited or waved over the ears. Nets were again adopted, and head—dresses which, whilst permitting a display of masses of false hair, hid the horsehair or padded puffs. And, lastly, the *escoffion* appeared—a heavy roll, which, being placed on a cap also padded, produced the most clumsy, outrageons, and ungraceful shapes (Fig. 424).

At the beginning of the fifteenth century men's dress was still very short. It consisted of a kind of tight waistcoat, fastened by tags, and of very close—fitting breeches, which displayed the outlines of the figure. In order to appear wide at the shoulders artificial pads were worn, called *mahoitres*. The hair was allowed to fall on the forehead in locks, which covered the eyebrows and eyes. The sleeves were slashed, the shoes armed with long metal points, and the conical hat, with turned—up rim, was ornamented with gold chains and various jewels. The ladies, during the reign of Charles VI., still wore long trains to their dresses, which they carried tucked up under their arms, unless they had pages or waiting—maids (see chapter on Ceremonials). The tendency, however, was to shorten these inconvenient trains, as well as the long hanging and embroidered or fringed sleeves. On the other hand, ladies' dresses on becoming shorter were trimmed in the most costly manner. Their head–dresses consisted of very large rolls, surmounted by a high conical bonnet called a *hennin*, the introduction of which into France was attributed to Queen Isabel of Bavaria, wife of Charles VI. It was at this period that they began to uncover the neck and to wear necklaces.

[Illustration: Fig. 425.—Italian Costumes of the Fifteenth Century: Notary and Sbirro.—From two Engravings in the Bonnart Collection.]

[Illustration: Fig. 426.—Costumes of a Mechanic's Wife and a rich Bourgeois in the latter part of the Fifteenth Century.—From Windows in the Cathedral of Moulins (Bourbonnais).]

Under Louis XI. this costume, already followed and adopted by the greatest slaves of fashion, became more general.

"In this year (1487)," says the chronicler Monstrelet, "ladies ceased to wear trains, substituting for them trimmings of grebe, of martens' fur, of velvet, and of other materials, of about eighteen inches in width; some wore on the top of their heads rolls nearly two feet high, shaped like a round cap, which closed in above. Others wore them lower, with veils hanging from the top, and reaching down to the feet. Others wore unusually wide silk bands, with very elegant buckles equally wide, and magnificent gold necklaces of various patterns.

"About this time, too, men took to wearing shorter clothes than ever, having them made to fit tightly to the body, after the manner of dressing monkeys, which was very shameful and immodest; and the sleeves of their coats and doublets were slit open so as to show their fine white shirts. They wore their hair so long that it concealed their face and even their eyes, and on their heads they wore cloth caps nearly a foot or more high. They also carried, according to fancy, very splendid gold chains. Knights and squires, and even the varlets, wore silk or velvet doublets; and almost every one, especially at court, wore poulaines nine inches or more in length. They also wore under their doublets large pads (*mahoitres*), in order to appear as if they had broad shoulders."

Under Charles VIII. the mantle, trimmed with fur, was open in front, its false sleeves being slit up above in order to allow the arms of the under coat to pass through. The cap was turned up; the breeches or long hose were made tight–fitting. The shoes with poulaines were superseded by a kind of large padded shoe of black leather, round or square at the toes, and gored over the foot with coloured material, a fashion imported from Italy, and which was as much exaggerated in France as the poulaine had formerly been. The women continued to wear conical caps (*hennins*) of great height, covered with immense veils; their gowns were made with tight–fitting bodies, which thus displayed the outlines of the figure (Figs. 427 and 428).

Under Louis XII., Queen Anne invented a low head–dress—or rather it was invented for her—consisting of strips of velvet or of black or violet silk over other bands of white linen, which encircled the face and fell down over the back and shoulders; the large sleeves of the dresses had a kind of turned–over borders, with trimmings of enormous width. Men adopted short tunics, plaited and tight at the waist. The upper part of the garments of both men and women was cut in the form of a square over the chest and shoulders, as most figures are represented in the pictures of Raphael and contemporary painters.

[Illustration: Italian Lacework, in Gold Thread.

The cypher and arms of Henry III. (16th century.)]

[Illustration: Fig. 427.—Costume of Charlotte of Savoy, second Wife of Louis XI.—From a Picture of the Period formerly in the Castle of Bourbon–l'Archambault, M. de Quedeville's Collection, in Paris. The Arms of Louis XI. and Charlotte are painted behind the picture.]

[Illustration: Fig. 428.—Costume of Mary of Burgundy, Daughter of Charles the Bold, Wife of Maximilian of Austria (end of the Fifteenth Century). From an old Engraving in the Collection of the Imperial Library, Paris.]

The introduction of Italian fashions, which in reality did not much differ from those which had been already adopted, but which exhibited better taste and a greater amount of elegance, dates from the famous expedition of Charles VIII. into Italy (Figs. 429 and 430). Full and gathered or puffed sleeves, which gave considerable gracefulness to the upper part of the body, succeeded to the *mahoitres*, which had been discarded since the time of Louis XI. A short and ornamental mantle, a broad–brimmed hat covered with feathers, and trunk hose, the ample dimensions of which earned for them the name of *trousses*, formed the male attire at the end of the fifteenth century. Women wore the bodies of their dresses closely fitting to the figure, embroidered, trimmed with lace, and covered with gilt ornaments; the sleeves were very large and open, and for the most part they still adhered to the heavy and ungraceful head–dress of Queen Anne of Brittany. The principal characteristic of female dress at the time was its fulness; men's, on the contrary, with the exception of the mantle or the upper garment, was usually tight and very scanty.

We find that a distinct separation between ancient and modern dress took place as early as the sixteenth century; in fact, our present fashions may be said to have taken their origin from about that time. It was during this century that men adopted clothes closely fitting to the body; overcoats with tight sleeves, felt hats with more or less wide brims, and closed shoes and boots. The women also wore their dresses closely fitting to the figure, with tight sleeves, low–crowned hats, and richly–trimmed petticoats. These garments, which differ altogether from those of antiquity, constitute, as it were, the common type from which have since arisen the endless varieties of male and female dress; and there is no doubt that fashion will thus be continually changing backwards and forwards from time to time, sometimes returning to its original model, and sometimes departing from it.

[Illustration: Figs. 429 and 430.—Costumes of Young Nobles of the Court of Charles VIII., before and after the Expedition into Italy.—From Miniatures in two Manuscripts of the Period in the National Library of Paris.]

During the sixteenth century, ladies wore the skirts of their dresses, which were tight at the waist and open in front, very wide, displaying the lower part of a very rich under petticoat, which reached to the ground, completely concealing the feet. This, like the sleeves with puffs, which fell in circles to the wrists, was altogether an Italian fashion. Frequently the hair was turned over in rolls, and adorned with precious stones, and was surmounted by a small cap, coquettishly placed either on one side or on the top of the head, and ornamented with gold chains, jewels, and feathers. The body of the dress was always long, and pointed in front. Men wore their coats cut somewhat after the same shape: their trunk hose were tight, but round the waist they were puffed out. They wore a cloak, which only reached as far as the hips, and was always much ornamented; they carried a smooth or ribbed cap on one side of the head, and a small upright collar adorned the coat. This collar was replaced, after the first half of the sixteenth century, by the high, starched ruff, which was kept out by wires; ladies wore it still larger, when it had somewhat the appearance of an open fan at the back of the neck.

If we take a retrospective glance at the numerous changes of costume which we have endeavoured to describe in this hurried sketch, we shall find that amongst European nations, during the Middle Ages, there was but one common standard of fashion, which varied from time to time according to the particular custom of each country, and according to the peculiarities of each race. In Italy, for instance, dress always maintained a certain character of grandeur, ever recalling the fact that the influence of antiquity was not quite lost. In Germany and Switzerland, garments had generally a heavy and massive appearance; in Holland, still more so (Figs. 436 and 437). England uniformly studied a kind of instinctive elegance and propriety. It is a curious fact that Spain invariably partook of the heaviness peculiar to Germany, either because the Gothic element still prevailed there, or that the Walloon fashions had a special attraction to her owing to associations and general usage. France was then, as it is now, fickle and capricious, fantastical and wavering, but not from indifference, but because she was always ready to borrow from every quarter anything which pleased her. She, however, never failed to put her own stamp on whatever she adopted, thus making any fashion essentially French, even though she had only just borrowed it from Spain, England, Germany, or Italy. In all these countries we have seen, and still see, entire provinces adhering to some ancient costume, causing them to differ altogether in character from the rest of the nation. This is simply owing to the fact that the fashions have become obsolete in the neighbouring places, for every local costume faithfully and rigorously preserved by any community at a distance from the centre of political action or government, must have been originally brought there by the nobles of the country. Thus the head–dress of Anne of Brittany is still that of the peasant–women of Penhoet and of Labrevack, and the *hennin* of Isabel of Bavaria is still the head–dress of Normandy.

[Illustration: Fig. 431.—Costumes of a Nobleman or a very rich Bourgeois, of a Bourgeois or Merchant, and of a Noble Lady or rich Bourgeoise, of the Time of Louis XII.—From Miniatures in Manuscripts of the Period, in the Imperial Library of Paris.]

[Illustration: Fig. 432.—Costume of a rich Bourgeoise, and of a Noble, or Person of Distinction, of the Time of Francis I.—From a Window in the Church of St. Ouen at Rouen, by Gaignieres (National Library of Paris).]

Although the subject has reached the limits we have by the very nature of this work assigned to it, we think it well to overstep them somewhat, in order briefly to indicate the last connecting link between modern fashions and those of former periods.

[Illustration: Figs. 433 and 434.—Costumes of the Ladies and Damsels of the Court of Catherine de Medicis.—After Cesare Vecellio.]

Under Francis I., the costumes adopted from Italy remained almost stationary (Fig. 432). Under Henri II. (Figs. 433 and 434), and especially after the death of that prince, the taste for frivolities made immense progress, and the style of dress in ordinary use seemed day by day to lose the few traces of dignity which it had previously possessed.

Catherine de Medicis had introduced into France the fashion of ruffs, and at the beginning of the fourteenth century, Marie de Medicis that of small collars. Dresses tight at the waist began to be made very full round the hips, by means of large padded rolls, and these were still more enlarged, under the name of *vertugadins* (corrupted from *vertu–gardiens)*, by a monstrous arrangement of padded whalebone and steel, which subsequently became the ridiculous *paniers*, which were worn almost down to the commencement of the present century; and the fashion seems likely to come into vogue again.

[Illustration: Fig. 435.—Costume of a Gentleman of the French Court, of the End of the Sixteenth Century.—Fac–simile of a Miniature in the "Livre de Poesies," Manuscript dedicated to Henry IV.]

Under the last of the Valois, men's dress was short, the jacket was pointed and trimmed round with small peaks, the velvet cap was trimmed with aigrettes; the beard was pointed, a pearl hung from the left ear, and a small cloak or mantle was carried on the shoulder, which only reached to the waist. The use of gloves made of scented leather became universal. Ladies wore their dresses long, very full, and very costly, little or no change being made in these respects during the reign of Henry IV. At this period, the men's high hose were made longer and fuller, especially in Spain and the Low Countries, and the fashion of large soft boots, made of doeskin or of black morocco, became universal, on account of their being so comfortable.

We may remark that the costume of the bourgeois was for a long time almost unchanged, even in the towns. Never having adopted either the tight–fitting hose or the balloon trousers, they wore an easy jerkin, a large cloak, and a felt hat, which the English made conical and with a broad brim.

Towards the beginning of the seventeenth century, the high hose which were worn by the northern nations, profusely trimmed, was transformed into the *culotte*, which was full and open at the knees. A division was thus suddenly made between the lower and the upper part of the hose, as if the garment which covered the lower limbs had been cut in two, and garters were then necessarily invented. The felt hat became over almost the whole of Europe a cap, taking the exact form of the head, and having a wide, flat brim turned up on one side. High heels were added to boots and shoes, which up to that time had been flat and with single soles.... Two centuries later, a terrible social agitation took place all over Europe, after which male attire became mean, ungraceful, plain and more paltry than ever; whereas female dress, the fashions of which were perpetually changing from day to day, became graceful and elegant, though too often approaching to the extravagant and absurd.

[Illustration: Figs. 436 and 437.—Costumes of the German Bourgeoisie in the Middle of the Sixteenth Century.—Drawings attributed to Holbein.]

Printed in the United States
69755LV00004B/249